Human-Computer Interface Design

SUCCESS STORIES, EMERGING METHODS, AND REAL-WORLD CONTEXT

Edited by

MARIANNE RUDISILL
NASA Langley Research Center

CLAYTON LEWIS
University of Colorado

PETER G. POLSON
University of Colorado

TIMOTHY D. MCKAY
Gateway 2000

MORGAN KAUFMANN PUBLISHERS, INC.
SAN FRANCISCO, CALIFORNIA

Sponsoring Editor Michael B. Morgan
Production Manager Yonie Overton
Production Editor Cheri Palmer
Editorial Coordinator Marilyn Uffner Allen
Production Books By Design, Inc.
Cover Design Ross Carron, Carron Design
Text Design Books By Design, Inc.
Compositor Sue Cologgi
Copyeditor Robert Fiske
Proofreader Megan McDowell
Indexer Marilyn Rowland
Printer Courier Corporation

Morgan Kaufmann Publishers, Inc.
Editorial and Sales Office
340 Pine Street, Sixth Floor
San Francisco, CA 94104-3205
USA
Telephone 415 / 392-2665
Facsimile 415 / 982-2665
Internet mkp@mkp.com
Web site http://mkp.com

© 1996 by Morgan Kaufmann Publishers, Inc.

Library of Congress Cataloging-in-Publication Data

Human-computer interface design : success stories, emerging methods,
  and real-world context / edited by Marianne Rudisill...[et al.].
      p.   cm.
    Report of a workshop held July 1991 in Boulder, Colo.
    Includes bibliographical references and index.
    ISBN 1-55860-310-7
    1. Human-computer interaction.   2. User interfaces (Computer
  systems)   I. Rudisill, Marianne.
  QA76.9.H85H8653   1995
  005.1'2—dc20
                                                95-20362
                                                    CIP

Contents

Preface   *vii*

P A R T   I   **Success Cases**

Usability for Fun and Profit:
A Case Study of the Design of DEC Rally Version 2   *3*
Dennis Wixon and Sandy Jones

Rapid, Integrated Design of a Multimedia Communication System   *36*
Ellen Francik

The Xerox Star: An Influential User Interface Design   *70*
Lawrence H. Miller and Jeff Johnson

Project Ernestine: Analytic and
Empirical Methods Applied to a Real-World CHI Problem   *101*
Michael E. Atwood, Wayne D. Gray, and Bonnie E. John

Pioneers and Settlers:
Methods Used in Successful User Interface Design   *122*
Stuart K. Card

P A R T   I I   **Emerging Methods**

**Improving User Interfaces and Application Productivity
by Using the ITS Application Development Environment**   *173*
John D. Gould, Jacob Ukelson, and Stephen J. Boies

**Lessons in Choosing Methods for
Designing Complex Graphical User Interfaces**   *198*
Carrie Rudman and George Engelbeck

**Getting Around the Task-Artifact Cycle:
How to Make Claims and Design by Scenario**   *229*
John M. Carroll and Mary Beth Rosson

**Mapping the Method Muddle:
Guidance in Using Methods for User Interface Design**   *269*
Judith S. Olson and Thomas P. Moran

P A R T   I I I   **Real-World Context**

**Organizational Obstacles to Interface Design
and Development: Two Participant Observer Studies**   *303*
Steven E. Poltrock and Jonathan Grudin

**System Design Practice, Emerging Development
Acceleration Strategies, and the Role of User-Centered Design**   *338*
R. Jay Ritchie and Judith A. List

Bringing Usability Effectively into Product Development   *367*
Peter F. Conklin

Accepting the Challenge   *375*
John L. Bennett

P A R T   I V   **Synthesis and Closing Discussion**

Respect and Beyond   *389*
Clayton Lewis and Peter Polson

Index   *395*

Preface

This book is the report of a workshop, titled Human-Computer Interface Design: Success Cases, Emerging Methods, and Real-World Context, held in Boulder, Colorado, on July 24–26, 1991, with sponsorship from the Institute of Cognitive Science at the University of Colorado, Boulder, and the Human-Computer Interaction Laboratory at the NASA Johnson Space Center. The organizers were Lee Gugerty, then at Lockheed Engineering and Sciences Co., Clayton Lewis, University of Colorado, Tim McKay, then at Lockheed Engineering and Sciences Co., Peter G. Polson, University of Colorado, and Marianne Rudisill, then at NASA Johnson Space Center, Human-Computer Interaction Laboratory.

The workshop grew out of discussions among the organizers of how we could most effectively encourage further progress in user interface design in practical settings. We concluded we should not only promote consideration of new methods in design and evaluation, as is usual in workshops and symposia, but also focus attention on two aspects of our work not so often discussed. First, we wanted to hear about success cases: user interface projects that had achieved success in real life, not just in the research lab, on the basis of some identifiable methods. Second, we wanted to consider the organizational context in which user interface design is done and reflect on how our work might be better accommodated to this context.

The resulting workshop format was a sandwich, with presentations on emerging methods falling between a historical review of success cases and discussion of the pragmatic context of design. Presenters in the success cases session were required to describe methods for designing and developing user interfaces for which there is convincing evidence of success. The methods were not required to have a theoretical basis or rationale but had to be sufficiently coherent that other workers might reasonably hope to apply them. Evidence of success could include commercial sales, realistic test data, clear statements of user satisfaction, or other information that would be accepted by a prudent judge as indicating that the method actually worked. Success of a design on which a method was used was not considered sufficient evidence in itself; there had to be a persuasive argument that the method actually contributed to the success.

Presenters in the emerging methods session were asked to describe new methods for designing and developing user interfaces. It was not required that these methods be proven successes, like those discussed in the first session. But we did ask for a persuasive argument that the method has the potential to improve significantly user interface design and development.

Presenters in the real-world context session were asked to discuss how work in user interface design and development accommodates or fails to accommodate real-world organizational, commercial, or practical requirements, and how this accommodation could be improved. Presentations had to be grounded in actual project experience or studies of such projects.

Each of the sessions included a discussion, written presentations of which we include here.

We thank the Human-Computer Interface Laboratory at NASA's Johnson Space Center for financial support for the workshop that formed the basis for the book. We also thank Dr. Martha Polson, Assistant Director of the Institute of Cognitive Science at the University of Colorado, where the workshop was held, and Dr. Lee Gugerty, who participated in the planning of the workshop. During preparation of the book, the various authors also served as reviewers, and we thank them for their comments. The following outside reviewers also provided many useful suggestions: Ron Baecker, Randolph Bias, Peter Foltz, Bill Hefley, Marilyn Mantei, Michael Muller, William Newman, Jakob Nielsen, Dan Olsen, Jr., John F. Patterson, Bruce Tognazzini, Terry Winograd, and Richard Young.

Success Cases

Usability for Fun and Profit: A Case Study of the Design of DEC Rally Version 2

DENNIS WIXON

Digital Equipment Corporation

SANDY JONES

Boston College

Introduction

Summary

The user interface design of DEC Rally Version 2 represents an important case study in improving the usability of a product from several perspectives:

- **Methodological**—Contextual inquiry (Holtzblatt and Jones, 1990) at customer sites was effectively combined with other methods to redesign the user interface.

- **Organizational**—A large part (40 percent) of development effort was devoted to user interface changes, and these changes were supported by various levels of management.

- **Outcome**—Product revenues increased dramatically (80 percent) for the new version; customers who were independently polled during field testing cited improved usability as the second most significant aspect of version 2.

To introduce the design changes, we briefly review the product origins, planning methods, and usability methods that were used in the redesign. We discuss the interface redesign in terms of eight problems, their solutions, and the conclusions we draw about user interface design and process from our experience in addressing each problem. In addition, we present an overview of the problem tracking system. In the conclusion section, we discuss revenue, usability theory and method, and future directions.

Product Origins

DEC Rally is a fourth-generation application generator. Rally is designed to optimize the production of interactive database applications and to run in a character cell environment. The development system includes:

- An object-based nonprocedural set of tools
- A procedural language with a Pascal-like syntax
- Interfaces to programs written in 3GL languages

The application generator itself is a Rally application. Thus, the developers of the application generator share some experiences of those who use Rally to develop other applications. Although Rally contains both a definition system (used to develop applications) and a run-time system (provides the environment for the developed applications to run in), our focus here is on the definition system.

The original Rally V1.0 was intended to be easy to use. Specifically, it attempted to minimize typing and human memory demands by providing (Lasher, 1988; Shneiderman, 1983) an interface using menus and forms. Use of menus was quite flexible, allowing users to select using numbers, keywords, or arrow keys. In addition, the menus allowed for type-ahead and learn sequences. Type-ahead provided expert users with a way of navigating through the menu hierarchy quickly since intermediate menus were not displayed. Experienced users referred to specific menu items by numeric sequences that uniquely identified them (for example, Good, 1989; Gilb, 1988; Ehn, 1988; Bennett, 1984). Form fields could be filled in by selecting from a list of values provided on the right side of each form. Once an object had been named, it could be referred to again by simple selection. A fundamental insight in the original design was the concept of a form/report. The system treated forms and reports in exactly the same way. This approach reduced the conceptual burden on the user. Prompting was provided at the bottom of each screen, and access to on-line help was provided throughout the product. Within the constraints of a character cell interface, this approach seemed state of the art.

However, in practice, the system proved to be challenging to users. There was a fundamental gap between the theory with which the system had been designed and the actual user interface. Many of the strengths of the initial design were obscured by interface problems that the users experienced when actually developing applications. No doubt some of these problems could have been avoided with a more careful initial design. However, a large number of the design issues could be uncovered only by observing the product in use at customer sites.

Version 2 Planning

The Rally development team, including the documentation group, had a better sense of the user's point of view than many development teams. There were several reasons for this. First, they used the product. This not only contributed to seeing the product from the end user's viewpoint, but it also made it relatively easy to develop prototypes for both informal and formal tests. Second, they were in contact with several of their customers both on a regular basis and at special events like DECUS. Third, they were in continuous communication with the people who supported the product and trained the users. These internal groups related customer issues to the development team. Finally, the team actively followed the trade press and kept up with the competitive products and customer reaction to these products.

From all these sources, the team developed a list of problems to be fixed. These included such items as shortening the menu hierarchy, improving the on-screen information, reducing the number of steps to perform common operations, and making the application reporting more effective. Thus, a redesign of the first version of the product was already under way when the usability group was asked to contribute. Most of the changes incorporated into version 2 were under active consideration. An early presentation of "usability engineering" (Whiteside, 1986; Gilb, 1988) was instrumental in gaining the support and confidence of senior members of the development group.

In the process of developing the second version of DEC Rally, we decided to try a number of methods: usability engineering, contextual inquiry, review of the design, and testing the prototype. We also decided to use both formal and informal channels of information exchange. Specifically, we supplemented the traditional method of writing reports by making videotapes of our customer visits and showing these to the Rally team over lunch. This provided for quick and vivid feedback to the development group. Even before a test plan was developed, we arranged some early visits to customer sites to understand how the product was currently being used. These visits provided data to the team early in the design process.

In addition to our informal methods, we developed a formal test plan that specified customer site visits. Each user was interviewed twice. In the first interview, the focus was on how they worked with the current product. We wanted to uncover mismatches between the existing product design and the work. Although we did not suggest it, some customers prepared for these interviews by keeping a diary of problems, and they proceeded to walk us through these examples using the product. This approach was often helpful since it expanded the range of the data that we saw. The second interview was more complex. We used a prototype of the newly designed system. We showed the users the system and solicited their comments. We then conducted a set of timed benchmark tests. We allowed the users to comment freely during the benchmarks. Since the sessions were videotaped, we were able to remove the "comment time," and this corrected time was used to measure performance.

The benchmark tasks we used examined how people learned the system and used a repeated measures design. Within each task, subtasks tested specific aspects of the prototype. These aspects were areas of the design where we suspected that our approach might need further refinement. We also used limited benchmark tasks because our prototype did not contain the full functionality of the system. In fact, it was a limited interface shell.

All the usability tests were planned in the development schedule. In one base level, the prototype of the system was developed. During the next base level, the customer site visits were conducted while the functionality unrelated to the interface was developed. Following the customer site visits, a base level was dedicated to addressing usability issues and fixing bugs that were uncovered during these site visits. This plan maximized the use of resources.

In this process, usability was completely integrated into product planning. The usability plan was directly incorporated into the development plan. The usability requirements and tests were directly incorporated into the product requirements.

Usability Methods

At the time that Rally was being redesigned, the Software Usability Engineering group had successfully applied usability engineering (Bennett, 1984; Good et al., 1986; Whiteside, Bennett, and Holtzblatt, 1988) to a number of products. The relative strengths of methods like usability engineering were clear, as were its limitations. We were in the process of investigating new methods (Good, 1989; Holtzblatt and Jones, 1990; Winograd and Flores, 1986; Wixon, Holtzblatt, and Knox, 1990). Some new methods like contextual inquiry showed promise. We decided to employ usability engineering, contextual inquiry, prototyping, and the systematic tracking and prioritizing of usability problems.

Usability Engineering

Usability engineering is a method for designing usability into products. It involves the specification of usability metrics and goals. These goals and metrics are considered "objective" because they are stated operationally. The metrics and goals are then used to systematically evaluate user interface designs. The usability engineering approach is derived from classical engineering and management by objectives, and it assumes that usability can be operationally specified. In practice, these operationally specified usability goals often involve performance measures and responses to written questionnaires. The operational specification of usability serves to provide a basis for a common understanding of the usability goals of a product. This common understanding can inform a design team and can serve as the basis for evaluation of proposed designs or working prototypes.

In practice, usability engineering efforts usually measure performance on an early prototype or a base level of a product. Benchmark tasks are developed from the operational specification of usability. Although objective and laboratory oriented, the method differs from classical experimental approaches in that no hypothesis testing or statistical decision making is involved. Instead, the testing is undertaken to assess whether the product meets its goal and to discover the problems that inhibit product usability. The importance of these problems is empirically assessed using a continuous scale, and the results are often presented to development groups using simple graphical methods like the Pareto chart (Ishikawa, 1982).

The development team can then address usability issues case by case, making decisions based not only on effort involved (which they assess independently) but also on the potential usability impact as presented in the Pareto chart. Usability engineering usually produces a measurable improvement in the usability of a product of about 30 percent (Whiteside, 1986; Whiteside, Bennett, and Holtzblatt, 1988).

Some of the strengths of usability engineering are:

- Establishing an agreed upon definition for usability
- Setting this definition in terms of metrics and goals for usability
- Putting usability on a par with other engineering goals
- Providing a context for the discussion of usability of a product independent of design decisions

- Providing a context for an agreed upon assessment for the usability of a product
- Providing a method for prioritizing usability problems

  Some of the weaknesses of usability engineering are:

- The assumption that usability can be operationalized
- The requirement that the practitioner be familiar with laboratory methods
- The establishment of usability goals independent of customer input
- The assessment of usability goals outside the customer's work environment
- The cost of conducting usability tests
- The stage of the engineering cycle at which the tests can be made (usually late)
- The failure to address usefulness

These methods work well if your goals and metrics are well grounded in the user's work. Partly because of our awareness of the weaknesses of usability engineering and because of a request from our management to "improve products by 300 percent" and make them successful in the marketplace, we were led to search for other methods that were more field oriented and took a broader perspective.

Contextual Inquiry

Contextual inquiry is a means of gathering information from users about their work practices and experiences. The contextual inquiry approach is based on field research techniques and focuses on interviewing users in their context as they work. The technique contributes to initial design concepts to form a valid understanding of the nature of user work. This understanding can then be used for effective design action. Contextual inquiry is based on the key concepts of context, partnership, and focus.

We begin with a recognition that our products are used within particular contexts. We need to understand users' needs in the context of their work. The work context includes the tools and other artifacts that people use during work, the people they work with, the culture of the organization they are in, the physical environment, and the work demands associated with particular activities. Being in context means that we go to the user site and talk with users about the work they are currently doing while they are doing it.

Because users are the experts in their work, they become partners in the inquiry. Together with the users, we develop interpretations about their work experience. We don't use preplanned questions and are careful not to "overcontrol" the interview. Rather, we engage users in a partnership to articulate their work process and needs. We enable the users to direct the conversation to those things that are central to their work experiences by using open-ended questions. In this way, we create an understanding of the users' work that informs the interface design.

Whenever we design, we have assumptions about what will solve a problem and the nature of the customers' work. These assumptions can be blind spots that prevent us from seeing information that challenges our assumptions. Contextual inquiry provides a way to align our understanding of work with the customers' understanding by constantly challenging our entering assumptions. We probe the things we don't understand, the things that contradict our assumptions, and the problems behind solutions. We share our interpretations with users to validate and reshape them.

Contextual inquiry is used within an iterative contextual design process. Throughout the design process, we use specific techniques in response to design issues. Prototyping is a key technique in iterative design. A prototype is an effective way to focus dialog with users during a contextual interview. As users explore the prototype, they provide insights that inform our designs.

The key benefits of contextual inquiry are that it:

- Can be used early in the development cycle
- Defines user work problems and opportunities for improved products and services
- Develops a partnership between engineering and customers
- Creates a shared system vision for the whole design team
- Combines with other processes to support decision making, prototyping, and team design
- Identifies both short-term and long-term product enhancements

The key limits of contextual inquiry are that it:

- Requires additional time and expense to set up customer site visits
- Requires interviewing and analysis skills
- Requires a method of tracking the large number of design ideas that result

Prototyping

The architecture of Rally made the development of prototypes relatively easy. A number of the user interface features were prototyped and reviewed informally. In addition, a prototype of the new interface was developed for customer site visits and formed the basis of our user interface testing.

Tracking Problems

Part of the usability plan included using the traditional software quality reporting system to track usability issues. Traditionally, this system focused on reliability of software. Problems relating to the functionality, usability, or documentation were often assigned a low priority.

For the work on Rally, a new system for prioritizing usability problems was developed. It incorporated high-priority ratings for usability problems. For example, if a problem was experienced by most of our interview participants, it was given a high rating. The priority system for usability issues was supported by a process developed from the traditional process for handling software problems. All problems entered the tracking system. They were classified according to which member of the development team was responsible for addressing them and whether they were usability issues. If problems were judged to be usability related, they were assigned to the usability consultant for prioritization. This priority scheme was developed jointly by the software team and the usability engineer.

Rally Design Changes and Reflections

In this section, we present eight interface design problems and their resolutions. For each problem and resolution, we offer conclusions about user interface design theory and practice.

The problems and their analysis divide themselves into two subgroups. The first five problems focus on specific components of the system. The last three problems focus on empirical analysis of the redesign and the overall development process.

Menu Navigation Problem

The Problem

One of the most visible problems with Rally version 1.1 was its menu structure. It consisted of over 80 separate menus arranged in a complex menu tree. This "organization" resulted in a system that was difficult to learn, easy to get lost in, and required many keystrokes to navigate to a given choice. In fact, among expert users, locations in the menu structure became identified with a number sequence that represented the menu path used to access the particular set of choices or forms, for example, 5 2 2 3 2 7 7 1. Many of the menu branches were obscure and poorly labeled. Finally, the number of items in a single menu was restricted to six (based on human factors principles); this not only proliferated menus, but led to menus with such quaint titles as "additional attributes."

As part of the version 1.1 product development effort, it was suggested that users be provided with a map of the menu structure on a poster to alleviate the confusion. The members of the documentation team argued strongly against such an approach. They contended that such a complex design could not be adequately represented in any poster and that the problem lay in the complexity of the menu system. Figure 1 shows an overview of version 1 and a single subset of the system in detail.

This illustrates an important principle of design: *You can't fix a usability design problem with documentation.* There is often a tendency in engineering management to assume that design problems can be addressed with training or documentation. In fact, over the years we have found that carefully documenting an unnecessarily complex user interface can increase user confusion and antipathy. Good documentation clarifies the inadequacies of suboptimal designs. The suggestion that the user manual be written early (Rubinstein and Hersh, 1984) in the development cycle is based on this insight. Writing the manual early contributes to the development effort by clarifying design problems early.

Redesign

The literature on menu design (Snowberry, 1983) suggested that navigation is quicker with broad, flat menu hierarchies than with deep menu hierarchies. We could accomplish this by placing more items on individual menus. In addition, changes in the menu organization would provide an opportunity to facilitate the learning of the product by demonstrating the product organization with the menu structure. Drawing from direct manipulation systems, we developed the concept of the *object-operation* menu. It was an unusual approach that combined objects and operations on a single screen. This menu incorporated grouping of items and provided headers for subgroups. As such, it provided a simple overview of the major objects of the system and what you could do with them. It is pictured in Figure 2.

The menu allowed users to select items by typing numbers or keywords (highlighted in bold) or by using the arrow keys. This menu alone eliminated almost 20 menus. It also served to present the primary objects and operations of the product in an organized way with clear category labels.

An interesting design issue with the object-operation menu was that it required users to make two choices from a single screen. They had to choose both an object and an operation. For example, to create a menu, users would type "menu create" or "2 1" (they could also select items with the arrow keys). This requirement was new to Rally users and departed from traditional single-choice menu design. (However, it was somewhat consistent with the

FIGURE 1

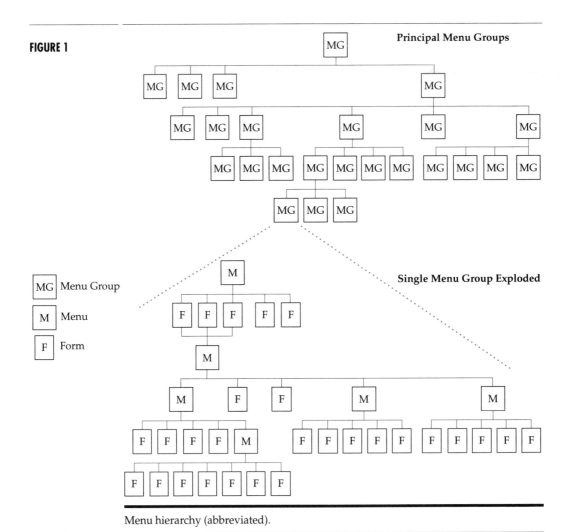

Menu hierarchy (abbreviated).

type-ahead feature incorporated into version 1.1.) To ease this transition, we provided not only an on-screen prompt, but we also provided for effective error recovery. If the user typed a single number, the system accepted the number, highlighted the chosen item, and changed the prompt to "Select an operation" (Figure 3).

Thus, the menus became context sensitive. If the user selected a choice from the left column, the choices on the right column would change to only those that were appropriate. For example, if the user selected "Message," the choices "Rename" and "Verify" would be removed, as in Figure 4.

By making the menu "selection sensitive," the user was directly led through the choices.

FIGURE 2

Primary objects:
1 **Task**
2 **Menu**
3 **Form/report**
4 Form/report **packet**
5 **Data** source definition
6 **Message**

Procedural objects:
7 **ADL** procedure
8 Global **variable**
9 External program **link**
10 **Parameter** packet
11 **Action** list

Format objects:
12 **Date** format
13 **Number** format
14 Number character **set**

Operations:
1 **Create**
2 **Edit**
3 **Delete**
4 **Rename**
5 **Copy**
6 **Verify**

GOLD-Q   Exit menu without
making a choice

Help   For more help

Select an object and an operation: _____

"Objects-operations" menu.

The concept of an object-operation menu was used whenever possible to reduce and simplify the menu hierarchy.

Flattening the menu hierarchy was only a partial approach to the problem of navigation. In a number of cases, the menu/form structure of the product could not adequately support work flow. In some cases, users would find themselves at the bottom of a menu tree in a form. Once the form was completed, the next logical operation would require navigation back up the menu tree and down another path to reach a form containing related information. For example, if the user were editing a menu and the menu contained a form/report name, the user might want to edit the form/report and then return to editing the menu.

Supporting this natural work flow required that users be allowed to "jump" across menus, preserving context of the present work (such as editing menus) and automatically specifying the new object of the work (such as editing a form/report). The preservation of context and new object specification are critical factors in supporting user work. The underlying architecture of Rally was stack-based; that is, forms could be stacked up and then popped off

FIGURE 3

Primary objects:
1 Task
2 Menu
3 Form/report
4 Form/report packet
5 Data source definition
6 Message

Procedural objects:
7 ADL procedure
8 Global variable
9 External program link
10 Parameter packet
11 Action list

Format objects:
12 Date format
13 Number format
14 Number character set

Select an operation:

Operations:
1 **Create**
2 **Edit**
3 **Delete**
4 **Rename**
5 **Copy**
6 **Verify**

GOLD-Q   Exit menu without
            making a choice

Help   For more help

Menu _____

Single selection from "objects column."

the stack as the user completed them. This stack-based approach provided the underlying support for jumping across the menu tree. In the previous version, users could type ahead in the menu structure and thus quickly navigate to the appropriate menu choice (provided they remembered the path). However, such navigation required them to specify the relevant object even though it was the currently selected one. Thus, an approach of allowing the users to directly access the functions when an object was selected significantly reduced users' memory load and allowed them to easily return to the present context. Such an approach "converted" the menu hierarchy into a network, minimized unnecessary navigation, and took the system closer to a direct manipulation approach. In effect, users could jump across the hierarchy, complete a task, and return to their point of departure. It was termed *edit-object*.

This was a fairly radical departure from a traditional menu structure. As the engineering manager put it:

One of the things that has always fascinated me about the DEC Rally Version 2 changes is that from the tool's point of view the menu tree became, technically, not a tree. It became a network, some nodes have more than one path that leads to them. To a computer scientist, having a menu tree with nodes that can be

FIGURE 4

Primary objects: Operations:
  1 Task   1 **Create**
  2 Menu   2 **Edit**
  3 Form/report   3 **Delete**
  4 Form/report packet
  5 Data source definition   5 **Copy**
  <mark>6 Message</mark>

Procedural objects:
  7 ADL procedure
  8 Global variable
  9 External program link   GOLD-Q Exit menu without
  10 Parameter packet   making a choice
  11 Action list
                                              Help   For more help
Format objects:
  12 Date format
  13 Number format
  14 Number character set

Select an operation: Message _____

"Selection sensitive" menu.

reached through more than one path might seem unorganized and confusing; to the users, it was exactly what they needed.

The ability to leap across the hierarchy was received enthusiastically by users and became a "delighting factor" in the interface.

Flattening the menu hierarchy and providing the edit-object approach significantly improved the menu interface. However, these design approaches did not specify the particular organization that the menu should take. The menu organization is determined by the "semantic structure" of the menu items and the flow of user work. The semantic structure of the product was well understood. An effective organization required an analysis of work flow. To review the work flow requirements against the menu design, we drew from the principles of usability engineering. A metric was suggested: number of menu transitions. A set of a dozen hypothetical tasks were devised and potential menu organizations were evaluated using the transition metric and the hypothetical task set. A menu structure that minimized the number of transitions was selected. The hypothetical tasks were devised by the development team. Since they actively used the product, this was reasonable; however, collecting scenarios from users would have been better.

Design Reflections

In the menu redesign, the following factors were important:

- Usability engineering applied early in the process
- Experience with other systems
- Familiarity with other systems
- Knowledge of the human factors literature
- The ability to prototype
- A flexible underlying architecture

The optimization of menu paths illustrates an interesting and often unappreciated aspect of usability engineering. One need not wait until a working prototype is constructed to evaluate a design. With a clear metric and a set of work tasks, one can evaluate design alternatives using the derived metric. No empirical lab tests need be run. Thus, usability engineering can have an impact on the early design phase of a project. Often this early impact is the most important. A clear statement of a metric and a goal serves as an "unconscious reminder" to the development group. It makes clear one of the goals of the design (Bennett, 1984). In some cases, like this one, it can provide specific data with respect to design alternatives.

One subtle contributor to the design of the menus was experience with other systems. The object operation was drawn from direct manipulation systems and applied in the context of a traditional character cell menu organization, changing its character radically.

Drawing from the human factors literature was a mixed blessing for our menu design efforts. Although the new design drew on the empirical literature of menu organization, the original design was hampered by a misunderstanding of the psychological literature. At least part of the depth of the original menu structure was attributed to the "psychological law" that menus should contain only seven items. This misunderstanding is apparently quite pervasive; it has even found its way into the academic literature (Kiger, 1984). In fact, short-term memory is completely unrelated to a menu system, whose aim is to facilitate recall.

A system that allowed for easy prototyping was a tremendous benefit in the menu redesign effort. The person responsible for the menu interface had reservations about the effectiveness of an object-operation menu for users, but because of the low effort involved he was willing to try it. In practice, it worked fine.

The menu changes such as the object-operation menu were accomplished with relatively little development work. The architecture of the system and the creativity of the team provided a simple and elegant approach to the problem. In this case, the two separate menu screens were simply overlaid on each other. Thus, though it looked like a single menu to the user, it was actually two menus.

List of Values Problem

The Problem

One of the features that was intended to make Rally easier to use was the list of values. The interface for Rally contained many forms. Fields in the forms could be filled in by selecting from a list of values that was contained at the right of the screen. (The list of values was affectionately known as LOV, pronounced "love.") A form with a list of values is depicted in Figure 5.

The list of values was dynamic and reflected variables in the application being developed. For example, once a user defined the fields in a database, the field names would be presented in the list of values at the right of the screen. This minimized both typing and remembering. Some of our earliest visits to customer sites uncovered unanticipated difficulties with the list of values. We found that many users developed large applications with many

FIGURE 5

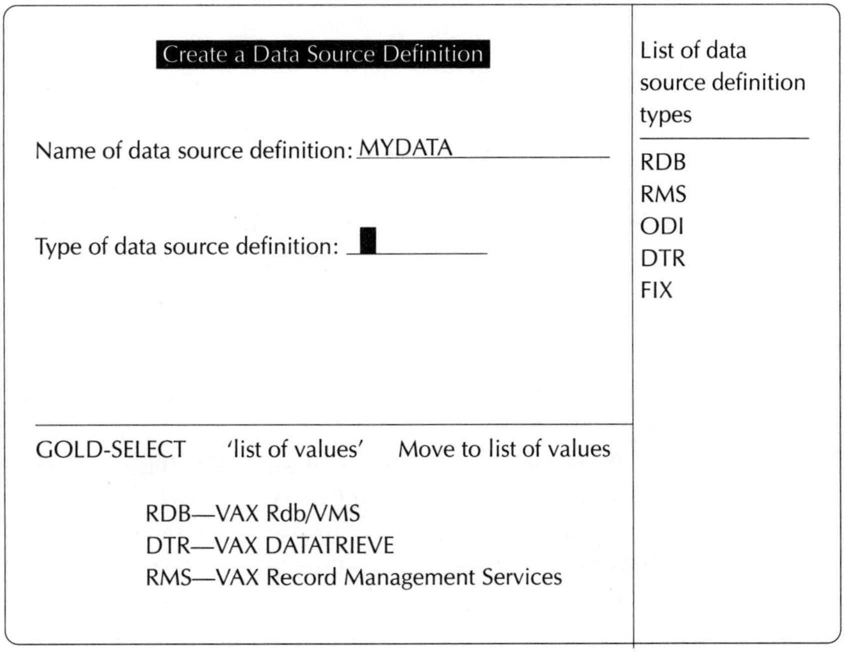

Create a Data Source Definition

Name of data source definition: MYDATA

Type of data source definition: ▮

List of data source definition types

RDB
RMS
ODI
DTR
FIX

GOLD-SELECT   'list of values'   Move to list of values

RDB—VAX Rdb/VMS
DTR—VAX DATATRIEVE
RMS—VAX Record Management Services

Example of list of values (LOV).

variables. Often the names of these variables were determined by corporate standards and approved by committees. The result was very long variable names in which the information became progressively more differentiated as one moved to the right of each name. A list might contain items like the following:

billing_information_customer_id_no

billing_information_customer_name_first

billing_information_customer_name_last

billing_information_customer_name_middle_initial

billing_information_customer_address_aptno

billing_information_customer_address_streetno

billing_information_customer_address_street_name

billing_information_customer_address_town

billing_information_customer_address_city

billing_information_customer_address_state

billing_information_customer_address_postal_code

billing_information_customer_address_nation

billing_information_customer_building

billing_information_customer_floor

billing_information_customer_mail_stop

Confronted with such terms, the list of values was of limited use because it displayed only the leftmost 17 characters. The user would see only "billing_informat" repeated 20 times. The design was constrained by the requirement that the system run on character cell terminals, with limited screen size (80 characters). Implementation concerns ruled out a pop-up window.

The system was designed to allow the user to scroll information in the list of values horizontally, but when users demonstrated how the scrolling worked it became painfully clear how frustrating this solution was. The user could scroll only a single line at a time. As a result, they could see only the differentiating information for a single line (Figure 6). In addition, if the line that they had scrolled did not contain the desired choice, they could move the cursor up or down a line. However, when the user moved to a new line the new line would not be scrolled, and the line they had just scrolled would revert to its previous position. Thus, users would scroll a line to the right, discover it was not the one they were looking for, and then have to repeat the process. This could happen many times. It was frustrating to users and

FIGURE 6

Hypothetical form to be filled in	Field names
Name of field:_____	billing_informati billing_informati billing_informati billing_informati name_middle_in▮
Type of data field:_____	billing_informati billing_informati billing_informati billing_informati billing_informati billing_informati
GOLD-SELECT 'list of values' Move to list of values	billing_informati billing_informati billing_informati billing_informati billing_informati

List of values single item scrolled.

painful to watch. An example narrated by an important customer was the "major feature" of one of our first video lunches.

Redesign

Two features were added to the product that alleviated the long variable name problem. First, the list as a whole was scrolled to the right when the user scrolled a single line. This gave the user a complete picture of the choices available. In effect, they were scrolling 20 lines instead of one. Moving up or down this list did not affect the left or right position. Second, with a single keystroke, the user could fill the screen with the list in question (Figure 7). A user could then scroll up or down the list and select a variable name. When the name was chosen, the original form was re-presented with the appropriate field filled in. Together, these features served to significantly alleviate the long variable name problem.

Design Reflections

From the viewpoint of the design process, there are three significant points about the long variable name problem.

The first is that we would have uncovered this problem only by visiting customers and seeing their real work. At the site visits, we discovered not

FIGURE 7

Hypothetical form to be filled in	Field names
	billing_information_customer_id_no
	billing_information_customer_name_first
Name of field: _____	billing_information_customer_name_last
	billing_information_customer_name_mid
	billing_information_customer_address_ap
Type of data field: _____	billing_information_customer_address_str
	billing_information_customer_addresses_s
	billing_information_customer_address_to
	billing_information_customer_address_cit
	billing_information_customer_address_sta
	billing_information_customer_address_po
GOLD-SELECT 'list of values' Mov	billing_information_customer_address_na
	billing_information_customer_building
	billing_information_customer_floor

List of values scrolled.

only that customers used long variable names but that these long variable names were determined by a companywide policy and process. Once entered into Rally, database names were subsequently automatically displayed as Rally objects and were defined by corporate database groups. Individual organizations did not have the latitude to change the way they worked to accommodate the limitations of a tool. We would never have discovered this problem with a benchmark test in our lab. Our task would never have included such long variable names.

Second, the use of videotape proved invaluable in this and many other cases. The problem of long variable names was a known problem. We had discussed it in design meetings prior to our site visit. But it had not been addressed because its relative importance was unclear. However, when we showed a video of a user at an important customer site walking through all the painful steps of scrolling an item to see the differentiating information, finding this was not the desired item, and then repeating the process, the significance of this limitation was impressed on all of us.

Finally, from the implementor point of view, this problem turned out to be easy to fix. It involved changing 3 characters in about 50 places in 500,000 lines of code. This illustrates another principle of design: *There is little or no correlation between the usability impact of a design change and the amount of effort involved in producing it.* (In some cases, the "better design" already existed in the code but had been commented out.)

Programming Environment Problem

The Problem

Like many 4GLs, Rally was designed with an embedded programming language called ADL. This programming language included its own screen editor that allowed a user to create code without leaving the development environment. It was assumed in the design that the programming language would be used only rarely and to a limited extent. As is often the case with 4GLs, the programming language was included almost grudgingly.

Our visits to customer sites showed that the assumptions of the designers with respect to the programming language were not justified. The customers made extensive use of the programming language, and many depended on it. As a result, the interface to the programming language was closely examined and found to be inadequate and inconsistent with the design of the rest of the product.

Throughout the product, memory and typing requirements were minimized by the use of the list of values. However, in the programming environment no list of values was provided. There was no simple interactive way to determine the variables used in the system under development. In developing traditional programs, one can cut and paste variable names from one module to another. However, as is the practice with many 4GLs, Rally did not produce source code. It did produce reports, but these were of limited value and could not be readily used in developing ADL code.

Confronted with this situation, the users had resorted to a series of complex work-arounds. The most popular was printing out copies of screens that contained the variable names. However, this work-around was inadequate in many cases since the variable names were long and the screens presented only the first 17 characters. It also failed to solve the problem of having to retype names that the system already had stored.

Redesign

The solution to this problem was not as simple as the long variable names problem. Although in one sense it was clear that something like a "list of values" was needed, its design was not straightforward. In the case of forms, information previously filled in on the current form and the position of the cursor on a particular field provided the system with the needed data to select the appropriate list to present. In the case of writing code, this type of information was missing. A number of categories of information could be provided. To provide an undifferentiated list would not be useful.

FIGURE 8

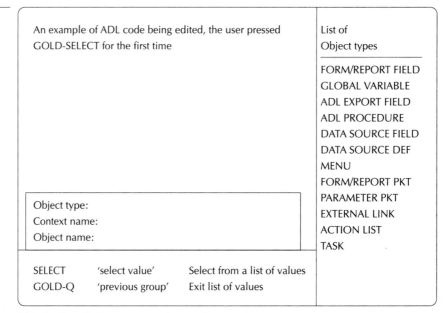

An example of ADL code being edited, the user pressed GOLD-SELECT for the first time	List of Object types
	FORM/REPORT FIELD
	GLOBAL VARIABLE
	ADL EXPORT FIELD
	ADL PROCEDURE
	DATA SOURCE FIELD
	DATA SOURCE DEF
	MENU
	FORM/REPORT PKT
Object type: Context name: Object name:	PARAMETER PKT EXTERNAL LINK ACTION LIST TASK

| SELECT | 'select value' | Select from a list of values |
| GOLD-Q | 'previous group' | Exit list of values |

List of values in the programming environment.

Eventually, we developed an approach in which users selected from successively presented lists of values, thereby gradually narrowing the search space. The choices that they had made up to that point could be reversed by pressing the backspace key. For example, users would ask to see a list and be given the values shown in Figure 8.

When they chose an alternative (for example, FORM/REPORT FIELD), they would be presented with a new list (Figure 9).

The process would then continue to the third step. At this point, the final entry would be made. This approach worked well and was incorporated into the product.

Design Reflections

From a design perspective, there were two interesting lessons here. First, users may suggest a design that is actually suboptimal—a work-around. This illustrates that it is necessary to probe behind users' design solutions and understand the problem before designing a solution. The example here can also be seen in terms of Pelle Ehn's (1988) tradition and transcendence distinction. People ask for support of their current work (tradition) even if it is suboptimal. *It requires a more reflective approach that probes behind offered solutions to create new alternatives (transcendence).*

The example of the list of values in the programming environment also illustrates that *successful solutions may obscure new approaches.* It was very

FIGURE 9

An example of ADL code being edited, the user pressed GOLD-SELECT for the first time	List of form/reports fields
	ALPHA
	GAMMA
	HYDRA
	DELTA
	SIGMA
	PHI
	SUMMA
	FRED
	BILL
	SUE

Object type: FORM/REPORT FIELD
Context name:
Object name:

| SELECT | 'select value' | Select from a list of values |
| GOLD-Q | 'previous group' | Exit list of values |

List of values with name selected.

difficult for the design team to think about the list of values concept in a context other than forms fill-in. Once the conceptual breakthrough had occurred, the design and implementation were straightforward. As one of the developers put it, "a novel and interesting engineering concept; a very small amount of engineering effort."

Finally, these coding examples illustrate again the misconceptions designers can have about their product until they see how it is used. Coding was not seen as important or needed until we visited customers.

Useless Information Problem

The Problem

Version 1.1 of Rally provided a potentially useful feature of prompting the user at the bottom of the screen with some context-sensitive help. This feature has been subsequently incorporated into later products such as Microsoft Excel. It can be very effective.

Unfortunately, in the first version of the Rally interface, its potential was not realized. The information provided at the bottom of the screen described the appropriate command. The information was presented in a paragraphlike format. Although it specified commands, it did not present accelerator keys.

In fact, most users made extensive use of these keys. The rationale for presenting commands only was that we could not be sure of the keyboard that the user was working on, so information about accelerator keys would not be appropriate. It would contain information like:

Use the 'list_of_values' and 'select value' commands to select a data type. Or, type the name of a data type followed by <RETURN>.

The Solution

The new system presented three types of information: which key to press, what the relevant command was, and a brief description of the effect of the command. The information was presented in a three-column format and was kept succinct. For example:

GOLD-SELECT	'list_of_values'	Move to the list of values
SELECT	'local_function'	Edit the object names

The leftmost column provided a keyboard assignment of the keys. The center column provided the command that one could type in if he or she was running on a keyboard that lacked the appropriate function key. The rightmost column was an abbreviated description of what the command did. We never formally tested this new format. It seemed obvious that the information was more effective given this presentation.

This design change seems very straightforward. It was not made sooner because there was a concern that some users of the product might not be using traditional Digital keyboards (VT100), and there was a reluctance to point to function keys that these users might not have or be aware of. This illustrates that software engineers tend to be influenced by low frequency events. Possibly training in mathematics, where thinking is categorical rather than probabilistic, or experience in programming, which demands attention to excruciating levels of detail, explains this phenomenon.

The final design actually served all the users since it presented the key accelerators, the command, and a one-line description. It also served to encourage users to buy the latest Digital terminal.

The solution here was based on a relatively straightforward application of some of the basic principles of documentation: *Be succinct, be clear, lay out your information in a useful way based on the context in which it is presented.* Another principle is *don't begin by compromising the design in consideration of low frequency data; it is often possible to design for everyone.*

Long Lists of Values Problem

One problem that had been uncovered during our customer visits was that lists of values would often contain many items. To select a value, users had to scroll through many items using cursor arrows. Graphical user interfaces have standard mechanisms such as scroll bars to address this problem, but in our environment this solution was not possible. At least two approaches were suggested for the long list problem. One was to allow the page keys (next and previous screen) to work on the list of values. This would make navigation quicker. A second alternative was to provide dynamic subsetting of the list of values such that typing a letter or set of letters would reduce the list of values to those items that matched the set typed. Both of these alternatives were eventually adopted. However, the dynamic subsetting was not implemented until version 2.1 of the product.

This experience illustrates another aspect of design work: *What doesn't get done in this version will get done in the next version, provided that the product survives and the design change is kept salient. Or do tomorrow what you have put off today.*

Expert Learning Problem

The redesign of Rally involved a number of extensive changes to the look and the feel of the product. One of the early concerns (cf. Telles, 1990) was for the impact that this would have on the efficiency of experts and on their opinion of the system. Well-practiced users of Rally were very familiar with the menu hierarchy and by using the type-ahead feature could navigate through the system quickly. This hierarchy was being radically altered.

One of the goals of the redesign was to have a minimal impact on experts. However, what is a minimal impact? Clearly, the most minimal impact would involve no redesign at all; however, given the state of the system, this was not acceptable. An empirical assessment of the learning of the new system by experts was conducted during the customer site visits. Performance was measured in terms of time to complete a task. Our minimum acceptable level was an equality between the new and old systems. (Equality was selected because the comparison was between performance on a system that these users had used daily for over a year and were acknowledged experts with and performance on a system that they had just been introduced to.) Our target level was a 25 percent improvement, and our best case was a 50 percent improvement.

FIGURE 10

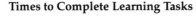

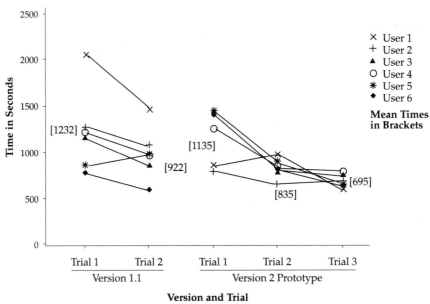

Learning times with prototype and version 1.1.

Five equivalent tasks were developed. The users—all of whom had over a year of experience with the version 1 product and used it daily—were asked to do two of the tasks on the current system and three of the tasks on the new system. In conducting the tests, the order of version and the task were balanced as closely as possible.

Figure 10 depicts the results. The time to complete tasks in seconds is represented on the Y axis, and the trials with the original system and the new system are represented on the X axis. The lines connect the performance figures for each user. The means are presented in brackets at the appropriate positions along the Y axis. With such a small sample, we decided to plot all the data to provide a clear picture of the variability in performance for different users.

The variability among users and the small sample size preclude any statistical comparisons. However, there are a couple of interesting observations one can make. First, variability among experts with version 1.1 is quite high in comparison with version 2. Five of the six experts show better times on the prototype than on version 1.1. With such a small sample, the average performance needs to be interpreted with caution. Nevertheless, the average time for the prototype version on the final trial is about 30 percent less than for version 1.1. Even on the second trial, performance is about 15 percent faster, and the trend that five of the six experts were quicker on the prototype is maintained. Interestingly, these data are consistent with some spontaneous comments that experienced users voiced with respect to the product. One said, "Once I learn it, I think I can be about 25 percent more efficient with the new version."

As a general principle, *a focused test be can used to address a general concern about the interface.* As the product manager put it, "it was great to know that the product would actually be usable before we shipped it."

Preferences

Differences in performance would have been of little consequence if the experienced users had disliked the new system. We asked users to rate each system on a series of 7-point scales. The differences are shown in Figure 11. The experienced users were generally more positive in their ratings of the prototype. Each user's ratings is shown in a single bar. If the user rated version 1.1 and the version 2 prototype equally, a bar does not appear.

Version 2 prototype was rated more positively than version 1.1 on 44 of 50 preference ratings.

Specific Design Issues

In developing the new menu system, access to some of the functionality was significantly changed. In certain specific areas, we were concerned that the redesign had made the features less accessible. We decided to conduct a diagnostic test of the performance of users on the current version and the prototype in just those areas where we had made substantial changes. Our measure was the speed with which users could complete a task. Our specific test areas were:

- Making a field invisible on a form
- Creating a legend (text to appear at the bottom of a form) and associating it with a field
- Creating a data field
- Changing the default format for the display of dates
- Creating a two-group form report with a control break

FIGURE 11

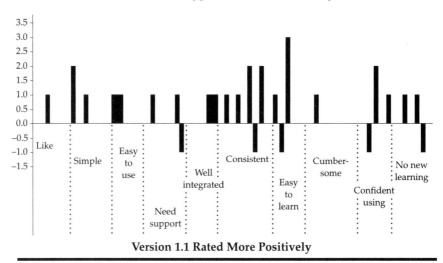

Preference rating by experts for version 2 prototype versus version 1.1.

The results are depicted in Figure 12. The squares reflect individual data points for the prototype. Triangles reflect times for version 1.1, crosses for the prototype of version 2. Averages for the V2 prototype are depicted by a plus sign, whereas averages for V1.1 are depicted by a cross.

In four of the five tests, performance was poorer with the V2 prototype. We had hoped for better. We had chosen to look at problematic parts of the new design, and our test was very stringent; we did not give these users any training in or explanation of the prototype. The data for legends, fields, and date format are roughly comparable. Two sets of data stood out from the rest. First, we had succeeded in making the creation of a two-group report significantly easier with a reduction in time of about 80 percent. At the same time, we had made making a field nondisplayed significantly harder, with an increase in time of 600 percent! Whereas in version 1.1 making a field nondisplayed had been a specific menu choice, in the prototype it was accessed by a function key in the screen editor.

We responded to the nondisplayed problem, which we had created in the version 2 prototype, by implementing a suggestion made by several customers. First, we allowed users to make fields nondisplayed simply by deleting them from the layout screen. As one developer put it, "the change was so damn obvious we had to have the users suggest it." We also added a way to make fields nondisplayed on a form that included specifying the position of items. Finally, we included a menu choice of "editing a form/report

FIGURE 12

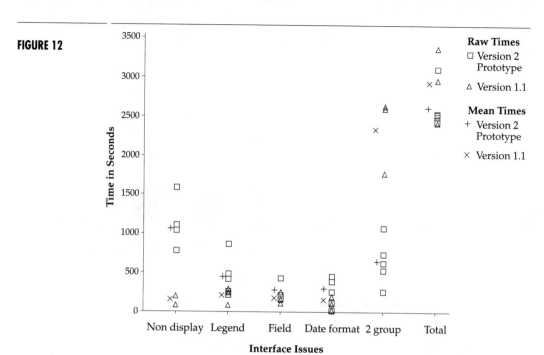

Performance on specific interface issues.

field" in a place where users would expect it. Informal observations suggested that these changes eliminated the problem.

This brings up an interesting point about design. Informal and formal tests can often work in tandem. We learned from the more formal tests what the important problems in the new design were, but the informal channels of communication with users gave us the best solution. One conclusion is *a mix of methods is better than relying on any method in isolation.*

Usability "Bugs"

Earlier, we mentioned that we had included usability problems in the tracking system for software bugs. We used this system throughout the version 2 development process. Figure 13 shows the relative frequency of usability problems at various priority levels and their disposition, where 1 is a high priority and 5 is a low priority.

Clearly, prioritization served to effectively allocate resources. Generally, high-priority issues were addressed, and low-priority issues were not. The prioritization scheme put usability problems on a par with reliability issues.

FIGURE 13

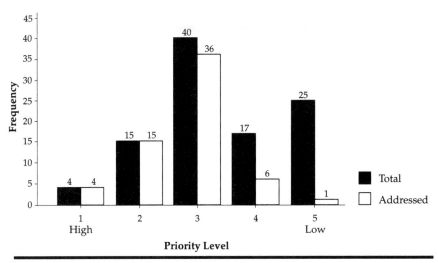

Usability problems.

In the software development cycle at Digital, products must pass certain quality levels to continue through the development cycle. Consequently, there were additional strong incentives to address usability issues. Once issues had been prioritized, it was not necessary to continue to lobby for the resources to address them.

Overall, the prioritization gave the usability consultant a strong role in the development process and reflected the confidence and trust the team had in the process and the people. In addition, strong management support was critical in implementing this process. Some other groups have been unwilling to incorporate a usability priority system in their quality tracking process.

The process principle here is that *one can use existing quality tools and methods in novel ways to solidify a commitment to usability.*

Conclusions

Impact on Revenue

A dramatic change in the interface of a product is a substantial risk. Users often prefer a familiar interface to one that is "improved" (Telles, 1990).

Deciding on the right changes is not an easy task, particularly in a large corporation where there are many barriers between product development engineering and the customer. Although prototype testing and contextual inquiry can provide one with some basis for confidence about an extensively redefined interface, in the final analysis acceptance by the customer is the ultimate test, not just of the interface but of the product as a whole and its marketing and support strategy. Even some of the most innovative products like the Macintosh experienced disappointing sales performance until they were "refined" with customer input.

The sales of version 2 of DEC Rally demonstrate that the product as a whole was a success. The data are shown in Figure 14, which plots revenue over time. The dashed line indicates a rough projection of revenue growth.

Revenues for version 2 of DEC Rally increased, on average, by about 80 percent. One could argue that revenues for a version 2 product should increase. However, the revenues for version 2 of Rally are about 30 to 60 percent over an optimistic projection. In surveys conducted by an independent quality group at Digital, improved usability is cited as the second most important aspect of the version 2 product (with improved database support listed first). Our usability efforts provided Digital with an excellent return on our investment. At the same time, the work was enjoyable.

Process, Methods, and Theory

While developing version 2 of Rally, we used a number of techniques: usability engineering, prototyping, formal software quality tracking, highly focused empirical tests, and contextual inquiry. Each method made a unique contribution to the overall product evolution. Usability engineering was most effective in the menu redesign where specific metrics could be readily applied to test alternatives. Contextual inquiry contributed most to the solution of the list of values problem because the engineering team could see the details of the cumbersome interaction with version 1.1 and came to appreciate that the simple work-around of shortening menu names would not work in the user's cultural environment. With respect to the overall design, we believe that the methods worked synergistically to produce a better design.

The development team was not merely receptive to input from user interface designers. They originated a number of the user interface changes before the Software Usability Group was involved. The role of the usability engineer was more in terms of focusing some parts of the design effort with data and providing some counseling on UI design practice in other systems. The effort developed into a true team approach in which we all were committed to improving the product.

FIGURE 14

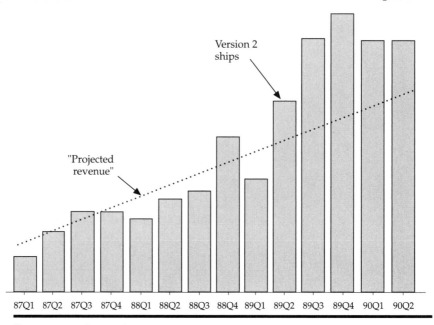

DEC Rally Revenue by Quarter

30%–60% revenue growth

Version 2
ships

"Projected
revenue"

87Q1 87Q2 87Q3 87Q4 88Q1 88Q2 88Q3 88Q4 89Q1 89Q2 89Q3 89Q4 90Q1 90Q2

Revenue growth over time.

In version 1.1, we consistently saw a gap between the potential of a UI and its practice. The relative role of theory and practice in design is the source of much discussion (Lewis, 1990). Suffice it to say that theory devoid of detailed design is insufficient to produce a successful product. On the other hand, simply an iterative approach without any grounding in design theory can result in unproductive changes.

Changes late in a design effort are often thought to be restricted to trivial details. Our experience here is not consistent with that generalization. Important changes came late in the development work, but they were planned for in the schedule and did not come as a surprise. Also the fundamental architecture of the product made changes easy. (It also made some methods possible like prototyping the interface.) We saw again that there was little or no correlation between the impact of user interface changes and the effort involved in making them.

In practice, major categories of user interfaces (command, menu icon) (Shneiderman, 1983) do not fully apply to a product. In fact, many of the successful aspects of the design of this product are the result of blurring these distinctions.

Finally, we had strong management support for a major user interface effort. This was due both to group culture—they used the product and were aware of the limitations of version 1.1—and to customer input—they asked for UI changes. Management experience with incorporating usability into products also played a role.

Future Directions

Gould, Boies, and Lewis (1991) have suggested that the success of a product depends on usability (how the product works, its usefulness), what the product does, and productivity (what the user can accomplish from a corporate viewpoint). Each of these needs to be addressed in context. Some contextual questions are:

- Who are the competitors, and how well do they address these issues?
- What are the customers' current practices and expectations for this product in this space?
- What is the prevailing user interface culture, and what expectations does it set?

The environment for software products is changing rapidly. In the past, design theory and formal articulation of method have lagged behind practice. This can be healthy to the extent that effective methods and theories are tested, not in isolated laboratories or dry theoretical papers, but in the crucible of the marketplace.

Acknowledgments

We wish to thank the following people:

The original Rally team consisted of Lew Lasher, Tony Rogers, Ruth Parker, Daryl Gleason, Chris Schuetz, Jackie Gosselin, Chuck Murray, Tom Wright, and Ray Giroux. John Henning was the supervisor. They all contributed substantially to the success of Rally V2.0.

Members of the Software Usability Group who assisted in the original Rally project include Tom Spine and Charles Frean.

Reviewers of this manuscript were Chauncey Wilson, Leo Treggiari, Anne Duncan, Michael Good, and Mary Beth Raven.

We want to express a special thanks to the customers who participated in the prototype reviews.

Finally, a thanks to Karen Holtzblatt and John Whiteside, who provided the foundations for many of the methods used here.

The following are trademarks of Digital Equipment Corporation: DEC Rally, Digital, RDB, VAX, Rdb/VMS, DTR, DATATRIEVE, RMS, and VMS. Excel is a trademark of Microsoft Corporation. Macintosh is a trademark of Apple Corporation.

References

Bennett, J. A. (1984). Managing to meet usability requirements: Establishing and meeting software development goals. In J. Bennett, D. Case, J. Sandelin, and M. Smith, *Video Display Terminals,* Englewood Cliffs, NJ: Prentice Hall.

Ehn, P. (1988). *Work-Oriented Design of Computer Artifacts.* Stockholm: Arbetlivscentrum.

Gilb, T. (1988). *Principles of Software Engineering Management.* New York: Addison-Wesley.

Good, M. (1989). Seven experiences with contextual field research. *SIGCHI Bulletin* 20(4), 25–33.

Good, M., Spine, T. M., Whiteside, J., and George, P. (1986). User-derived impact analysis as a tool for usability engineering. In *Proceedings of CHI'86, Human Factors in Computing Systems* (Boston, April 13–17, 1986). New York: ACM, 241–246.

Gould, J., Boies S. J., and Lewis, C. (1991). Making usable, useful, productivity-enhancing computer applications. *Communications of the ACM* 34(1), 74–85.

Holtzblatt, K. and Jones, S. (1990). *Contextual Inquiry: Principles and Practice,* Digital Equipment Corporation, Technical Report, October 1990, DEC-TR 729.

Ishikawa, K. (1982). *Guide to Quality Control.* Tokyo: Asian Productivity Organization, 2d. ed., 42–50.

Kiger, J. (1984). The depth/breadth trade-off in the design of menu-driven user interfaces. *International Journal of Man Machine Studies* 20, 201–213.

Lasher, L. (1988). The VAX Rally system—A relational fourth-generation language. *Digital Technical Journal* 6.

Lewis, C. (1990). A research agenda for the nineties in human-computer interaction. *Human Computer Interaction* 5(2 and 3). Hillsdale, NJ: Lawrence Erlbaum Associates.

Miller, G. (1956). The magical number seven plus or minus two: Some limits on our capacity for processing information. *Psychological Review* 63, 81–97.

Rubinstein, R. and Hersh, H. (1984). *The Human Factor.* Burlington, MA: Digital Press.

Shneiderman, B. (1983). Direct manipulation: A step beyond programming languages. *Computer* 16(8), 57–69.

Snowberry, K. (1983). Computer display menus. *Ergonomics* 26(7), 699–712.

Telles, M. (1990). Updating an older interface. In *Proceedings of CHI'90, Human Factors in Computing Systems* (Seattle, April 1–5, 1990). New York: ACM, 243–247.

Whiteside, J. A. (1986). Usability engineering. *UNIX Review* 4(6), 22–37.

Whiteside, J., Bennett, J. and Holtzblatt, K. (1988). Usability engineering our experience and evolution. In M. Helander (ed.), *Handbook of Human Computer Interaction.* New York: North Holland, 791–817.

Whiteside, J. and Wixon, D. (1987). Improving human-computer interaction—a quest for cognitive science. In J. M. Carroll (ed.), *Interfacing Thought: Cognitive Aspects of Human Computer Interaction.* Cambridge, MA: Bradford/MIT Press, 337–352.

Winograd, T. and Flores, F. (1986). *Understanding Computers and Cognition.* Norwood, NJ: Ablex.

Wixon, D., Holtzblatt, K., and Knox, S. (1990). Contextual design: An emergent view of system design. In *Proceedings of CHI'90, Human Factors in Computing Systems* (Seattle, April 1–5, 1990). New York: ACM, 329–336.

Rapid, Integrated Design of a Multimedia Communication System

ELLEN FRANCIK
Pacific Bell

Practitioners in human-computer interaction (HCI) are urged to go beyond usability testing to address all aspects of product design and use. However, we must continue to do this work within tight development schedules. In recent years, there have been reassurances that rapid evaluations, thoughtfully done, do in fact identify the most pressing design issues. These methods include contextual interviews with a small but diverse sample (Wixon, Holtzblatt, and Knox, 1990), heuristic interface evaluations by trained HCI specialists (Nielsen, 1992), and small-n usability studies (Nielsen, 1989; Virzi, 1990).

The first two techniques rely on depth rather than breadth. Contextual interviews combine observation at the user's place of work with active engagement and discussion during the interview. The interviewer's goal is to understand user requirements for a given system in the context of the user's many other activities and the meaning of those activities. The power of this technique lies in the quality of observation and interviewing and the careful selection of a diverse set of users. Heuristic evaluations of system usability depend on the converging opinions of several usability experts, who ideally are also experts in the domain of the user's work. The third technique, running usability studies with just a few participants (also called "discount" usability engineering), assumes that major usability problems are quickly identified and fixed so that the interface can be tested repeatedly.

When rapid methods can be used together, they are yet more powerful. The work of an IBM team designing the 1984 Olympic Messaging System (Gould et al., 1987) is deservedly cited as an example of rapid, integrated design. The OMS team, a small interdisciplinary group, was responsible for all aspects of usability for a multilingual messaging kiosk for Olympic athletes and their families. Their methods included physical site surveys, participatory design, lab prototyping, walk-up-and-test kiosk mockups, and full-blown field trials. Their findings influenced all facets of the system: operator assistance for family members calling from abroad, design of supporting material including athletes' nametags, and expansion in the number of languages supported by the kiosk.

The present case study also illustrates the successful use of several HCI methods in the design of a commercial product, a pen-based multimedia communication system. It shows the interdependence of laboratory and field methods; of hardware, software, and documentation design; of development, marketing, and sales support. But this case study goes beyond the scope of the Olympic Messaging System case study. It describes how HCI results were used in strategies to create new markets and encourage long-term use of the product.

Work on this multimedia system began in the mid-1980s as a technology experiment. After repeated demos, it became a fully funded project with a swiftly growing development team and an aggressive product schedule. Only two and one-half years elapsed between the first proof-of-concept demos and release 1.0—and that included design and manufacturing of custom hardware. The design process was informal and iterative. Software and hardware engineers formed the core team, joined by human factors engineers, industrial designers, technical writers, and marketers.

The methods evolved as the project grew and provided converging information. In fact, it's difficult to separate the laboratory and field methods. Instead, the upcoming sections are organized by the areas affected by the methods: hardware design, software design, and workgroup support. First, however, we begin with a system description.

The Completed Design and Original Concept

In 1988, Wang Laboratories bundled together the familiar technologies of image capture, voice recording, and electronic mail and added pen annotation and high-resolution graphics. The result was the Freestyle system, providing multimedia communication for networked personal computers (Wang, 1989). People captured computer screens or scanned-in paper as images, applied synchronized handwritten and voice annotations using a graphics tablet and a voice handset, and mailed these messages to other PCs. A special-purpose desktop environment was used to store, organize, and mail the images (Figure 1).

Images were created in four ways: capturing any screenful of information displayed on the PC; scanning in existing paper information such as forms or diagrams; receiving a fax via a fax card in the PC; or sketching and writing on

FIGURE 1

Freestyle image desktop; handwriting and voice annotation tools.

a blank screen ("electronic paper"). Scanners and fax cards linked Freestyle workgroups to established paper processes.

Freestyle recorded not only handwriting but also stylus cursor movement, allowing the user to point while talking. The combined inputs produced a dynamic multimedia message that was mailed to others and played back. Graphic buttons above the image controlled the playback of synchronized voice, hand-drawn, and typed messages. As a result, people pointed at things they were talking about rather than describing them verbally. For instance, a user reviewing a budget spreadsheet would point and say, "*This* number seems out of line compared to last month's figures."

Freestyle captured work not typically done on computers, using familiar skills such as writing, sketching, and talking on the phone. It was suited for rapid, complex communication: problem solving, commenting, negotiating, planning, and design. This image-based annotation tool thus supported distributed workgroups who otherwise required more expensive, bandwidth-intensive computer or videoconferencing systems. For example, design and manufacturing groups in different cities could use these technologies to communicate more clearly about changes to design drawings, eliminating the need to travel for face-to-face meetings.

Freestyle owed much of its design to Stephen Levine, its dynamic development manager, and his vision of a computer that even his father-in-law Leonard could use (Levin, 1988). Design team members learned that Leonard, a prototypical keyboard-phobic executive, spent much of his day meeting with people, reviewing documents, and talking on the phone. The goal of the Freestyle system was to support these needs with advanced technology (imaging, electronic mail, voice annotation, pen-based computing), packaged in a form that Leonard could love (Levine and Ehrlich, 1991).

This design concept had four corollaries with far-reaching consequences for hardware design, software design, and workgroup support:

- Support use of familiar skills.
- Benchmark the system against the physical world.
- Emphasize innovation.
- Provide flexibility and encourage customization.

Support Use of Familiar Skills

The development team sought to make the product easy to use by taking advantage of people's knowledge of the physical world, minimizing the number of required commands, and providing great flexibility. Physical objects and operations were mirrored throughout the Freestyle system. PC screens were captured as images by bringing the pen close to the tablet. Users could begin to write immediately, with no mode switch or menu navigation, and use a pink eraser on the pen to erase annotations. Synchronized voice annotations were added through a voice handset, based on a speakerphone for more spontaneous hands-free operation. However, controlling the playback of recorded speech could not mimic turn-taking in conversations—no raised eyebrows or polite interruptions—so standard tape recorder controls were used instead.

Real-world desks are covered with paper and folders. People maintain mental models of the spatial locations of papers and categories of papers on their desks and in their offices (Malone, 1983). People overlap paper, they create piles, they put things in folders, and they put critical documents in prominent places. Freestyle directly and flexibly mimicked these activities. Annotated documents stored on the graphical desktop could be haphazardly overlapped, neatly piled, moved into folders, stapled together, or separated by unstapling. The document images were recognizable one-eighth-size miniatures. No labels or PC file names were required. The miniatures could be quickly, fluidly moved around the screen; the entire miniature moved, not just the outline, so the illusion of control over concrete objects was maintained. Other common functions were represented by desktop icons: copier, printer, scanner, phone book for addresses, individual mail slots, additional blank and ruled paper notepads, and a file cabinet for archival storage. Because of this flexibility, the desktop reflected the changing work patterns both of individuals and of workgroups.

Benchmark the System Against the Physical World

The physical world set high standards for this new multimedia system. As a result, Freestyle was optimized for graphical fidelity and high performance. A host of hardware and software inventions ensured that rapid handwriting was signature quality without jagged curves or missing strokes; that voice and handwriting were exactly synchronized, and played back as quickly or slowly as they had been created; and that document miniatures were recognizable and could be rapidly dragged around the desktop without flickering.

Emphasize Innovation

These stringent performance requirements, plus the challenge of making multimedia computing truly accessible to novices, led the design team to emphasize innovation. Freestyle's target platform was the (then) widely available 286 PC. However, standard windowing interfaces for those PCs couldn't support dynamic, high-fidelity playback of synchronized voice and handwriting. Moreover, those interfaces weren't Leonard-proof. If Leonard had to name his documents mydoc.txt, he wasn't going to use the system. And mice, the standard input devices for windowing systems, were ill-suited to handwriting and sketching. (The development team's view of mice was reflected in its name, the Computer Annotation Technologies or CAT group.)

Instead, the Freestyle system co-existed with PC and minicomputer applications. Users could capture, annotate, store, and share information from any of these other applications. Freestyle behaved like a TSR (terminate and stay resident) utility, suspending the current application when the pen touched the tablet. The user could annotate the captured screen image or proceed to the Freestyle desktop. When the user left Freestyle, the suspended application resumed.

Note the apparent tension between this design principle (emphasize innovation) and the first (support use of familiar skills). But in fact, many innovations were technical. Hardware and software advances—more responsive tablets, improved image rendering, an operating environment separate from Microsoft Windows—made it possible to create a computer environment whose paperlike operation would be familiar to users.

Provide Flexibility and Encourage Customization

The Freestyle system was intended to support spontaneous communication rather than structured work flows—as the name implied. Its interface encouraged customization of workspaces to fit individual work styles and communication patterns. The desktop was entirely malleable. Not only documents but also icons could be rearranged. Most functions were installed by dragging icons out of a "catalog," and deinstalled by moving the icons to the wastebasket.

The address book contained both shared and personal sections. The personal book contained a subset of frequently used addresses from the corporate book, plus any fax numbers. The most frequently used addresses or distribution lists could be turned into "mail slot" icons residing directly on the desktop. A profile editor allowed users to change cursor shape, pop-up menu timing, and the proximity required between documents so that they would snap into neat piles (rather than overlapping). Finally, modular design of hardware and software options such as voice, fax, and personal scanners allowed users to choose only those options they needed.

These four design concepts (familiarity, flexibility, innovation, customization) focused on individuals' use of the system, on personal choice and productivity. Later in the project, we were able to emphasize workgroups' use of the system. In the meantime, there was plenty of work to do to ensure that the system *was* usable for individuals, and these design concepts drove the design of the hardware and software.

Hardware Design

Hardware design began early—two years before Freestyle was released (1986). Based on the initial design concept, the goal was to have electronic devices that were as expressive and easy to write with as pen and paper. This meant that the tablet needed to have quick response, fine resolution, and accuracy, and that the pen had to have a responsive, natural feel. The design efforts began by assessing system performance, proceeded to physical design of the hardware, and concluded by studying use of the system for real work.

Assessment of Existing Products

Engineers from the development team bought off-the-shelf tablets varying in size, performance, and resolution—and tried to break them. It wasn't hard. A battery of informal tests, ranging from natural handwriting to frantic scribbles to slow, straight lines drawn with rulers, quickly proved that most of the tablets had not been designed with handwriting in mind.

Many of the problems that emerged during these try-to-destroy-it tests (as Gould, 1988, calls them) were obvious: jagged lines, missing line segments, or other graphical artifacts. These were serious problems arising from the fact that handwriting was a very demanding use of these tablets; handwriting is precise, dynamic, angular, and involves rapid changes of direction. Compensating for the limitations of these tablets meant writing slowly, retracing parts of some letters, and having to erase large lines that the computer automatically drew between points. Other problems, such as timing lags, were more subtle, but there were extra loops in handwriting where people were redoing strokes they thought the tablet had missed, such as N's becoming M's. The lag made the system feel slow, which was vaguely disconcerting and somewhat difficult.

None of the tablets was ideal. However, one computer-aided design (CAD) tablet seemed likely to provide the necessary speed and resolution. We worked with the vendor to continue to improve the hardware's performance and to redesign the bulky tablet and pen—a process that was more than cosmetic since it eventually required re-engineering every component. The hardware design was based on laboratory tests of working and model components, prototyped, and then evaluated during long-term use in internal and customer sites (Francik and Akagi, 1989).

Laboratory Testing

Based on the try-to-destroy-it tests, paperlike performance was a lofty goal indeed. Nevertheless, the development team continued to push hardware and software design as close to that goal as time, budget, and technology would permit. In keeping with that goal, the human factors lab evaluations used real pens and paper as a basis for design and testing.

Thirteen evaluators participated. In their daily work, these people frequently commented on documents or otherwise preferred handwriting and speaking to typing. The session began with a benchmark task in which evaluators filled in a paper form as we noted how they positioned the paper. Next came a series of drawing, writing, and annotation tasks on the working CAD-tablet system. Finally, everyone completed a questionnaire. It covered four topics: ease of writing on an opaque tablet; "feel" of the working pen and tablet; proposed (foam board model) tablets of various sizes; and proposed (wooden model) pens of various lengths, thicknesses, and cord placements.

Pen Design

The CAD pen had been designed for pointing, menu selection, and tracing in CAD applications. Its size, shape, balance, feel, and texture were not suited for handwriting. As a real-world benchmark, we gathered a variety of ink pens, from fat felt-tips to slender ball-points, and had evaluators select their favorite: The average diameter was 7.2 mm. Not surprisingly, the CAD pen's 12 mm diameter was rated "too thick" for handwriting (5.92 on a 7-point scale, where 1–3 = too thin, 4 = neutral, and 5–7 = too thick). Of five models ranging from 8 to 12 mm, evaluators preferred the 9 mm model (ranked 1.69 out of 5) and unanimously rejected the 12 mm model (5.00). We recommended 10 mm, the smallest diameter electrically possible.

The pen's feel also needed work. Evaluators said that writing required too much pressure and a near-vertical pen angle. The steel tip scraped and jittered across the tablet's textured surface. Finally, the shaft of the pen was a very glossy plastic, difficult to grip. For the new design, we tapered the barrel of the writing end so that the pen could be held at a writing angle, changed the tip from steel to plastic for a smoother writing feel, and added a matte texture and ribbed grip area. Minimum and maximum writing pressure were determined from additional brief tests of ball-point pens, felt-tip pens, and pencils.

Cord placement and pen length both depended on erasure. The development team expected erasure to be relatively frequent, and wanted an easily accessed, easily learned switch on the pen that wouldn't be accidentally activated while writing—in other words, a pink eraser for Leonard. This meant moving the "pencil's" cord to the side. But evaluators were sharply divided on this issue, some favoring the change and others arguing that a side cord would unbalance the pen, drape across the back of the hand, or hinder rapid writing. Based on evaluators' rankings of model pens with side cords, we recommended a length of 160 mm and lengthened the cord restrainer to guide the cord away from the user's hand. Four channels for the pen cord were added to the bottom of the tablet to keep the cord out of the way; the cord could be routed toward any of the tablet's edges.

Tablet Design

The CAD tablet was large, heavy, and wedge-shaped, too big for most standard office furniture and too unwieldy to hold in one's lap (rated 6.46 on a 7-point scale, where 1–3 = too small, 4 = neutral, and 5–7 = too large). Evaluators ranked five flat foam board tablets. A paper-sized 21.5×28 cm model, corresponding to the size of the half-page monitor, was preferred (ranked 1.46). We also recommended a 31×31 cm tablet to correspond to a full-page screen; a similar model had been ranked second best. That full-page tablet, the production model, was 25 percent smaller than the CAD tablet and weighed half as much. In addition, we eliminated the tablet angle; added rubber feet to the underside to keep this smaller, lighter tablet from skidding on the desktop; made the tablet's surface smooth to minimize jitter in handwriting; and indicated the active area with a slight recess.

Writing and Drawing Tasks

Evaluators rated the working system as moderately easy to use (3.15 on a 7-point scale, where 1 = very easy). They also found it moderately easy to look at the screen while writing on the tablet (3.50) though they commented that this new skill required practice. For all evaluators, the hardest part was drawing and writing at the desired orientation, especially horizontally (5.23). Eleven out of 13 people slanted the tablet to the left, as if writing on a sheet of paper. Seven of those 11 moved the monitor as well to align it with the tablet. Four people mentioned that lines that were straight but not quite horizontal looked more jagged on the system than they would have on paper (although this was due to the display's resolution).

These issues needed to be followed up during long-term observation. In the meantime, ergonomic specifications derived from the study were provided to the tablet vendor, and soon prototype tablets became available for another round of try-to-destroy-it tests. As the handbuilt prototypes became more stable, they were placed in workgroups.

Field Observation

We observed tablet and pen use as part of an extensive program of field research (Francik et al., 1991). For both internal and external sites, we helped new users plan equipment placement, observed installation and training, and collected comments through interviews and written design change requests. We also observed how the hardware was used in a variety of office settings.

Hardware Configuration

Slanting the tablet like a sheet of paper, though common in the laboratory experiment, rarely occurred in actual use. Limited desk space was one reason, but work patterns also played a role. For example, people who did a lot of typing when not using Freestyle tended to place their keyboard in front of their monitor and the tablet squarely beside the keyboard.

At several sites, people added accessories to their desks to help them manage the tablet, keyboard, and monitor. Among these were keyboard shelves, keyboard arms, and small platforms for the monitor under which either the keyboard or tablet could slide. The challenge of configuring hardware options for multimedia systems is well illustrated by the MERMAID system pictured in the CSCW 90 proceedings (Watabe et al., 1990). The desktop in the photo barely holds the MERMAID monitor, tablet, mouse, microphone, and video equipment; the keyboard and optional scanner are not shown.

Pencil and Tablet Design

Several electrical changes to the tablet made it larger. In the laboratory study, evaluators had preferred to angle larger tablets 4 to 7 degrees for better forearm support. Therefore, we specified retractable feet and beveled the front edge so that the arm could rest comfortably on it. Another change was based on observed use of the pen and tablet. Since some people often moved the tablet aside in order to work with the PC keyboard, we designed a secure pen clip. The clip was an accessory that could be attached to the left, right, or top edges of the tablet. It also had a slot that served as a "well" to hold the pen upright. People who did not frequently move their tablets around stored the pen upright and grasped it easily when needed.

Writing and Drawing Tasks

People did need to practice the skill of looking at the screen while writing on the tablet. Most users' first reaction was, in fact, to treat the tablet like a sheet of paper. Many people initially tended to look at the tablet while writing. Those that did requested paperlike features such as lines on the tablet even though no writing would appear on the tablet. Some experimented with slanting the tablet at an angle, but this behavior didn't persist.

To minimize the effort required for handwritten messages, users slanted their *writing* at a comfortable writing angle. The diagonal writing was eye-catching and was used for informal notes. Other situations did require more precise alignment of handwriting on the page. The most common was filling out or signing forms, which a broad range of people did with minimal practice.

Erasing with the pen required no training. In fact, transfer of skills from the paper environment was so great that some people, after erasing, would brush away "eraser crumbs" with the side of their hand! The side cord placement did have one drawback: Over time, turning the pen in the same direction could curl the pen cord.

What We Learned Using These Methods

In summary, we found that the Freestyle tablet and pen did support a wide range of writing and drawing tasks as well as menu selection and object manipulation. Uses of Freestyle included filling out and signing forms, annotating draft documents, and sketching. The many improvements made to the original pen—especially diameter, grip, and writing tip—made this fine control possible.

Another design goal was to minimize training time and effort. We found both in field observation and in usability testing (see Software Design) that the use of the pen and eraser was intuitive.[1] However, nearly all users required some initial instruction on looking at the screen while writing on the tablet. Users varied greatly in how quickly they acquired this skill although with experience the differences between users appeared to diminish. Some qualitative differences between writing on the tablet and writing on paper remained: Informal notes on blank electronic "paper" tended to be written on a slant, and the characters were larger than those on actual paper.

Even so, whether experienced users decided to write or type in Freestyle depended on several factors. Individuals' skill with the pen was only one of these. Others included:

- Typing ability.
- Need to type when using other applications, such as spreadsheets. Tablets placed to the side of the keyboard were more difficult to reach.
- Type of annotation required. A typed annotation might be lost against a typed background; a drawing might better illustrate a point than any text; or the user might need to circle or highlight something already in the image.
- Social constraints that determined whether a note could be informally handwritten or had to be "neatly" typed.

The hardware design clearly showed the influence of Levine's original design concept. An imperative had been issued: Design this system to match the performance and fidelity of handwriting on paper; then streamline hardware design as much as possible *without* sacrificing performance. The Freestyle tablet—though much smaller than the original CAD tablet—was still large enough that some users had added keyboard shelves or monitor platforms to help them juggle the hardware. But inside that Cadillac tablet were electronics that accurately captured the dynamics of handwriting at a resolution even greater than most PC monitors could display. The streamlined pen design, in turn, enabled users to take full advantage of the tablet's capabilities. The pen's design had been determined mostly from the laboratory study. Finally, field testing provided information on sustained use of the system, leading to refinements that made the pen and tablet more durable as well as more easily managed in the office environment. It also confirmed that users could easily write, draw, and manipulate graphical objects.

Software Design

Freestyle's capabilities could not be duplicated with existing PC prototyping tools. Instead, the development team provided demos of working code every four to six weeks. When a minimal but useful system was available, prototypes were given to friendly internal (alpha) workgroups, and sites were expanded and upgraded as new software and hardware versions became available. These efforts lasted approximately one year. During the last part of that year, customer (beta) sites were identified and equipped.

Because it was easier to build the system than to prototype it, usability testing was done on this working code. This meant that laboratory testing and field evaluation of the software happened *in parallel,* and the two sets of data could be juxtaposed. Detailed observations of ease of learning and fine motor coordination were supplemented with contextual information about long-term use.

Let's begin with a discussion of a familiar method, usability testing—though with a twist—then consider broader user interface issues that emerged with prolonged use of the system.

Iterative Usability Testing of Interface and Tutorial

Does a system modeled so explicitly on the familiar paper world need a tutorial? Documentation? Help text? If so, what kind? To find out, we tested software and help materials together.

Twenty-five evaluators participated in five rounds of testing, with five evaluators per round (Perkins et al., 1989). An exploratory study was run on the initial prototype (P1) software and hardware. P1 had basic mail and annotation capabilities and used modified off-the-shelf hardware. This exploratory study showed which aspects of Freestyle were intuitive and which needed to be explicitly taught.

Based on these results, changes were made to the P1 software to address some usability issues. This new version of the software, P2, also contained additional features (for example, icon graphics and screen-based voice controls). A tutorial was developed for P2, called T2 to match the software version. T2 provided two kinds of training: instruction on nonintuitive features that had not changed in the P2 software, and instruction on new features that appeared for the first time in P2. The T2 tutorial was tested with the P2 software.

These test results led to revisions in both the tutorial and the software, giving rise to T3 and P3. Another round of testing led to T4 and P4. The P4 software was also tested without the tutorial as a control to determine the usability of this final version of the software.

- *Tutorial.* The tutorial required no extra code. It was a multiple-page, stapled Freestyle document made up of scanned-in drawings. Its first page, legible from the desktop, featured a bullseye and told how to open the document to full-screen size: "Touch and Lift Here." Instructions positioned on the drawings pointed to the system's superimposed menus and annotation controls. Freestyle even demonstrated itself: Synchronized handwritten and voice annotations gave "live" explanations of the annotation features.

- *Task.* The experimental task covered all basic system functions: opening documents; scrolling; adding synchronized annotations; closing documents to move to the desktop; piling and stapling pages; mailing, copying, and deleting documents; and exiting the system. Evaluators were asked to think aloud as they worked. Everyone completed the task, with coaching provided as necessary. Task time, error frequencies, and comments were collected and scored by an independent judge.

- *Results.* The exploratory study showed that several features were obvious and required *no* training: writing and erasing with the pen, the correspondence of the screen cursor to the pen point on the tablet, the availability of the voice handset for spoken annotation, and even the operation of many of the desktop objects when identified with labels.[2]

Some usability problems were solved by changing the system, some by changing the documentation, and some by changing both at once. Icon targeting was a clear example of the first kind of problem, one requiring a software change. On the P1 desktop, documents were dragged to various box-shaped "icons," such as the mailer or the copier. Any overlap activated the function. In P2, graphic icons were introduced, and the targeting scheme was changed to one in which the cursor—a hand holding one corner of the document—had to be over the target icon. Errors proliferated. Even people who knew what their error was found themselves making it repeatedly, missing targets an average of 7.8 times during the task. The overlap scheme was reinstated for P3, and errors dropped to 1.6. P4 also used overlap targeting, and errors remained low at 0.2 for the task.

Scrolling problems, by contrast, were solved with a documentation change. Freestyle had no scroll bars infringing on space for image display. Instead, the user moved the pen to the tablet's edge until the cursor changed to a hand grasping the document's edge. Dragging up or down scrolled that page. The exploratory study showed that nobody could learn scrolling without training. Unlike icon targeting, though, scrolling was easily taught and remembered. Scrolling was described in the T2 tutorial and the description revised until scrolling errors disappeared in T4/P4. No evaluators who went through the tutorial had problems scrolling, and this was confirmed by the final control test on the P4 software (7.8 errors without the tutorial versus 1.6 errors with it).

One usability problem needed both new software and new documentation. Voice controls began with a red Record button on the P1 handset, whose function was not obvious. In P2 software, a Voice On/Off control at the top of the screen was substituted, which greatly reduced errors. By P4, however, more detailed control over recording and playback was added, presented using international symbols generally found on audio or video equipment. These features needed to be labeled and described in documentation. Evaluators made fewer errors on voice controls when going through the tutorial first (2.2 errors without the tutorial versus 0.5 error with it).

Finally, one usability problem was solved by making the system more *self-documenting*. The Info icon on the P1 desktop provided document information (annotation and mailing history) of documents dragged to it. However, most evaluators erroneously touched Info to get help on the system. In P2, the Info icon was movable, so people tried to use it to get information about individual icons as well as documents. In P3, information about the desktop icons was available in the *tutorial,* and errors decreased (1.4 versus 0.4). Finally, in P4, Info provided help on any desktop icon, resulting in an immediate reduction in errors.

In general, this series of usability tests confirmed that Freestyle was easy for users to learn given brief instruction. Usability was improved by simultaneous changes to software and documentation—and coordinating the design and testing helped software engineers and technical writers work more effectively together.

"Rapid Prototyping" of System Use

Lowell Steele, an R&D veteran from General Electric, wrote: "Because the greatest barriers to innovation are diffusion of effort and uncertainty over performance, there is no substitute for real-life demonstrations in high-leverage applications.... Seeking refinement of properties without a specific application in mind is an invitation to failure. To let the learning curve begin to work, you have to get on it" (Steele, 1983, p. 139). In keeping with that principle, a very early version of Freestyle was given to internal workgroups and its use observed over time. Although the system was constantly changing, its evolution had three basic stages:

- *Minimal system.* The large off-the-shelf CAD tablet, a standard PC with half-page monitor, and a modified black phone serving as voice handset provided basic functions. The desktop had no icons and few features, but captured screens and scanned-in paper could be annotated and mailed. No multiple-page (stapled) documents could be created, nor could labeled folders. Even so, organization emerged on users' desktops. Blank papers with large handwritten legends, legible on the desktop, were used to label columns of documents. Critical items were set aside in their own area of the desktop.

- *Evolving prototype.* Prototype tablets based on the dimensions specified in the hardware laboratory study became available. Voice controls were provided in software and the black phone handset with the red button was exchanged for a buttonless model. Three-dimensional piles with drop shadows, stapled documents, and labeled folders provided new ways to organize information on the desktop. Mail slots, icons for rapid mailing to selected individuals or groups, were added and were widely used. The Info icon provided document histories, and later, information about other desktop objects. Performance for image display, movement, and annotation was continually improved.

- *Near-release system.* The final tablet and voice handset—with speakerphone option—were finished. A fax option provided new ways for images to enter and leave the system. Most important, bridges to other systems were built, including Wang's character-based e-mail system and its centralized, large-scale imaging system. The latter was used for archival storage of Freestyle documents through an icon on the Freestyle desktop.

Minimal systems were first provided to a small group of administrators and managers in Research and Development. The system was initially used to speed up forms approval—an attractive application for many customers as well. The site grew to include a maintenance engineering group that generated many of the forms. This group was geographically distributed over two buildings and several floors. They began using the system to conduct budget negotiations, making written and spoken annotations on images of spreadsheets, and attaching other documents to buttress their arguments. They used Freestyle to substitute for the face-to-face meetings that were so hard to schedule, and in place of visually impoverished voice mail messages. In addition to this core workgroup, other managers throughout the company, including the senior executives, were added to the network.

The internal site provided the luxury of extended study. Just before the first systems were installed, we used structured interviews to gather information on the existing forms approval process. Then as each system was delivered, we observed the informal, brief training given by one of the developers and watched people's first use of the system. One week later, we returned to ask about system use and answer any questions. Over the next few months, user roundtables were held to discuss evolving system use and gather suggestions for design changes. And, of course, there was the system itself; Levine received many suggestions directly in his Freestyle inbox.

Involvement in beta sites was more targeted. Once a site had been selected and a workgroup proposed by the customer, Wang's beta site team would visit. This visit typically took two days. We began by interviewing key managers in the customer site about their plans for the system, then met with each of the potential system users. One month later, we returned to meet with the users, individually and in a discussion group. We documented their use of the system, gathered their design comments, and offered suggestions on improving work flow and finding new uses for the system.

Field observation complemented and extended the laboratory results for software design, as it had for hardware design. Our findings included the following:

- *Basic functions were rapidly learned.* Freestyle's marketing slogan was "You already know how to use it." That was more a statement about the familiarity of the design than a precise measurement of the learning curve! Even so, within 10 to 15 minutes, novices could learn to create, mail, read, and file multimedia mail messages. Even people who had never used a graphical interface could accomplish these tasks. In later exploration, users did take advantage of the brief help text provided for each icon by the Info function. This introduced them to new features.

- *Motor performance difficulties had social consequences.* Perhaps this should be no surprise. But for the developers, users' stories of embarrassment and frustration were the best incentives for tuning the system design. For instance, the laboratory study had certainly provided data that the new icon targeting scheme in P2 was a problem. Then corroborating stories from the field clinched it. In fact, one user said she'd mistakenly sent a memo to the CEO because the CEO's mail slot was next to the one she really wanted. With that evidence, the change back to overlap targeting was decided.

- *Voice controls provided flexibility without too much complexity.* As sites matured, workgroups began to use the system for discussion, planning, and negotiation rather than simple forms approval. Messages went back and forth, and multiple voice annotations could be found on a single message. So that users could easily move between annotations (and avoid listening to the message's entire history), the simple record and play buttons were replaced with a full set of icons like those found on videocassette recorders or compact disc players. These controls did require some explanation. In particular, the controls for skipping between "tracks" (speakers) and for jumping to the start or end of the recording were CD controls—and most of our system's users didn't have CD players in 1988. With some coaching, users began to take advantage of these controls.

- *Desktop customization was widely used.* Freestyle's design emphasized flexible spatial organization of the desktop and visual recognition of the images. People really used and enjoyed this flexibility. Some desktops were cluttered, others tidy, but each person developed a scheme for clustering documents and visually isolating important pieces of work. On one desk, four critical documents were grouped in a 2×2 square, new documents replacing the ones that were dealt with. Another desk had a handwritten *To Do!* list prominently placed. Piles of overlapping documents, organized by task, were common, and task categories were shared. For example, a secretary–manager team from one of the early internal pilot sites agreed on common categories for piles of scanned travel request authorization forms (TRAs). The secretary then created more specific variants ("TRAs today," "TRAs tomorrow") since her role in the workgroup was to expedite work in progress, including travel (Levine and Ehrlich, 1991). Similarly, users created and clustered mail slot icons for frequently used addresses in their workgroup; this was another clue to collaboration patterns.

- *Desktop customization provided clues to new features.* Freestyle's malleability led people to improvise and to combine features in new ways. We could see the evidence of users' needs on their desktops and in their documents. This was exactly what the development team had hoped for in deploying an early, minimal system. Some clues pointed to features that needed improvement. For example, when message recipients couldn't tell whether a document had voice annotation, senders began writing "VOICE" on the cover page. But other clues led to new features, particularly in the filing and retrieval of documents. The earliest version of the system had no filing aids—just the flat desktop. Users improvised: They took blank sheets of electronic paper, wrote category names (for example, "Criticals") in large letters that were visible when the page was shrunk to a desktop miniature, and used that page to label a column or group of overlapping documents! In response to that need, labeled folders were added to the system. Some users then quickly filled their desktop with folders and so needed off-desktop storage. Yet others wanted text labels for documents, particularly look-alike forms that were being hand-labeled in large letters. In response to those needs, Freestyle was tied to Wang's existing image database, accessed via a desktop icon, which enabled users to label, archive, and search for stored documents.

- *Many features needed for specific work processes were identified.* Users began to propose features that would support forms approval and other emerging uses of the system. Many of these suggestions were role specific. Secretaries asked for a tracking database so that they could tell where forms were in the approval process (and, therefore, who needed to be lobbied). Financial analysts and managers responsible for budgets wanted links from forms to spreadsheets. Employees unfamiliar with certain work processes asked for built-in work flow rules. The development team was flooded with suggestions for shaping the product; the biggest challenge was deciding which suggestions to take.

What We Learned Using These Methods

The software design, like the hardware design, remained deeply faithful to the original design concept. Freestyle closely mimicked the physical world, and much engineering effort went into making the system's performance as fluid as the movement of physical objects. The result: Novices, with minutes of training, were creating and managing multimedia messages. Data from iterative usability testing and from "rapid prototyping" in the field had combined to make this possible.

The laboratory testing had enabled us to look at details of interaction with the system and to fine-tune its behavior. We had simultaneously lab-tested a tutorial, which by its final iteration was greatly streamlined. That tutorial was not part of the final product but formed the basis of a quick reference card and other training materials.

Field observation had provided complementary long-term data on usability issues. Yet even more important, we had observed patterns of work: how features were used and combined, which new features were needed, and how communication flowed through groups. The opportunity to observe Freestyle workgroups over many months led us beyond the design of specific features, to evaluating workgroups' use of the system, and eventually to customer consulting.

Workgroup Support

When the project began, no one had planned on a human factors team doing customer consulting. First of all, it wasn't our job. There was already a Consulting Services group; in fact, they worked on Wang's large imaging system, helping customers redesign their business processes in preparation for the system's introduction.

Which brings us to the second point: Freestyle, unlike that larger system, was not intended to require business process redesign. It was designed to co-exist with other systems, to draw on familiar skills, to enhance and speed individuals' work. Field observation was supposed to address the greatest challenge, usability, and to collect suggestions for features to add to the minimal system.

But Freestyle wasn't just an individual productivity tool. It was a communication tool, a multimedia mail system. Its success would depend on workgroups, not just individuals. This became clear to designers and users alike when the first few handbuilt systems were introduced into R&D's (paper) forms approval process. Users quickly became aware of their communication paths. For example, a financial analyst who used to sign 20 forms a day now had to scan each one into the system before signing. The clerical staff who were sending her the forms didn't have systems and so a temporary bottleneck was created. Later, these people also received systems. They were quite willing to scan in the forms; it eliminated handcarrying the forms from their building to the analyst's.

Such workgroup issues were familiar. Members of the human factors department had worked on the introduction of other novel communication tools, such as voice mail and electronic calendars (Ehrlich, 1987). When these new communication systems first became available in the marketplace, potential customers typically encountered three problems:[3]

- *Identifying appropriate uses for the system.* Voice mail could reduce telephone tag by allowing people to leave content-rich messages. However, the first users of this new technology treated voice mail like pink message slips: They left only name-and-number messages, and telephone tag continued.

- *Selecting workgroups and identifying workgroup members.* During the early years of voice mail's availability, systems were often given to inappropriate workgroups, such as those who sat on the same floor and could easily communicate by just walking down the hall.

- *Configuring the system (equipment and/or software options) for each user to support the flow of work.* Some early sites treated voice mail as a replacement for executive receptionists. Unanswered calls to executives went straight to voice mail—and influential customers, unable to get help locating the executives, complained.

To help customers solve these problems for Freestyle, we first had to refine our own understanding of its uses—and users (Francik et al., 1991). The field research team included two experimental psychologists, an MBA/sociologist with extensive background in technology introduction and a consulting anthropologist.

Understanding Uses and Users

Designing "a system for Leonard" was convenient shorthand for an intuitive, highly graphical interface. And the system certainly needed to appeal to senior executives like Leonard (so that they would allocate funds to purchase such innovative hardware and software). But Leonard wasn't going to be the only, or even the most typical, user. Any Freestyle site including an executive was likely to include clerical and professional staff in the same workgroup.

And certainly there were other workgroups outside the executive suite, workgroups that could really take advantage of Freestyle's unique features.

We did needs-finding interviews in several organizations such as building construction, graphic arts, and manufacturing. These groups didn't receive equipment, but they did represent markets that might have a high need for annotation during complex design tasks. We were particularly interested in the use of graphic materials—sketches, pictures, page layouts, engineering drawings—that were usually transmitted via paper mail or fax. We asked about discussions or negotiations on those graphics, about time pressures, and about communicating with people in other locations. The goal was to uncover scenarios where Freestyle's combination of features (voice and handwritten annotations on complex backgrounds, electronically transmitted) would show a clear advantage over other communication media.[4]

The results were encouraging. The most compelling examples came from a manufacturing group where design team members in different buildings had difficulty setting up meetings to discuss changes to engineering drawings. These delays were costly, but even more costly were unresolved ambiguities in the drawings. (Was that line a *fold* or a *cut* in the sheet metal? If the wrong design were manufactured, the engineering change order could cost hundreds of thousands of dollars.)

Based on the scenarios uncovered in these interviews, the Freestyle marketing group wrote brochures describing possible uses of the system. Each one illustrated the system's use in a different vertical market. All the brochures emphasized complex uses of Freestyle for negotiation, planning, and design.

But new users needed to be encouraged to see Freestyle as a tool for complex communication. Routine, structured processes were often proposed for pilot sites. Perhaps the simplest use of the system was for electronic distribution of scanned-in paper, much like an easy-to-use fax machine. One step up from that would be forms approval or document review, processes that involved handwriting as well as rapid electronic transport. Freestyle could certainly meet these needs, but so could other technologies.

For the system to find its competitive niche, people needed to use it not only for rapid electronic transport but also for conversation, gesturing, commenting. Freestyle was to meetings as voice mail is to telephone conversations: an asynchronous counterpart, capable of rich communication, but likely to be used for too-simple messages. As in the voice mail case, we would need to develop strategies to help customers understand Freestyle's uses and place it productively in organizations. These strategies were based on long-term observation of the alpha site.

Understanding and Supporting Work Processes

After several months, the alpha site had grown from 4 systems to nearly 40. The benefits of the system were clearest for the maintenance engineering group, spread over two buildings, who had greatly benefited from the speedy electronic routing of forms and had then expanded their use of the system to include budget negotiations. Through interviews in other organizations, we had identified similar communication needs in several vertical markets. These investigations had redefined the product concept. Freestyle was no longer an executive workstation, or even a general annotation tool: It was a system for group work.

Through experimentation, the maintenance engineering group had also overcome initial difficulties in three key areas: identifying uses for the system, selecting workgroups, and placing equipment to support the flow of work. Based on long-term observation of that group, we developed a list of those issues for the development team, particularly for the beta site manager who would need to guide customers through the same difficulties. At the beta site manager's request, we began to provide targeted consulting to potential customers. That consulting is described in detail elsewhere (Francik et al., 1991).

But from an HCI methods perspective, we still had two problems to solve. First: how to quickly uncover workgroups' informal communication patterns, particularly the negotiation, planning, and design activities to which Freestyle was best suited? Second: how to transfer our understanding of these issues to sales support analysts and to customers, thereby reducing or eliminating the need for consulting?

Rapid Workgroup Assessment

The success of this method depended on gathering background information about each customer's company and the proposed Freestyle workgroup. By the time that the site visit began, we had a good idea of the customer's business goals, the organization (and other possible Freestyle workgroups), and the target work process. Most of the two-day visit was taken up by one-hour interviews with prospective users.

We needed to make sure that no key people were missing from the proposed pilot site. From our experience with the alpha site, we knew that people would tend to see the organization chart as the workgroup—and that was a trap. But there wasn't time to diagram the whole communication network, that is, to detail all communication media and frequencies throughout the organization to see how people really clustered into workgroups (Figure 2).

FIGURE 2

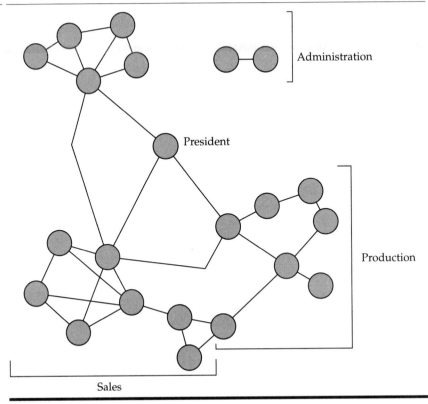

Administration

President

Production

Sales

A communication network diagram. This network shows communication frequencies in an organization with three functional departments. Each circle is a person, and lines connect people who communicate. The longer the line between two people, the less frequently they communicate. *After Rogers and Agarwala-Rogers (1976).*

We could, however, spot-check the network, focusing our brief interviews on the proposed workgroup and Freestyle application. This meant shifting users' thinking from structured processes to networks of communicators, from organization charts to cross-functional workgroups.

So in each interview, we sketched the part of the network centered on the interviewee (Figure 3). "Here you are at the center of the universe," the conversation began. "Now, whom do you communicate with most often on this work process? Who's the next most important person? And after that? Who else do you communicate with for other reasons? What about people outside the company?"

Our notation captured the following:

FIGURE 3   Communication constellation from a purchasing department. Not all detail is shown.

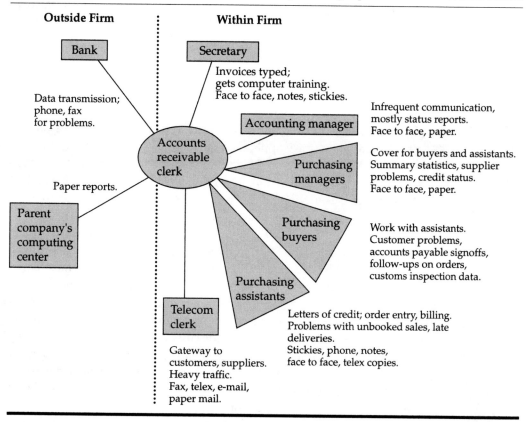

- Names of individuals or groups, ordered from top to bottom by importance (frequency or urgency of communication). The use of a triangle to denote a group is borrowed from linguistics, where a wedge-shaped structure in a tree diagram represents a part of the tree whose details aren't displayed. We often went back to ask, "Is there anyone in that group that you work with more often than the others?"
- Whether the communication was one-way or two-way.
- What the reasons were for communicating.
- What media were used.
- Where the other people were. (We were especially interested in workgroup members who were far away since Freestyle might help overcome barriers of distance.)

These sketches were most useful in helping people reflect on their informal, and often overlooked, communication needs. The interviews suggested ways in which proposed workgroups needed to be changed or "stretched" to other organizations.

Transferring Methods

A more ambitious goal was to teach this analysis to sales support analysts and customers. Even though we were working with very experienced analysts and visionary customers, this proved to be difficult. One reason was that it's hard to recognize applications that are based on spontaneous communication. Constance Perin, the anthropologist who was part of the adoption team, has elsewhere (Perin, 1991) described organizational biases that lead bureaucracies to view their work processes in structured, centralized, controlling ways.

In addition, the analysts who supported the test sites were used to looking for structured work flows. Computer systems have historically been most effective for highly structured information processing and are most easily cost-justified when small, predictable productivity gains accumulate over thousands of transactions. In contrast, matching Freestyle to a customer's organization meant uncovering the unpredictable. It meant understanding how people go through iterations, discuss options, and spontaneously include related material to buttress their arguments. It meant looking for phone calls, face-to-face conversations, yellow stickies, and scribbled notes on documents. Even experienced analysts who knew their customers well weren't used to tracking this kind of "data."

We created a structured questionnaire based on our diagrams and tried both giving it directly to potential users and having analysts work with users to gather the information. But with limited time available to work with thousands of analysts and customers, it was much easier to raise general awareness of communication issues than to teach specific techniques. So we produced a video (Wang, 1990). It was distributed to the sales force and was designed to be shared with customers.

The video was a crash course in sociotechnical analysis centered on Freestyle. It outlined how to select a business process suited to the product, how to trace out the work process, and how to place equipment (printers, scanners, voice boards, fax boards) so that information flowed freely into and through the workgroup. The video summarized Freestyle's key features and its suitability for rapid, complex communication involving both graphical information and annotation. It provided tips on how to look for those materials in existing work processes. It listed pitfalls in choosing workgroups such as mistaking organization chart boxes for workgroups or forgetting support staff. Finally, it discussed printers, scanners, and fax machines as ways to get information into and out of a Freestyle workgroup. To make all these issues concrete and compelling, testimonials from the alpha sites were combined with anecdotes from the beta sites. We hoped that these stories would help new customers avoid the pitfalls and adopt Freestyle more quickly.

What We Learned Using These Methods

The field interviews and observations had not only provided data to improve hardware and software design, but had also helped redefine the product and its potential markets. From working with alpha and beta sites, the project team had found new ways to describe and communicate the benefits of this novel system, and to guide its introduction into workgroups. To be sure, Freestyle's ease of use for *individuals* was still important, but throughout development and marketing there was now an awareness of Freestyle's use by *groups*. Glossy brochures, live demonstrations, and demo videos all illustrated the system's use for complex communication. Product managers could easily articulate to sales representatives the pitfalls of placing systems solely on executives' desks. Each customer's proposed workgroup configuration was fine-tuned to better match the actual work flow.

Workgroup issues directly affected design as well. The development team took several steps to reduce per-user hardware cost, thereby allowing customers to purchase more systems and include all workgroup members. One step was to develop software that could be used with commonly available monitors so that purchase of a full-page, high-resolution monitor was an option rather than a requirement. A second crucial step was the development of software for mouse control of annotation, eliminating the expense of the tablet. As a result, an off-the-shelf 286 PC could serve as the base workstation. Networks of users were extended by developing a version of the software that worked on local area networks (LANs) as well as on centralized hosts. It was also during the beta site period that the fax software and hardware were developed. These cost-reduction strategies allowed customers to take advantage of existing fax and LANs to reach other organizations cost effectively, thus making it easier to increase the number of systems and achieve critical mass.

These lessons were the hardest to learn. Thinking of Freestyle as a groupware system meant changing not only product features, but also changing the ways in which the R&D and marketing organizations talked about the product and supported the product. It meant working with the sales force to help them understand the product, and then in turn working with customers to overcome all the barriers to adoption. These are significant challenges shared by many new products. They're especially hard, though, when the initial product concept is an easy-to-use single user application, and the final product is in fact a communication system that depends on workgroup dynamics for its acceptance.

A Success Case?

The main purpose of the Freestyle project was to develop a system and sell it to customers—not to test HCI methods. Our methods were necessarily streamlined to fit into a whirlwind development process. We used the physical world and existing paper processes not only as a source for design ideas, but as an easily accessed source of data for benchmarking. We did discount usability testing (Nielsen, 1989) but with a twist: Interface and tutorial evolved together as test results were incorporated into the design and new features were added for testing. We developed a "discount sociotech" tool, the rapid network diagrams, that enabled us to quickly assess work flows and reconfigure pilot sites. Table 1 summarizes the methods and findings from the Freestyle project.

Crucial to the success of all these efforts was the early deployment of the system, with a minimum number of features, to a friendly internal workgroup. Long-term study of this workgroup created a deep familiarity with the system and its effects on work processes. Because of that familiarity, we could more confidently interpret the discount data. We could assess which problems of hand–eye coordination were serious usability problems and which would fade with more experience. We understood the true usability of visual filing on the desktop and how the need for more structured storage depended on message volume and work roles. We knew the pitfalls in application selection and workgroup configuration, and could rapidly check for them during customer interviews.

As in IBM's Olympic Messaging System case study, the Freestyle project benefited from integrating laboratory and field methods, as well as hardware and software evaluations. Some of us were, over time, involved in more than one aspect of the project and that carryover was essential. For example, I was involved in early hardware laboratory testing, then in software design, and finally in field research and customer consulting. So when evaluating users' ability to do fine handwriting, I could assess the relative roles of the electrical and physical design of the pen, the behavior of the software, and the long-term use of the pen and tablet in various office environments and work processes.

It's tempting to claim that successful HCI methods lead to successful products. However, in our experience, good methods may be necessary but certainly aren't sufficient. Among the other considerations are:

- *Engineering.* Good methods quickly uncover design problems—which may not be solvable for *this* product, at *this* price, with *this* technology. As one analyst noted, "[Freestyle's] proprietary graphics environment cries out for integration with the kind of graphics-based software that would be possible under Windows and Presentation Manager. Yet Freestyle's speed couldn't be achieved under Windows, and the time hasn't come for OS/2" (Bonner, 1990). And tying your new product to other emerging technology is risky. As of this writing, in 1994, IBM is still trying to gain wider acceptance for OS/2; Microsoft Windows NT seems to be the next PC platform.

- *Competition.* Freestyle entered the market in the late 1980s, when new graphical user interfaces abounded. Although Freestyle was intended to co-exist with other PC interfaces, it still looked like one more environment for users and developers to grapple with: " 'The last thing the world needs is another user interface,' said Stewart Alsop 2d, editor of the PC Letter newsletter, referring to Wang's attempt to enter a field recently stirred up by OS/2 Presentation Manager, NextStep, NewWave, Metaphor, Windows, Deskmate, the Mac Desktop [sic], mice, and other technologies designed to make it easier to use computers" (Lewis, 1988).

- *Timing.* How long can a company wait for its innovation to catch on? *PC/Computing,* even while commending the system for technical excellence, noted: "As impressive as Freestyle is, the system that finally brings its wonders to the masses will probably be Freestyle-inspired rather than Freestyle itself. Wang's sorry financial condition may preclude it from devoting the resources necessary to establish Freestyle's new technology in the PC marketplace" (Bonner, 1990). In casual conversation, more than one person has dubbed Freestyle "the Xerox Star of pen-based computing." There is both flattery and irony in that comparison.

Effective HCI methods play just one part in products' technological, economic, and social development. As Stuart Card notes, successful systems are indebted to many less successful predecessors (Card, this volume). Products that are successful today have taken years, even decades, to become so.[5] The typewriter, an early communication technology, took over 100 years to be engineered, marketed, and widely accepted. E. Remington & Sons invested 13 years in typewriter development and marketing, but went bankrupt before it could benefit from accelerating sales; a new firm, Remington Typewriter Company, soon realized the profit (Cooper, 1983). Fax, that now-essential business tool, began to flourish in the 1980s, but was hardly an

TABLE 1	HCI Activities, Methods, and Results During Development of Freestyle	
Area	**Methods**	**Results**
HARDWARE	Try to break it.	Identified performance requirements for tablet to support fluid handwriting.
		Selected vendor to work with on tablet design.
	Laboratory evaluation of off-the-shelf equipment and of prototype tablets and pens. Rating, ranking, observation, questionnaire.	Specified detailed design for pen and tablet. Led to working prototype hardware that was distributed to internal test site participants.
		Gathered initial information on hand–eye coordination difficulties in writing on a tablet while looking at the display.
	Internal sites: observation of training, follow-up interviews, ongoing observation, user roundtables.	Uncovered issues with hardware configuration on desk. Refined design and developed accessories. Made improvements for final design to improve durability.
		Assessed long-term ease of use, particularly hand–eye coordination, as shown in documents produced by users. Some initial behavior observed in laboratory study did not persist in actual use. Gathered contextual information on use of handwriting vs. typing.
	Customer sites: follow-up interviews and observation one month after installation.	Confirmed information on equipment configuration, use of accessories, general ease of use.
SOFTWARE	Iterative usability tests of interface and tutorial.	Collected converging information on hand–eye coordination based on initial use and detailed observation.
		Assessed which features required no training, minimal training, some training, or redesign. (Juxtaposed these findings with long-term findings from field sites.) Tested both new and redesigned features for usability.
		Refined documentation, online help, and quick reference card. Coordinated changes to product with those to documentation.
	Internal sites: preinstallation interviews, observation of training, follow-up interviews, ongoing observation, user roundtables.	Assessed fit between initial (minimal) system and existing paper process. Prioritized design change requests.
		Collected evidence for long-term usability of product features. Iterated design of features such as voice annotation controls and filing aids.
		Customization provided clues to new features.
		Discovered need to prompt workgroup to take full advantage of product for complex communication. This led into strategies for encouraging adoption of product.

Area	Methods	Results
	Customer sites: follow-up interviews and observation one month after installation.	Gathered broader, but less detailed, information than that received from internal sites. Conflicting requests for product changes came from many different organizations, industries, and work processes. Opportunity to see how new users do with the product; by this time, the internal sites were very experienced with it.
WORKGROUP SUPPORT	Needs-finding interviews with workgroups representing potential markets.	Uncovered new, richer scenarios of use; incorporated into marketing literature. Also used by customer site teams. Beginning of changes in how the development team thought about the product.
	Internal sites: preinstallation interviews, observation of training, follow-up interviews, ongoing observation, user roundtables.	Developed deep understanding of barriers to product introduction, use, and success. Clear evidence that the product depends on workgroup selection and configuration. Examples of pitfalls and of successful use would help customers think about similar issues in their organizations. Beta (customer) test manager became committed to workgroup analysis.
	Customer sites: work with sales support staff, preinstallation interviews, follow-up interviews, and observation one month after installation.	Encountered the same barriers to product introduction, use, and success. Provided targeted consulting to customers before and after installation. Streamlined interview techniques for rapid workgroup assessment. Attempts to teach workgroup assessment were unsuccessful; instead, summarized consulting information in a video.

overnight success: "Life Begins at 50," quipped *Forbes* magazine (Schreiber, 1983). And the jury is still out on the videophone. Bell Laboratories demonstrated it in 1927. Field trials beginning in the mid-1950s culminated in AT&T's product (Carson, 1968), which failed in the marketplace. AT&T has recently re-engineered and re-introduced the videophone. It might be accepted in residences, but in businesses it must now compete with computer-based videoconferencing.

Freestyle itself is now no longer a product, but a potential contributor to future products' success. Wang's financial difficulties caused the company to declare bankruptcy. The new and much smaller Wang that emerged from Chapter 11 does not offer Freestyle as a product—but the company *has* focused its product line on imaging technology and work flow products for open systems. Meanwhile, other companies may take design ideas from Freestyle and reinvent them to take advantage of more powerful computers and networks. I saw one such system in the spring of 1994. Two PCs were connected by a telephone line; each had a special integrated display so that the user could write directly on the flat screen with a pen. Conversation and annotation were happening fluidly in real time. And, although there wasn't a full-featured graphical desktop, miniature versions of the documents were visible in a document gallery. "We took a lot of ideas from Freestyle," the designer said. "We hope you don't mind."

But even with these larger historical forces at work, let us not understate the case for HCI methods. They are tools to help designers and marketers gain market acceptance for new technologies. As Peter Conklin has noted, HCI methods that improve *usability* can help companies achieve volume sales earlier and may even speed up the development process itself (Conklin, this volume). To that, we would add that HCI methods can be aimed directly at *market creation* and *product acceptance*. Designing innovative products means understanding potential contexts of use. That understanding gives product teams the information needed to support and influence technology introduction into organizations.

Acknowledgments

This chapter is based on four previous articles on the Freestyle project, and I thank the authors of those articles for their contributions to this historical overview, with special thanks to Carrie Rudman for valuable discussions. I would also like to acknowledge the other evaluation team members: for hardware design, Kenichi Akagi, Barbara Kelly, Thom Tedham, Mike Schirpke, and Mary Jane Boyd; for software design, Ron Perkins, Dan Workman, Louis Blatt, Alex Harui, Karen Donoghue, and Peter Nolan; and for field research, Donna Cooper, Constance Perin, Sharon Dodson, and Amy Bucklin. The organization that built Freestyle included these people and 80 more; my thanks to all of them for the opportunity to work on this project. Marilyn Mantei kindly reviewed this manuscript, and Stuart Card helped me take the long, historical view.

Freestyle is a trademark of Wang Laboratories, Inc. OS/2 and Presentation Manager are trademarks of International Business Machines Corporation. Windows and Windows NT are trademarks of Microsoft Corporation. NextStep is a trademark of NeXT, Inc. NewWave is a trademark of Hewlett-Packard. Macintosh is a trademark of Apple Computer, Inc. Star is a trademark of Xerox Corporation. Other product names are trademarks of their respective companies.

This work was done at Wang Laboratories. Ellen Francik is now at Pacific Bell. Current address: 2600 Camino Ramon / Rm. 4N250J / San Ramon, CA 94583. Electronic mail: epfrancik@pacbell.com.

This paper represents personal and professional opinions of the author. It does not necessarily represent the views of Wang Laboratories, Inc. or of Pacific Bell.

Notes

1. Jef Raskin (Raskin, 1994) urges developers to value innovation in user interfaces, even if these novel interfaces require some initial training. He argues that we should replace the glowing term *intuitive* with the more neutral *familiar,* meaning "using readily transferable existing skills." Freestyle *was* explicitly designed to be familiar by drawing on users' knowledge of the paper and telephone worlds. Some aspects of the product were more innovative and did require more training, such as the ability to synchronize handwritten and voice annotation and send that as an electronic mail package.

2. Icon design was not an issue until the P2 test since the P1 software used only labeled boxes. Some P2 icons were not immediately recognizable. The icon designer did separate rating and ranking studies on alternative icon designs, and revised icons were rolled into the P3 and P4 software.

3. Introducing systems for group work is especially tricky since the system must succeed with a critical mass of co-workers having different tasks and goals. But any new technology requires care in its introduction. Leonard-Barton and Kraus (1985) highlight well-established principles of site management. Opper and Fersko-Weiss (1992) outline adoption strategies for groupware products from the perspective of the adopting organization.

4. This approach, which emphasizes the kinds of information that can be conveyed by various channels, is referred to as a "media richness" perspective. It can be contrasted with a "social presence" perspective, which describes media in terms of support for interpersonal relationships (Fish, Kraut, and Root, 1992).

5. Steele (1983), in an HBR paper titled "Managers' Misconceptions About Technology," notes that most innovations are unsuccessful and gives examples of the re-engineering and adoption efforts required for successful products. His examples range from frozen food to plastics. Rogers's thorough *Diffusion of Innovations* (1983) emphasizes the role of social networks in individuals' and organizations' adoption of new practices.

References

Bonner, P. (1990). Most valuable products of the year / Freestyle. *PC/Computing* 3(1) (January 1990), 78–79.

Card, S. Pioneers and settlers: Methods used in successful user interface design. (This volume.)

Carson, D. L. (1968). The evolution of PICTUREPHONE service. *Bell Laboratories Record* (October), 282–291.

Conklin, P. Bringing usability effectively into product development. (This volume.)

Cooper, W. E., ed. (1983). *Cognitive Aspects of Skilled Typing.* New York: Springer-Verlag.

Ehrlich, S. F. (1987). Strategies for encouraging successful adoption of office communication systems. *ACM Transactions on Office Information Systems* 5(4) (October), 340–357.

Fish, R. S., Kraut, R. E., and Root, R. W. (1992). Evaluating video as a technology for informal communication. In *Proceedings of CHI '92* (Monterey, CA, May 3–7). New York: ACM, 37–48.

Francik, E. and Akagi, K. (1989). Designing a computer pencil and tablet for handwriting. In *Proceedings of the 33rd Human Factors Society Annual Meeting* (Denver, October 16–20). Santa Monica, CA: Human Factors Society, 445–449.

Francik, E., Rudman, S. E., Cooper, D., and Levine, S. (1991). Putting innovation to work: Adoption strategies for multimedia communication systems. *Communications of the ACM* 34(12) (December), 52–63.

Gould, J. D. (1988). How to design usable systems. In M. Helander (ed.), *Handbook of Human-Computer Interaction.* Amsterdam: Elsevier Science Publishers, 757–789.

Gould, J. D., Boies, S. J., Levy, S., Richards, J. T., and Schoonard, J. (1987). The 1984 Olympic Message System: A test of behavioral principles of system design. *Communications of the ACM* 30(9) (September), 758–769.

Leonard-Barton, D. and Kraus, W. A. (1985). Implementing new technology. *Harvard Business Review* 63(6) (November–December), 102–110.

Levin, P. (1988). In-law inspires computer idea. *The Las Vegas Sun* (November 18), 6A.

Levine, S. R. and Ehrlich, S. F. (1991). The Freestyle system: A design perspective. In A. Klinger (ed.), *Human-Machine Interactive Systems.* New York: Plenum Press.

Lewis, P. H. (1988). Exotic gizmos for aiding workers. *The New York Times* (November 20), F11.

Malone, T. (1983). How do people organize their desks? Implications for the design of office information systems. *ACM Transactions on Office Information Systems* 1, 99–112.

Nielsen, J. (1989). Usability engineering at a discount. In G. Salvendy and M. J. Smith (eds.), *Designing and Using Human-Computer Interfaces and Knowledge Based Systems.* Amsterdam: Elsevier Science Publishers, 394–401.

———. (1992). Finding usability problems through heuristic evaluation. In *Proceedings of CHI '92* (Monterey, CA, May 3–7). New York: ACM, 373–380.

Opper, S. and Fersko-Weiss, H. (1992). *Technology for Teams: Enhancing Productivity in Networked Organizations.* New York: Van Nostrand Reinhold.

Perin, C. (1991). Electronic social fields in bureaucracies. *CACM* (December), 74–82.

Perkins, R., Blatt, L. A., Workman, D., and Ehrlich, S. F. (1989). Iterative tutorial design in the product development cycle. In *Proceedings of the 33rd Human Factors Society Annual Meeting* (Denver, October 16–20). Santa Monica, CA: Human Factors Society, 268–272.

Raskin, J. (1994). Intuitive equals familiar. *Communications of the ACM* 37(9) (September), 17–18.

Rogers, E. M. (1983). *Diffusion of Innovations.* New York: The Free Press.

Rogers, E. M. and Agarwala-Rogers, R. (1976). *Communication in Organizations.* New York: The Free Press.

Schreiber, J. (1983). Life begins at 50. *Forbes* 132(5) (August 29), 130–132.

Steele, L. (1983). Managers' misconceptions about technology. *Harvard Business Review* 61(6) (November–December), 133–140.

Virzi, R. A. (1990). Streamlining the design process: Running fewer subjects. In *Proceedings of the 34th Human Factors Society Annual Meeting* (Orlando, October 8–12). Santa Monica, CA: Human Factors Society, 287–290.

Wang Laboratories, Inc. (1989). Freestyle. *ACM SIGGRAPH Video Review Supplement to Computer Graphics,* 45(4), New York: ACM.

———. (1990). Putting Freestyle to work. Videotape No. 741-7372. Wang Media Services, Lowell, MA.

Watabe, K., Sakata, S., Maeno, K., Fukuoka, H., and Ohmori, T. (1990). Distributed multiparty desktop conferencing system: MERMAID. In *Proceedings of CSCW 90, Conference on Computer-Supported Cooperative Work* (Los Angeles, October 7–10). New York: ACM, 27–38.

Wixon, D., Holtzblatt, K., and Knox, S. (1990). Contextual design: An emergent view of system design. In *Proceedings of CHI '90* (Seattle, April 1–5). New York: ACM, 329–336.

The Xerox Star:
An Influential User Interface Design

LAWRENCE H. MILLER
The Aerospace Corporation

JEFF JOHNSON
Sun Microsystems

In April of 1981, Xerox introduced the 8010 "Star" Information System. Though Star was not the market success that its designers or Xerox had hoped it would be, its introduction was an important event in the history of personal computing because it changed notions of how interactive systems should be designed. Unique when it was introduced, Star's user interface has been widely imitated—more or less—in computer systems that have been more successful in the marketplace. Largely because of Star, the combination of a bitmapped display, a desktop metaphor, graphical controls, WYSIWYG applications, multiple application windows, and a mouse pointer has become the defacto standard of a good user-interface design.

It is worthwhile to try to understand how a design as influential as Star's came about. The purpose of this paper is to examine the design process that led to Star in the hopes that lessons will emerge that can be applied to the design of future interactive computer systems. Detailed discussions of the important aspects of Star—particularly its user interface—have been published previously (Smith et al., 1982; Smith, 1985; Johnson et al., 1989) and will not be repeated here. Here, our subject is the *process* that produced Star.

Purpose of Star

Star was designed as an office automation system. The target users were office professionals and their support staff, all nontechnical in background and job function. The idea was that professionals and clericals in a business organization would have workstations on their desks and would use them to produce, retrieve, distribute, and organize documentation, presentations, memos, and reports. All the workstations in an organization would be connected via Ethernet and would share access to file servers, printers, and so forth.

Star's designers assumed that office workers are interested in getting their work done and not at all interested in computers. Therefore, an important design goal was to make the "computer" as invisible to users as possible. The applications included in the system were those that office workers would supposedly need: documents, business graphics, tables, personal database, and electronic mail. The set was fixed, always loaded, and automatically associated with data files, eliminating the need for users to worry about obtaining, installing, and starting the right application for a given task or data file. Users could focus on their work, oblivious of concepts like software, operating systems, applications, and programs.

Another important assumption was that Star's users would be casual, occasional users rather than people who spent most of their time at the machine. This assumption led to the goal of having Star be easy to learn and remember.

Design of Star

The design process that produced Star had three primary components:

1. Incorporation of ideas based on experience with previous computer systems, particularly research systems developed at Xerox PARC

2. Strong commitment to put a lot of effort into producing a good design before implementing

3. Extensive use of prototyping and user testing to check design decisions and suggest improvements

In the following sections, we elaborate on each of these components.

Design-Process Component 1: Incorporating Ideas from Previous Computer Systems

The design process that led to Star began long before Star itself was conceived. The Star design team included people who had been exposed, in one way or another, to a variety of innovative computer systems. Though some aspects of Star were totally new, Star's design incorporated many ideas that had been manifested in these previous systems. Some of these systems were ones that members of Star's design team had themselves previously created. Others had been designed by others, for example, at Xerox Palo Alto Research Center. Of course, Star's designers had also been exposed to a variety of *non-innovative* computer systems. From this experience, Star's designers had developed strong opinions about what did and didn't work and about interactive computing in general. The impact of this experience on Star's design cannot be overstated (Figure 1).

Pre-Xerox Forerunners of Star

Some of the ideas that distinguished Star from other computer systems of its day are traceable to early writings on interactive computing by Vannovar Bush (1945) and Alan Kay (1969). However, the most important pre-Xerox ancestors of Star are two research prototypes built during the 1960s: Sketchpad and NLS.

Sketchpad. In the 1960s, when interactive computing was just beginning to catch on, Ivan Sutherland built an interactive graphics system called Sketchpad (Sutherland, 1963). Sketchpad allowed users to create graphical figures on a CRT display using a light pen. The geometric shapes users put on the screen were treated as objects: After being created, they could be moved, copied, shrunk, expanded, and rotated. They could also be joined to make larger, more complex objects that could then be operated on as units. Sketchpad influenced Star's user interface as a whole as well as its graphics applications.

NLS. Also in the 1960s, Douglas Engelbart established a research program at Stanford Research Institute (now called SRI International) for exploring the use of computers "to augment the knowledge worker" and human intellect in general. He and his colleagues experimented with different types of displays and input devices—inventing the mouse when other pointing devices proved inadequate—and developed a system commonly known as NLS (Engelbart and English, 1968).[1] NLS was unique in several respects. It used CRT displays when most computers used teletypes. It was interactive (that is, on-line) when

FIGURE 1

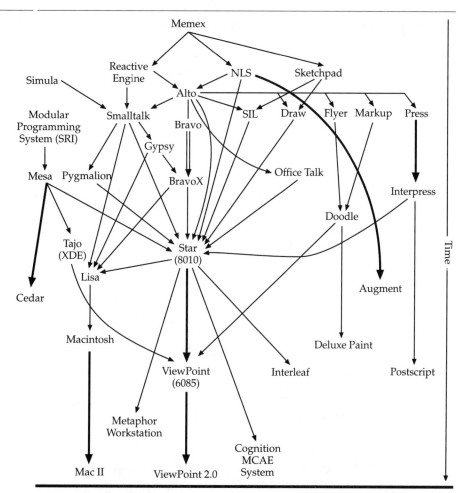

How systems influenced later systems. This graph summarizes how various systems related to Star have influenced one another over the years. Time progresses downward. Double (heavy) arrows indicate direct successors (follow-on versions). Many "influence arrows" are due to key designers changing jobs or applying concepts from their graduate research to products.

almost all computing was batch. It was full-screen oriented when the few systems that were interactive were line oriented. It used a mouse when all other graphic interactive systems used cursor keys, light pens, joy sticks, or digitizing tablets. Finally, it was the first system to organize textual and graphical information in trees and networks, which today would be called an "idea processor" or a "hypertext system."

Forerunners of Star Developed at Xerox PARC

In 1970, Xerox established a research center in Palo Alto to explore technologies that would be important not only for the further development of Xerox's then-existing product line (copiers), but also for Xerox's planned expansion into the office systems business. The Palo Alto Research Center (PARC) was organized into several laboratories, each devoted to basic and applied research in a field related to the goals mentioned. The names and organization of the labs have changed over the years, but the research topics have stayed the same: materials science, laser physics, integrated circuitry, CAD/CAM, user interface (not necessarily to computers), and computer science (including networking, databases, operating systems, languages and programming environments, graphics, document systems, groupware, and artificial intelligence).

The computer scientists at PARC were fond of the slogan "The best way to predict the future is to invent it." After some initial experiments with time-shared systems, they began searching for a new approach to computing. Among the founding members of PARC was Alan Kay. He and his colleagues were acquainted with NLS and liked its novel approach to human-computer interaction. Soon, PARC hired several people who had worked on NLS and in 1971 signed an agreement with SRI licensing Xerox to use the mouse. Kay and others were dedicated to a vision of personal computers in a distributed environment. In fact, they coined the term *personal computer* in 1973, long before microcomputers started what has been called the "personal computer revolution."

Alto Workstation. One result of the search for a new approach was the Alto (Thacker et al., 1982). The Alto was a minicomputer that had a removable, 2.5 megabyte hard disk pack (floppy disks did not exist at the time) and 128 to 256 kilobytes of memory. Unlike most machines of its day, the Alto also had a microprogrammable instruction set, a "full-page" (10 1/2 × 8 1/4 inch; 600 × 800 pixel) bitmapped graphic display, about 50 kilobytes of high-speed display memory, and a mouse (Figure 2).

The first Alto was operational in 1972. At first, only a half dozen or so Altos were built. After software that exploited the Alto's capabilities became available, demand for them grew tremendously, spreading beyond PARC into Xerox as a whole and even to external customers. Eventually, over a thousand Altos were built.

Smalltalk. Alan Kay had been one of the main advocates of the Alto. His Learning Research Group (LRG) began using the Alto to build prototypes for a personal computing system "of the future": a portable machine that would

FIGURE 2

The Xerox Alto. The Alto, developed at Xerox PARC in the 1970s, was a prototype for Star. Both its hardware and the many programs written for it by PARC researchers strongly influenced Star's designers. *Photo courtesy of Xerox Corporation.*

provide—rather than a canned set of applications—the building blocks necessary for users to build the tools and applications they need to solve their own information processing problems (Kay, 1977; Kay and Goldberg, 1977). The technologies needed to build a lap computer with the power of the DynaBook (as the envisioned system was called) were unavailable at the time. The prototypes developed by Kay's group evolved into the Smalltalk language and programming environment (Ingalls, 1981; Tesler, 1981; Goldberg, 1984;

Goldberg and Robson, 1984). They further promoted the notion of personal computing, pioneered complete, interactive programming environments, and refined and solidified concepts of object-oriented programming that had been extant only in vestigial form in previous systems. Most important for Star, they demonstrated the power of graphical, bitmapped displays, mouse-driven input, windows, and simultaneous applications. This is the most visible link between Smalltalk and Star, and is perhaps why many people wrongly believe that Star was written in Smalltalk.

Pygmalion. The first large program to be written in Smalltalk was Pygmalion, the doctoral thesis project of David C. Smith (1977). One goal of Pygmalion was to show that programming a computer does not have to be primarily a textual activity: It can be accomplished, given the appropriate system, by interacting with graphical elements on a screen. A second goal was to show that computers can be programmed in the language of the user interface, that is, by demonstrating what one wants done and having the computer remember and reproduce it. The idea of using icons—images that allow users to manipulate them and in so doing act on the data they represent—came mainly from Pygmalion. After completing Pygmalion, Smith worked briefly on the NLS project at SRI before joining the Star development team at Xerox.

Bravo, Gypsy, and BravoX. At the same time that LRG was developing Smalltalk for the Alto, others at PARC, mainly Charles Simonyi and Butler Lampson, were writing an advanced document editing system for it: Bravo. Because it made heavy use of the Alto's bitmapped screen, Bravo was unquestionably the most WYSIWYG text editor of its day, with on-screen underlining, boldfacing, italics, variable font families and sizes, and variable-width characters. It allowed the screen to be split so that different documents or different parts of the same document could be edited at once, but it did not operate in a windowed environment as we use the term today. Bravo was widely used at PARC and in Xerox as a whole.

In 1976–1978, Simonyi and others rewrote Bravo, incorporating many of the new user-interface ideas floating around PARC at the time. One such idea was modelessness, promoted by Larry Tesler (1981) and exemplified in Telser's prototype text editor Gypsy. They also added styles, enhancing users' ability to control the appearance of their documents. The new version was called BravoX. Shortly thereafter, Simonyi joined Microsoft, where he led the development of Microsoft Word, a direct descendent of BravoX. Another member of the BravoX team, Tom Malloy, went to Apple and wrote LisaWrite.

Draw, SIL, Markup, Flyer, and Doodle. Star's graphics capability (that is, its provisions for users to create graphical images for incorporation into documents, as opposed to its graphical user interface) owes a great deal to several graphics editors that were written for the Alto and later machines.

Draw, by Patrick Beaudelaire and Bob Sproull, and SIL (for Simple Illustrator) were intellectual successors of Sutherland's Sketchpad: graphical object editors that allowed users to construct figures out of selectable, movable, stretchable geometric forms and text. In turn, Star's graphic frames capability (Lipkie et al., 1982) is in large measure an intellectual successor of Draw and SIL.

Markup was a bitmap graphics editor (a paint program) written by William Newman in BCPL for the Alto. Flyer was another paint program, written in Smalltalk for the Alto by Bob Flegel and Bill Bowman. These programs inspired Doodle, a paint program written for a later machine by Dan Silva. Doodle eventually evolved into the Free-Hand Drawing application for Star's successor, ViewPoint. Silva went on to write DeluxePaint, a paint program for PCs.

Laurel and Hardy. A network of personal workstations suggests electronic mail. Though electronic mail was not invented at PARC, PARC researchers (mainly Doug Brotz) made it user friendly for the first time by creating Laurel, a display-oriented tool for sending, receiving, and organizing e-mail. The experience of using Laurel, which was named after a tree, inspired others to write Hardy, named after Laurel, for an Alto successor machine. Laurel and Hardy were instrumental in getting nonengineers at Xerox to use e-mail. The use of e-mail spread further when Star and ViewPoint spread throughout Xerox. Today, Xerox employees depend heavily on the company's global e-mail network for communication with other employees.

OfficeTalk. One more Alto program that influenced Star was OfficeTalk, a prototype office automation system written by Clarence "Skip" Ellis and Gary Nutt (1979). OfficeTalk supported standard office automation tasks and tracked "jobs" as they went from person to person in an organization. Experience with OfficeTalk provided ideas for Star because of the two systems' similar target applications.

The debt that Star owes to the Alto and its software is best summed up by quoting from the original designers, who wrote in 1982:

> Alto served as a valuable prototype for Star.... Alto users have had several thousand work-years of experience with them over a period of eight years, making Alto perhaps the largest prototyping effort in history. There were dozens of experimental programs written for the Alto by members of the Xerox Palo Alto Research Center. Without the creative ideas of the authors

of these systems, Star in its present form would have been impossible. (Smith et al., 1982).

Design-Process Component 2: Large Design Effort

Although Star incorporated ideas from a number of predecessors, it still required a mammoth design effort to pull all those ideas together—and, where existing ideas didn't suffice, develop new ones—to produce a coherent design. According to the original designers, "...it was a real challenge to bring some order to the different user interfaces on the Alto" (Smith et al., 1982). Fortunately, Star's designers had, in the late 1970s, a rare luxury in the development of commercial computer systems: No one else was developing anything like Star, so they felt no pressure to rush a product to market before they were satisfied with it. They took advantage of this situation to think through what they wanted to develop and how they wanted to develop it.

To develop Star and other office systems products, Xerox created the Systems Development Department (SDD). SDD was staffed by transferring people from other parts of Xerox, including PARC, as well as by hiring from outside. Thus, contrary to what has often been stated in the industry press, Star was not developed at PARC, but rather in a separate product development organization.

To foster thoughtful and uniform design, Star's designers developed a strict format for functional specifications. Applications and system features were first described in terms of the objects that users would manipulate via the software and the actions that the software provided for manipulating objects. This "objects and actions" analysis was performed at a fairly high level without regard to how the objects would actually be presented or how the actions would be invoked by users. In the terminology of Card, Moran, and Newell (1983), systems and applications were first specified only at the task-domain level of analysis rather than at lower levels. A full specification was then written from the objects and actions version. In contrast, many user-interface designers begin by specifying user actions and screen displays. The approach used by Star's designers forced them to think clearly about the purpose of each application or feature and fostered recognition of similar operations across specifications, allowing what might have seemed like new operations to be handled via existing commands.

Using the objects and actions design approach, Star's designers produced specifications for the overall system user interface and for each of the applications. These were collected into one large reference, the Star Functional Specification. Referred to internally as the Red Book, it included whole chapters on design philosophy as well as design details. It brought the specifications for all of Star's applications (at least, all that were conceived at the time) together in one place to promote oversight and uniformity.

An important aspect of the Star design and development process is that the Star designers *were* the system architects and project managers. This arrangement contrasts sharply with how user-interface designers and human-factors specialists usually participate in product development projects: as team members or consultants having no more power (and usually less) than the programmers. In Star's case, the user-interface designers had the ultimate authority: They could enforce their vision of the system and had the power to delay a release if they didn't like something.

Another important aspect of the Star design process was that the software was designed, and then the hardware was designed to meet the needs of the software specification. The display, keyboard, mouse, and even processor were custom-designed to best support the software design.

A third important aspect of the Star design process was the high priority placed on good graphic design, with the resulting heavy involvement of professional graphic designers. Though this was unique at the time, having graphic designers as part of the design team is now fairly common in the industry. For Star, Norm Cox designed the file icons, desktop, property displays, window borders, and many other aspects of the screen appearance; Doris Wells was responsible for most of the graphic refinements in the ViewPoint release of the system. Some graphic design decisions were made based on the recommendations of these and other designers, but many were based on prototyping and user testing of alternative designs that these people and others had proposed (Bewley et al., 1983; Verplank, 1988). The design of the desktop icons is a good example of this (see "Star Prototyping and User Testing"). Had graphic designers not contributed their expertise, the Star user interface would no doubt have been far less worthy of being imitated as much as it has been.

In all, about 30 person-years went into the design of Star's user interface, functionality, and hardware (Harslem and Nelson, 1982). The Star development effort:

- Involved developing new network protocols and data-encoding schemes when those used in PARC's research environment proved inadequate

- Included a late redesign of the processor

- Included several software redesigns, rewrites, and late additions, some based on results from user testing, some based on marketing considerations, and some based on systems considerations

- Included a level of attention to the requirements of international customers that was—and remains—unmatched in the industry (Becker, 1984, 1985, 1987)

- Left much of what was in the Star Functional Specification unimplemented
- Involved a great deal of prototyping and user testing

Design-Process Component 3: Star Prototyping and User Testing

The goal of user interface testing was to answer specific design questions. It was used when the experience and intuition of the designers were inadequate to resolve certain design issues. Such issues included:

- Selection schemes
- Mouse buttons
- Screen color (phosphor) and refresh rate
- Desktop icon designs
- Customer programming language (called CUSP)

Notice that this list is void of any tests related to either more global issues of learnability, usability, user satisfaction, productivity, and so on or questions specific to individual application programs. Part of the effort at that time was in defining appropriate testing methodologies (Miller, 1979a and 1979b). Many of the lab methods were based on very early work in user interface testing and modeling, with emphasis on the work of one of the authors in performance assessment and attitude (subjective) measures (Miller, 1977).

Nielsen and Molich (1990) describe four methods of evaluating user interfaces:

1. Formal analysis. Based on a model of computer-human interaction.
2. Automatic evaluation. By this they mean that the interactions are monitored or simulated, and a computer-generated scoring method is used.
3. Empirical evaluation. Experiments are conducted with users exercising the system, or part of the system, and design comparisons are evaluated using standard experimental designs.
4. Heuristic evaluation. Experienced UI designers rate the system.

Lewis et al. (1990) also describe a systematic way of evaluating user interfaces using a technique they call *cognitive walkthroughs.*

Methodology

The user interface tests for Star used the third of Nielsen and Molich's ways of evaluating user interfaces: experimental methods. By training and background, the members of the user interface testing group[2] were predisposed to experimental evaluations, with model development a goal, given a sufficient body of experimental and observational work (as in Miller, 1979a). Performance measures were typically time to learn a task, time to complete a task, errors made in performing tasks, confusions among similar methods in performing a task, and attitude measures of satisfaction with the system. Statistical analyses were conducted with appropriate experimental designs (Winer, 1971), and were reported to the user interface prototyping group.

Where tests involved subjects performing a task on the system, they were either drawn from the secretarial and administrative staff at Xerox or were clerical and secretarial temporaries hired as test subjects. We believed the subjects represented a valid sampling of Star's ultimate end users. There was some disagreement among Star's designers and Xerox marketing and management about who the target users were: business professionals or office clerical workers. The prototype designers and the user testing group focused on secretarial and clerical users because we felt that word processing pools, legal secretaries, and other clerical personnel represented the major marketing opportunity for Star.

Tests

Low-level[3] tests were conducted on several aspects of the Star system.

This section briefly discusses some of these tests,[4] the methods used, and the results. We discuss their impact on the Star product in a later section.

Labels Tests. Usability studies on Star quickly established that names and labels that made sense to the designers did not necessarily make sense to users. A labeling study was conducted (McBain, 1979) to ascertain the difficulties users had with function key labels, object names, and their meanings. A later study (Miller, 1981) involving writing procedures for repetitive office tasks also examined the question of multiple names. Notice that the human computer interaction literature also has subsequently considered this an important area of study (Furnas et al., 1982).

METHOD. Several tests were conducted that attempted to understand the names that potential Star users would use for performing various tasks in the system. These were tasks for which there were already labeled function keys. We wanted to see how users' names for functions corresponded to labels we chose. There were 21 function keys, with proposed labels that included: **Font, Move, Copy, Delete, Again, Special, Help,** and several others.

The first test involved a series of 23 scenarios, and the subject was expected to provide a name for the operation. Scenarios included descriptions such as:

Let's say you plan to type the expression "Short Term Memory" several times in a report. If the system has been programmed to do so, you can type STM and the system will automatically type the remaining letters for each word. What is the name of the key you would press to *program* the system?

The second test repeated the same scenarios but required the subject to select his or her answer from a list of 36 labels. For each of the questions, there already existed a function key, so each question had a "correct" answer.

RESULTS. Labels such as **Delete** and **Repeat** were found to occur spontaneously with 70 to 80 percent of the subjects (unfortunately, there was no key labeled **Repeat**—it was labeled **Again**). Labels such as **Move, Again, Global Replace, Change,** and **Undo** were spontaneously generated less than 30 percent of the time. Clearly, some labels needed rethinking, and they were changed.

Property Sheets. A study was conducted to ascertain the meaningfulness of names used on property sheets (Schroit, 1979). A property sheet is a table of information giving relevant attributes of a selected object. There are text and document property sheets, graphics property sheets, and so on. Text properties include font family, size, bold, italics, and others. Document properties include page numbering, headers and footers, and others.

METHOD. Subjects were given a description of some feature or property (29 questions in all) and asked to select, from a list of 8 supplied names, the name of the property sheet that would be used to display or alter the described property. There was no training on the property sheets.

A second task required the subjects to describe what they believed to be the function of each named property. Again, there was no training period.

RESULTS. The first task indicated problems with understanding just what each property sheet does. Especially difficult were descriptions such as Alignment, Keep on, Hyphenation and Spacing between Lines (found on Paragraph sheet); Show Nonprinting Characters and Scale (found on the Window sheet); Spacing between Columns (on the Tab Settings sheet); and Number of Columns (on the Page Layout sheet).

On task two, 100 percent of the subjects made errors on labels such as Outer, Reset, Tab Types, and Before/After Paragraph Spacing. Reset is an interesting one since it is commonly found on property sheets in software for the Apple Macintosh. Fewer subjects (but greater than 60 percent) had problems with Defaults, Footings, Other, Same, Different, Keep on, Display, Subscript, and Superscript.

Combined with the function key labels tests, this test suggested, long before it became well accepted, that there are potential difficulties in any simple labeling scheme. It also suggested that the number and variety of function keys and property sheets should be greatly limited. What was the motivation of separating Star properties into so many property sheets? Could several of these have been combined, simplified, replaced with other command forms, or eliminated?

Icon Tests. Star's user interface is permeated with icons. However, the term *icon* in Star does not refer to any graphical label (for example, a scrolling button) but is restricted to the small graphical representations of closed data files that appear on user's desktops and in folders. The recognition, manipulation, naming, and placing of icons form a major part of the user's interaction with Star. To the extent that icons are recognizable, distinguishable, simple and natural to manipulate, and free of surprises or dangerous side effects, the system ought to be easier to learn and use, and ought to lead to better user performance and attitudes. These concerns formed the basis of an extensive and elaborate series of tests on several different proposed icon designs (Bewley et al., 1983; Verplank, 1979).

METHOD. Four sets of icons were used in a series of tests that required subjects to learn, recognize, and distinguish icons in one set, then to give opinions about icons in other sets. (Samples from the four sets are shown in Figure 3.) There were eight tests, and all subjects participated in all eight. Tests involved describing what each icon means, picking a name for each icon, matching names to icons, a timed name–icon matching test, and a set of ratings, first on one set of icons, and then on all four comparison sets.

RESULTS. Substantial confusion was shown across all icon sets. Confusion can be ascribed to the uniqueness of the idea of icons and, in several cases, to the uniqueness of the indicated concept. (There were icons for recording a macro, shaped somewhat like a reel-to-reel tape recorder, for example.) However, two strong tendencies did emerge from the tests: Icons with labels indicating their function were preferred over those without; icon sets with more clearly distinguished visual properties (less uniformity of size and shape) were preferred over those with less distinguishable properties.

Free response naming tests again indicated the great variety of labels people use. They also indicate amazing diversity of ideas on what designers thought were perfectly clear depictions. For example, an icon representing a relational database (and labeled 1979 Xerox Employees) was called variously a badge, a roster, a title for view graphs, a bulletin board, a label on a file drawer, a report card, a display unit, and more accurately, a file containing

FIGURE 3 Four icon sets used in the Star icon tests. *Courtesy of Xerox Corporation.*

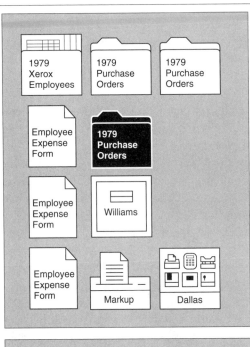

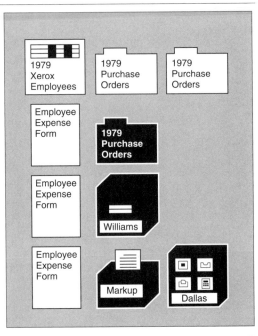

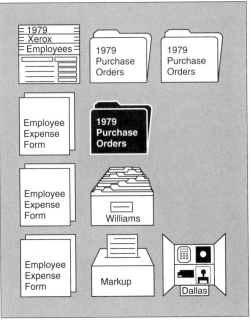

data and a tabulation of employees. Something we take for granted today, a calculator icon (labeled, oddly enough, Business) was called buttons with slot, security bin, no idea, and instrument timer. Some subjects confused out-baskets and in-baskets. An arrow coming out of a basketlike design was thought to be an in-basket because you take things out of an in-basket. Another subject thought it was an in-basket, but "...don't know what the arrow means."

It is important to note, as Verplank (1979) did, that "These tests did not consider whether the basic functionality of icons ... is valid or effective. Other tests will be required to see how people take to the use of icons." No such other tests were performed.

Text and Graphics Selection Schemes Tests. One of the many novel aspects of Star was the mouse. Finding the best mouse configuration—number of buttons and their meaning—was an important concern. The selection scheme tests (Bewley et al., 1979) evaluated one-, two- and three-button mice, and several alternative text selection methods. Separate tests were performed for text objects and for graphics objects. Typical text selection methods included character-oriented schemes (select an individual character, then draw or otherwise extend the selection to get a block of text) and entity schemes (select character, word, sentence, paragraph, or whole document through multiple clicks; then extend the selection in units of the selected object). Methods of extending the selection included draw through, select start then end of block, combined mouse keys and keyboard actions, and so on.

In addition to the test selection methods, we were interested in ways of highlighting the selected text: box, underline, or inverse video.

METHOD. Six selection methods and three selection-feedback methods were tested. Performance measures included time to complete tasks, errors, and user preference.

Text editing tasks included inserting text and moving single and multiple characters, words, sentences, or paragraphs. Graphics editing included selecting a control point on a line, selecting a line, and selecting a graphics frame (an embedded drawing area in the text editor).

RESULTS. The results indicated that on both time and errors, one scheme was superior: a two-button scheme that used the left button to select a character and the right button to extend the selection (see "Sidebar: Star's Mouse"). On highlighting, there was a strong preference for inverse video for text and boxed feedback for graphics.

S I D E B A R	**STAR'S MOUSE**

An interactive computer system must provide a way for users to indicate which operations they want and what data they want those operations to be performed on. Users of early interactive systems specified operations and operands via commands and data descriptors (for example, text line numbers). As video display terminals became common, it became clear that it was often better for users to specify operands—and sometimes operations—by pointing to them on the screen. It also became clear that graphic applications should not be controlled solely via a keyboard. In the 1960s and 1970s, many different pointing devices were invented and tested: light pen, track ball, joy stick, cursor keys, digitizing tablet, touch screen, and mouse (English, Engelbart, and Berman, 1967).

Star's incorporation of a mouse required an explicit decision to break with both industry convention (where mice were unknown) and Xerox PARC convention (where mice had three buttons). To justify such a dual break, the designers had to justify their design with compelling evidence that their design was superior to alternatives. To this end, they performed extensive user testing (Bewley et al., 1983). In this section, we discuss several important aspects of Star's mouse, explaining why Star's designers decided as they did.

THE MOUSE VS. CURSOR KEYS

Some people argue over the merits of the mouse compared to those of the cursor keys. Cursor key proponents argue that cursor keys are faster because of the time required to move one's hands from the keyboard to the mouse and back. Mouse advocates argue that the mouse is faster because of the many keystrokes required to move the cursor with cursor keys. The facts are:

- The time to moves one's hands to the mouse depends on where they start. If one's hand is usually on the keyboard, then it does take time to move it to the mouse. However, Star is designed to minimize the use of the main keyboard array. In fact, Star can be operated for extended periods without touching the main keyboard, which is used primarily to enter text. Unless a user is entering text, his or her hands stay mainly on the mouse and function keys. Further, though systems often embed the cursor keys in the main keyboard array as control characters, cursor keys are usually positioned apart from the main keyboard array. Moving one's hand to a separate cursor key pad takes just as long as moving it to the mouse because the time to move the hand is dominated by precise positioning movements at the end of the movement.

- Each cursor-movement mechanism is superior in certain situations. The time to move the insertion point with a mouse is a log function of distance and size of target (Card, Moran, and Newell, 1983). Moving the insertion point to the next character using a mouse takes as much time as moving it to a distant one because the time is dominated by precise movements to home-in on the target. With cursor keys, the time required is a linear function of distance. Moving the insertion point to the next character is much faster than moving it a long distance. Thus, if the insertion point is to be moved a few characters, cursor keys are faster; if it is to be moved a long distance, the mouse is faster.

Though Star originally had no cursor keys, they were added in ViewPoint, Star's successor.

THE MOUSE VS. OTHER POINTING DEVICES

Like other pointing devices, the mouse allows easy selection of objects and triggering of sensitive areas on the screen. The mouse differs from touch screens, light pens, and digitizing pads in that it is a relative pointing device: The movement of the pointer on the screen depends on mouse movement rather than on its position. Unlike light pens, joy sticks, and digitizing pads, the mouse (and the corresponding pointer on the screen) stays put when the user lets go of it to do something else.

TWO MOUSE-BUTTONS VS. ONE OR THREE

Star uses a two-button mouse, in contrast with the one-button mouse used by Apple and the three-button mouse used by most other vendors. Though predecessors of Star developed at Xerox PARC (see "Incorporating Ideas from Previous Computer Systems") use a three-button mouse, Star's designers wanted to reduce the number of buttons to alleviate confusion over which button did what. The functions invoked via the Alto's middle button are, in Star, invoked in other ways. Why did Star's designers stop at two buttons instead of reducing the number to one, as Apple did? Because in the studies they conducted, having a one-button mouse eliminated button-confusion errors only at the cost of increasing selection errors to undesirable levels (see "Text and Graphics Selection Schemes Tests").

The major commercial vendors today have made different decisions regarding the number of mouse buttons: one button for the Macintosh, two buttons for mice designed for IBM-compatible PCs (for example, the Microsoft mouse), and three buttons for Unix workstations.

LOW VS. HIGH-LEVEL MOUSE-HANDLING

To achieve satisfactory mouse-tracking performance, Star's mouse is handled at a very low level and has a very high priority. In some workstations, mouse tracking is handled in the window system, with the result that the mouse pointer often jerks around the screen and may even freeze for seconds at a time, depending on what else the system is doing. The mouse is a hand–eye coordination device, so if the pointer lags, users just keep moving the mouse, and when the system catches up, the mouse moves beyond the user's target. This was considered unacceptable by Star's designers and at Xerox in general.

Writing Arithmetic Expressions. Although Star, being initially a closed system, did not run any of the spreadsheet programs that were available in the early 1980s (for example, VisiCalc), it did offer spreadsheetlike capabilities in its document-tables facility. Users could create expressions to calculate the value of specified table cells automatically. A test was conducted in an attempt to understand the difficulties Star users might have in writing these expressions (Roberts, 1980).

Today, we know that spreadsheet expressions can be quite complex, involving several operators of different precedence, functions of one or more cells (variables), functions of a range of cells (such as sum, max, and min), and expressions containing conditionals. How good would the expected Star user population be at writing these kinds of expressions? The literature at that time was very scant on such questions. (There had been some work in assessing abilities in writing complex database queries involving the boolean operators AND, OR, and NOT.)

METHOD. Subjects were trained on a set of training materials, then given a set of problems. After each problem, the experimenter indicated whether the solution was correct and, if not, gave some assistance in completing the problem. There was substantial interaction between experimenter and subjects; the goal of the tests was an informal, not rigorous, look at the potential problems.

The prototype Star system used for these tests also provided a calculator-like interface to writing expressions, a potentially powerful bridge between inexperienced users and the powerful expression syntax Star allowed. Subjects were required to write expressions using this calculator interface.

RESULTS. Time to complete tasks was recorded. Additionally, a 6-point scale was used to indicate the correctness of the solution. A questionnaire was also administered providing information on a user's feelings of comfort in writing expressions, assessment of alternative forms, and so on.

The results indicate that "most secretaries will be able to write extremely simple arithmetic expressions, those containing one operator. The 'average' secretary probably could not solve problems of more difficulty than that...." Virtually all subjects had difficulty at some point, as the expressions became more complex, and all had some difficulty with the syntax used for conditionals.

The results with the calculator interface appear to be mixed: "The subjects seemed to like it for simple problems; but for difficult problems they preferred writing, which was easier for them to 'visualize.'"

A reasonable predictor of a subject's performance was his or her own self-assessment of mathematical abilities. This suggests that end-user programming—writing procedures, macros, spreadsheet formulas—is a self-selecting process and that someone's own professed abilities (or lack of) are a good indicator of performance.

Other Tests. Several other tests were conducted for which original reports and data are no longer available. These include screen refresh rate, screen phosphor, keyboard design and layout, and others. For each of these, the overall methods, experimental designs, data gathering, analysis, and reporting were similar to the studies reported here.

Evaluation of Star Design Method: Lessons Learned

What is to be learned from our examination of the Star design process? The popularity of the user interface that Star pioneered makes it clear that Star's designers did many things right. The user interface of Apple's Lisa computer borrowed heavily from Star (Williams, 1983; Johnson et al., 1989). The interfaces of the Metaphor workstation, the Cognition MCAE CAD/CAM system, and Open Software Foundation's Open Look were developed with the direct involvement or consulting services of many of the same software and graphic designers who designed Star, and so share important features with it. Still other systems imitate Star indirectly by imitating its imitators, for example, Interleaf and FrameMaker document systems, Microsoft Windows, and the OSF/Motif user-interface style. At the same time, the popularity of the Star user interface mainly in systems other than Star indicates that Star's designers did some things wrong. We now review those aspects of the design process—first right, then wrong—that affected the user interface.

What Was Right About the Star Design Process?

As we have seen, an important part of what was right about the design of the Star user interface was that it rested on so much innovative research in interactive computer systems. This research, especially that coming from Xerox PARC, provided not only design ideas that were useful in designing Star, but also the mindset necessary to keep innovating, to not be satisfied with conventional designs, even when the conventions were unconventional Xerox PARC conventions. The context in which their design effort began is, of course, something Star's designers cannot take credit for, except to the degree that some of them had done some of the prior research. More of the credit for the unique context is due to Xerox management, which created PARC, and then started the Star effort in order to get some of the ideas floating around at PARC into products.

Though Star's designers were fortunate to have many ideas and much experience to draw on, producing a product from them was by no means straightforward. They made the most of their good starting position by adopting a unique design process. We believe that the following are the aspects of Star's design process that designers would do well to emulate:

- *Commitment to design first, then code.* Often, developers feel pressure to begin writing code before really knowing what the interface or even the functionality of the system or application is to be. This is even though development effort is usually greatly reduced when designers figure out in advance what they want instead of making the design up as they go. The Star development effort was not exempt from such pressures and, in fact, succumbed to them to a certain extent. Nevertheless, the relative lack of time pressure, combined with the resolve of Star's designers to produce a very usable, highly consistent system, fostered the commitment to a well-thought-out design.

- *Use of objects-and-actions design methodology.* Several people who were involved in the design of Star (either directly or indirectly) claim that the most valuable thing they learned from that experience is to perform an objects-and-actions analysis of an application's target task domain prior to designing the user interface. Beginning by considering the conceptual design of applications and functions—ignoring the temptation to jump straight to laying out buttons, scroll bars, and menus, and specifying keystroke-level aspects of the interface—is extremely beneficial. Not only does it improve the design of an individual application or function by making it fit the target task-domain better (Zarmer and Johnson, 1990; Nardi and Johnson, 1994), it improves the design of the overall system by promoting simplicity and consistency, for example, the use of generic commands (Rosenberg and Moran, 1984; Johnson et al., 1989).

- *Attention to detail.* It has been said that "God is in the details." In the case of Star, it is certainly true that attention to detail (for example, making sure that all text is edited in the same way, regardless of where it is, or that mouse clicks give feedback on button-down but don't take effect until button-up) is largely responsible for Star's clean, consistent, easy-to-learn user interface. Without such attention to detail, the interface might well have been innovative anyway, but it would not have been as clean. However, we believe that the level of detail embodied in the Star design was and still is extremely rare in the computer industry.

- *Participation of graphic designers.* An important part of paying attention to detail is getting the screen graphics right. Screen graphics designed by computer programmers will not satisfy customers. The Star designers recognized their limitations in this regard and hired the right people for the job. The graphic designers hired to devise the appearance of Star's interface followed and, in many cases, developed the graphic principles described in Verplank (1988) and Johnson et al. (1989).

- *Commitment to user testing and subsequent redesign.* In the late 1970s, when Star was being designed, it was much less common for computer product developers to include user testing in their design process. Star was thus one of the first commercial computer products for which user testing played an important part in the design. Since user testing is expensive and time consuming, one can ask whether it paid off. How much better was the product compared to how it would have been with no testing? Were any design catastrophes avoided through testing? Would Star have been perceived differently by the marketplace or the CHI community without the tests? Given Star's relative lack of success in the commercial market but immense success as a source of ideas for future designers, did the user testing focus on the right questions? Obviously, these questions cannot be answered conclusively. Suffice it to say that Star's designers believe that the benefits received from the user testing were worth the costs.

In addition to affecting the product's design, those involved in Star's user testing established:

- A collection of baseline data that can be used by future practitioners[5]

- The notion that some performance could be predicted from parametric descriptions of user interfaces

- That performance in some tasks differed substantially among individuals, that is, that any effective interactive system must tolerate individual differences

---

SIDEBAR | **STAR'S DOCUMENT-CENTRIC DESIGN**

Most personal computers and computer workstations give no special status to any particular application. They run dozens, even hundreds, of applications, many of which are incompatible with each other.

Star's designers, in contrast, assumed that the primary use of the system is to create and manage documents. The document editor is therefore the primary application. All other applications exist mainly to provide or manipulate information that will ultimately reside in some document. Thus, most applications are integrated into the document editor, operating within frames embedded in documents. Those applications that are not part of the document editor support transfer of their data to documents.

What Was Wrong About the Star Design Process?

These are the aspects of the design process that we believe—with the benefit of 20/20 hindsight—that Star's designers should have done differently and that subsequent designers should avoid:

- *Insufficient attention to industry trends.* Partly out of excitement over what they were doing, PARC researchers and Star's designers didn't pay enough attention to the "other" personal computer revolution that was occurring outside of Xerox. By the late 1970s, Xerox had its own powerful technical tradition (mouse-driven, networked workstations with large bitmapped screens and multiple, simultaneous applications), blinding Star's designers to the need to approach the market via cheap, standalone PCs. The result was a product that was highly unfamiliar. Nowadays, of course, user interfaces like Star's are no longer unusual.

- *Insufficient attention to what customers want.* The personal computer revolution has shown that it is futile to try to anticipate all the applications that customers will want. Star should have been designed to be open and extensible by users from the start, as the Alto was. In hindsight, extensibility was one of the keys to the Alto's popularity. The problem wasn't that Star lacked functionality, it was that it didn't have the functionality customers wanted. Eventually realizing that Star's closedness was a problem, Xerox replaced it with ViewPoint, a more open system that allows users to pick and choose applications that they need, including a spreadsheet and IBM PC software. Apple Computer learned the same lesson with its Lisa computer and similarly replaced it with a cheaper one having a more open software architecture: Macintosh.

- *Insufficient attention to interactive responsiveness.* Star's designers were greatly disappointed in the poor responsiveness exhibited by prerelease versions of the system. Star's designers should have established performance goals, documented them in the functional specifications, and stuck to them as Star was being developed. Where performance goals couldn't be met, the corresponding functionality should have been cut. Instead of speed, the user interface should have been designed to be more responsive. By designing the system to handle user input more intelligently, systems can be made more responsive without necessarily making them execute functions faster (Duis and Johnson, 1990). They can anticipate likely user commands and prepare the responses in advance. They can operate asynchronously with respect to user input, making use of background processes, keeping up with important user actions, delaying unimportant tasks (for example, refreshing irrelevant areas of the screen) until time permits, and skipping tasks called for by early user actions but rendered moot by later ones.

- *Overreliance on physical metaphors.* Star's designers were perhaps over dogmatic about the desktop metaphor and direct manipulation. Some interfaces that have imitated Star (either directly or by imitating interfaces that imitated Star) aren't so strict and are more usable as a result. Direct manipulation and the desktop metaphor aren't the best way to do everything (Halasz and Moran, 1982; Houston, 1983; Johnson, 1985; Johnson, 1987). Remembering and typing is sometimes better than seeing and pointing. For example, if a user wants to open a file that is one of several hundred in a directory (folder), the system should let users type its name rather than forcing them to scroll through the directory trying to spot it so that they can select it.

- *Testing the wrong user population.* It is clear that the designers and user-testing people were heavily influenced by a marketing perception of stereotypical Star users: clerical, secretarial, or steno pool personnel, computer naive if not computer aversive. Studies at potential customer sites (law offices, insurance companies, and others) reinforced this view because of the prevalence at that time of large word processing centers, with high turnover rates.

Over and over again, questions were asked and tests conducted with subjects variously described as: "…from the…secretarial population…" or "…the subjects were chosen from the naive subjects who participated [in an earlier test]." Another study: "Ten subjects participated in the test. Eight subjects had experience on the IBM Selectric…." Or another study: "Two [subjects] were secretarial *students* and one…was a homemaker who had been a secretary previously. None were supposed to have any word processing or computing experience…" [emphasis added]. Yet another test: "Each group [of subjects] consisted of three secretaries and two non-secretaries…"

What are we to infer from such subject selection methods? In Campbell and Stanley's (1963) terms, what is the external validity of tests run with such subjects? Would different subject selection methods have changed the perception or qualitative value of the results? Unfortunately, those conducting user tests for Star were pioneers in the rigorous and systematic application of experimental techniques to the design and refinement of commercial interactive computer systems.

Conclusions

Star has had an indisputable influence on the design of computer systems. For example, the Lisa and Macintosh might have been very different had Apple's designers not borrowed ideas from Star, as the following excerpt of a *Byte* magazine interview of Lisa's designers shows (Williams, 1983):

Byte: Do you have a Xerox Star here that you work with?

Tesler: No, we didn't have one here. We went to the NCC [National Computer Conference] when the Star was announced and looked at it. And in fact it did have an immediate impact. A few months after looking at it we made some changes to our user interface based on ideas that we got from it. For example, the desktop manager we had before was completely different; it didn't use icons at all, and we never liked it very much. We decided to change ours to the icon base. That was probably the only thing we got from Star, I think. Most of our Xerox inspiration was Smalltalk rather than Star.

Elements of the desktop metaphor approach also appear in many other systems. The history presented here has shown, however, that just as Star influenced systems that came after it, Star was influenced by ideas and systems that came before it; it was not designed from scratch. One might then ask: Was Star's landmark and influential design due primarily to the experience of the designers, the support for innovation provided by their working environment, the specification methodology that they devised and employed, the unprecedented amount of user testing that they conducted, or some combination of these?

The foregoing analysis shows that the answer depends on which aspect of Star's user interface one is discussing. The ideas of a desktop metaphor, a mouse, windows, and icons clearly did not come from the specification regimen or from user testing; they came from the experience of the designers and the innovative culture in which they worked. If those ideas are the essence of the Star user interface, then much of the comprehensive design approach developed for the purpose of developing Star did not actually contribute much to what is important about Star. However, if what is important about Star is its high degree of consistency, its access to a great deal of functionality through the mouse and a few generic function keys, its providing the information users require to do their work (not too much; not too little), its graphical clarity, and its high level of general polish, greatly exceeding what is seen in most mouse-and-window-based systems, then the user testing and the strict specification regimen were important.

| SIDEBAR | **TILED VS. OVERLAPPING WINDOWS** |

It is now common for systems to allow several programs to display information simultaneously in separate areas of the screen rather than each taking up the entire display. Star was the first commercially available system to provide this capability.

One controversial issue Star's designers had to face was should application windows overlap or not? Some windowing systems allow windows to overlap one another. Other systems don't; the size and position of windows are adjusted by the system as windows are opened and closed. At Xerox PARC, whether windows should overlap was a hotly debated issue. How it was decided for each of the window-based systems developed there depended on the personal preferences of the window-system implementors, who, of course, had the last word.

In contrast, Star's designers applied user testing to resolve the issue. Star's windowing system was initially designed such that it could overlap windows. However, Star's designers observed in early testing that users spent a lot of time adjusting windows and usually adjusted them so that they did not overlap. Because of this, the designers decided that application windows should be constrained so as not to overlap. However, not all windows in Star were constrained in this way. For example, property and option sheets were displayed in windows that overlapped application windows. They were not special other than not being subject to the tiling constraint. This contrasts with windowing systems that were designed from the ground up to be tiled, for example, Cedar (Teitelman, 1984).

When ViewPoint, Star's successor, was being designed, market pressure to allow application windows to overlap grew stronger. Further, new user testing convinced designers that there are situations in which overlapping application windows are preferable (Bly and Rosenberg, 1986). For these reasons, the tiling constraints were made optional in ViewPoint, with the default setting being that application windows can overlap one another.

Without all the aspects of the design process we have described, Star would not be regarded today as a seminal—that is, influential—design. It would not have been as widely imitated.

With all these positive influences on Star's design process, why didn't Star succeed in the marketplace as well as it has in influencing subsequent system designs? The answer lies only partially in mistakes made in the design process. A multitude of factors influence a product's degree of market success, only a small fraction of which have to do with the product's design. In the computer systems business, marketing, sales, support, and reputation are four important factors. Perhaps the most important factor hindering Star's success in the marketplace was the fact that it was totally new, both in what it was for and in how users interacted with it. As is explained in Card's discussion of the "success cases" in this section, radically new products almost never succeed in the marketplace; most marketing successes are products that follow and incrementally improve on a prior design.

Of course, to ask why Star didn't succeed in the marketplace—despite its obvious success as a source of "genetic material" for later systems—is to ask a metaphysical question. We cannot turn the clock back to 1976. We cannot run the experiment again with a different design or different management decisions. We can speculate endlessly, but we can never really know why. Therefore, the right thing to do is to document the Star experience as well as we can and move forward.

One conclusion that the authors drew from their experience with Star and Viewpoint is that developing the style of user interface that Star pioneered—what is now called the graphical user interface (GUI)—shouldn't be as difficult as it was with Star. Nonetheless, development of GUIs for commercial applications remains as difficult today as it was then. To move forward, we need to explore methods of automatically generating interfaces that follow accepted look-and-feel guidelines, but that don't require hundreds of man-years of effort (Arens et al., 1991; Johnson, 1992).

Acknowledgments

We are pleased that the Xerox Corporation has cooperated in producing this paper. Figures and quotations from Xerox reports are used with permission. We are indebted to the extensive and insightful comments of an anonymous reviewer.

Notes

1. The actual name of the system was On-Line System. There was a second system called Off-Line System (abbreviated FLS), hence NLS's strange abbreviation. NLS is now marketed by McDonnell-Douglas under the name Augment.

2. Bill Bewley, Dave Cooper, Dexter Fletcher, Cookie McBain, Larry Miller, Terry Roberts, Dave Schroit, Bill Verplank, Rex Walden.

3. By "low-level" test, we mean a test that was designed to compare time and errors on specific aspects of the Star system—keyboard, mouse, object selection—as opposed to

application, systemwide, productivity, or other tests that measure effectiveness in completing a job-oriented set of procedures.

4. The ones for which we still have original materials.

5. Assuming they can get by Xerox's proprietary concerns.

References

Pre-Xerox PARC

Bush, V. (1945). As we may think. *Atlantic Monthly* 176(1), 101–108.

Engelbart, D. and English, W. (1968). A research center for augmenting human intellect. *AFIPS Proceedings of the Fall Joint Computer Conference*, vol. 33, 395–410.

English, W., Engelbart, D., and Berman, M. (1967). Display-selection techniques for text manipulation. *IEEE Transactions on Human Factors in Electronics*, HFE-8, 21–31.

Kay, A. (1969). *The Reactive Engine.* Ph.D. thesis, University of Utah.

Sutherland, I. (1963). *Sketchpad: A Man-Machine Graphical Communications System.* Ph.D. thesis, MIT.

Xerox Pre-Star

Card, S., English, W., and Burr, B. (1978). Evaluation of mouse, rate-controlled isometric joystick, step keys, and text keys for text selection on a CRT. *Ergonomics* 21, 601–613.

Ellis, C. and Nutt, G. (1979). *Computer Science and Office Information Systems.* Xerox PARC Tech. Report SSL-79-6.

Ingalls, D. (1981). The smalltalk graphics kernel. *Byte* 6(8) (August), 168–194.

Kay, A. (1977). Microelectronics and the personal computer. *Scientific American* 237(3) (September).

Kay, A. and Goldberg, A. (1977). Personal dynamic media. *IEEE Computer* 10(3) (March), 31–41.

Smith, D. (1977) *Pygmalion: A Computer Program to Model and Simulate Creative Thought.* Basel and Stuttgart: Birkhäuser Verlag.

Tesler, L. (1981). The smalltalk environment. *Byte* 6(8) (August), 90–147.

Thacker, C., McCreight, E., Lampson, B., Sproull, R., and Boggs, D. (1982). Alto: A personal computer. In D. Siewioek, C. G. Bell, and A. Newell (eds.), *Computer Structures: Principles and Examples.* New York: McGraw-Hill.

Star

Becker, J. (1984). Multilingual word processing. *Scientific American* 251(1) (July), 96–107.

———. (1985). Typing Chinese, Japanese, and Korean. *IEEE Computer* (January), 27–34.

———. (1987). Arabic word processing. *Communications of the ACM* 30(7) (July), 600–610.

Bewley, W., Roberts, T., Schroit, D., Verplank, W. (1983). Human factors testing in the design of Xerox's 8010 Star office workstation. *Proceedings of the ACM Conference on Human Factors in Computing Systems,* 72–77.

Bewley, W. (1979). *The Star Selection Schemes Test: Final Report.* Xerox Internal Report FA Report-79-1, El Segundo, CA (January).

Harslem, E. and Nelson, L. (1982). A retrospective on the development of Star. *Proceedings of the Sixth International Conference on Software Engineering,* Tokyo, Japan.

Johnson, J., Roberts, T., Verplank, W., Smith, D., Irby, C., Beard, M., and Mackey, K. (1989). The Xerox Star: A retrospective. *IEEE Computer* 22(9), (September) 11–26.

Lipkie, D., Evans, S., Newlin, J., and Weissman, R. (1982). Star Graphics: An object-oriented implementation. *Computer Graphics* 16(3) (July), 115–124.

McBain, C. (1979). *The Star Keyboard Test: Labels Test.* Xerox Internal Report FT Report 79-2, El Segundo, CA (April).

Roberts, T. (1980). *Arithmetic Expression Writing Experiments.* Xerox Internal Memo, El Segundo, CA (July).

Schroit, D. (1979). *Status of Property Sheet Testing.* Xerox Internal Memo, El Segundo, CA (February).

Smith, D. (1985). Origins of the desktop metaphor: A brief history. Panel: The Desktop Metaphor as an Approach to User Interface Design. In *Proceedings of the ACM Annual Conference,* 548.

Smith, D., Irby, C., Kimball, R., Verplank, W., and Harslem, E. (1982). Designing the Star user interface. *Byte* 7(4), 242–282.

Verplank, W. (1979). *Results of: Star Icon Tests.* Xerox Internal Report FA Report-79-8, El Segundo, CA (December).

———. (1988). Designing Graphical User Interfaces. Tutorial notes, *ACM Conference on Computer-Human Interaction.*

Miscellaneous

Arens, Y., Miller, L., and Sonheimer, N. (1991). Presentation design using an integrated knowledge base. In J. W. Sullivan and S. W. Tyler (eds.), *Architectures for Intelligent Interfaces: Elements and Prototypes.* Reading, MA: Addison-Wesley.

Bly, S. and Rosenberg, J. (1986). A comparison of tiled and overlapping windows. *Proceedings of the ACM Conference on Computer-Human Interaction,* 101–106.

Campbell, D. and Stanley, J. (1963). *Experimental and Quasi-Experimental Designs for Research.* Chicago: Rand-McNally.

Card, S., Moran, T., and Newell, A. (1983). *The Psychology of Human-Computer Interaction.* Hillsdale, NJ: Lawrence Erlbaum.

Card, S., Moran, T., and Newell, A. (1979). *The Keystroke-Level Model for User Performance Time with Interactive Systems.* PARC Report SSL-79-1, Palo Alto, CA (March).

Duis, D. and Johnson, J. (1990). Improving user-interface responsiveness despite performance limitations. *Proceedings of IEEE CompCon '90* (San Francisco).

Furnas, G., Gomez, L., Landauer, T., and Dumais, S. (1982). Statistical semantics: How can a computer use what people name things to guess what things people mean when they name things? *Proceedings of the Conference on Human Factors in Computer Systems* (Gaithersburg, MD, March), 251–254.

Gentner, D. and Grudin, J. (1990). Why good engineers (sometimes) create bad interfaces. *Proceedings of the ACM Conference on Human Factors in Computing Systems,* 277–282.

Goldberg, A. (1984). *Smalltalk-80: The Interactive Programming Environment.* Reading, MA: Addison-Wesley.

Goldberg, A. and Robson, D. (1984). *Smalltalk-80: The Language and Its Implementation.* Reading, MA: Addison-Wesley.

Halasz, F. and Moran, T. (1982). Analogy considered harmful. *Proceedings of the Conference on Human Factors in Computing Systems* (Gaithersburg, MD), 383–386.

Houston, T. (1983). The allegory of software: Beyond, behind, and beneath the electronic desk. *Byte* (December), 210–214.

Johnson, J. (1985). Calculator functions on bitmapped computers. *SIGCHI Bulletin* 17(1) (July), 23–28.

———. (1987). How closely should the electronic desktop simulate the real one? *SIGCHI Bulletin* 19(2) (October), 21–25.

———. (1992). Selectors: Moving beyond user interface widgets. *Proceedings of the Conference on Human Factors in Computing Systems,* 273–279.

Keen, P. (1981). Information systems and organizational change. *Communications of the ACM*, vol. 24, no. 1 (January), 24–33.

Lewis, C., Polson, P., Wharton, C., and Rieman, J. (1990). Testing a walkthrough methodology for theory-based design of walk-up-and-use interfaces. *Proceedings of the ACM Conference on Human Factors in Computing Systems*, 235–242.

Malone, T. (1983). How do people organize their desks? Implications for the design of office information systems. *ACM Transactions on Office Information Systems*, vol. 1, no. 1 (January), 99–112.

Miller, L. (1977). A study in man-machine interaction. *Proceedings, National Computer Conference*, vol. 46, Montvale, NJ: AFIPS Press, 409.

———. (1979a). Experimental validation of cognitive models for man-machine interaction. In E. J. Boutmy and A. Danthine (eds.), *Teleinformatics '79*, Amsterdam: North-Holland Publishing, 195–200.

———. (1979b). The use of empirical observations in the development of formal models. *ACM SIGSOC Bulletin*, vol. 11, no. 1, Association for Computing Machinery (July).

———. (1981). Procedure specification by non-programmers. *ACM SIGSOC Bulletin*, Association for Computing Machinery, Presented at 5th International Conference on Easier and More Productive Use of Computers, Ann Arbor, MI (May).

Molich, R. and Nielsen, J. (1990). Improving a human-computer dialogue. *Communications of the ACM*, vol. 33, no. 3 (March), 338–348.

Nardi, B. and Johnson, J. (1994). User preferences for task-specific vs. generic application software. *Proceedings of the ACM Conference on Human Factors in Computing Systems*, 392–398.

Nielsen, J. and Molich, R. (1990). Heuristic evaluation of user interfaces. *Proceedings of the ACM Conference on Human Factors in Computing Systems*, 249–260.

Rosenberg, J. and Moran, T. (1984). Generic commands. *Proceedings of the First International Conference on Human-Computer Interaction (INTERACT-84)*.

Teitelman, W. (1984). A tour through Cedar. *Proceedings of the 7th International Conference on Software Engineering*. Silver Spring, MD: IEEE Computer Society Press, 181–195.

Williams, G. (1983). The Lisa computer system. *Byte* 8(2) (February), 33–50.

Winer, B. J. (1971). *Statistical Principles in Experimental Design*. New York: McGraw-Hill.

Zarmer, C. and Johnson, J. (1990). User interface tools: Past, present, and future trends. *Hewlett-Packard Laboratories Technical Report, HPL-90-20.*

Project Ernestine: Analytic and Empirical Methods Applied to a Real-World CHI Problem

MICHAEL E. ATWOOD, WAYNE D. GRAY

NYNEX Science & Technology, Inc.

BONNIE E. JOHN

Carnegie Mellon University

Introduction

Human performance is affected by the hardware and software systems that are used, and it is our job, as computer-human interaction researchers and practitioners, to determine which system produces the best performance. In addition, it is our job to refine tools to produce better systems. It is rare that we have a chance to evaluate and refine both systems and tools on a single, real-world project of significance. Project Ernestine was such a project; it let us compare different systems and their adequacy in a real-world context, evaluate and extend tools for use in system design, and have significant practical, as well as theoretical, impact.

Project Ernestine empirically compared two different workstations for telephone company operators and validated GOMS analysis, an analytic formulation that was introduced a decade ago (Card, Moran, and Newell, 1983), and that has shown a history of theoretical refinement (Olson and Olson, 1990). Like many of its predecessors, Project Ernestine was an attempt to "harden the science of human-computer interaction" (Newell and Card, 1985); unlike many of its predecessors, Project Ernestine applied GOMS to a real-world, not a laboratory, setting.

Applying analytic modeling efforts to real-world settings is an enterprise laden with paradox. If models predict results that designers consider "intuitive," then models are perceived to be of little value. On the other hand, if models predict results that are counterintuitive, why, in the absence of empirical data, should they be believed? More important, why should an expensive empirical trial be conducted to validate a counterintuitive prediction of an analytic model? Understandably, opportunities to demonstrate the value of analytic modeling are rare.

In Project Ernestine, we examined the performance of telephone company toll-and-assistance operators (TAO), the operators who answer when you dial 0, using both a *current* and a *proposed* workstation. The *current* workstation is several years old and is a 300-baud, character-oriented system. The *proposed* workstation has an ergonomically designed keyboard and graphic-oriented display that paints the screen at 1200 baud while reducing the number of keystrokes that TAOs must make.

The TAO task involves the exercise of routine cognitive skills. The typical TAO has had sufficient practice to become expert at this task, makes few errors, and considers his or her average work time per call to be very important. The nature of the task, combined with the comparison of the two workstations, provided an excellent opportunity to evaluate GOMS models. Preliminary GOMS analyses (Gray et al., 1990), however, predicted that the *proposed* ergonomically superior workstation would, at best, be no faster than the older, *current* workstation. When trial data confirmed this prediction, GOMS models were used to explain this result.

Initially, there were several reasons we were excited about this project and believed that it would eventually develop into a CHI success story. Project Ernestine formed a collaboration of academic researchers, industrial researchers, and a sponsoring organization that provided the real-world setting. From this collaboration, with its different expertise, goals, and criteria for success, came unique opportunities for contributing to the field of CHI:

1. It provided what we believe to be the first real-world validation of the GOMS style of analytic modeling that has generated academic interest for the past decade. Within CHI, few topics match GOMS in terms of number of papers, years as a "key topic," or general interest. Although there have been some laboratory evaluations of the style of modeling, to date, we are aware of no evaluations that have shown significant benefit in nonlaboratory settings.

2. It provided an opportunity to extend the GOMS modeling techniques to include speech input and output and tasks where required information is

obtained during task performance rather than being available before the task begins. The initial GOMS models were developed for expert, error-free performance in tasks where the human controlled the speed of task execution and where human behavior was basically taking actions in a serial fashion. John (1988) extended this framework to account for parallelism of behavior; here we have the opportunity to further extend this framework by shifting the locus of control away from one person and toward the interaction of two people.

3. Project Ernestine provided a rare opportunity to demonstrate experimental methods and techniques in a real-world setting. CHI is an applied science concerned with constructing artifacts and validating the usefulness of those artifacts. Although field trials are fairly common in industry, operational constraints frequently prevent exercising the same amount of experimental control that would be used in laboratory settings. For example, participant selection, control procedures, or defining what data are collected are outside the control of many field trials. In this project, we were able to control all relevant experimental parameters.

4. Project Ernestine offered the promise of saving the sponsoring organization, NYNEX, many millions of dollars. The cost of purchasing TAO workstations is high, but the cost of operating those workstations is even higher. Estimates for NYNEX put the cost of each second of TAO work time gained or lost around $3 million per year. Empirical data on the effectiveness of workstations would be useful since it could either support a wise decision or recommend against an unwise decision. Further, models that could predict work times for different workstations, and possibly suggest more efficient designs, would also be of immediate use.

5. Project Ernestine had the promise of leading to additional real-world opportunities to test and extend this methodology. If the supporting organizations see great value in this project, they should provide us with other opportunities to conduct empirical trials and develop analytic models of performance. Being asked to do a second project is typically a good indicator of the success of the first project.

Although these are the criteria that we would expect a CHI success story to meet, there are different perspectives from which success can be viewed, and the criteria are valued differently by different participants in a project. These perspectives arise from the nature of CHI, and all are represented in Project Ernestine.

CHI is an applied science. It relies on basic sciences, but advances come from applying and validating theories and techniques in a real-world setting. In CHI projects, academic researchers typically provide in-depth knowledge of theories and techniques developed in laboratory settings. Corporate researchers typically provide expertise in field experiments and are familiar both with theoretical techniques and real-world tasks. The sponsoring organization provides the real-world setting and in-depth task expertise.

Each of these groups, however, has a different perspective from which to define success. Success for the academic researcher, for example, is in demonstrating that a theory or technique developed in a laboratory has predictive validity in a real-world situation. Further, extensions to those theories or techniques made during the application to the real-world task, which can then be used to explain other unrelated tasks, are viewed as success by the academic researcher. Corporate researchers may define success in terms of demonstrating that the theories and techniques are valuable tools for examining the types of tasks undertaken by their corporation. The value is assessed not only according to the predictive validity, but also according to the ease with which the tools can be used for the next problem facing the corporation. The sponsoring organization has a particular problem to solve in this particular project, and the input into that problem is their main determinant of success.

Although their perspectives for viewing success differ, collaboration among academic researchers, corporate researchers, and sponsoring organizations is crucial to projects such as Project Ernestine. For a project to be labeled a total success, all three groups must benefit from their participation.

In this paper, we describe the Project Ernestine field trial, describe the GOMS models that were used and the extensions to the models that were developed, discuss the pragmatics of applying these technologies in a real-world setting, and discuss why we believe Project Ernestine represents a major success in applying CHI technologies. Finally, we present an overview of where we believe this work is leading.

Project Ernestine: The Trial and GOMS Analyses

There were two principal aspects of Project Ernestine: conducting the field trial and developing the analytic models. For exposition, we present these as separate sections. The reader should be aware, however, that these two aspects occurred in parallel. While the field trial was being conducted, the models were being developed. In fact, models developed before the field trial was concluded very accurately predicted the results that we later observed in the empirical data. Moreover, when people were skeptical of what they considered to be the counterintuitive results of the empirical trial, the models were used to explain the results and support the trial's accuracy. This situation, models used to confirm the empirical data, is unlike the more typical case where an empirical trial is used to support the accuracy of the models. (For details of the field trials and GOMS analysis, see Gray, John, and Atwood, 1993.)

The Task and Workstations

TAOs are the operators you get when you dial 0. Their job is to assist the customer in completing calls and to record the correct billing. Among other tasks, TAOs handle person-to-person calls, collect calls, calling-card calls, and calls billed to a third number. The TAO does not handle directory assistance calls.

Two TAO workstations were evaluated: the *current* workstation and a *proposed* workstation. The *current* workstation had been in use for several years and employed a 300-baud, character-oriented display and a keyboard on which functionally related keys were color coded and spatially grouped. This functional grouping often separated common sequences of keys by large distances on the keyboard.

In contrast, the *proposed* workstation was ergonomically designed with sequential as well as functional considerations. The graphic, high-resolution display operated at 1200 baud, used icons, and in general, is a good example of a graphical user interface whose designers paid careful attention to human-computer interaction issues. For example, when the phone being called is ringing, an icon of a telephone with its receiver on-hook appears next to the called number; when the phone is answered, the icon changes to a telephone with its receiver lying next to it. In the *current* workstation, this is indicated by the ASCII characters CLD 1 (standing for "CalLeD line 1") appearing far away from the called number, in the lower part of the screen. Similar care went into the design of the keyboard, where an effort was made to minimize travel distance among the most frequent key sequences and to reduce the number of keystrokes required to complete a call by replacing common two-key sequences with a single function key.

The Field Trial

Methodology

Participants. The phone company office used in the study employs about 100 TAOs and handles traffic in the Boston, Massachusetts, area. For purposes of the study, 12 *current* workstations were removed and 12 *proposed* workstations installed.

All participants were New England Telephone (NET) employees who had worked as TAOs for a minimum of two years. Twenty-four participants were selected for the *proposed* workstations from a list of approximately 60 volunteers. Selection was influenced by work performance, work schedules, seniority, and trial needs. Each *proposed* participant was paired with a control participant matching for shift worked (that is, time of day) and average work time on the *current* workstation.

Trial Procedures. *Proposed* and *current* participants worked their normal shifts during the four-month trial. From the perspective of the *proposed* participants, their tasks and duties as a TAO were identical to their pretrial job in all respects but one, namely, a new workstation was used. For the *current* participants, nothing had changed.

We collect data by accessing the NYNEX database maintained for billing purposes, which records completed customer requests handled by every TAO in an office. Reports generated for each office randomly sample one out of every ten calls that pass through that office. We used this office database to extract data on the calls handled by our 24 *proposed* and 24 *current* participants.

Call Categories. To concentrate our effort for both the empirical and analytic comparisons, we focused on a subset of all calls, ones that were either high volume or of special interest to NYNEX Operator Services. The list of 20 call categories accounted for 88 percent of all completed calls, based on one month's frequency data for all calls handled by all NET TAOs.

Results

For the 48 TAOs (24 *proposed* and 24 *current*) over the 4 months of the study, our 20 call categories sampled a total of 78,240 calls. Five call categories were eliminated for some analyses because of insufficient occurrence of those call categories.

Collapsing over call category to look at the median work time per call for each participant, for each month, the data show that the *proposed* group is slower than the *current* group by 4 percent; that is, the *proposed* workstation requires 0.8 second more time on an average call than does the *current* workstation. This 0.8 second is both statistically and financially significant. This work time deficit translates into a cost of $2.4 million a year in additional operating costs if the *proposed* workstation were to be installed across the NYNEX operating area.

Reflecting seasonal variations in call mix, the main effect of month is significant, but not the interaction of groups by month. This lack of a significant interaction suggests that TAOs using the *proposed* workstation mastered it very quickly, reaching asymptote within the first month of performance. This result is not unreasonable. All participants in this study were experienced TAOs. In most respects, their job did not change as a function of the workstation they used; the call categories and customers were the same. The basic difference was that the *proposed* workstation used displays and a keyboard that were ergonomically superior to those of the *current* workstation.

For the analysis by call category, we looked at the 15 sufficiently represented call categories. This analysis yielded significant effects of group, call category, and their interaction. The effect of call category was expected because of the different nature of the calls. The interaction shows that the advantage of the *current* workstation over the *proposed* is not constant for all call categories. For some call categories this difference is small (0.2 second), whereas for others it is quite large (3.7 seconds). This is an interesting result that cannot be explained by the field data. This is a result on which analytic models may shed much light.

The GOMS Analyses

Benchmark Tasks

Rather than model every possible procedure executed by the TAOs, for each call category we modeled one common, or important, variation. With the help of NYNEX Operator Services personnel, we wrote a single script for each of the 20 call categories originally chosen for study, called *benchmarks*. These benchmarks were validated against observed calls and were found to be representative of the average work time for these call categories.

The GOMS Models

To model these benchmarks, two different approaches were used: observation-based models and specification-based models. The models of the *current* workstation were based on videotapes of experienced TAOs handling calls for each of the benchmark tasks. In contrast, TAOs were never observed using the *proposed* workstation. Rather, these models were specification based; that is, they were constructed based on system response time estimates and TAO procedures provided by the manufacturer.

TAOs do several things in parallel when processing a customer's request: They listen or talk to the customer, they perceive information on the CRT screen, they move their hands to appropriate keys and strike them. To model this situation, we turned to John's critical path method extension of GOMS, which we call *CPM-GOMS* (John, 1988).

In CPM-GOMS, the parallelism of the TAO's task is represented in a *schedule chart* (Figures 1 and 2). Each activity in handling a call is represented as a box with an associated duration. The durations for all pausing and speaking, both by the TAOs and the customers, are set by the benchmarks and taken directly from the videotapes. The duration of hand movements for pressing keys for the *current* workstation is also set from the videotapes, as are the system response times for the *current* workstation. Normative estimates were obtained from the literature (Card, Moran, and Newell, 1983; John and Newell, 1989a, 1989b) for cognitive operators, eye movements, and perceptual operators. Dependencies between activities are represented as lines connecting the boxes. For example, the TAO cannot hit the *collect-billing* key until he or she hears the customer request a collect call. Therefore, there is a dependency line drawn between the box representing the perception of the word *collect* and the boxes representing the cognitive operators that verify the word *collect* and initiate pressing the *collect-billing* key. The boxes and their dependency lines are drawn according to a detailed understanding of the TAO's task, goal decomposition, and operator-placement heuristics (John, 1990).

An important concept in analyzing the total task time for complex parallel tasks is the *critical path.* In project management, the critical path is "the

FIGURE 1

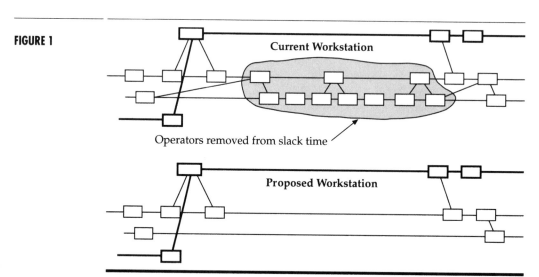

Section of CPM-GOMS analysis from near the beginning of the call. Notice that the proposed workstation has removed two keystrokes (which had required seven motor and three cognitive operators) from this part of the call. However, none of the ten operators removed were along the critical path (shown in bold).

FIGURE 2

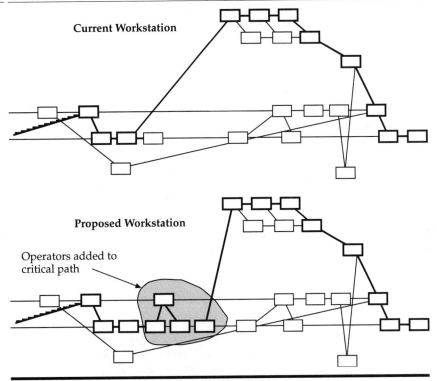

Current Workstation

Proposed Workstation

Operators added to
critical path

Section of GPM-GOMS analysis from the end of the call. Notice that the proposed
workstation has added one keystroke to this part of the call, which results in four operators (three motor and one cognitive) being added to the critical path (shown in bold).

sequence of tasks that determines the soonest the project can finish" (p. 6,
CLARIS Corp., 1987). In CPM-GOMS analyses, the duration of activities on
the critical path determines the total time for the task. Each schedule chart is
the CPM-GOMS model of the call it depicts. We constructed 30 such models,
yielding performance predictions for the 15 benchmarks on the *current* workstation and the 15 benchmarks on the *proposed* workstation, corresponding to
the 15 call categories finally analyzed in the empirical data.

Workstation design features and call handling procedures have an impact
on the length of a call, which is reflected in the critical path. For example,
Figures 1 and 2 show the first and last segments of a CPM-GOMS analysis for
one 15-second calling-card call for both the *current* and *proposed* workstations.
Figure 1 has two striking features. First, the analysis for the *proposed* workstation has ten fewer boxes than the analysis for the *current*, representing two
fewer keystrokes. Second, none of the deleted boxes were on the critical path;
all were performed in slack time. At this point in the task, the critical path is

determined by the TAO greeting and getting information from the customer. Removing keystrokes that occur during slack time does nothing to affect the TAO's work time; that is, work time is controlled by the conversation, not by the keystrokes and not by the ergonomics of the keyboard.

For the *proposed* workstation, one of the keystrokes eliminated at the beginning of the call (Figure 1) now occurs later in the call (Figure 2). In this analysis, the keystroke goes from being performed during slack time to being performed on the critical path. As a result, the cognitive and motor time required for this keystroke now adds to the time required to process this call, and CPM-GOMS predicts that, for this call category, despite requiring one less keystroke than the *current*, the *proposed* will require more time.

CPM-GOMS Predictions versus the Trial Data

Overall Prediction of Performance Time

The trial data showed that the *proposed* workstation was 4 percent slower than the *current* workstation, slower by 0.8 second. The CPM-GOMS models predict that the *proposed* workstation would be 3 percent slower than the *current* workstation, slower by 0.6 second. Looking at each of the 15 call categories that were analyzed, the correlation between predicted and observed work times was significant for both the *current* workstation, $r^2 = 0.69$, and the *proposed* workstation, $r^2 = 0.65$, showing that the models adequately reflected the variation in work time as a function of call type.

Models as Explanation

Including the CPM-GOMS modeling effort in Project Ernestine had one welcome, but unanticipated, result. The trial data were so counterintuitive that, in the absence of a compelling explanation of why the *proposed* workstation was slower than the *current,* there was a tendency to try to find fault with the trial rather than with the workstation.

The manufacturer had predicted that the *proposed* workstation would be, on average, 2 seconds faster than the *current* workstation. Given the general expectation that an ergonomically engineered, modern workstation should be faster than a five-year-old, ergonomically indifferent one, this estimate seemed reasonable. When the trial data began to accumulate, the immediate and widely held conclusion (by people unfamiliar with the GOMS analyses) was that something (training, procedures, or equipment) was wrong with the trial.

An initial model of just one call category (Gray et al., 1990) showed us why this general expectation was wrong. For example, as shown above in Figures 1 and 2, although the *proposed* workstation generally had fewer keystrokes than the *current* workstation, the new procedure put more keystrokes on the critical path, rather than in the slack time, increasing the length of the call. In addition, the close spacing of the function keys on the *proposed* keyboard encouraged the use of the right hand for pressing all keys; CPM-GOMS predicted that this would be slower than the old procedure of using the left hand for certain keys that was encouraged by the layout of the old keyboard. Further, although the *proposed* workstation was faster than the *current* workstation in displaying a whole screen of information, the first line of information was displayed more quickly on the *current* workstation. The CPM-GOMS models showed that important information is displayed on the first line of the screen at the beginning of every call. Since this system event is on the critical path, it adds to the average work time on the *proposed* workstation.

The CPM-GOMS models enable us to see the forest rather than the trees. We now understand the TAO's task as a complex interaction involving the TAO, the customer, and various hardware and software. Trying to optimize one component of this interaction, without considering how it interacts with the others, is unlikely to reduce work time.

Project Ernestine Pragmatics

Since CHI is an applied science, validating the science requires experiments in the real world. Since we were interested in applying analytic models to the evaluation of TAO workstations, our studies were done in a TAO office. In this section, we summarize what we have learned about conducting studies in the real world and how the attitudes of our sponsoring organization, and others, are influenced by such studies.

Real-World Experiments

We consider three aspects of real-world experiments: selecting participants, collecting data, and generalizing results. Experiments involve groups of people (participants) who are selected on the basis of their characteristics so that we can compare their performance, attitudes, or other metrics with groups that have other characteristics, or so that we can compare their performance with model or theory-based predictions. In the prototypical case, we compare the *experimental* group with the *control* group, and these two differ with respect to what conditions they operate under during the experiment. In laboratory studies, we recruit participants to meet these conditions; in real-world settings, we do not have this luxury, but we gain some important advantages.

For the empirical trial, we needed two groups of participants: one that would use the *proposed* workstation and one that would use the *current* workstation. Each participant in each of these groups would use only the indicated workstation for the duration of the trial. In addition to these two groups, there was a third group that made this trial possible.

Since the trial was conducted in a functioning TAO office, telephone company policies, and public utilities commission regulations, dictate that certain levels of performance are to be maintained, and restricting TAOs to certain workstations might jeopardize this level of performance. For example, there is an expectation that a certain percentage of the customer calls to the office will be answered within a certain number of rings. To ensure that these expectations were met, a certain number of TAOs must be assigned to a third group that could quickly be assigned to use either the *proposed* or *current* workstation, as required to meet office performance goals. Although this group is not typically viewed as part of the *experiment*, at least as it is reported, the experiment would not have been possible without them. In practice, the size of the group that is needed to maintain operational performance is determined first and dictates the number of people available for the other groups.

Participant selection also needed to be sensitive to labor union regulations. Labor union regulations require that TAOs be given work assignments on the basis of seniority. Since this trial was planned for a period during contract negotiations, concern for labor union regulations was very high.

Two nonexperimental factors, then, affect assigning participants to groups: operational requirements and labor union requirements. These factors prevent us from doing what we would typically do in a laboratory experiment, that is, randomly assign participants into *experimental* and *control* groups. Random assignment is, however, not the issue. Random assignment is done in the laboratory when there is no information on what characteristics a person has that would make him or her better able or less able to perform the experimental task; random assignment evens out such characteristics across groups. In real-world experiments, we have a very good idea what characteristics are important, and having *equal* groups is more important than having *randomly assigned* groups.

In real-world experiments, random assignment would typically be a disadvantage. Assigning participants to *equal* groups requires (1) understanding what characteristics are important, (2) having sufficient data on potential participants, and (3) having a sufficiently large population of participants. For Project Ernestine, the first issue was easy to resolve; since we were interested in TAO work times, groups were made equal with respect to this characteristic, as well as experience, work shift, and similar factors. The second issue, having sufficient data on this characteristic, was addressed by analyzing TAO work times for the six months preceding the trial start. The third issue was also resolved; since 54 of the approximately 100 TAOs volunteered to participate in this study (that is, use the *proposed* workstation), we were able to select 24 TAOs who met all operational and labor union requirements.

For future real-world studies, there are three lessons to be learned. First, operational requirements may dictate that standard *two group* experiments become *three group* experiments, with the third group maintaining operational requirements. Second, labor union requirements may effect assigning participants to groups. Third, it is important to have equal groups, not randomly assigned groups. Given a sufficiently large population of participants and data on important participant characteristics, these factors are not prohibitive, and we were able to select 24 TAOs to use the *proposed* workstation while maintaining the *experimental* and *control* group division expected by experimental psychologists, meeting labor union requirements, and maintaining enough TAOs in a third group to meet operational requirements.

Although there are some potential pitfalls in selecting participants for real-world studies, there is one decided advantage: We can address skilled performance over an extended period. All the participants in this study had a minimum of two years experience, and all worked their normal schedule for the four-month trial period. This allows us to investigate issues that are impractical to address in the laboratory.

A second advantage of real-world studies is that we can be very unobtrusive in data collection. Since participants are doing their normal job and are not aware of having their performance monitored by other than the normal means and since the experimenters were rarely on-site, the participants' behavior was minimally affected by their "being in an experiment." Operator work times that are routinely recorded in a NYNEX database provided the data for this experiment.

Having unobtrusive measures is an advantage, but it did prevent us from collecting all the data that might be relevant. We would have liked, for example, to measure keying performance, screen display information, TAO–customer dialogues, and so forth. Although we collected some such data with videotape, this method is not satisfactory for collecting vast amounts of data, such as the thousands of calls used in this study. Collecting large amounts of data at this level requires interfacing with the equipment that the TAOs use. For example, collecting keying performance requires that we can detect and record keystrokes. In this case, however, the manufacturer, who made both the *current* and *proposed* workstations, considered the workstation software and their communication protocols to be proprietary, and we did not have access to this information.

The only keystroke-level data we have is from the benchmark calls. Our GOMS models, which are based on these benchmark calls, predict some work time differences based on keying behavior. Though our predictions are supported by the observed work times, we cannot say conclusively that keying behavior is the source of the differences. For the purposes of evaluating the *proposed* and *current* workstations and of validating GOMS models, this was an inconvenience, but it was not a serious problem.

Organizational Attitudes and Expectations

We can trace attitudes and expectations through three phases on each of two tracks. The three phases are *pretrial, during trial,* and *after trial.* The two tracks are the telephone company who managed the office in which we did this study and the manufacturer of the *current* and *proposed* workstations.

In the *pretrial* phase, both tracks were in parallel. When the manufacturer offered to loan workstations to the telephone company for evaluation and the telephone company asked us to be involved in evaluating the workstations, all parties were somewhat comfortable with our role as empirical trial coordinator. All were comfortable with ground rules that specified that we would provide results to the manufacturer and conduct a trial without disrupting normal operations in the TAO office. When we presented the idea of using this trial as an opportunity to validate the GOMS-style of analytic models, the attitude of the other parties involved can best be described as curious interest. All parties assumed that the *proposed* workstation would be superior to the *current* and that this was an interesting opportunity to use analytic models to validate and justify this assumption.

In the *during trial* phase, both tracks were similar but began to show signs of diverging. When preliminary GOMS analyses predicted that the *proposed* workstation would be slower than the *current* workstation, both tracks showed only mild interest and some doubt. Since both tracks did not, at this point, expect the models to add anything of value to this study, what was perceived as an "off-the-wall" prediction could be disregarded as irrelevant to evaluation of the workstations. Note that had the predictions confirmed the manufacturer's claims and the telephone company's expectations that the *proposed* workstation would be faster, the models could also be disregarded since they predicted only what was "common sense."

Once the empirical trial results confirmed the predictions, both tracks asked why this counterintuitive result occurred. The point of divergence was in how they took the answer. For the telephone company, their appraisal of the GOMS models shifted to strong support. The manufacturer of the two workstations has yet to accept these models or the results of this study.

In the *after trial* phase, the telephone company looked to the GOMS models to explain this result and to suggest how to design a better workstation. The telephone company involved in this study (and its sister company in NYNEX) are now strong supporters of the GOMS modeling approach. The most positive statement of this confidence is that they selected not to purchase the *proposed* workstation and to give us a central role in designing the next generation of telephone company operator work environment. We will return to this topic later in discussing future directions of this work.

The manufacturer of the *current* and *proposed* workstations, in the *after trial* phase, questioned both the trial and the models. To a degree, some such reaction would be expected since we conveyed an unwelcome and unexpected result. To a large degree, however, it was unexpected since the empirical data and models gave converging evidence, and the models provided clear explanations for the empirical result. The empirical data showed that the *proposed* workstation was slower than the *current* workstation; GOMS showed why this was so and suggested how to fix this problem.

We would like to emphasize two conclusions that we have drawn from these exchanges. First, the manufacturer did not do an irresponsible, incomplete, or inappropriate job of designing the *proposed* workstation. Given the state-of-the-art of interface design at the time of their design, they used appropriate, industry-standard human factors design and evaluation techniques. We believe that the deficits in this design could have been identified a priori by GOMS modeling (as, indeed, they later were), but until Project Ernestine, GOMS modeling had not been verified as a methodology for design and evaluation in the real world. The manufacturer could not be expected to anticipate the benefits of an unproven methodology. Second, our design, execution, and analysis of the trial has been subjected to very close scrutiny, and the results are explained by the GOMS models; no one can credibly dispute the fact that TAO performance is slower with the *proposed* workstation than with the *current*.

Is Project Ernestine a CHI Success Story?

In the introduction to this chapter, we listed five reasons Project Ernestine might be considered a success story and listed three perspectives from which success can be viewed. In this section, we consider each in turn.

1. Did Project Ernestine provide a real-world validation of the GOMS style of analytic modeling? Our answer to this question is obviously yes. The CPM-GOMS models for both the *current* and *proposed* workstations

accurately reflected the empirical trial data. It is important to emphasize that the models for the *proposed* workstation were developed without ever observing that workstation in use. That these models were based on knowledge of the task and the manufacturer's specifications for the new workstation demonstrates that CPM-GOMS can predict performance in a complex, cognitive task.

2. Did we usefully extend the GOMS modeling techniques? Our answer is yes. In Project Ernestine, we devised heuristics for modeling the perception of simple auditory signals, speech input and output, eye movements, and system response time (John, 1990), all missing from the original GOMS analyses. An extension of GOMS, CPM-GOMS, developed in an academic setting, on laboratory data (that is, transcription typing data; John, 1988), was shown to apply to real-time tasks where action is parallel and required information to be obtained during task performance. This project also showed the value of using benchmark tasks, a useful technique for simplifying large and complex analyses.

3. Was Project Ernestine a successful application of experimental methods and techniques in a real-world setting? Two unrelated reasons cause us to believe that we experienced a success in this area as well. First, the fact that the experimental design, analysis, and conclusions survived close scrutiny by several parties supports the fact that this was a well-designed and well-conducted experiment. Second, Project Ernestine convinced the sponsoring companies of the value of conducting real-world experiments. In addition, we, as experimenters, learned a lot about real-world experiments. For example, while in this experiment, we had to rely on videotapes of a few calls to capture keystroke information; we have now developed tools that let us capture all keystrokes by all TAOs on a constant basis, greatly improving the quality (and quantity) of the data we have to work with.

4. Did Project Ernestine save the sponsoring organization significant amounts of money? The answer is yes, but because an exact accounting requires information about maintenance, training, and other costs not available at this time, it is hard to name an exact dollar figure. Regarding operator work time alone, the GOMS models predicted, and the empirical data proved, that the *proposed* workstation was about six-tenths of a second slower per call, on average, than the *current* workstation. This increase in average work time would produce an operating cost deficit of about $2 million per year, as opposed to the $7 million savings originally estimated by the manufacturer. Based on this information, the sponsoring organization decided not to buy the *proposed* workstation, avoiding the additional operating costs.

Although we believe that Project Ernestine saved significant amounts of money in the present, we are convinced that it will save even more in the future. For reasons other than operating costs or purchase price, the sponsoring organization must replace the *current* workstations in the near future. Project Ernestine played a role in convincing the sponsoring organization to look beyond the *proposed* workstation and to work with another manufacturer to apply what we have learned to the design of a new workstation. With respect to this criterion, this is where the real success may occur; we expect to apply what we have learned and the techniques we have developed to the design of a more efficient workstation.

5. Did Project Ernestine lead to additional real-world opportunities to test and extend experimental trials and analytic modeling? The clearest indicator of success here is that we were asked to evaluate proposed changes in the TAO's work environment and to contribute to the design of a new workstation. Even though the supporting organization has long believed in the value of field trials, by participating in the design, conduct, and analysis of this project, they gained firsthand experience with field trials and now take a more active role in designing, conducting, and analyzing field trials in their organizations. What's more, they encourage and support the development and use of analytic models and view GOMS as a valuable tool. We may not have done what Brown (1991) calls "research that reinvents the corporation," but we believe we have done research that causes the corporation to improve their ability to conduct research and to reshape the way that they think about research.

As we noted in the introduction to this paper, achieving success on this project required the alignment of three groups of people, each of which views success from a different perspective, and each of which weights the importance of the criteria discussed differently.

1. From the perspective of academic research, Project Ernestine provided both predictive validity of the GOMS formalism in the real world and several extensions to GOMS modeling techniques. These results signify great success for academic CHI research.

2. From the perspective of corporate research, Project Ernestine was a success in two areas. First, it showed that we could effectively solve problems in an operational setting, and one measure of success is that we were asked to solve additional problems. In particular, since the telephone companies need a new workstation, we were asked to participate in the design of that workstation. Second, Project Ernestine was a successful transfer of technology into an applied setting. We have demonstrated that GOMS models apply to this environment, have learned to build these models, and plan to

extend them further so that they can be used for system design in this and other system development efforts.

3. From the perspective of the sponsoring organization, this project supported an appropriate buy–no-buy decision. Although supporting this decision was a benefit, a greater benefit derives from the fact that we demonstrated that we could collect and analyze the data and build the models that we need to design a workstation that is optimal for their environment. For reasons that are outside the scope of this discussion, but that include financial, regulatory, and labor issues, this must be done quickly. The techniques and results of Project Ernestine and its successors (see next section) assist in meeting this goal.

In general, our answer to the question, is Project Ernestine a CHI success story? is yes. Of the five criteria discussed, we believe all are met. From the three perspectives for viewing success, all are satisfied. By taking the first step to show that this was a good environment for the application of GOMS, we hope that we have opened the way for further applications that will lead to major benefits for the field of CHI.

Continuing Research

Project Ernestine convinced all concerned of the value of carefully controlled empirical trials and that GOMS models could be used to predict workstation performance in an operational environment since the models' predictions closely matched the results of an empirical trial. The obvious next question to ask is, could we have used only the models and avoided the trial? For Project Ernestine itself, the answer is clearly no, since the trial was necessary to validate the models. For future trials, the answer is yes; the number of trials we need to conduct is reduced.

Until Project Ernestine, we had no validation of GOMS models in a real-world setting, and understandably, no one would accept GOMS predictions instead of an empirical trial. This project provided the trial that was needed to validate this style of modeling. The fact that the models predicted the direction and size of the results found in the empirical trial indicates that the models can in the future be used to reduce the number of costly empirical trials.

As a concrete example, in the New Horizons Project, we are looking at design possibilities for a workstation that supports a mixture of routine TAO tasks and other tasks not previously performed by TAOs. With minor variations to account for hardware differences, the models developed in Project Ernestine can be applied to the New Horizons Project. For example, when the sponsoring organization wondered about the value of a "personal response system" (a recording of the TAO's voice greets the customer rather than a "live" TAO), we could predict the savings that would result for each of several proposed architectures for implementing this feature. We are currently constructing models for the new tasks so that more complete predictions can be made.

We have also improved our data collection capability. For Project Ernestine, we had work time data for about 80,000 calls and detailed keystroke data on relatively few benchmark tasks. For the New Horizons Project, new data collection techniques were developed that have provided detailed keystroke data on (as of this writing) more than 4 million calls, which were collected over several months in a controlled setting. The magnitude and detail of this data allow us to look at factors such as learning, errors, error recovery, transfer (since both routine and new tasks are involved), and selection rules for selecting among various methods to accomplish a given task.

As with Project Ernestine, we believe that the New Horizons Project will be a CHI success story. In fact, we believe it will be perceived as more successful. By contributing to the design of a new workstation, rather than relying on versions provided by others, the sponsoring organization has the potential to gain a workstation that reduces operational costs as well as purchase costs. By using GOMS to help design a new workstation, another step in applying psychological theory to CHI design will be demonstrated. Further, the New Horizons domain offers the opportunity to examine long-term learning and transfer effects in a real-world context, which may result in significant additions to the basic science underlying GOMS.

Conclusion

Project Ernestine compared the performance of TAOs on *current* and *proposed* workstations, both with empirical evaluation and GOMS models. The GOMS models were shown to predict the counterintuitive empirical results quite accurately, and explain them sufficiently, so that the sponsoring organization decided not to buy the *proposed* workstation. Rather, the sponsoring organization is applying both the empirical and modeling techniques to the design of a new workstation.

Project Ernestine provided the first real-world validation of GOMS modeling; it extended GOMS in several directions; it demonstrated empirical techniques in a real-world setting; it saved the sponsoring organization money; and it led to additional opportunities to use these techniques. The success of this project was due to a collaboration among academic research, industrial research, and the sponsoring organization, and to a large degree, all benefited from this work. What we have learned from this project promises to be even more beneficial in the future.

Acknowledgments

We wish to acknowledge the many people at New England Telephone and NYNEX Telesector Resources Group who made Project Ernestine possible and who, along with people from New York Telephone are supporting the New Horizons Project. In particular, we acknowledge Karen O'Brien who, as project manager for Project Ernestine, ensured that the highest standards for field research were followed and who continued to work with us on the New Horizons Project. We also acknowledge Warren Cook, Bill Ovberg, and Florence Lunny for their support at New Horizons, and the telephone company operators for participating in these studies. We also thank Debbie Lawrence for comments on this chapter and Heather Desurvire, Debbie Lawrence, Rory Stuart, Suzi Levas, Thea Turner, Tom Newman, Darlene Hart, Rob DiNardis, Craig Reding, Connie Carlson, Jan Stein, Rao Tanuka, Raj Saksena, Jack Lam, Menno Aartsen, Mike Metaxas, and Sandy Esch for their efforts on these projects.

Bonnie John's participation was supported, in part, by the Office of Naval Research, Cognitive Science Program, Contract Number N00014-89-J-1975N158. The views and conclusions contained in this document are those of the authors and should not be interpreted as representing the official policies, either expressed or implied, of the Office of Naval Research or the U.S. Government.

References

Brown, J. S. (1991). Research that reinvents the corporation. *Harvard Business Review* (January–February), 102–111.

Card, S. K., Moran, T. P., and Newell, A. (1983). *The Psychology of Human-Computer Interaction*. Hillsdale, NJ: Lawrence Erlbaum.

CLARIS Corporation (1987). *MacProject II Manual*. Mountain View, CA: CLARIS Corporation.

Gray, W. D., John, B. E., and Atwood, M. E. (1993). Project Ernestine: Validating a GOMS analysis for predicting and explaining real-world task performance. *Human-Computer Interaction* (8), 237–309.

Gray, W. D., John, B. E., Stuart, R., Lawrence, D., and Atwood, M. E. (1990). GOMS meets the phone company: Analytic modeling applied to real-world problems. In D. Diaper, D. Gilmore, G. Cockton, and B. Shackel (eds.), *Human-Computer Interaction—INTERACT '90.* North-Holland: Elsevier Science Publishers.

John, B. E. (1988). *Contributions to engineering models of human-computer interaction.* Doctoral dissertation, Carnegie Mellon University.

———. (1990). Extensions of GOMS analyses to expert performance requiring perception of dynamic visual and auditory information. *Proceedings of CHI '90* (Seattle, April 1-5). New York: ACM.

John, B. E., and Newell, A. (1989a). Cumulating the science of HCI: From -R compatability to transcription typing. *Proceedings of CHI '89* (Austin, April 30–May 4). New York: ACM.

———. (1989b). Toward an engineering model of stimulus-response compatability. In R. W. Proctor and T. G. Reeve (eds.), *Stimulus-Response Compatability: An Integrated Perspective.* New York: ACM.

Newell, A. and Card, S. K. (1985). The prospects for psychological science in human-computer interaction. *Human-Computer Interaction* (1), 209–242.

Olson, J. R. and Olson, G. M. (1990). The growth of cognitive modeling in human-computer interaction since GOMS. *Human-Computer Interaction* (5), 221–265.

Pioneers and Settlers: Methods Used in Successful User Interface Design

STUART K. CARD

Xerox Palo Alto Research Center

The pioneers get the arrows, and the settlers get the land.

GUY KAWASAKI
(former Apple evangelist, BayCHI meeting,
Palo Alto, California, April 14, 1992)

User interfaces, it has been said (Card, this volume), are an ineluctable part of interactive software systems. They are typically more than half the code, often far more. They typically cause more than half the problems, too—often far more. In short, they represent the sort of troublesome engineering problem that organizations would like to *do something* about.

This book is one of those attempts to do something. The premise of this section of the book is that by examining successful user interfaces of the past, we can spot and articulate methods that led to successful designs and then deploy these methods in the future, leading to more successful designs. This stratagem, of course, presupposes we know success, at least when we see it. Unfortunately, the world is not so simple. Many spreadsheet programs contain demonstrably successful user interfaces. Moreover, they were designed using a successful, reliable, repeatable method—simple theft. Are such programs examples of what we mean by successful interface design and the methods for producing them? In a sense, as we shall see, the answer is yes. But also no. Despite its obvious virtues, theft has the equally obvious limitation that the method works only on things previously created by some other method (and for a similar purpose). It also has the equally obvious limitation, observable in spreadsheet programs, that technological advance slows to a crawl and all systems begin to look alike.

In what follows, we attempt to understand what it means for a user interface to be successful. Perhaps it will be no surprise that this will cause us to expand the unit of analysis beyond a single design point to its historical roots and to its arena of commercial or mission engagement. In particular, it will suggest the difference between "Pioneer Systems," those aimed at advancing the state of the art and "Settler Systems," those aimed at exploiting existing techniques. Armed with a notion of success, we then set about to inventory the methods used by the designs described in other papers of this section. Finally, we attempt to taxonomize methods in our inventory, organizing them so as to gain insight into the structure of the space of methods available for building interactive computing systems. We suggest that below the surface of the methods there are a set of common mileposts or goals. That these mileposts be accomplished in some way is probably more important than the particular methods of accomplishing them.

In the small, success of HCI systems is focused on the next system being built. But in the large, success has to do with the whole process of technology evolution.

Success

Successful User Interfaces

Let us begin with the hard question: What do we mean by a successful user interface design? Or perhaps better stated: What do we mean by a successful design for an interactive computing system? In one sense, it is not problematic to find such designs. Both the popular press and informal professional discussions list them frequently. This is fortunate since identifying the methods underlying successful designs would be much harder in a field where it was generally thought that there weren't any. Table 1 is my (incomplete) list of successful interfaces. This list, like any, is a bit idiosyncratic, but it would be surprising if there weren't considerable overlap with the lists of others.

For each of the systems in Table 1, we can give a reason for listing it as a success. The first groups of these develop the notion of the electronic workspace:

Sketchpad (Sutherland, 1963) originated the concepts of virtual reality and constraint-based interfaces and most of the rest of computer graphics. The

TABLE 1   **Some Successful HCI Interfaces**

• Sketchpad	Virtual reality and constraint-based interfaces
• AAMRL Virtual Reality	Virtual reality
• NASA Virtual Reality	Cost-reduced virtual reality
• NLS	Mouse, hypertext, point and click, groupware
• Smalltalk	Overlapping windows, menus, objects, icons, desktop metaphor
• Star	Menu bar, generic functions, integrated functions, large-scale UI
• Mac	Third-party commonality
• Dataland	Large desktop data space
• Rooms	Multiple shared workspace
• FreeStyle	Image-based synchronized documents
• PenPoint	Pen-based integrated UI environment
• X	Client–server model applied to user interfaces
• Olympic Message System	Multilingual kiosk interaction with thousands of walkup users
• Emacs	User-extensible editor
• Unix shell scripts	User-extensible operating system
• VisiCalc	Spreadsheet metaphor
• HyperCard	User programmability

AAMRL Virtual Reality System (Furness, 1986) developed practical versions of virtual reality, especially in the cockpit context. The NASA Virtual Reality System (Fisher, 1989) produced cost-reduced components for virtual reality and led to its popularization.

Along the path that eventually led to the GUI (graphical user interface) paradigm, NLS (Engelbart and English, 1968) was one of the major precursors to direct manipulation. It introduced the mouse, hypertext, the point-and-click style of text editing, and groupware. Expert users could work collaboratively at unbelievably rapid rates. Smalltalk (Kay, 1977; Kay and Goldberg, 1977; Smith, 1977; Tesler, 1981) took the mouse from NLS; further developed the window concept into overlapping windows; and added menus, objects from Simula (Dahl and Nygaard, 1966), and the desktop metaphor. The result was the invention of the direct manipulation interface and the principled integration of different media, such as text, graphics, music, and animation. Star (Smith et al., 1982; Johnson et al., 1989; Miller and Johnson, this volume) added the notions of the menu bar, generic functions whose interpretation depended on the object to which they were applied, and strong integration. It was the first commercial expression of the desktop–icon interface. The achievement of Star was that a noncomputer professional could begin operating a high-functionality mixed-media interface in about 30 minutes. The Macintosh interface (really the Lisa interface, Williams, 1983) was the first commercially successful exploitation of this new sort of interface. It added user interface commonality across third-party applications and dialog boxes. The achievement of the Macintosh was that it provided a mixed-media environment in which there was high transfer of learning among third-party applications.

Dataland (Herot, 1980; Bolt, 1984) explored the notion of the interface being a window into a large data space. Rooms chopped this space into regions organized around tasks, in order to get rapid task switching in a large space without search, and allowed objects to be simultaneously in different regions.

The next groups of user interfaces go beyond the usual workstation:

FreeStyle was a groupware system that originated the use of coordinated audio and gesture annotation to image-based documents. PenPoint (Carr and Shafer, 1991) introduced the pen-based notebook metaphor.

The X protocol (Scheifler, Gettys, and Newman, 1988), though not itself a user interface, is notable because X-based user interfaces swept user interaction in the Unix industry into a client–server model, thereby allowing for user interfaces whose backends ran on distributed machines.

The Olympic Message System (Gould et al., 1987) developed techniques that allowed multicultural, multilingual, walkup users of an information kiosk to exchange messages and access information. It also demonstrated the feasibility and value of user prototyping, even under the most demanding schedule constraints.

Finally, a last group of user interfaces developed the notion of user-tailorable systems:

Emacs (Stallman, 1987) and Unix Shell Scripts (Kaare, 1983) were both successful attempts to make extensible systems that are user programmable and tailorable. They have proved powerful and highly adaptable over a number of years despite their lack of either aesthetics or human factors. VisiCalc originated the spreadsheet—a paradigm so powerful that it overcame human factors shortcomings in the command language.

HyperCard (Apple Computer, 1987) brought a version of hypertext and frame-based interface (Robertson, Newell, and Ramakrishna, 1981) to the mass market, provided good media integration for sound, CD-ROM, video, and animation, and in particular, was successful at simplifying programming for at least some end users.

To this list of systems, we can add the examples of systems discussed as successful systems in other papers in this book (Table 2). For these systems, we have specific information on the methods by which they were produced. Two of these, Star (Miller and Johnson, this volume) and FreeStyle (Francik, this volume) also appear in Table 1 and have been mentioned. The system described by Atwood, Gray, and John (this volume) is a proposed toll-and-assistance operator workstation (we call it the New TAO Workstation). Their claim is not for the success of the workstation, but of their method, CPM-GOMS, for evaluating it. This is one of the first studies in HCI to document commercial return for using an analytical method; in this case they claim to have saved the phone company more than $2 million. Rally (Wixon and Jones, this volume) is a fourth-generation application generator. Wixon and Jones discuss the revision of this system's existing user interface. Their claim is that their methods had large and measurable effects on the product's commercial success. Whiteside presents a user-customized meeting room and training system, custom-fit to each user (we call it Meetingware).[1] The claim is that the methods described led to a new class of products.

For all the systems in Table 1 and Table 2, there is some reason, as we have outlined, for counting the system a success. But looking at these systems as a collection, success seems to be something of a mixed bag. Some were important commercially. Some were hailed by reviews of the time and received awards, but were commercially unsuccessful. Some were known only to academic specialists, but were heavily imitated. Clearly, creative success and business success are not the same. We need to distinguish the varieties of success that are possible before we can discuss the methods underlying that

TABLE 2 **Successful HCI Systems as Represented at the Workshop**

Paper	System	Description	SSI
Atwood, Gray, and John	New TAO Workstation	Proposed toll-and-assistance operator workstation	1
	CPM-GOMS	Analysis into GOMS methods and critical path method analysis	(4)
Wixon and Jones	Rally	Fourth-generation application generator	1
Whiteside, as presented at the workshop	Meetingware	Custom meeting room and training	3
Francik	FreeStyle	Pen-based groupware	6
Miller and Johnson	Star	Networked document processing	8

success. There is also a more subtle lesson to be learned. In a sense, focusing on point designs, such as those listed in Tables 1 and 2, is the wrong unit of analysis. Actually, the methods that produce successful, especially novel, user interfaces can best be seen by expanding the context and examining the *sequence* of inventions that led to those designs—the *food chain of innovation*.

The Food Chain of Innovation

Figure 1 gives a reasonably accepted account of the history of the graphical user interface as compiled by the editors of *IEEE Spectrum* (Perry and Voelcker, 1989). Several of the systems in Table 1 appear in the figure. From the figure, we can see that development of the graphical user interface went through four stages: (1) scattered research at various university and government-financed laboratories, (2) the classical definition of this interface at Xerox PARC, from which all commercial versions descend, (3) the introduction of initial products into the marketplace, and (4) standardization. Those systems that were commercial successes are marked in the figure. An obvious conclusion stands out: *Commercial success occurred only at the very last stages of this process, long after major technical invention had ceased.*

FIGURE 1

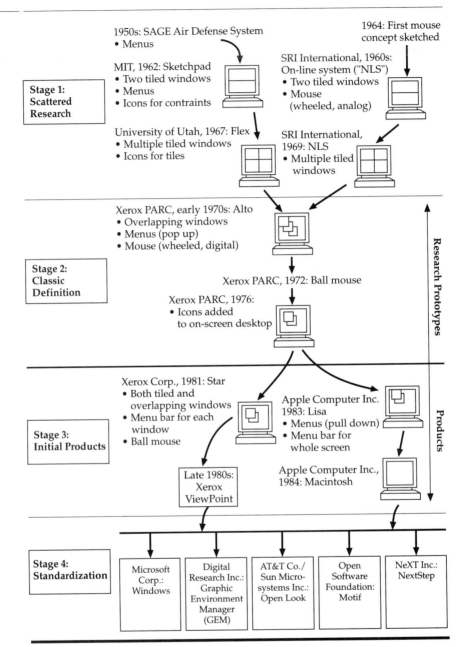

Development of the graphical user interface according to the editors of *IEEE Spectrum* (Perry and Voelcker, 1989). The interface went from scattered exploratory research, to development of a series of classic systems, to initial product, to standardization. The graphical user interface is now an entrenched incumbent technology, resistant to innovation.

For example, consider the Apple Macintosh, widely cited as the first commercially successful use of a graphical user interface. The first Apple introduction of this technology on the Lisa failed, as did the second, the Lisa 2, as did the third, the Macintosh 128. Only on the fourth try, the Macintosh 512, was there commercial success. But this machine had no user interface invention, it just used the design settled earlier in the series. Most of the real invention in this design, in turn, actually occurred in the designs of the Xerox Smalltalk and the Xerox Star systems and related design at Xerox PARC, especially Bravo (Lampson, 1976), Gypsy (Lampson, 1988), Draw (Lampson, 1976), and SuperPaint (SIGGRAPH, 1990). Some ideas in these systems can be traced even further, as Figure 1 shows. In fact, it should be noted, a major set of the precursor ideas derive from government-funded university and research institute laboratories or major industry research laboratories. Virtually all the user interface invention occurred in the predecessors to systems that were commercial successes.

The Macintosh 512 was a commercial user interface success, but it was not an invention success. Smalltalk and Star, and perhaps Lisa, were invention successes, but they were not commercial successes.[2] These invention successes were of dominating importance in making possible the success of later user interface designs, but they may have occurred in previous research or in a previous commercial system. Furthermore, many of them worked well in the sense of allowing users to accomplish the task the system was built to do—that is, they were also engineering successes. *If we were simply to examine a system that was a commercial success, we would miss many of the key methods that gave rise to that success because they occurred earlier in the food chain.*

It is useful to distinguish at least three types of successes in user interface design: (1) an *invention success,* (2) an *engineering success,* and (3) a *commercial innovation success.* An *invention success* brings into existence something that did not previously exist. It usually relieves or avoids some major constraint inherent in the previous art, or it contrives a way to perform some new function. Inventions can be things, like a computer input device, or they can be processes, like a technique for testing user interfaces. Closely related is a *discovery,* which brings something into known existence that previously existed, but was unknown. An *engineering success* brings into existence a system that meets its objectives and does so using a specified level of resources. An *innovation success* brings a new product or service to the market and derives commercial gain from so doing.

In adopting these terms, we have followed the conventional distinction between *invention,* the creative act of bringing new things into existence, and *innovation,* the particular new marketable product or process or service that eventually results (see, for example, Burgleman and Maidique, 1988, p. 31). The one is the beginning, the other the end, of the innovation process. As anyone with any experience with this process has learned, there's a lot that goes in the middle.

Invention

The success of an invention may be assessed by the extent to which it made a difference—its impact. Of course we know this largely in retrospect—the extent to which the impact of some invention shook the existing state of the art like an earthquake, overturning existing practice. In fact, earthquakes are such a good metaphor we can adopt the phenomenological scaling of earthquakes literally and scale inventions the same way. Newell (1992) used this technique to invent the NOV scale for expressing the novelty of a theoretical prediction. Each level on the NOV scale, from 1 (a reformulation) to 3 (a confirmation of existing theory) to 6 (a new discovery) and beyond indexed successively greater impacts of a theory on the existing state of knowledge. In a similar vein, Table 3 proposes a new Seismic Scale of Innovation (SSI). The table pairs terms from the phenomenological Modified Mercali earthquake magnitude scale to describe successively greater impacts of the invention on the existing state of the art. Since it is a phenomenological scale, the Modified Mercali scale is pretty good at describing metaphorically just about anything whose foundations are being shaken. For convenience, equivalents to the more familiar Richter scale (an objective scale based on ground shaking) are used to set numerical scale points. An important characteristic of the earthquake scale is the relative frequency with which the different scale events occur: Smaller scale events occur frequently, and great events on rare occasions. I have therefore given a very rough guess of relative frequency using the exponential distribution of the Richter scale and anchoring the end points so as to produce the 50,000 programs that are said to have come into existence at the one end and the field-transforming development of the GUI at the other end. Of course, such approximations are necessarily crude, but they do produce a feel for relative invention in HCI.

A Class 0 Invention on the SSI scale ("No earthquake") is a program that just clones another without modification; the clones of VisiCalc come to mind. Then come SSI Class 1 Inventions ("Not felt, but recorded"), which make minor modifications to existing user interfaces or user interface techniques in order to handle similar problems. Microsoft Word for the PC was essentially BravoX for the Alto (Lampson, 1988), for example. In a Class 2 Invention ("Hanging objects swing"), known techniques are applied to new problems. PowerPoint, a program for making presentations that

TABLE 3   **Seismic Scale of Innovation**

Earthquakes				User Interfaces	
PHENOMENA	MM	RICHTER	SSI	CHARACTERISTICS	N/YR
No earthquake.	0	0	0	Clone (Example: VisiCalc clones)	—
Not felt, but recorded.	I	0–1.9	1.0	Reimplementation of existing technique to similar problem (Examples: Microsoft Word, New TAO Workstation, Rally)	4000
Hanging objects swing.	II–III	2.0–3.4	2.0	Application of existing technique to new problem or minor additions to technique (Example: PowerPoint)	830
Felt by some. Like a passing light truck.	III	3.5–4.2	3.0	Nonobvious use of existing techniques (Examples: Cosmic Osmo, Meetingware)	170
Felt by many. Dishes rattle.	IV	4.3–4.8	4.0	Refinement of existing paradigms by substantial new invention (Example: Macromind Director)	36
Felt by all. Sleepers awake.	V–VI	4.9–5.4	5.0	New idea for minor component (Examples: Dataland, Rooms)	7.5
Slight building damage. Books fall. Liquids spill. Windows break. Walking is difficult.	VI–VII	5.5–6.1	6.0	Discovery of new major component (Examples: Rocky's Boots, Emacs, FreeStyle)	1.6
Considerable building damage. Chimneys fall. Some houses knocked from foundations.	VIII	6.2–6.9	6.5	Trendsetter. Imitated by others (Examples: Spreadsheet, Shells, HyperCard, Macintosh UI)	0.66
Serious damage. Rails are bent. General panic. Partial collapse.	IX	7.0–7.4	7.0	Course change for industry (Example: X)	0.32
Great damage. Masonry buildings destroyed. Bridges fall.	X	7.4–7.9	7.5	Major paradigm shift (Examples: NLS, PenPoint)	0.13
Damage nearly total. Most works of construction destroyed.	XI–XII	8.0	8.0	Restructuring of field (Examples: Sketchpad, Smalltalk, Star)	0.067

combines a drawing tool with templates, color palettes, and a slide sorter, might be an example here. The vast number of user interfaces produced are Class 0, 1, or 2—their intention is to use known techniques in a new product or service.

In the next band of levels, the user interface begins to receive some notice for inventiveness. In a Class 3 Invention ("Felt by some. Like a passing light truck"), nonobvious use is made of existing techniques. Cosmic Osmo's (Miller, Miller, and Lovick, 1989) clever creation of a world that can be explored without instruction by three-year-olds might be an example here. In a Class 4 Invention ("Felt by many. Dishes rattle"), there is refinement of existing paradigms by substantial new invention. The set of techniques used in the Olympic Message System (Gould et al., 1987) might qualify here. In a Class 5 Invention ("Felt by all. Sleepers awake"), there is a new idea for some component of the user interface. An example would be the large data space in the MIT Dataland system (Bolt, 1984). In a Class 6 Invention ("Slight building damage....Walking is difficult"), there is the discovery of some major new component. Emacs's (Stallman, 1987) extensible editor paradigm might be an example.

In the last band, there is substantial impact on the field of user interface design. In a Class 6.5 Invention ("Considerable building damage.... Some houses knocked from foundations"), a user interface emerges that is a trendsetter, widely imitated by others, for example, spreadsheets from VisiCalc. In a Class 7 Invention, there is a course change for at least part of the industry. In fact, the gloss for this level ("Serious damage. Rails are bent. General panic. Partial collapse") is a pretty good description of the impact of X (Sheifler, Gettys, and Newman, 1988). In a Class 7.5 Invention ("Great damage.... Bridges fall"), there is a major paradigm shift. The NLS system, which introduced the mouse, point-and-click editing, and hypertext is an example. Finally, in a Class 8 Invention ("Damage nearly total.... Most works of construction destroyed"), there is a restructuring of the field. Fifteen years later, most new user interfaces do bear a resemblance to those pioneered by the Smalltalk system.

The systems indexed by Table 3 seem to fall into two broad groups that we will call Pioneer Systems and Settler Systems. In one group (SSI ≥ 3), the Pioneer Systems, are Star, HyperCard, PenPoint, and NLS, user interface designs that pioneered new user interface techniques or uses. In the other group (SSI < 3), the Settler Systems, are interfaces that apply existing interface techniques to new problems. The systems of the first group are concerned to a greater extent with user interface invention. The systems of the latter group are concerned mostly with exploiting existing techniques for other ends, hence with good engineering. (Note, however, that all user interfaces must be concerned with engineering to some extent, or even good inventions will fail in the implementation.) In Table 2, Star, FreeStyle, and Meetingware are examples of Pioneer Systems. The New TAO Workstation and Rally are examples of Settler Systems.

Engineering

Whereas the success of an *invention* may be measured by its impact, the success of an *engineering* project may be assessed by the extent to which it meets its objectives (and by whether those objectives are adequate). Engineering is about having enough control over technique that a desired objective can be predictably and reliably achieved for a given resource cost. Usability is an important engineering objective. In the spirit of the SSI scale, I also offer a validated scale for usability: the *Cooper–Harper Scale* (Table 4), drawn from the testing of airplanes (Cooper and Harper, 1969). Since it is a phenomenological scale, the Cooper-Harper is also pretty good at describing just about any machine where usability is important in order to get it to fly. The user is assumed to be able to compensate for some of the deficiencies of the machine, and the scale essentially indexes how hard the user must work to achieve a well-defined level of success with the system (not crashing). The 10-point scale breaks into four regions: Satisfactory without improvement (1–3), Deficiencies warrant improvement (4–6), Adequate performance not attainable without improvement (7–9), and Not controllable (10).

It is not so useful to try to rate the systems in Tables 1 and 2 because rather than looking at a single system, engineering progress would usually be seen within *versions* of the same system. For the Rally system, however, this is, in fact, what we have. Redesign improved the system from perhaps a 6 ("Very objectionable but tolerable deficiencies requiring extensive user compensation") to perhaps a 2 ("Good—Negligible deficiencies, user compensation not required"). For the New TAO Workstation system, the principle engineering metric of improvement was time per call. The CPM-GOMS method predicted that, to everyone's surprise, this metric was expected actually to worsen. In both cases, it is not the invention of novel functionality that is at issue; it is better performance on usability or efficiency for the defined system.

Table 3 suggests that most user interfaces are Settler Systems, dominated by engineering (96 percent of the systems will be SSI 0, 1, or 2, according to the table) and that therefore methods for engineering, including usability engineering, will be of most interest to most designers. On the other hand, it also suggests that methods that aid invention will have a disproportionately large impact.

Innovation

But what of the other ingredients that lead from invention and engineering to commercial success? What makes this other part of the difference? Here it is

TABLE 4   **Cooper–Harper Scale**

Score	Aircraft Characteristics	Demand on Pilot
SATISFACTORY WITHOUT IMPROVEMENT		
1	Excellent—highly desirable	
2	Good—negligible deficiencies	No pilot compensation required
3	Fair—some mildly unpleasant deficiencies	Minimal pilot compensation required
DEFICIENCIES WARRANT IMPROVEMENT		
4	Minor but annoying deficiencies	Moderate pilot compensation
5	Moderately objectionable deficiencies	Considerable pilot compensation
6	Very objectionable, but tolerable deficiencies	Extensive pilot compensation
ADEQUATE PERFORMANCE NOT ATTAINABLE WITHOUT IMPROVEMENT		
7	Major deficiency	Adequate performance not attainable with maximum tolerable pilot compensation. Controllability not a question
8	Major deficiency	Considerable pilot compensation required for control
9	Major deficiency	Intense pilot compensation required to control
NOT CONTROLLABLE		
10	Major deficiencies	Control will be lost during some portion of required operation

useful to broaden our view and look at user interfaces as just another class of technological innovation. White and Graham (1978) have suggested that four factors determine the success of a technical innovation. These are inventive merit, embodiment merit, operational merit, and market merit (Figure 2). *Inventive merit* is the technological invention that makes a difference, as we have previously discussed. Usually the invention relieves or avoids major constraints inherent in the previous art. In the case of the transistor (Table 5), the electronic amplification function could be provided with smaller size,

FIGURE 2

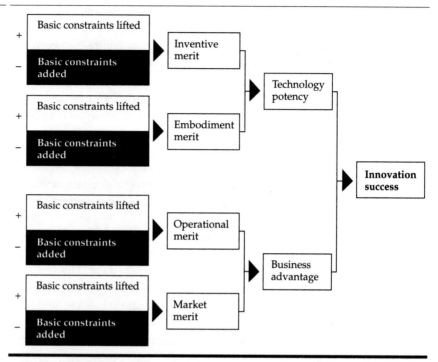

White and Graham's (1978) model of innovation success. Success depends on the extent to which innovations exhibit four kinds of merit. Innovations often fail in the market because they are lacking merit in one or more of these categories, despite strengths in other areas.

TABLE 5

Innovation Criteria for Transistor Radio

1. Inventive merit	+	Improves size, weight, power, reliability
2. Embodiment merit	+	Miniaturization of antenna, tuning capacity, batteries, loudspeaker permits pocket radio
3. Operational merit	+	Removes need for franchised dealer service network and dealer channels because of higher reliability and can ship through the mail
4. Market merit	+	Captures major new growth market with go-anywhere, play-as-you-go characteristics

After White and Graham, 1978.

less power, and more reliability. Of course an invention may have disadvantages, too. Transistors had low yield, causing them to be more costly than vacuum tubes. So it is important, as in Figure 2, to keep track of those factors detracting from innovation success (marked with a minus in Figure 2) as well as those contributing to innovation success (marked with a plus).

Embodiment merit refers to the way the invention is embodied in its surrounding systems. An embodiment can either leverage off the opportunity of an invention or dissipate it. Japanese manufacturers leveraged the size and power advantages of the transistor by miniaturizing the antenna, the speaker, and the capacitors as well. This made possible the transistor radio, a radio with new uses. On the contrary, American manufacturers just made slightly smaller radios and thereby dissipated the invention merit of the transistor in their embodiment.

Operational merit is how the invention affects the business practices of the company selling it. Again, the operations of a business can leverage off the advantages of an invention or dissipate them. The small size and greater reliability of transistor radios made it possible for transistor radio manufacturers to avoid having to establish a franchised dealer and service network. The radios didn't need as much service, and they could be mailed to a central facility. This allowed the manufacturers to overcome a major barrier to the entry of new companies into the radio business.

Finally, *market merit* is how the invention is leveraged to increase demand. The small, lightweight transistor radios could be carried in a pocket. This allowed new uses for the radio: It could be carried to the beach or to a ballgame; people could listen to sports or music while they did construction work or washed the car. These new uses expanded the market even though transistor radios were at a cost disadvantage. The new markets' expanded volumes helped to lead to lower prices, and lower prices expanded the markets further.

We can use White and Graham's analysis to help us understand the relationship between success in technological innovation for HCI and commercial innovation success. Table 6 shows the case of the Xerox Star, the system that first commercially introduced graphical user interfaces. The Star system had spectacularly strong technological merit. It introduced windows, generic functions, menus, and personal networking, all the basic ingredients that would become the standard user interface ten years later. Its embodiment, on the other hand, was more mixed. Experience had shown that larger screens were much more desirable for productivity, and marketing analyses had concluded that price was less important than functionality, so the machine was given a larger display, faster network, and integrated applications, but these raised the price. The heavy emphasis on the machine as a network citizen meant that it did not work well without the net and hence was expensive in

TABLE 6   **Innovation Criteria for Xerox Star**

1. Inventive merit	+	Windows (multiple processes share display). Generic functions (fewer commands, faster learning). Menus (recognition instead of recall). Networking (group interaction). More function, less learning
2. Embodiment merit	+	Larger screen, faster Ethernet, integrated applications for higher productivity
	–	Embodiment led to high entry cost, blocked third-party software. Underpowered
	–	Not intended to look like general computer
3. Operational merit	–	System product not well-matched to Xerox sales, service force. High evolution cost
4. Market merit	+	Opened new markets. Strong customer loyalty
	–	Embodiment means must sell against IBM in MIS department. No cheap entry. Can't develop enough software

small installations. The decision not to sell it as a general-purpose computer or to enable third-party development meant that its uses could not grow as fast as those machines that did this. Finally, the machine was not fast enough to leverage the productivity gains inherent in its inventive merit.

Operationally, the Star was not well matched to the capabilities of the sales and service force. The heavily integrated design led to high evolution costs for the machine. Still, the machine had strong market merits. It opened new markets and developed a very loyal customer base. But the embodiment, which was aimed at selling to large corporations rather than individuals, meant that it was forced to sell against IBM in MIS departments dominated by IBM. The lack of adequate third-party development meant that others could not open new applications for it. Thus, the Star system was a strong technical success for HCI, but not a commercial innovation success.

The Apple Macintosh (Table 7) presents a different story. The Macintosh had more modest inventive merit. The essentials of the graphical user interface came from Smalltalk and Star, to which were added a dialog box scheme and a scheme of generic pull-down menus that eventually allowed transfer of learning by users from one application to another. Apple embodied the technology in a general-purpose computer at a low price that was open to third-party developers. This was an important leveraging of the technological merit. In fact, this orientation toward third-party software was probably deciding in the end. It was a third-party software company, not Apple itself, that found the "killer-ap" of desktop publishing, which turned the invention merit of the bitmapped graphical interface into a major advantage for the machine. On the other hand, there were also negatives to the embodiment: The machine was underpowered, the screen was too small, there was no serious network, and there was little integration. Operationally, the machine was compatible with the company's marketing and service channels, which was a plus. Apple was already a computer company with a dealer network. But it was in the marketing merit that Apple was able to derive from the technical invention that really helped bring success. The interface gave the machine market differentiation from all PC companies. Ease of use became a major selling point. The machine attracted innovative third-party developers and opened up the desktop publishing market and desktop graphics design markets.

Wang FreeStyle (Table 8) is still another case. FreeStyle also had good inventive merit. It allowed users to attach synchronized speech and gestures as annotations to image-based electronic mail, and the whole was embodied in an image-based desktop. The basic innovation capability was partially enhanced by its embodiment. The electronic mail embodiment allowed a new kind of collaboration at a distance. Synchronized interactions that would normally have required a high-bandwidth video conference installation ("Why is this number here lower than this number over here?") could be done with low bandwidth over existing networks with no synchronous requirement. The image desktop part of the embodiment allowed integration of scanning, fax,

TABLE 7	**Innovation Criteria for Apple Macintosh**		
1. Inventive merit	+	(From Smalltalk and Star): Graphic orientation, windows, menus, mouse	
	+	Generic pull-down menus allow transfer of learning among third-party applications	
2. Embodiment merit	+	General-purpose computer at a cheap price	
	−	Screen too small, underpowered, no network, lack of integration	
3. Operational merit	+	Compatible with channels	
4. Market merit	+	Market differentiation from PC. Ease of use major selling point. Positioned as the "other PC." Attracted innovative third-party developers. Opened up desktop publishing	

TABLE 8	**Innovation Criteria for Wang FreeStyle**		
1. Inventive merit	+	Synchronous speech acts in asynchronous medium: synchronized speech, gesture annotations to image-based electronic mail
2. Embodiment merit	+	Electronic mail embodiment allows new kind of collaboration at a distance, but with lower bandwidth, existing nets, no synchronous requirement. Image desktop allows integration of scanning, fax, drawing, image capture from PC applications
	–	Constrained by Wang proprietary systems
3. Operational merit	–	Not compatible with Wang channels, products, PC products
4. Market merit	+	Market differentiation, new market development
	–	Confusion about what product is and for whom

drawing, and image capture from PC applications. Alas, some of the inventive merit was dissipated by the requirement that it had to be embedded in Wang proprietary systems. Operationally, FreeStyle was not well-matched or compatible with Wang channels, products, or with PC products. This fact did not allow Wang to leverage the invention well. Market merit was also mixed. On the one hand, it was a market differentiator and opened up new areas for potential market expansion. On the other hand, there was considerable confusion about what the product was and for whom it was meant.

It is easy to see why invention success and commercial innovation success are very separate things. Even starting with a strong invention, it may take several tries before the right embodiment, operational use, and market positioning of an invention are hit upon. Worse, generally only invention success and embodiment success are assessable from within the research and development organizations. Even the best set of methods in the hands of the best people can therefore fail commercially.

To summarize, by expanding our focus beyond individual point design first to the food chain of ideas, then to the larger innovation context, we can now finally state more about what it means for an interactive system to be successful: *An interactive system design is successful if it is an **invention success** (that is, it relieves major constraints inherent in previous art or captures some new function) or if it is an **engineering success** (that is, it accomplishes its design objectives, such as usability or speed, within its resource constraints) or if it is an **innovation success** (that is, it produces a return on investment, namely, it has an adequate*

FIGURE 3

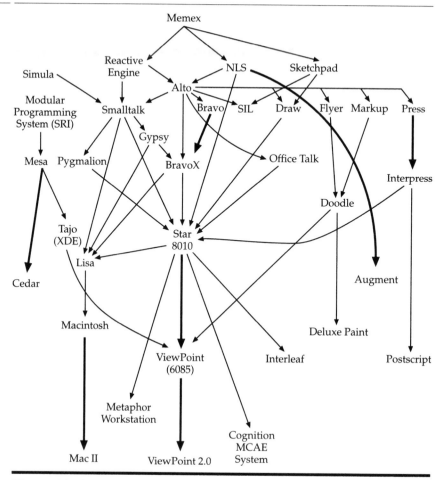

History of the Star user interface (Miller and Johnson, this volume). Star benefited from the food chain of ideas and, in turn, was a very strong contributor to later systems.

combination of technological merit, embodiment merit operational merit, and market merit) or if it is a **link on the food chain** *to the above.*

An invention's success is usually shown by its being widely imitated, often in modified form, over generations of systems. This is clearly seen in the diagrams that are often drawn tracing the food chain of invention ideas. Figure 1 is one such diagram. Figure 3 is another. Each step is a stage in the evolution of the technology. A successful invention *makes a difference* in the history of the technology. The systems listed in Figures 1 and 3 have achieved some measure of success by virtue of appearing in these diagrams: They led to something.

An engineering success is shown by the fit that is achieved to its purpose. Unlike invention success, which is best seen across generations of the technology, engineering success occurs within the design process of a single system, possibly over several versions. It is usually achieved by some combination of analytical methods (that predict the parameters of a design that will fit the situation) and the empirical test–fix cycle that studies the design in idealized or realistic environments to discover areas of misfit and plan remedies.

An innovation success is shown by the extent to which the organizational success of the sponsoring organization is affected by the introduction of the innovation. In the commercial world, this is in the form of profit return on investment, or perhaps strategic positioning or some other subtle surrogate for profit. In the noncommercial world, the analogue might be in terms of organizational growth or in terms of mission success (for example, battles won, disease deaths reduced). An innovation success is a successful engagement with the larger context surrounding an invention.

Methods

We have seen that different sorts of success can be associated with user interface design. Design methods are somewhat relative to these. Methods that support engineering, for example, might not be suitable for invention. Methods are also relative to different aspects of the invention process itself. We therefore continue our analysis of the food chain of invention by considering briefly the nature of the invention process that gives rise to it.

Methods and the Invention Process

Studies in the history of technology help us see patterns underlying technological evolution. Hughes (1983) studied the activities of professional inventors whose inventions resulted in the electric power industry. He identified five phases of invention: (1) problem identification, (2) solution as idea, (3) research, (4) development, and (5) introduction. In *problem identification,* the inventor perceives a situation that can be defined as a problem. This implies that a solution is likely to be found. Identifying a problem in a situation is an important perception. Experienced inventors realize that in many situations, problems cannot be defined because of the inadequate state of technology or for nontechnical reasons. *Solution as idea* refers to the idealized functioning of some solution in some idealized environment. The idea is often represented as a sketch. *Research* is an information-gathering exercise done by literature search or experiments, possibly with prototypes. *Development* may involve the redefinition of the problem and new ideas (and perhaps additional research). The invention is tried in environments increasingly similar to the one in which the innovation must function. Finally, *introduction* brings the invention to market or otherwise to real users. Of course, this process is neither straight-forward nor linear. Still Hughes's phases are useful in helping us recognize that innovation is an activity of parts, not a single homogeneous act.

Hughes's phases are applied to the invention process for the papers in this section (Table 2) in Table 9. The New TAO Workstation, for example, is at the point of introduction. The analysis methods described are trials determining whether it should be introduced or not. The Rally system is concerned with introduction but also with engineering out problems of usability. This is done by trying to understand and appreciate the use of the system in the environ-ment in which it must actually function. Both these systems (at least in this phase of their development) are Settler Systems. They are primarily con-cerned with engineering performance and usability using known user inter-face techniques on defined problems.

By contrast, the other three systems in Table 2 are Pioneer Systems. In Table 9, this is reflected by the number of phases with which the systems are involved. The FreeStyle system and the Star system are more concerned with the invention of new technology for a new problem. The Meetingware system is concerned with integrating existing technology to solve a new problem; the invention here is a method for running meetings, eventually introduced as consulting service business.

TABLE 9   **Phases of Invention (Hughes) Applied to Systems in Table 2**

	Settler Systems		Pioneer Systems		
	[1]	[2]	[3]	[4]	[5]
SSI	1.0	1.0	3.0	6.0	8.0
Problem identification				●	●
Solution as idea				●	●
Research			●	●	●
Development		●	●	●	●
Introduction	●	●	●	●	●

[1] New TAO Workstation, [2] Rally, [3] Meetingware, [4] FreeStyle, [5] Star

FIGURE 4

Resources   Demand

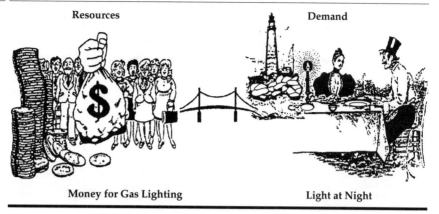

Money for Gas Lighting   Light at Night

An interpretation of the nature of invention according to Hughes (1983). An invention is a technology that uses some resource efficiently to meet a demand precisely.

Let us consider more closely the problem identification phase. Of course, invention may follow many courses and have many origins, but Hughes noticed some frequent patterns in the methods used by professional inventors that are useful to us. These inventors often sought to identify a demand or function to be performed on the one hand and a resource on the other (Figure 4). Then they would try to develop new technology that used the resource efficiently to meet the demand precisely. If the demand is stipulated and the search is for technology to fill it, then the invention is "demand pull." If the technology is stipulated and the search is for a demand, then it is "technology push." Both exist and can lead to successful systems.

According to Hughes, inventors identified a problem by looking for a "reverse salient," a weakness in the technology. They then tried to identify a "critical problem," that is, a problem to be solved that would correct the reverse salient. For Edison, the reverse salient was usually economic, the critical problem usually technical, thus linking the parameters of invention success to some of those for innovation success.

What is important to realize is that the process of bringing out an innovation may focus on either of these activities: searching for a new function ("application" in the computer industry) that utilizes a technology or searching for a technology that is a good fit to a defined problem.

Now we turn to the five systems of Table 2 in order to discover the methods used in their design. The phases of problem as idea, research, and development can intermingle, and their disentangling requires more detailed information than is available to us from the reports we have of their development. To simplify matters, we will distinguish the more easily separated methods surrounding artifact construction and evaluation. Introduction, as we have seen from White and Graham's analysis earlier, is a very complex topic in its own right and one whose methods are not dealt with in detail by these accounts. We therefore consider it outside the scope of our current analysis. As a consequence, we are left with three aspects of the design process:

1. *Problem identification*
2. *Artifact construction*
3. *Evaluation*

We use these to give initial organization to the inventory of methods we discover in the subject systems of our analysis.

New TAO Workstation (Atwood, Gray, and John)

In the design of the New TAO Workstation, the functional demand has been stipulated as minimizing time to service a call. Atwood, Gray, and John are evaluating the system on this basis. They use several methods: The *Comparative Field Experiment* is used for a comparison between the existing and proposed workstations. CPM-GOMS (*Analytic Calculation*) is used to predict the performance of the new system and to find a hidden bottleneck that is the cause of the differences. To do the calculation, *Scenarios* are developed from videotaped analysis of operators doing benchmark tasks (*Benchmark Laboratory Experiment*). The analysis is also used to interpret and reinforce the results of an empirical experiment that would otherwise be uninterpretable. We can summarize their methods categorized by design aspects as follows:

METHODS USED:

Problem Identification
- *Scenarios*

Evaluation
- *Benchmark Laboratory Experiment*
- *Comparative Field Experiment*
- *Analytic Calculation: GOMS*

Rally (Wixon and Jones)

In this system, again, the functional demand has already been established. Wixon and Jones are called in to engineer an improvement in usability. They use a large number of methods. First, they use some evaluation methods at the site of use to locate problems in fit between the uses of the system in context and its design: They do *Field Interviews* with users at their site of work and *User Observation* of users attempting to use the original system. Then they use another set of methods for constructing a prototype of the artifact: Users are encouraged to make suggestions and to evaluate the prototypes (*Participatory Design*). The designers use their own experience with other systems (*Steal and Modify*) for ideas as well as their own experience as users (*Use What You Build*). They set up some *Agreed Formal Usability Metrics* and design to these as targets (usability engineering). For their design, they make use of a form of *Object and Action Analysis* and use *Generic Functions* to reduce the command count and simplify the design. The design is iterated (*Cut and Try*), and iterations are evaluated with *Field Interviews, User Observations, Benchmark Laboratory Experiments* to measure performance time, *Comparative Field Experiments* to compare versions, and *Analytic Calculations* to evaluate designs on the basis of number of menu transitions. *Comparative User Preferences* between original and proposed design is used as a wide-band technique to pick up unanticipated problems, especially among the important expert user population. Finally, usability problems are put into the problem tracking system with the rest of the engineering problems (*Usability Problem Tracking*).

METHODS USED:

Artifact Construction

- *Steal and Modify*
- *Cut and Try*
- *Participatory Design*
- *Formal Usability Targets (UE)*
- *Usability Problem Tracking*
- *Object/Action analysis*
- *Generic Functions*

Evaluation

- *Field Interviews* (videotaped)
- *User Observation* (videotaped)
- *Benchmark Laboratory Experiments* (Time)
- *Analytic Calculations* (Number of menu transitions)
- *Comparative User Preferences*

Meetingware (Whiteside)

This is a case of demand pull. Whiteside starts from a relatively fixed notion of functional demand: use of emerging computer and communications technologies to produce better synchronous, real-time meetings both local and geographically distributed. His search is for better meeting methods and technologies. His group used their own actual meetings (*Design for Yourself*) with many iterations (*Cut and Try*) to discover techniques for improving meetings and to try out the technologies. They also invited other people to their design meetings and went to meetings of others (*Participatory Design*) and used *Special Projects* to expand the meetings beyond the group. Building was mainly *Cut and Try* systems integration. Evaluation was by *Use What You Build*.

The project has several good examples of finding and resolving reverse salients: The need for a portable, high-resolution color projector is identified as a bottleneck and is developed through encouragement of a third-party manufacturer; system integration is identified as another bottleneck blocking the development of meeting room tools. Finally, the role of new meeting methods is identified as an enabling factor for integrating the technology, and this is addressed. In fact, its identification shows that instead of a simple software or hardware business, a successful business model is likely to come as part of a custom consulting business.

METHODS USED:

Problem Identification
- *Design for Yourself*
- *Cut and Try*
- *Use What You Build*
- *Participatory Design*
- *Special Projects*

Artifact Building
- *Cut and Try*
- *Participatory Design*
- *Special Projects*

Evaluation
- *Use What You Build*
- *Special Projects*

FreeStyle (Francik)

This is a case of technology push.[3] The technologies (image capture, voice recording, electronic mail, fax, pen annotation, high-resolution graphics) were established early based on a very generic notion of usefulness; the development attempts both to engineer these to acceptable levels of performance and to search for a more precise notion of demand. To develop a prototype, the designers use a version of the *Design for Yourself* method in which a particular user or very few users are selected and the design made to satisfy them (within the group the slogan was, "Design for Leonard," the manager) through repeated iterations (*Cut and Try*). The voice and gesture annotations are integrated with fax documents and screen images of computer-generated documents. A principal operation on these documents is a technique for combined handwriting, voice, and gesture annotation. With this technique, a number of group work interactions that would have required high-bandwidth synchronous communications can now be done with low-bandwidth asynchronous communications. But the emphasis this brings to group communications makes it necessary to search for and understand the parameters of demand.

The Wang team had a double burden. They needed good human engineering to make the system sufficiently paperlike that the concept did not die on issues of system response (for example, a tablet with a "bad feel" relative to paper), and they needed to reshape the feature-set of the system to bring such added value to its users that it could bring a new computing paradigm into the marketplace. The team used many methods for these tasks. They used the *Try to Break It* method to reveal some shortcomings in their test of candidate tablets. *Benchmark Laboratory Experiments* were used to test the tablet and the whole system. Among other things, task time, error frequencies, and comments were collected. *Questionnaires* were used in the design of the hardware. *User Preferences* were assessed using 7-point *ratings* of important attributes (such as pen thickness), and *rankings* were done among alternative designs.

Parallel to the laboratory tests, a number of field methods were used with both *Alpha Testing* in house and *Beta Testing* outside. The team and their colleagues used the system (*Use What You Build*). An extensive set of *Field Interviews* and *Field User Observations* were made at different sites. *Participatory Design* was undertaken with users, and "Communication Constellation Analysis," a variant on Sociogram Analysis, was done to identify communication patterns (*Work Flow Analysis*). To describe possible uses uncovered in their field studies, the team wrote brochures describing possible system applications, a form of *Scenario*.

METHODS USED:

Problem Identification
- *Field Interviews*
- *User Observation*
- *Scenarios*
- *Design for Yourself*

- *Cut and Try*
- *Use What You Build*
- *Work Flow Analysis* (Sociogram)
- *Participatory Design*

Artifact Building
- *Steal and Modify*
- *Cut and Try*
- *Participatory Design*

Evaluation
- *Benchmark Laboratory Experiments*
- *Alpha Testing*
- *Beta Testing*
- *Try to Break It*
- *Use What You Build*
- *User Observation*
- *Questionnaires*
- *Comparative User Preferences* (Rankings)
- *Absolute User Preferences* (Rankings)

Star (Miller and Johnson)

Star was a technology push effort.[4] It arose not so much from a particular demand as from a vision whose pedigree extended from Vanevar Bush, through Doug Engelbart and Ivan Sutherland, Alan Kay, and others. This led to a long series of prototypes conducted by the *Design for Yourself* and *Use What You Build* methods in which an entire community of people experienced several thousand person-years in an environment of networked, bitmapped, personal computing. The results were several new genres of software: point-and-click editing (derived from NLS), bitmap-based paint programs, geometric primitive-based drawing programs, laser printing, client–server networking, page description languages, work-flow-based computing, object-oriented graphical user interfaces, icons, pull-down menus, and the desktop metaphor. Problem identification took the form of integrating this experience, formal market analyses, and designer fieldwork. In addition to the *Use What You Build* prototyping method, the directions of the PARC technology and Star were partially guided by an extensive market analysis in which Xerox employees did extensive *Field Interviews* and analyses with about 60 businesses, including a *Work Flow Analysis* for each. This was followed by designed mockups of technical solutions to customer problems, which were brought back to customers for their reaction, including queries about pricing. One result is that it was concluded that customers were relatively price insensitive and were more interested in functionality. As a consequence, the Star design point improved usability (for example, going to a larger display) at the expense of price. The Star interface designers then went to customer sites, preselected by the market analysis, conducted *Field Interviews* and *Work Flow Analysis*, and wrote *Scenarios*.

As Miller and Johnson illustrate, the Star designers had a large amount of accumulated exposure and experience going into the design, and this was heavily used (*Steal and Modify*). It is this experience that provided grounding for the larger ideas (which probably couldn't have been tested experimentally, anyway). The fundamental technique for getting the design clean was to produce a set of abstractions that captured the essence of user work using *Objects and Actions Analysis* (Newman and Sproull, 1973). The methods of *Design Before Coding* and *Comprehensive Design Description* were techniques for achieving global consistency in the design. This was appropriate because the extensive prototyping effort preceding the Star design had already provided the experience needed for this step. From there, *Cut and Try* was used to prototype very rapidly and to try out design variants that the group was undecided about or to validate that some idea was likely to work. Only if it was not obvious from looking at the prototypes were *Comparative Laboratory Benchmark Experiments* necessary. In some cases, *Theoretical Calculations* were used to supplement or confirm the experiments. For example, *Benchmark Laboratory Experiments* compared novice users on several alternative methods for determining the optimum number of buttons on the mouse for text selection, but *Analytical Calculations* were used to compute likely expert performance (since the design was new, experts didn't, of course, exist to run in experiments). In another case, the maximum velocity that the user would move the mouse was calculated (Card, Moran, and Newell, 1983, pp. 252–255) and found to be greater than the hardware could support, forcing a redesign. (The calculation was done in a discussion during lunch and a confirming experiment completed by the early afternoon.) Usability problems were put into the prioritized fix-it list with other system problems (*Usability Problem Tracking*), and a *Try to Break It* method was used as part of the release process. But one of the principal methods for building the interface was *UI Constraints First,* that is, the user interface constraints were set before other constraints of the system, forcing other subsystems to adapt. This was partially enabled by the method of *Designer Management*, in which the user interface designer is also the product manager and has clear control of the design.

METHODS USED:

Problem Identification
- *Design for Yourself*
- *Use What You Build*
- *Scenarios*
- *Work Flow Analysis*
- *Field Interviews*
- *User Reaction to System Mockups*

Artifact Building
- *Steal and Modify*
- *Objects and Actions Analysis*
- *Generic Functions*
- *Comprehensive Design Description*
- *Design Before Coding*
- *Cut and Try*
- *UI Constraints First*
- *Usability Problem Tracking*
- *Designer Management*

Evaluation
- *Alpha Testing*
- *Use What You Build*
- *Benchmark Laboratory Experiments*
- *Try to Break It*
- *Analytical Calculations*

The Ecology of Methods

Patterns of Method Use

Now that we have analyzed each of the systems in Table 2 to discover the methods used in each, we can note some larger patterns of use. Table 10 summarizes the methods used for each of the systems of Table 2, broken out by whether they were used in Problem Identification, Artifact Creation, or Evaluation. There are several patterns to note. First, the same method can appear in several roles. *Field Interviews,* for example, were used in both problem identification and evaluation.

Second, methods can be classified into either *analytic methods* (understanding is extracted by analysis) or *synthetic methods* (understanding is extracted by building something). These are marked A or S in the table. Both analytic and synthetic methods were used in all three roles, problem identification, abstract creation, and evaluation. In developing the FreeStyle system, for example, the demand and functionality to be performed was investigated by building prototypes and using them, a synthetic method (*Use What You Build*). But the same sort of information was also sought by *Field Interviews,* an analytic method. The different methods are presumably complementary. Several projects used suites of methods with similar aims to gather deeper insights and correct for any misleading impressions gained from a particular method.

Finally, it is interesting to note that the combinations of methods used were more eclectic than ideological. For example, on the Rally project, methods associated with the "contextualist" school were used (for example, *Participatory Design, Field Interviews, User Observation*), but so were *Benchmark Laboratory Experiments* and *Analytic Calculations* that are sometimes considered part of an opposing philosophy. Similarly, the Star project, often associated with *Benchmark Laboratory Experiments* (Bewley et al., 1983) and sometimes with *Analytic Calculations,* also used extensive *Field Interviews and User Observation.* Whiteside discusses the contextualist approach at length in his paper on Meetingware, but a major part of the designers' demand identification was done using themselves as subjects rather than using external field groups, as might be thought from the philosophy. The FreeStyle system used all flavors of methods. Even the New TAO Workstation group, primarily interested in *Analytic Calculations* with GOMS models, used *User Observation.*

Although methods from supposedly opposing philosophies were used together, I detect no contradictions here. The designers and evaluators of these systems are simply sophisticated enough to employ methods within their limitations. The Rally group, for example, used contextualist methods to understand the design problem but were able to use *Analytic Calculations* to search the design space cheaply for promising menu designs. They then used more expensive contextualist methods to evaluate their design. Likewise, the Meetingware group used themselves to iterate their understanding as rapidly and cheaply as possible but then looked at other groups and used *Special Projects* to validate and generalize their findings. Rather than thinking of methods as ideological opponents of each other, these groups use combinations of methods to complement each other and cheaper methods to conserve resources so that the more expensive methods could be deployed in the most vital places.

TABLE 10 **Summary of Methods Used**

Method	Type*	New TAO Workstation	Rally	Meeting System	FreeStyle	Star	Total
PROBLEM/DEMAND IDENTIFICATION							
Design for Yourself	S			●	●	●	3
Use What You Build	S			●	●	●	3
Scenarios	A	●			●	●	3
Participatory Design	S			●	●		2
Field Interviews	A				●	●	2
Work Flow Analysis	A				●	●	2
Cut and Try	S			●	●		2
User Observations	A				●		1
Special Projects	S			●			1
User Reaction to Mockups	S					●	1
ARTIFACT CREATION							
Cut and Try	S		●	●	●	●	4
Steal and Modify	S		●		●	●	3
Participatory Design	S		●	●	●		3
Object and Actions Analysis	A		●			●	2
Generic Functions	S		●			●	2
Usability Problem Tracking	S		●			●	2
Formal Usability Targets	A		●				1
Special Projects	S			●			1
Design Before Coding	S					●	1
Comprehensive Design Description	S					●	1
UI Constraints First	S					●	1
Designer Management	S					●	1
EVALUATION							
Benchmark Laboratory Experiments	A	●	●		●	●	4
Use What You Build	S		●	●	●	●	4

Method	Type*	New TAO Workstation	Rally	Meeting System	FreeStyle	Star	Total
Analytic Calculations	A	●	●			●	3
Field Interviews	A		●		●		2
User Observation	A		●		●		2
Comparative User Preferences (rankings)	A		●		●		2
Alpha Testing	S				●	●	2
Try to Break It	S				●	●	2
Comparative Field Experiments	A	●	●				2
Special Projects	S			●			1
Beta Testing	S				●		1
Questionnaires	A				●		1
Absolute User Preferences (attribute ratings)	A				●		1

*A = analytical method, S = synthetic method

It is interesting to note the most popular methods. If we restrict ourselves to methods used by a majority of the projects (or more projects), the chief methods for problem and demand identification were:

Design for Yourself

Use What You Build

Field Interview

Scenarios

The most popular methods for artifact creation were:

Steal and Modify

Cut and Try

Participatory Design

Thus, to come back to a question we began with: Is simple theft an example of what we mean by a successful method? The answer according to these projects is clearly, yes. The reason is that, as we have noted, technology advances by the food chain of ideas, so good designers are also designers knowledgeable about the designs of other systems, and there is probably at least as much power in this method as in participatory design or any of the methods aimed at contextual understanding of the problem to be solved. But although theft is the engine that carries good ideas forward in the chain, other methods are necessary in order to add to the stock of good ideas.

The most popular evaluation methods were:

Benchmark Laboratory Experiments

Use What You Build

Analytic Calculations

Table 11 breaks out the methods used by Analysis vs. Synthesis and phase of the design process. This table shows that about 5 of the 23 methods (about a fifth) are used in more than one role. It also shows the heavy use of *Cut and Try* and *Use What You Build,* two of the more pragmatic methods.

Dimensions of Variation

The eclecticism of methods displayed by designers of these real systems suggests looking more closely at the morphological space (Card, Mackinlay, and Robertson, 1991) occupied by the methods. We can describe the space of methods on at least four dimensions (Figure 5):

1. *Analytic vs. Synthetic Methods*
2. *Idealization of Context*
3. *Idealization of Representation*
4. *Development Milepost*

First is the distinction between *Analytic Methods* and *Synthetic Methods* that we referred to earlier. Second is the amount of *Idealization of Context* involved. At the one extreme are methods in which there is little idealization of context. The methods are aimed at the direct external setting in which a system will actually be used. *Field Interviews* and *User Observation* are examples. These methods attempt to tap the richly textured, contextualized information that comes from the natural setting without any intermediate abstraction or encoding. A less expensive alternative to dealing directly with an external cost is the use of the self or local group as a context. Methods like *Use What You Build* and *Alpha Testing* attempt to exploit this lower-cost resource. At the other extreme is a constructed, artificial context. *Benchmark Laboratory Experiments* is an example. The context is idealized by underlying parameters of variation in order to make inference easier. These methods attempt to address a space of possible situations rather than just particular situations that have been seen.

TABLE 11   **Methods Used in Different Design Activities**

Method	Problem	Artifact	Evaluation	Total
ANALYSIS				
Field Interviews	3		2	5
Benchmark Lab Experience			4	4
User Observations	1		2	3
Scenarios	3			3
Analytic Calculations			3	3
Work Flow Analysis	2			2
Objects and Actions		2		2
Comparative User Preferences			2	2
Formal Usability Targets		1		1
Comparative Field Experience			1	1
Questionnaires			1	1
Absolute User Preferences			1	1
SYNTHESIS				
Cut and Try		4	5	9
Use What You Build	3		4	7
Steal and Modify		4		4
Design for Yourself	3			3
Participatory Design	2			2
Generic Functions		2		2
Special Projects	1		1	2
Alpha Testing			2	2
Try to Break It			2	2
Reaction to Mockups	1			1
Beta Testing			1	1

A third dimension is the *Idealization of Representation.* At one end are methods that do not use a representational articulation of the design or the situation or the behavior. *Use What You Build* and *Field Interviews* are examples of these. At the other end are methods that have a notational representation,

FIGURE 5

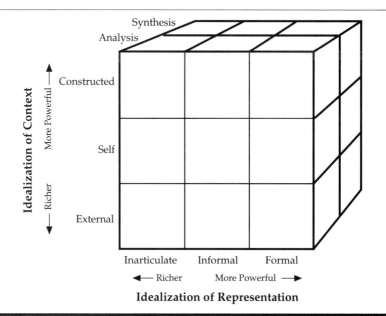

Three dimensions of variation along which methods for developing human-computer interaction systems can be placed. A fourth dimension, not shown here, concerns the purpose of the method.

such as *Analytic Calculations* or *Objects and Actions*. In between are methods that have some sort of informal representation, as the use of *Scenarios* to represent a situation.

When we categorize all the methods of Table 11 by these three dimensions, we obtain Table 12. A few synthetic methods, such as *Steal and Modify*, are applied across contexts, and they have been listed in a new row, "Context-Free Methods" in the table. Otherwise, the methods of our inventory fit into the scheme. Figure 6 takes this analysis one step further and shows miniaturized versions of Table 12 for each of the papers in Table 2. A cell in the table is shaded in if the paper used at least one method in that cell. The analysis of the New TAO Workstation used only Analytic methods; the design of the Meetingware system used only Inarticulate Synthetic methods. Otherwise, the rest of the systems used an eclectic combination of different cells.

Essentially, these three dimensions of methods—Analytic vs. Synthetic, Idealization of Context, and Idealization of Representation—represent tradeoffs among three pragmatic variables: (1) power, (2) richness, and (3) cost. Methods oriented toward the external context and the methods with inarticulate representation have access to the full, richly textured experience of users and situations. But the analysis that can be done with these is limited. As the

TABLE 12   **Dimensions of Variation for Methods Used**

Idealization of Context	Idealization of Representation		
	INARTICULATE	**INFORMAL**	**FORMAL**
ANALYTIC METHODS			
Constructed		• *Benchmark Laboratory Experiments* • *Comparative User Preferences (ranking)* • *Absolute User Preferences (rating)* • *Questionnaires*	• *Analytic Calculations*
Self			
External	• *Field Interviews* • *User Observations*	• *Scenarios* • *Work Flow Analysis* • *Comparative Field Experiment*	
SYNTHETIC METHODS			
Constructed			
Self	• *Design for Yourself* • *Use What You Build* • *Alpha Testing* • *Try to Break It*	• *Design Before Coding* • *Comprehensive Design Description*	• *Formal Usability Targets* • *Objects and Actions Analysis* • *Generic Functions*
External	• *Participatory Design* • *Special Projects* • *User Reaction to Mockups* • *Beta Testing*	• *Usability Problem Tracking*	
Context-Free Methods	• *Steal and Modify* • *Cut and Try* • *UI Constraints First* • *Designer Management*		

FIGURE 6 Miniaturized versions of Table 12, showing which cells of the table are occupied by methods used in building the systems in this section.

TAO

Idealization of Context	Idealization of Representation		
	Inarticulate	Informal	Formal
ANALYTIC			
Constructed			●
Self		●	
External		●	
SYNTHETIC			
Constructed			
Self			
External	●		
Context-Free			

Rally

Idealization of Context	Idealization of Representation		
	Inarticulate	Informal	Formal
ANALYTIC			
Constructed			●
Self			
External		●	●
Context-Free		●	
SYNTHETIC			
Constructed			
Self			●
External			
Context-Free		●	

Meetingware

Idealization of Context	Idealization of Representation		
	Inarticulate	Informal	Formal
ANALYTIC			
Constructed			
Self			
External			
SYNTHETIC			
Constructed	●		
Self	●		
External	●		
Context-Free	●		

FreeStyle

Idealization of Context	Idealization of Representation		
	Inarticulate	Informal	Formal
ANALYTIC			
Constructed		●	
Self			
External	●	●	
SYNTHETIC			
Constructed			
Self	●		
External	●		
Context-Free	●		

Star

Idealization of Context	Idealization of Representation		
	Inarticulate	Informal	Formal
ANALYTIC			
Constructed		●	●
Self			
External		●	●
SYNTHETIC			
Constructed			
Self		●	●
External		●	●
Context-Free		●	

Total

Idealization of Context	Idealization of Representation		
	Inarticulate	Informal	Formal
ANALYTIC			
Constructed		●●●●	●●●
Self			
External	●●●	●	●
SYNTHETIC			
Constructed		●	
Self	●●●	●●	●●
External	●●●	●●	●●
Context-Free	●●●●		

representation of the situation moves toward more constructed context or toward more formal representations, they employ abstractions that selectively omit information (Restnikoff, 1989). These abstractions introduce real possibilities for error in understanding a situation. In return, they enable the use of more powerful operations on the representations. For example, in the Rally case, representing the design in terms of menu crossings enabled the team to construct a counting metric to rapidly eliminate many inferior designs. The alternative would have been direct inarticulate reactions from users experience of each in the field. In the case of Star, using the Keystroke Model allowed calculations to be done to predict expert performance at a time when no experts existed. Wisely, many projects resolve this tension by using combinations of methods situated along this tradeoff curve. This is the classic tradeoff in engineering and in science: *Analysis and deeper understanding depend on idealized representations that abstract away from the thing itself in all its particularity.*

The other tradeoff is cost. Methods vary enormously in cost. Fielding a full prototype with its customer relations and technical support team may be very expensive, for example, but also very revealing. Again, wisely, many projects deploy combinations of methods along the tradeoff curve. *Use What You Build,* for example, may be a cheap way to uncover many of the same flaws that would be discovered much more expensively by fielded prototypes. By using this cheap method, the fielded prototype can be used to uncover the more subtle problems.

The fourth dimension of methods concerns the things they are trying to accomplish. At any time, the design is in some state from problem identification through introduction (and beyond, actually). The methods are essentially techniques for determining that state or moving it to the next state. We have classified these by Problem Identification, Artifact Construction, and Evaluation. There is no accepted list that further breaks out the things to be accomplished in a design. Table 13, therefore, puts forward a proposal for a set of mileposts in each of these categories. Up to this point, the analysis has been confined to methods that were actually used to develop the systems in Table 2. The mileposts in the table reflect, in addition, experiences in systems research at Xerox PARC.[5] The first column in the table lists the milepost, the second column lists evidence (not the only possible) that the milepost has been reached. The last column in the table lists methods from this paper that either can help to reach the milepost or could help to tell if the milepost had been reached. Projects can, of course, skip some of the mileposts by assuming that attempted demonstration would be positive. This saves time, but adds risk. Thus, some projects are done intuitively and succeed, showing that the intuitions were correct about the state of the project. But other projects assume mileposts that later turn out not to be true. The classic example is for the

TABLE 13   **State-of-the-Design Mileposts**

Milepost	Evidence for	Applicable Methods
PROBLEM MILEPOSTS		
1. What is the work practice?	Naturalistic descriptions that explicate interrelationships and context	• *Field Interviews* • *User Observation* • *Participatory Design* • *Design for Yourself*
2. How can the essence of the activity be abstractly characterized?	Abstractions that characterize the essence of the activity. Identification of key factors and parameters of variation	• *Scenarios* • *Work Flow Analysis* • *User Reaction to Mockup* • *Objects and Actions*
3. What is the critical problem?	Identification of solvable problem that will lead to high payoff	
ARTIFACT CONSTRUCTION MILEPOSTS		
1. What is the basic invention idea?	Inspiration for invention, expressed notebook drawing, napkin, seminar, or hallway conversation	
2. What is the Application Internal Model?	Internal clockworks model of the application worked out	• *Objects and Actions* • *Steal and Modify* • *Comprehensive Design Description*
3. What is the Design User's Conceptual Model?	Model of the application as intended to be seen from the user	• *Objects and Actions* • *Steal and Modify* • *Comprehensive Design Description* • *Generic Functions*
4. Is the artifact feasible?	Wizard can use	• *Design for Yourself*
5. Can the grubby details be overcome?	Friends of Wizard can use	• *Cut and Try* • *Use What You Build*
6. Is the artifact robust?	People who don't even know the Wizard can use	• *Alpha Testing* • *Try to Break It*

Milepost	Evidence for	Applicable Methods
7. Has the artifact been modularized and packaged?	Documented API	
8. Is the technology use replicable?	Demonstration that same technique can reliably be applied again with the same good result	

EVALUATION MILEPOSTS

Milepost	Evidence for	Applicable Methods
1. Is the artifact usable?	Users can actually put to use (including opening box and setting up)	• *Benchmark Laboratory Experiments* • *Alpha Testing*
2. Is the artifact useful?	Evidence it has solved the problem. Voluntary regular use	• *Use What You Build*
3. Has the artifact solved a problem in a significant domain?	Propagation of system to larger groups of users	• *Field Interviews* • *User Reaction to Mockups*
4. Does the solution have commercial utility?	Sales	

designers to assume they understand the problem the design is to solve without actually taking the time to visit the field and understand the users.

The list in Table 13 is a tentative reorganization of the analysis of Table 12. The point it tries to make is that: *Methods are not ends in themselves, but means to certain ends.*

There are alternative means to accomplish those ends. The demand for a certain function, for example, could be examined analytically through interviews and observation, or it could be examined synthetically by trying to build experimental prototypes and iterating based on experience. Systems and user interfaces that are successful are not successful because they use a particular magic method, but because, using some collection of methods, they managed to accomplish certain ends, such as identifying the demand, making the system usable, and making the system robust. There are alternative means by which these ends could be accomplished, probably including methods associated with radically different philosophies. But there are not alternative ends to accomplish. This list of ends (and some practical ways of accomplishing them) is the real thing for which we are looking. Table 13 is a first attempt.

Pioneers and Settlers

A theme that comes through these analyses is the difference between Settler Systems seeking incremental advances in user interface technology by using known or incrementally improved techniques on new problems and those Pioneer Systems seeking larger increments in the state of the art. This division is one of degree and continuum since many systems combine a little Pioneering with a lot of Settling. Because of the difficulty of developing Pioneer Systems, many companies avoid investing in them. This is expressed in the quotation: *The Pioneers get the arrows, the Settlers get the land,* from Guy Kawasaki at the beginning of this paper. But many of the breakthroughs in human interfaces that have enabled the expansions of entire industries have come from such pioneering research. It is doubtful whether the new industrial research philosophies, such as "third-generation research management" or "research as part of development," which stress the tight coupling of research to product development, would have produced such Pioneering advances although they might have been more efficient at producing incremental Settler advances.

Figure 7 again shows Figure 1, only this time the SSI Invention rating has been indicated for each system and also the funding sponsorship. We have also added to the figure an indication of funding sources.

From the figure, we note the critical role of federal government sponsorship of the early Pioneer Systems. This relationship stands out quite distinctly when we plot SSI Invention rating as a function of development phase (Figure 8). On the figure, we have indicated funding source. High innovation occurs early. In essence, government, especially ARPA, funding laid the seeds of the graphical user interface revolution of the 1970s and 1980s. Department of Defense program managers, especially ARPA program managers, did actually *do something* about the problems and potential of human interfaces with computers. Government funding of advanced human-computer interaction technologies built the intellectual capital and trained the research teams for the Pioneer Systems that, over a period of 25 years, revolutionized how people interact with computers. Industrial research laboratories at the corporate level in Xerox, IBM, AT&T, and others played a strong role in developing this technology and bringing it into a form suitable for the commercial arena. The really big advances in human-computer interaction were worked out in these Pioneering Systems.

Most systems (as we saw from Table 3) are Settler Systems, and so these systems are an important consumer of methods, especially engineering methods, for the routine production of new designs. But the Pioneer Systems drive the technology. Pioneer Systems are more likely to be associated with methods for getting deep understanding of their task domains or to be associated

FIGURE 7   Each system in Figure 1 has been assigned an approximate magnitude on the invention scale and has been annotated with respect to funding source. Much of the earlier work with the highest impact was government funded. Work funded by development organizations tended to be lower on the SSI scale.

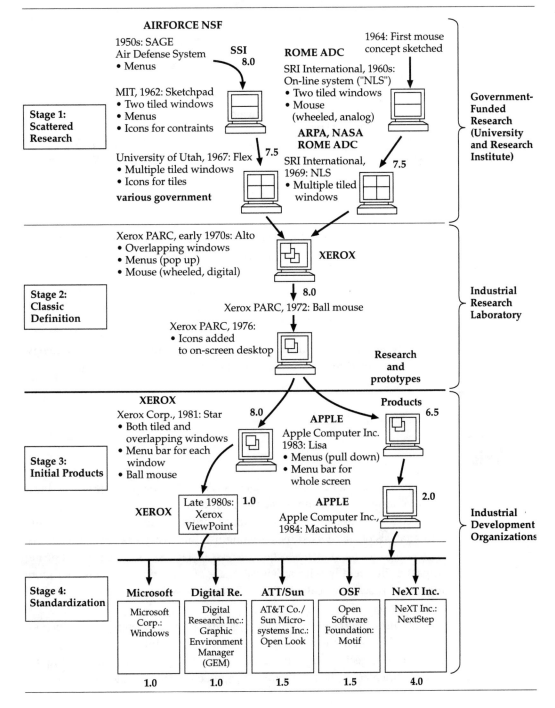

FIGURE 8

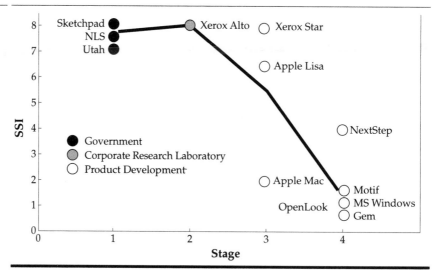

Ratings on the Seismic Scale of Invention (in Figure 7) as a function of user interface stage and funding source. Although based on subjective ratings, the basic pattern is clear: Pioneering invention for the cases examined tended to take place in federally funded research projects and central corporate research centers. *Based on data collected from the research community by Brad Myers and on listed acknowledgments.*

with new technology or deep understanding of some aspect of technology. Methods oriented toward developing the next Settler System are likely to be inadequate for some aspects of Pioneer Systems.

Conclusions

Now let us summarize our conclusions. We began by looking for methods used to design successful interactive computing systems. As a consequence, we needed to characterize what it means for such a system to be successful. Our analysis of success led us to distinguish three varieties: *invention success, engineering success,* and *innovation success.* In fact, we suggested measuring impact quite literally with a Seismic Scale of Invention. Systems that score high on this scale we called *Pioneer Systems;* those that score low we called *Settler Systems.*

Most user interfaces are Settler Systems. They seek engineering success: systems that meet their defined objectives for usability or human performance (and objectives that are reasonable). Most methods in the HCI literature are oriented to the production of engineered Settler Systems.

Innovation success, success in the arena of engagement between a system and its public, is the third kind of success we considered. Innovation success is an outcome of a much wider set of factors. An innovation success requires four basic ingredients to come together: technical merit, embodiment merit, operational merit, and market merit. Although invention success and engineering success are forces for innovation success, excellent methods used by excellent designers can nevertheless fail to produce innovation success because the failure can derive from business failures in the larger context, such as market position, distribution alliances, resources, or regulatory action. The converse can also be true.

The design of an interactive system can have any and perhaps several of invention, engineering, and innovation success, but methods that produce engineering success for Settler Systems, usability testing, for example, are not themselves sufficient for producing invention success for Pioneer Systems.

To illuminate the role of methods in successful system design, we noted that the process of invention flows through several phases. We simplified the phases down to three principal ones: problem identification, artifact building, and evaluation. We used these phases to organize the methods used to build the systems under analysis. Most systems used several methods. We noted particularly the wide use of the *Cut and Try* method for iterating designs and the *Steal and Modify* method for harvesting experience built up earlier in the food chain of ideas.

Beyond the roles they support, we suggested methods could be classified along four dimensions. First is whether the method is analytic or synthetic. Second is the degree of idealization of design context, and third is the degree of idealization in the design representation. These latter two dimensions reflect the tension between the richness of direct contact with a design situation, on the one hand, versus, on the other hand, the analytical power that arises by working with idealized abstractions. A related tension is between using better, but costlier, methods versus less good, but cheaper, ones. These tensions were addressed in the designs under examination by using combinations of methods differing in their tradeoffs. The fourth dimension of method classification is what the method is trying to accomplish. The desired accomplishments can be arranged as design mileposts. It is really these mileposts that are the goal of the methods. There are many alternative methods that can be used to achieve the same milepost, but there are not alternative mileposts.

Let us now come back to our original problem of identifying the methods that produced successful HCI systems. As we have seen, we cannot simply peer into systems that are successful in their markets or missions and hope to derive directly the methods that made them so—the original premise of this book. The critical seeds of success were often sown long ago in a Pioneer predecessor system and may even, in some cases, form tacit or embedded art from which the current system was built. Only by examining the larger context of technological evolution and mission engagement can we see through to the lessons we seek to learn. In summary, the lessons might be stated:

If you are interested in just a single point design, exploit the food chain of ideas, and employ established methods to accomplish the design mileposts. Some mileposts may be assumed, but this always increases risk. Analyze the design in terms of the four types of merit underlying innovation success in order to identify vulnerabilities.

If you are a company or funding agency taking the long view, fund research in Pioneer Systems to build up the food chain of ideas.

At any rate, adopt a combination of methods in order to diversify risks, minimize cost, and accumulate as much insight into the design as practical.

A few caveats about the limitations of our analysis: The analysis in this paper has been confined to methods in the systems studied. Of necessity, a certain amount of interpretation is involved in extracting and assigning methods, but I believe that we are still able to use this intrinsically noisy data to discover the larger patterns of methods for successful systems. I believe these larger patterns would still hold, even in the face of some particular errors of interpretation for a particular system. Further, there are other methods in use that did not happen to occur visibly in these systems. I believe that these could largely be fitted into the patterns described, but it would be an interesting exercise to see if other patterns emerged as well.

We have discussed and rated HCI dialogue techniques as the basic inventions units of HCI. We could do the same for methods themselves although this would be far harder. There is a food chain of ideas in methods just as there is for systems; processes can be key innovations just as much as things. An analysis of this sort would be required to do full justice to the Atwood, Gray, and John paper on CPM-GOMS instead of focusing on the system for which the method was used, as we have had to do here.

Finally, a word about timing and how it affects success. Good engineering of Settler Systems is always relevant, but the timing of Pioneer Systems is more complex. Technologies proceed by punctuated evolution: They go through relatively short periods of rapid change followed by long periods of stability. The impact of Pioneering systems, therefore, depends, in part, on timing. At certain periods, new ideas (such as scroll bars on windows) slip easily into the new technology, but later superior ideas find it difficult to dislodge the incumbent. Methods selected for design must always be sensitive to their ecological context and tread skillfully between new species and established competitors.

Notes

1. John Whiteside presented this work at the workshop, but the paper is not included in this volume. See Whiteside (1993).

2. Smalltalk was not commercially available, so it could not have been a commercial success during the period referred to.

3. To get the fullest possible picture of the design process for FreeStyle, in addition to the paper in this section, I have drawn on Francik and Akagi (1989), Francik et al. (1991), and Levine and Ehrlich (1991).

4. To get the fullest possible picture of the design process for Star, in addition to the paper in this section, I have drawn on Bewley et al. (1983), Smith et al. (1982), Verplank, (1988), Johnson et al. (1989), a lengthy telephone interview with Charles Irby, the head of the design team, and my own recollections.

5. The Artifact Construction and Evaluation lists derive from discussions with, and are the inspiration of Rick Beach. They partially reflect PARC experience in commercial printer development. The scale items "Wizard can use," "Friends of Wizard can use," "People who don't even know the Wizard can use" are traditional PARC measures of research system maturity, invented by Ed McCreight.

References

Apple Computer (1987). *HyperCard User's Guide.* Cupertino, CA: Apple Computer.

Bewley, W. L., Roberts, T. L., Schroit, D., and Verplank, W. L. (1983). Human factors testing in the design of Xerox's 8010 Star office workstation. *Proceedings of the ACM Conference on Human Factors in Computing Systems,* 72–77.

Bolt, R. A. (1984). *The Human Interface.* Belmont, CA: Lifetime Learning Publications.

Burgleman, R. A. and Maidique, M. A. (1988). *Strategic Management and Technology of Innovation.* Homewood, IL: Irwin.

Card, S. K. (this volume). Pioneers and settlers: Methods used in successful user interface design.

Card, S. K., Mackinlay, J. D., and Robertson, G. G. (1991). A morphological analysis of the design space of input devices. *ACM Transactions on Information Systems* 9 (April 2), 99–122.

Card, S. K., Moran, T. P., and Newell, A. (1983). *The Psychology of Human-Computer Interaction.* Hillsdale, NJ: Lawrence Erlbaum.

Carr, R. and Shafer, D. (1991). *The Power of PenPoint.* Reading, MA: Addison-Wesley.

Cooper, G. E. and Harper, R. P., Jr. (1969). The use of pilot rating in the evaluation of aircraft handling qualities (AGARD-597). Paris, France: Advisory Group for Aerospace Research and Development. (DTIC No. AD689722).

Dahl, O.-J. and Nygaard, K. (1966). SIMULA—An Algol-based simulation language. *Communications of the ACM* 9(9), 671–678.

Engelbart, D. C. and English, W. K. (1968). A research center for augmenting human intellect. *AFIPS Proceedings of the Fall Joint Computer Conference* (Vol. 330), 395–410.

Francik, E. and Akagi, K. (1989). Designing a computer pencil and tablet for handwriting. In *Proceedings of the 33rd Human Factors Society Annual Meeting* (Denver, October 16–20). Santa Monica, CA: The Human Factors Society, 445–449.

Francik, E., Rudman, S. E., Cooper, D., and Levine, S. (1991). Putting innovation to work: Adoption strategies for multimedia communication systems. *Communications of the ACM* 34(12) (December), 52–63.

Fisher, S. (1989). The AMES Virtual Environment Workstation (VIEW). *SIGGRAPH '89*. Course #29 Notes.

Furness, T. A. (1986). The super cockpit and its human factors challenges. *Proceedings of the Human Factors Society, 30th Annual Meeting.* Santa Monica, CA: The Human Factors Society, 48–52.

Gould, J. D., Boies, S. J., Levy, S., Richards, J. T., and Schoonard, J. (1987). The 1984 Olympic Message System—A test of behavioral principles of system design. *Communications of the ACM* 30(9) (September), 758–769.

Herot, C. F. (1980). Spatial management of data. *ACM Transactions on Database Systems* 5 (December 4), 493–514.

Hughes, T. P. (1983). *Networks of Power, Electrification in Western Society, 1880–1930.* Baltimore, MD: The Johns Hopkins University Press.

Johnson, J., Roberts, T. L., Verplank, W., Smith, D. C., Irby, C., Beard, M., and Mackey, K. (1989). The Xerox Star: A retrospective. *IEEE Computer* 22 (September 9), 11–26.

Kaare, C. (1983). *The Unix Operating System.* New York: John Wiley & Sons.

Kay, A. C. (1977). Microelectronics and the personal computer. *Scientific American* 237(3) (September).

Kay, A. C. and Goldberg, A. (1977). Personal dynamic media. *IEEE Computer* 10 (March 3).

Lampson, B. W., ed. (1976). *Alto User's Handbook.* Palo Alto, CA: Xerox Palo Alto Research Center.

Lampson, B. W. (1988). Personal distributed computing: The Alto and Ethernet software. In A. Goldberg (ed.), *A History of Personal Workstations.* New York: ACM Press.

Levine, S. R. and Ehrlich, S. F. (1991). The FreeStyle system: A design perspective. In A. Klinger (ed.), *Human-Machine Interactive Systems.* New York: Plenum Press.

Miller, R., Miller, R., and Lovick, S. (1989). Cosmic Osmo. Computer program for Macintosh. Cyan Productions and Activision.

Newell, A. (1992). Unified theories of cognition and the role of Soar. In J. A. Michon and A. Akyurek (eds.), *Soar: A Cognitive Architecture in Perspective.* Dordrecht, The Netherlands: Kluwer Academic Publishers.

Newman, W. and Sproull, R. (1973). *Principles of Interactive Computer Graphics.* New York: McGraw-Hill.

Perry, T. S. and Voelcker, J. (1989). Of mice and menus: Designing the user-friendly interface. *IEEE Spectrum* (September) 46–51.

Restnikoff, H. L. (1989). *The Illusion of Reality.* New York: Springer-Verlag.

Robertson, G., Newell, A., and Ramakrishna, K. (1981). The ZOG approach to man-machine communication. *International Journal of Man-Machine Studies* 14(4) (May), 461–488.

Scheifler, R. W., Gettys, J., and Newman, R. (1988). *X Window System.* Bedford, MA: Digital Press.

SIGGRAPH (1990). Computer Graphics Achievement Award: Richard Shoup and Alvey Ray Smith. *Computer Graphics* 24 (August 4), 17–18.

Smith, D. C. (1977). *Pygmalion: A Computer Program to Model and Stimulate Creative Thought.* Basel: Birkhäuser Verlag.

Smith, D. C., Irby, C. H., Kimball, R. B., Verplank, W. H., and Harselm, E. F. (1982). Designing the Star user interface. *Byte* 7(4), 242–282.

Stallman, R. (1987). *GNU Emacs Manual, Sixth Edition, Version 18.* Cambridge, MA: Free Software Foundation.

Sutherland, I. E. (1963). *Sketchpad: A Man-Machine Graphical Communication System.* Ph.D. thesis, MIT. Reprinted by Garland Publishing, Inc., New York, 1980.

Tesler, Larry (1981). The Smalltalk environment. *Byte* (August).

Verplank, W. (1988). Designing graphical user interfaces. Tutorial notes, *ACM CHI '88 Conference on Human Factors of Computing Systems,* Washington, D.C.

White, G. R. and Graham, M. B. W. (1978). How to spot a technological winner. *Harvard Business Review* (March–April), 146–152.

Whiteside, John. (1993). The phoenix agenda: Power to transform your workplace. Essex Junction, VT: Omneo, xvi, 318p.: ill.; 24 cm.

Williams, G. (1983). The Lisa computer system. *Byte* 8 (February 2), 33–50.

Emerging Methods

Improving User Interfaces and Application Productivity by Using the ITS Application Development Environment

John D. Gould, Jacob Ukelson, Stephen J. Boies

IBM Research Center

ABSTRACT

This paper describes ITS, an innovative approach to application development (including user interface development), and summarizes case studies carried out by developers who have used ITS to develop real applications and user interfaces. Unlike with most tools, developers use ITS to create both user interface prototypes and complete applications. The results of these studies demonstrate that using ITS leads to dramatic improvements in application development productivity and suggest that ITS also leads to innovative user interfaces.

Introduction

User Interfaces

Designing and implementing a user interface is today half the work in developing an application (Myers and Rosson, 1992). It is hard to make good user interfaces. Look around. How many famous user interfaces or user interface designers can you name? Creating good user interfaces requires iterative design. Iterative design is, believe it or not, still not widely practiced. This past month, one developer asked me to evaluate informally his nearly completed important new user interface for large computer system operators. I asked him what the intended users thought of it so far. He had not shown it to any intended users. It is one screen. I told him the price of my helping him would be that he must get *one* (for starters anyway) intended user to join us. He has not done this yet. Yet, in his mind, he was very conscious of good usability. That's why he called. In a second example, a responsible person in a medium-size development organization explained to me with great conviction that they do all of their usability testing *before* they make their application so that it is guaranteed to be right and does not require user testing or iterative design later. When challenged, he defended this position with pride— even though he was simultaneously working with us on another effort where, by contrast, we would show him weekly what we were creating, he would critique it, we would make a bunch of changes, and then repeat the cycle. Iterative design requires tools and a work organization to facilitate it, and the motivation to do it.

The workstations that people use today differ greatly from one another. There are different operating systems (for example, OS/2, AIX), different user interface styles (for example, Macintosh, Motif, CUA), different graphic standards (for example, BGA, VGA), and different system response times. This variety presents great challenges to designers who want to make applications that run on a variety of workstations. A technical approach is needed that allows the same application to work in all these workstations.

There are powerful user preferences for the various user interface styles. Vendors have them, and customers have them. There are few new human-computer interaction techniques. Today, there is much more prototyping than there was a decade ago. What is now needed are tools and a development environment that allow these prototypes to evolve into real applications.

User interface styles are hard to maintain. Most people find it very difficult or impossible to modernize the user interface of an existing application, for example, add move and drag. What is needed is a way to easily update user interface styles—not just in a book, but in real applications.

Today, there are many expensive "usability labs." They contain serious data logging facilities, studio-quality video and audio recording, comfortable surroundings, one-way mirrors, and so on. In contrast to these, the usability labs of the next decade should be hallways and storefronts and cafeterias, where what is being made for people is seen and tried by them in ways that they want to use it. Better yet, don't just *show it* in the hallway, also *make it* in the hallway, and get suggestions early on. This has proved to be a good methodology (Gould et al., 1987).

Applications

The key problems in application development today center on productivity:

1. There is a need to make applications that increase the productivity of end users. This implies both an easy-to-use user interface style and a user interface that reveals powerful, appropriate content functions in each application.

2. There is a need to increase the productivity of development organizations making these applications.

3. Applications must be made in a way that, once in use, they are much easier to change and update, thus increasing the productivity of maintenance organizations.

This paper identifies the main factors affecting application development productivity; then describes ITS; then summarizes several case studies of developers using ITS to implement serious applications, with emphasis on the effects of ITS on development productivity and on creating innovative user interfaces. The results of these case studies demonstrate that ITS (1) greatly enhances application development productivity and (2) provides a mechanism for creating applications that can lead to improved end-user productivity and that of their work organizations.

Productivity in Application Development

Figure 1, based in part on studies by Curtis, Krasner, and Iscoe (1988) and Jones (1986), summarizes the main factors impairing development productivity. How ITS responds to these factors is described in Gould, Ukelson, and Boies (1991).

Brief Description of ITS

ITS is a research project started in May 1987. The key points of the ITS approach (described, for example, in Wiecha et al., 1990) are summarized in Figure 2.

FIGURE 1   **Problems in the Application Development Process**

Mainly Affecting Developers Themselves

- Huge individual differences in talent
- Communication and coordination breakdowns
- Fluctuating and conflicting requirements
- Existing tools are limited:
  Produce limited ranges of applications
  User interfaces do not benefit from code reuse
  Prototypes do not evolve into final application
  Applications lack system generality:
    Run in only one user interface style
    Run on only one operating system
    Run in only one graphic standard (resolution, display size)

Mainly Affecting End Users and Their Organizations

- Thin spread of application domain knowledge
- Hard to do iterative design
- Hard to do usability testing

Mainly Affecting Application Maintenance

- Hard to change the content of applications
- Hard to change the user interface styles of existing applications

Four User Interface Blocks

With ITS, application ("content") experts structure their applications in terms of form, choice, list, and info blocks. Style experts write rules about how these blocks will be rendered on an end-user's screen under various circumstances. These two groups can work in parallel and independently.

Separation of Content and User Interface Style

By "user interface style," we mean the collection of human-computer interaction techniques, including how they look, work, and feel, that render the substance (content) of an application on an end-user's screen. Apple's Macintosh, OSF's Motif, and IBM's CUA are examples of user interface styles. By "application content," we mean the substance of an application, that is, the elements that distinguish an automobile configurator application from a spelling verification application from a visualization application. Most user interface code

FIGURE 2   **Key Features of ITS**

- Four user interface blocks
- Separation of content and user interface style
- Rule-based, computer-executable styles
- Four work roles and four work products
- Prototyping and code reuse

has to do with style. By separating the user interface style and content, the need to write style code for each application can be eliminated.

With ITS, once an appropriate user interface style is developed, the content of many different applications can run in it (see CUA case study). This has the advantages of greatly reducing the amount of new work through style reuse, increasing the impact of the best styles, and creating more usable applications. This approach leads to consistent user interfaces and should facilitate users learning later releases of existing applications or new applications.

Conversely, with ITS, the same content application can run in several different styles (see spreadsheet package case study). This has the advantage of greatly reducing the amount of new work (the same excellent student registration application, for example, could run in one style at one university, a different style at a second university, and a different style at the government's customs and immigration bureau). It also provides the potential for leveraging the applications with insightful functions that lead to enhanced productivity for end users and their organizations.

With ITS, the same application—content and style—can run on several different operating systems (ITS has so far run on DOS, OS/2, Windows, and AIX), on several different video standards, and with several different display sizes (see Totals case study). This has the advantages of economy of scale, reduces the need to do an application over for each operating system, and makes the best work available to a larger number of individuals and organizations.

In ITS, the style of an application is separate from the content of an application, similar to that in presentation systems, for example, IBM Presentation Manager, Microsoft Windows, Mac Toolkit (Figure 3a). Unlike presentation systems, however, ITS does not limit applications (content) to a single fixed style. Further, in ITS the user interface (both the style and the content of it) is separate from the functions of application (content), similar to that in User Interface Management Systems (UIMS) (Figure 3b). Unlike UIMS, however, ITS can enforce user interface consistency from application to

FIGURE 3

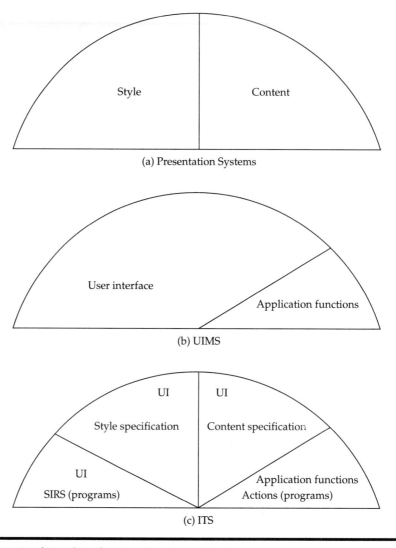

(a) Presentation Systems

(b) UIMS

(c) ITS

Schematic relationship of various development tools.

application. ITS (Figure 3c) has both of these splits just mentioned. Further, with ITS, human-computer interface styles are rule based and can be designed either to be general purpose and adequately handle a variety of applications, like IBM's CUA-2 style (see the CUA case study), or to be more specific and better handle certain types of specific applications (see the Expo'92 case study).

Rule-Based, Computer-Executable Styles

Today, developers have great difficulty locating, reading, understanding, recalling, and applying the massive amounts of required detail contained in user interface guidelines books. With ITS, reliance on guidelines books can be eliminated. Style rules are instantiated in computer executable rules rather than in textbooks. A new application is *automatically* shown in one or more styles. This allows very rapid prototyping, typically within an hour for the first few windows. Styles are not tuned to a specific application but contain general, executable rules controlled by a set of parameters. Each style has a different set of rules that (1) map content into human-computer interaction techniques and (2) determine the details of each interaction technique. Figure 4 shows that a style could render the same set of choices that lets users select Freshman, Sophomore, Junior, or Senior as a menu bar, a standard menu, or a half-pie menu. Within the same application, this choice block might be rendered one way in one context and another way in another context.

Four Work Roles and Four Work Products

With ITS, there are four work roles, and each produces a different work product.

FIGURE 4

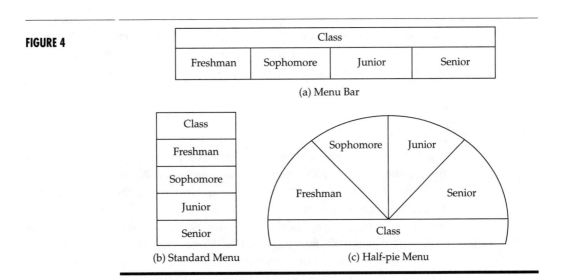

Three renditions of the same set of choices.

Content experts (or "domain experts" in Curtis, Krasner, and Iscoe, 1988) are assumed to understand the requirements of an application. Examples would be key managers, owners, analysts, requirements people, planners, even usability people. With ITS, content experts can be full-term, actively participating partners in the development process. They use a tag language (see Wiecha, et al., 1990) to write executable content specification files by structuring the content of their application in terms of choice, form, list, and info blocks, and by grouping these blocks into frames. Within these blocks, content experts place attributes that specify the text messages shown to users, flow of control, application semantics (style guidance), and how the user interface content will be bound to the application program. Content experts must know how to use an editor of their choice.

Content programmers are assumed to be skilled programmers. They write small C-language programs, called Actions, which implement backend functions and make the applications work, for example, get records from a database. We generally expect that, because of differing expertise, different individuals will carry out the work of content experts and content programmers.

Style designers are assumed to be skilled at designing user interfaces. They write style specifications files (presently using a tag language) that contain (1) all the human-computer interaction techniques that are used in a particular style and (2) the rules for determining how each content block will be rendered, that is, which interaction technique will be used to render each content block. We expect that there will be far fewer style designers than content designers.

Style programmers are assumed to be skilled programmers. Their job is similar to that of content programmers, except that they work on the style side. They write general-purpose C-language programs, called style implementation routines (SIRs), that make interaction techniques work, for example, make a list actually scroll when a user clicks on a scroll bar.

Prototyping and Code Reuse

The ITS development environment supports very rapid prototyping in which the very beginnings of an application, say, after a few hours work, automatically and immediately work in one or more styles because these styles are rule based. Of significance, unlike most prototyping tools, an ITS prototype evolves into the final application. There is no throw-away prototype. The ITS development environment greatly facilitates code reuse, which is responsible for much of the productivity enhancements described in the case studies that follow.

Case Studies of Productivity of Developers Using ITS

In this section, we describe six case studies of developers using ITS to implement significant work (summarized in Figure 5). In each study, members of the ITS project, sometimes working with others, used IBM PS/2 workstations with ITS running under OS/2. Each project was started to demonstrate the feasibility of the ITS approach in a new application domain. These studies were not carried out as detached, arm's-length, objective evaluations of ITS. Rather, they represent necessary hill-climbing research and development work, and reflect our desire to work with others and let the resulting feedback provide directions for the further development of ITS. Thus, the conclusions arrived at are open to more interpretations than are the results of a series of good laboratory experiments.

Measuring productivity is hard (see, for example, Jones, 1986). We use four measures here:

- Time to complete an application, measured in person-weeks.
- Comments of developers.
- Quality of the work. To date, we can judge this only by the informal judgments of informed developers and users.
- Quality of the work regarding subsequent application maintenance. To date, we judge this by comments of informed management and developers and by comments of people who maintain the work.

Continental Insurance Underwriting Application

At the end of 1989, Continental Insurance was trying to move their applications toward a workstation environment—after years of mainframe experience. Their application maintenance was very costly, and they needed to respond quicker (that is, be able to modify existing computer programs) to changes in state and federal insurance regulations and laws. They had heard about ITS and became interested in carrying out a joint study. IBM's ITS group, as a main part of their ITS research strategy, wanted, early on, to use the development environment they were making to do real applications and learn from this experience.

It was agreed that Continental would use ITS to implement the content of an important insurance industry application, and IBM would use ITS to implement the user interface style, as specified by Continental. The initial issues centered on feasibility:

FIGURE 5   **Summary of Key Points from Several Case Studies of Developers Using ITS**

IBM-CONTINENTAL INSURANCE UNDERWRITING APPLICATION

- Field study jointly carried out by Continental Insurance and IBM ITS group
- Results compared with ongoing traditional Continental development method
- ITS led to 25 times productivity improvement, higher quality user interface, anticipated lower maintenance

---

GENERAL-PURPOSE SPREADSHEET PACKAGE

- Lab study with college work-study student as participant
- With ITS, created much of a general-purpose spreadsheet package in 2 person-months
- Successfully separated content and style
- Implemented application in one style; used it in another style

---

IBM CUA USER INTERFACE STYLE

- Two ITS group members kept a diary as they used ITS to implement IBM's CUA user interface style
- Implemented all 14 CUA interaction techniques and 9 others in 7 person-weeks
- This style is reusable, and several ITS applications now use it

---

EXPO'92 MULTIMEDIA VISITOR SERVICES APPLICATIONS

- World's Fair in Seville, Spain, attended by 42 million visitors
- International development team used ITS to make integrated set of advanced multimedia applications for visitors to use
- Thirty-three kiosk buildings dedicated to, and networked for, these applications
- This was the largest, most diverse multimedia system ever developed and demonstrated the value of ITS for making such applications
- Data-logged results showed 5–15 million visitors used these multimedia applications

---

TIME AND ATTENDANCE RECORDING APPLICATION

- Three-site development effort using ITS to make a workstation version of existing mainframe time and attendance recording system
- ITS workstation version to run with same backend code as mainframe version uses
- Workstation version runs on both OS/2 and AIX, and in multiple graphic standards
- Project ultimately terminated because customer eliminated need for this application

---

ILLINOIS DEPARTMENT OF EMPLOYMENT SECURITY

- 600,000 unemployed people in Illinois and 1 million unemployment claims filed annually
- ITS group made highly graphic, "sit down and use" touch-screen user interface
- Citizens can now directly file their unemployment claims and search jobs databases instead of exclusively interacting with employment bureau staff workers
- Application ties into several existing very large government databases
- Additional huge databases used to facilitate novel human–computer interaction techniques
- Presently in use at a large Ilinois state employment office

---

- Could IBM use ITS to make a user interface style that:
  Looked like standard insurance industry paper (Acord) forms?
  Worked according to Continental's 100-page user interface guidelines?
  Would have generality, that is, would work with other, not yet defined, content applications?

- Could Continental programmers, all of whom programmed in Cobol only, learn ITS, C, OS/2, and use these to make worthy workstation applications?

- Could Continental programmers subsequently maintain ITS-implemented applications?

The results showed that the work was completed in 12 person-months, including Continental's learning time. Figure 6 shows one screen. At the time of this study, this same Continental application was being implemented with Continental's traditional development approach. A comparison showed that (1) ITS led to a huge productivity gain in time to complete the work (25 times faster); (2) Continental Insurance data processing management judged the ITS-implemented user interface to be of higher quality than that of the other implementation; and (3) Continental Insurance data processing management judged the ITS-implemented version to be much easier to maintain than their traditional Cobol approach. (See Boies et al., 1991, for a report of this work.)

General-Purpose Spreadsheet Package

The ITS group had made two strong claims that had not been fully demonstrated at the time of this study: (1) the content and the style of (almost) any

FIGURE 6

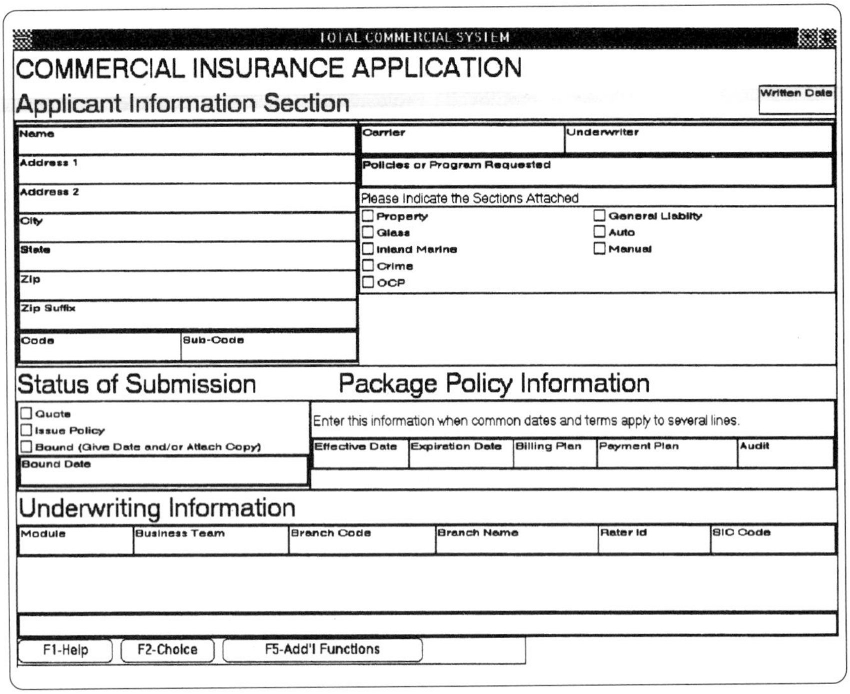

An ITS-implemented user interface screen in Continental's underwriting application. This is the top one-third of one page of the standard insurance industry paper Acord form. *Picture courtesy of Paul Matchen and Dale Georg.*

application can be separated, and (2) an application can be developed in one style and then subsequently run in another style. This study addressed both of these issues. A general-purpose spreadsheet package was chosen to be implemented because it (1) has well-known and used functions; (2) has well-known user interface characteristics; (3) seemed challenging, to some people, to determine what was content and what was style; and (4) emphasized, more than previous applications implemented in ITS, end-user "programming," end-user customization, and calculating. A further consideration was that the work-study student who did the work was motivated to implement a spreadsheet package. This student already knew ITS and did the work of content expert and content programmer. He worked 3 days per week throughout the summer (2 person-months).

The results showed that the participant successfully used ITS to implement most functions in a general-purpose spreadsheet package in these 2

FIGURE 7

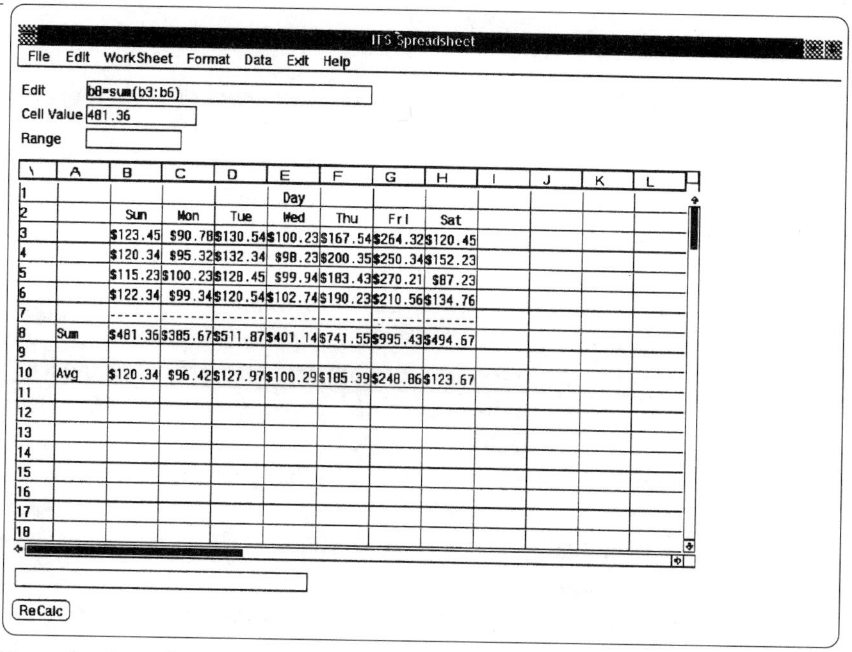

Example of small spreadsheet being implemented with the general-purpose spreadsheet package developed in this study. The participant's work was to create the general-purpose spreadsheet package. This figure shows an end user using the ITS-implemented spreadsheet package to make a small financial spreadsheet of her own. *Picture courtesy of Paul Matchen and Dale Georg.*

person-months. Figure 7 shows an example spreadsheet created with the participant's general-purpose spreadsheet package. The participant achieved this great productivity through code reuse and having the prototype, which he quickly created (and which evolved into the final application), identify the actions that he needed to write. This productivity presumably compares favorably to that using other development approaches. The participant successfully separated content and user interface style. This work also demonstrated that an application can be implemented in one style and then run in another. The participant implemented his spreadsheet package using the style written for Continental Insurance; afterward, with about a day's work, he ran his application in a new style (not available when he developed his application and therefore unknown to him). (See Sitnik, Gould, and Ukelson [1991] for a report of this study.)

IBM CUA User Interface Style

This study (Ukelson et al., 1991) centered on style only. The goal was to use ITS to implement IBM's CUA-1989 style (IBM, 1989) the then current IBM style, together with enough additional interaction techniques so that a wide variety of applications could run in it. Two ITS group members, one with a Ph.D. in computer science and the other with a Ph.D. in psychology, did this work. They kept a diary of what they did and how long it took.

The results showed that they implemented the 14 CUA interaction techniques and 9 additional interaction techniques in 7 person-weeks (Figures 8 and 9.) This productivity compares favorably with the length of time it takes to implement the interaction techniques for *any one* CUA-conforming application. However, this completed style work can be, and has since been, reused by many applications, thus eliminating about half the work that would otherwise have to have been done in each of them. These applications include a multilanguage spelling verifier (Marivel Jaramillo), a multimedia story-producer (Steve Boies), a national language translation application (Sharon Greene), a time and attendance recording system (described later), backend

FIGURE 8

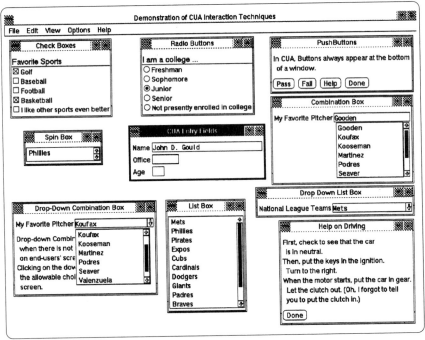

Examples of CUA interaction techniques made by the two participants. *Picture courtesy of Paul Matchen and Dale Georg.*

FIGURE 9

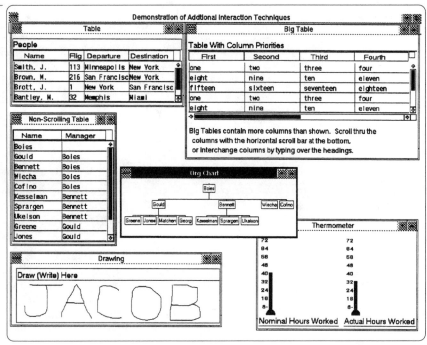

Examples of additional interaction techniques made by the two participants. *Picture courtesy of Paul Matchen and Dale Georg.*

services for the Expo'92 system (described next), a restaurant reservation system (Jacob Ukelson), and a television satellite application (Jeff Kelley).

Expo'92 Multimedia Visitor Services Applications

Background

The results of the first two studies, and a variety of other experiences in working with potential users of ITS, demonstrated that the ITS approach is successful with text-based, transaction-oriented applications and with so-called graphic applications like spreadsheet packages. Some observers doubted whether the ITS approach would work for very advanced, highly and quickly interactive, multimedia applications with thousands of images and high-quality audio. They felt that the separation between content and style would be less clear. We wanted to extend ITS in this direction. In addition, we

FIGURE 10

A user interface screen for Expo'92.

wanted to create an application in ITS that would be widely used. Thus, several members of the ITS group decided to work jointly with IBM Spain to create the highly pictorial Visitor Information Services applications for Expo'92. Expo'92 was the World's Fair held in Seville, Spain; average daily attendance was 250,000 guests. There were 33 kiosk buildings, made exclusively to house IBM Visitor Information Services, each containing seven high-resolution touch-screen systems for visitors to use.

The Expo'92 Visitor Information Services (Figure 10) offered information and services to an estimated 42 million visitors from April through October 1992. This multimedia "walk-up-and-use" system contained an integrated set of applications, including (1) several thousand high-resolution pictures and maps with directions for navigating around the two-square-kilometer site; (2) interactive, pictorial stories about participating countries and organizations; and (3) up-to-the-minute schedules of events. In addition, the system provided visitors with services beyond those traditionally found in information kiosks, including (1) person-to-person and group electronic messaging, (2) automated restaurant reservations, (3) public opinion polling,

(4) locators for lost family members, and (5) a variety of standalone and networked games for use during off-peak hours. (See Wiecha, et al., 1990, for more details.)

Besides the sheer magnitude of this highly visible project, developing an interactive user interface style for Expo'92 was a good test for the ITS approach because the application possessed several significant challenges. The application had to run in several national languages, including Spanish and English. The kiosks had to be walk-up-and-use; most visitors were inexperienced at using computers. To be visually attractive, the kiosk buildings and the applications had to contain world-class graphic design quality and operate with multiple types of media: high-quality text, graphics, and images.

The developers, too, posed challenges. This was the largest development team yet using ITS. About seven people from the American IBM ITS group, based in New York, worked full time and another five worked part time for two years, together with several people from IBM Spain, based in Seville, to use ITS to implement this original application. Unlike the other case studies in which the design goals (specifications) were relatively clear at the start, this work is based entirely on original design. Thus, the iterative design aspects of ITS were fully tested.

Results and Conclusions

Most of the functions were prototyped at least 12 months in advance of the opening of Expo'92. From the outset, working prototypes (in ITS, this means the entire application as it exists at the moment) were quickly created and regularly changed. Prototypes, working in Spanish and English, were placed in the hallway of IBM Research and at the Visitor Center at the Expo'92 construction site, and demonstrated at the August 1991 meeting of SIGGRAPH in Las Vegas. These prototypes attracted passersby to use them, thus providing the development team with useful feedback. Several notebooks of volunteered comments were obtained.

These prototypes were technically exciting enough to impress computer scientists that this application advanced the state of the art of multimedia applications. They were attractive enough to excite management support for this expensive project. They were satisfying to the ITS group in that the same tools were used to build this leading-edge multimedia application as were used to build the text-based applications described earlier. Running prototypes of the Expo application excited so much interest among visitors to the site and the popular press (for example, in 1991, it was referred to in *Business Week, Scientific American,* and on the ABC television show "Good Morning

America"), that it often obscured the motivation for doing the work—to improve the ITS approach.

The main result showed that with ITS as the development tool, this international team created the largest, most diverse multimedia application ever developed, one that was used by 5–15 million people with no training, and one that many users raved about.

This was a large system, with 230 networked guest stations, the largest LAN in Europe, a 2,000-square-foot system control center (which itself was often toured by visiting data processing people), and remote monitoring and broadcasting. The system was updated throughout the fair, as requests for new functions were made. Usage statistics were automatically data-logged. Most of the services ("functions") required guests to insert their tickets into the ticket-reader associated with a guest station. A ticket contained information about that guest, including which other tickets were issued with that one. This facilitated, for example, sending messages to other group members. Over the six months of Expo'92, five million log-ons to the system were recorded. One log-on typically involved about three people. That is, a group of about three people typically used the system at once, with two people looking on and collaborating, for example, on a group picture, a multimedia message, a restaurant reservation, or a painting. Thus, with these three corrections, we assume 5–15 million guests were actually involved with using the system, or between one-ninth and one-third of the World's Fair 42 million visitors.

Figure 11 presents the highlights of a typical week, based on data-logged values. The entire system was nearly always available during the 19-hour, 7-days-a-week fair. It is generally acknowledged that this was by far the most used multimedia application ever. The numbers are huge for a research project, for example, millions of users, billions of interactions throughout the fair. Each of the functions was heavily used, as can be seen in the figure. The guests really liked the system, and the public press rated it as one of the top attractions at Expo.

What about development productivity? Observers are more impressed that this integrated set of applications could be done at all, without regard to how much effort it took. About 25 person-years of work went into developing this application. Only a portion of this time was spent designing, implementing, and testing the Visitor Information Services application. Much, maybe most, of the time has been spent managing this international development effort, negotiating and developing the required infrastructure with the Expo authorities (buildings, power, servicing, signage, ticketing, and so on), and extending ITS in general ways that are now useful for future multimedia applications.

FIGURE 11   **Data-logged Results and Observed Reactions of Guests**

WEEKLY USAGE RESULTS

- 99.5% availability
- Highly interactive, common user interface
  92 million interactions/week
- Tied to personal identification
  231,000 log-ons/week
- Multilingual
  Spanish, English, French
- 100 interactive educational multimedia stories
  161,000 viewed/week
- Restaurant reservations
  Enhanced restaurant revenue
- Voice and picture messaging
  63,000 received/week; more sent
- Creative painting
  63,000 saved/week; many more made
- Take your picture
  126,000 saved/week; many more made
- On-line news services
  560,000 stories read/week (second "most read" newspaper in Andalucia)
- Handled a million images with instantaneous response

GUEST REACTIONS

- Over the whole Expo, 5–15 million guests used it (no training)
- Had fun and did serious transactions
- Most-used multimedia application ever
- Guests did not realize they were using a computer
- Rated one of the most useful attractions at Expo'92

Time and Attendance Recording Application

The goal of this study was to make an ITS application that would run on various types of workstations, in a variety of graphic standards, and on more than one operating system (OS/2 and AIX). The results show that these technical goals were achieved but that the project as a whole was not successful.

In 1991, 128,000 IBMers used a mainframe application (called Totals) each week to record the hours that they worked, the reasons they were absent, local travel expenses, and related other business facts (Figure 12). Most found that they spent more time using this application than they did when they simply

FIGURE 12

```
╔═══════════════════════════════════════════════════════════════╗
║ ▬                    A-A-3270 Emulator                    ☐█║
║ CFTG000A                 TOTALS Attendance                      ║
║                        IBM Internal Use Only                    ║
║ ─────────────────────────────────────────────────────────────  ║
║ Name               Serial #    Week Ending  Dept-Sfx/Shft   START-STOP ║
║ D V GEORG           067367       04/24/92    533C/1S      08:30 AM 05:12 PM ║
║ Enter Full Week and/or Daily Attendance EXCEPTIONS below:    Schedule ID/Week# ║
║ Full Week IWS(Flex) Start Time    _  :  _   A                  A0/01 ║
║ Full Week Same Absence Code   __    Normal Meal Period  12:00 PM TO 12:42 PM ║
║                                                                 ║
║    CODE  START AM/PM   STOP  AM/PM   NS   ABS    REG   OT  HRS WORKED ║
║ SA  _    _ : _   _     _ : _   _     X    0.0    0.0   0.0    0.0 ║
║ SU  _    _ : _   _     _ : _   _     X    0.0    0.0   0.0    0.0 ║
║                                                                 ║
║ MO  _    08 : 30  A    05 : 12  P    _    0.0    8.0   0.0    8.0 ║
║ TU  NL   08 : 00  A    02 : 00  P    _    0.0    6.0   0.0    6.0 ║
║ WE  _    08 : 30  A    05 : 12  P    _    0.0    8.0   0.0    8.0 ║
║ TH  NL   08 : 00  A    02 : 00  P    _    0.0    6.0   0.0    6.0 ║
║ FR  _    08 : 30  A    05 : 12  P    _    0.0    8.0   0.0    8.0 ║
║ To proceed to sign time card, press PF10.                       ║
║                             Total Hours   0.0   36.0   0.0   36.0 ║
║                                                                 ║
║                                                                 ║
║ PF2  =CODES       PF3  =Exit TOTALS  PF5  =Erase     PF6  =Add'l Entries ║
║ PF9  =HELP        PF10 =Next Screen  PF12 =Return               ║
║ PA█A                                                            ║
╚═══════════════════════════════════════════════════════════════╝
```

Mainframe version of totals.

filled out paper time cards. The organization within IBM responsible for this application received pressure to provide a workstation version of it. We (two members of the ITS group) jumped (too enthusiastically as it turned out) at the chance to use ITS to create this workstation version. We were enthusiastic about this opportunity because (1) we felt that ITS-made applications could outperform workstation applications developed with the tools that the customer (responsible IBM organization) was planning to use, (2) we could make a superior user interface to what existed, (3) this was a good opportunity to have an ITS-made application used throughout IBM, and (4) the application would likely have commercial value outside IBM.

In an effort to create a workstation version and make it easier to use than what existed, a three-site IBM development effort began in September 1991. After some initial competition and much customer management discussion, ITS was chosen as the tool to implement the workstation version. Two members of the ITS group did this work. A second site, IBM Southbury, had the responsibility of reconfiguring the existing 200,000 lines of PL/1 code and rewriting these in C code so that both the new mainframe user interface and the new workstation user interface (which were very different) could be frontends to it. A third site, IBM Stormytown, had the responsibility for connecting workstations to this backend C code. Figure 13 summarizes the research issues for ITS.

The development of the workstation version started in the typical fashion

FIGURE 13   **Research Issues in Making Totals**

- Use ITS in a three-site development effort for this database application.
- Workstation version must run on multiple operating systems, machines, video standards.
- Maintenance must be done by non-ITS people.
- Development productivity with ITS to be compared with parallel development effort using Easel.
- ITS-made workstation application to work with same backend code as mainframe terminals use.
- Study tradeoffs of local storage versus host storage of users' data.
- Work with real requirements people.
- Make new workstation application as easy to use as paper time cards, that is, much easier to use than presently existing mainframe application.

of other ITS-made applications. A prototype was quickly created and shown to the customer's requirements people (Figure 14). They made many requests for changes. These changes were implemented. This process was repeated every couple of weeks for several iterations. These iterations helped us better learn the customer's requirements. It also helped the customer's requirements people, who showed no interest in using ITS themselves, realize that what they had been claiming to be their "requirements" was really a mixture of what they wanted and what the mainframe programmers felt that they could provide. The ITS-made prototype was put in the Research building lobby after five months. Research employees were historically the loudest critics of the existing system. Passersby provided valuable comments, many of which were incorporated. Many bugs were found and fixed. In the meantime, the customer dropped workstation development with other previously favored tools because they judged the ITS work to be proceeding much faster, the user interface to be superior, and any significant changes could be made more quickly.

Then there was a pause. The ITS-made user interface was completed for all five work roles (employees, supplemental employees, managers, coordinators, reviewers) and awaited completion of the backend work. Putting this differently, about half the work is in the user interface (Myers and Rosson, 1992). This half was done in ITS in at most a person-year. The other half took several times longer in this case. Eventually, the backend work was completed sufficiently for a test. Everything worked. But it worked slowly in accessing data for individual users. Response time was poor due to the way the database was eventually organized. We redid the user interface, eliminating function, to compensate for slow database interactions. The customer then

FIGURE 14

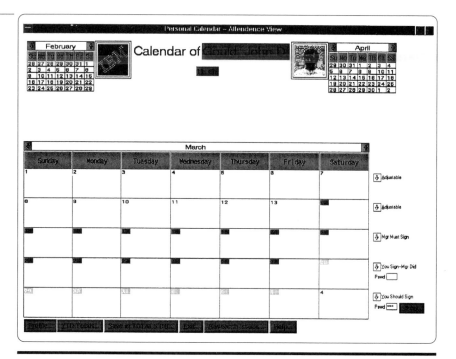

Workstation version of totals made with ITS.

took over the application to complete it. While this dragged on, IBM senior management decided that employees no longer needed to record their time and attendance. Hence there was no need for this application.

This project was a failure. In retrospect, the main reasons are not surprising:

1. We are much more serious about having very fast system response times than are many colleagues with whom we work; this was true here, as we discovered once the backend was implemented and testing could start.

2. Accessing existing older databases in acceptable response times is always difficult. It was particularly so here since the database work was also ongoing, and so little code was stable.

3. Our enthusiasm for this project outstripped the customer's commitment to it; hence, required backend work always favored the mainframe version over the workstation version.

4. We failed to monitor closely and control, where appropriate, the system architecture and database work.

Illinois Department of Employment Security

The goal of this study was to use ITS to develop, for pay, an important commercial application that would have clear displaceable costs and would be socially responsible. The Illinois Department of Employment Security (IDES) has the responsibilities for processing unemployment insurance claims and providing job services to employers and to potential employees. They asked the ITS group to provide a direct access system that would allow unemployment claimants to file their initial claims by themselves from a computer kiosk and to search for new jobs from computerized job listings. This request was based in part on their knowledge of the Expo'92 application. In a recent year, IDES processed over a million claims. Like many other public and private sector organizations, IDES is faced with the need to increase their level of client service while controlling, and perhaps even reducing, costs.

The ITS group used ITS to create a multilingual, "sit-down-and-use" touch-screen system that enables claimants to file unemployment insurance claims and search national job listings directly. This system, called Touch Illinois, is a line-of-business, transaction-based system that is expected to displace operating costs. In particular, this system for the first time allows people, with no training, to use highly interactive, graphic touch screens to enter data, fill out important forms, and submit the results in real time, with little or no help or intervention. As a new frontend to IDES's existing system mainframes, it extends and protects their investment in existing applications and databases.

Touch Illinois is currently in a pilot stage at a suburban Chicago IDES office (one of the busiest of the state's 62 employment offices). It features 25 direct access touch-screen kiosks for claimants and 20 networked stations for IDES staff that use touch screen, keyboard, and mouse. A majority of the claims being filed there are now done with this system. The staff stations are used to review the information entered by the claimants and to monitor the status of the networked system.

We believe that the key to the success so far of Touch Illinois rests on two factors: (1) an iteratively tested and improved user interface with very fast response times that enables novices to sit down and use the system successfully and (2) the reuse of much ITS code and functions developed for earlier ITS-made applications. Touch Illinois aids (and therefore speeds up) data entry by the claimants through the use of large computerized databases whenever possible. This includes aiding claimants in entering their first and last names, U.S. Postal Service addresses, Illinois employers, and any data that IDES has on claimants, such as their wage records. This not only makes the data entry quicker and easier, but also improves the quality of information that is entered.

Present Status of ITS

ITS is designed, implemented, and in use. Feasibility has been established, and productivity has been demonstrated. About 30 applications and serious prototypes have been implemented. Several user interface styles are available for application developers. Several applications use the same styles, and at least one application runs in more than one style. There is a continuous development of new ITS tools, such as tools for content experts (a story-maker), tools for content programmers (debugging aids), and database connections. Unlike many other projects that build tools for people to use, we use our own tools (ITS) to build new tools.

ITS is still a research project. ITS is not yet a commercially available product although more and more application developers are asking us for it. The limitations of ITS include *current ones* (not yet a product, insufficient documentation, using ITS to create a user interface style is hard for nonprogrammers to do), *perceived ones* (tag languages, not WYSIWYG), and *fundamental ones* (users must be computer literate, ITS is not for every application). These case studies eliminated several previously existing "current" limitations.

Summary

ITS is an innovative technical and organizational approach for developing computer applications, particularly novel user interfaces with good response times. To evaluate and improve ITS, several serious applications were developed using ITS, one involving millions of users. The results show that a variety of applications and user interfaces can be successfully developed with ITS, and most of them have proved to be valuable. This empirical approach to tool development is rare but important. It leads to improvements in the tool based upon what is actually needed for creating successful user interfaces rather than what tool designers might imagine would be useful.

Acknowledgments

Stephen Boies is the ITS chief designer (and senior manager). Jacob Ukelson is the ITS chief colleague. Their work gives John Gould something to write about in this paper.

References

Boies, S. J., Ukelson, J. U., Gould, J. D., Anderson, D., Babecki, M., and Clifford, J. (1991). Using ITS to Create an Insurance Industry Application—A Joint Case Study. *IBM Research Report, RC-16467.*

Continental Insurance Company (1989). *Standards and Guidelines for Screen Design.* Continental Data Center Standards Administration. Pub. No. CST017E.

Curtis, B., Krasner, H., and Iscoe, N. (1988). A field study of the software design process for large systems. *Communications of the ACM* 31, 1268–1287.

Diel, H., Duvenbeck, H., and Welsch, M. (1992). Overview of ScreenView. *IBM Development Laboratory Boeblingen–Technical Digest.*

Gould, J. D., Boies, S. J., Levy, S., Richards, J. T., and Schoonard, J. W. (1987). The 1984 Olympic Message System—A test of behavioral principles of system design. *Communications of the ACM* 30(9), 758–769.

Gould, J. D., Ukelson, J. P., and Boies, S. J. (1991). Improving Application Development Productivity by Using ITS. *IBM Research Report, RC-17496.*

IBM Corporation (1989). Systems Application Architecture: Common User Access. Basic Interface Design Guide, SC26-4583.

Jones, T. C. (1986). *Programming Productivity.* New York: McGraw-Hill.

Malcolm, J. (1992). WMS: Breaking the User Interface Coordinate Barrier. Personal communication, March 31.

Myers, B. A. and Rosson, M. B. (1992). Survey on User Interface Programming. *IBM Research Report, RC-17624.*

Sitnik, E., Gould, J. D., and Ukelson, J. P. (1991). Case Study: Using ITS to Make a General Purpose Spreadsheet Program. *IBM Research Report, RC-16696.*

Ukelson, J. P., Gould, J. D., Boies, S. J., and Wiecha, C. (1991). Case Study: Using ITS Style Tools to Implement IBM's CUA-2 User Interface Style. *Software Practice and Experience* 21(12), 1265–1288.

Ukelson, J. P., Gould, J. D., and Boies, S. J. (1992). User Navigation in Computer Applications. *IEEE Transactions on Software Engineering.*

Wiecha, C., Bennett, W., Boies, S., Gould, J., and Greene, S. (1990). ITS: A Tool for Rapidly Developing Interactive Applications. *ACM Transactions on Office Information Systems* 8, 204–236.

Lessons in Choosing Methods for Designing Complex Graphical User Interfaces

CARRIE RUDMAN, GEORGE ENGELBECK
US WEST Advanced Technologies

ABSTRACT

Five different methods were used to design the same complex graphical user interface for telephone company employees who provide telephone services to residential and small business customers. The methods included (1) on-site observation at the service centers, with current system review, (2) participatory prototyping, (3) decision tree interviews, (4) semantic net interviews, and (5) prototype-based role playing. We discovered unique requirements from particular methods that were not revealed by the other methods. On-site observation allowed us to understand the nature of the current business. Participatory prototyping allowed us to take advantage of the knowledge of the company employees. Semantic interviews allowed us to understand the nature of the complex data domain. Finally, decision tree interviews and prototype-based role playing allowed us to create a design that would support two-party negotiations. Each method revealed problem-solving strategies that were not obvious from any of the other methods but had important implications for design. We give concrete examples of the different types of information captured with each method, the differences in their influence on the ultimate design, the differences in the social roles they played, and their limitations. We conclude that methods must be tuned to the application domain and that multiple methods are needed to produce timely, effective designs.

Introduction

Our human factors engineering team was given the task of designing a graphical user interface for service representatives who carry out negotiations for telephone service with residential and small business customers over the telephone. The design involved identifying needed data elements and functions, grouping them into components, selecting Motif user interface components, and designing navigation techniques. The new X-windows-based user interface would replace several existing block mode user interfaces that were being used throughout US West's 14-state region.

We were aware of a wide range of vastly different approaches to user interface design to choose from (Karat, 1991). Some publications promote designing within the work context (Whiteside, Bennett, and Holtzblatt, 1988), some promote iterative prototyping with user participation (Bjerknes, Ehn, and Kyng, 1981; Whiteside, Bennett, and Holtzblatt, 1988), while others promote highly structured analysis of the users' representation of the domain before any design is attempted (Olson and Olson, 1990). Still others have promoted using evaluation methods like thinking aloud protocols to iteratively evolve user interface designs (for example, Mack, Lewis, and Carroll, 1983).

Over the course of a year, we selected a set of methods that progressively added to the design. We had access to service representatives who were using the current systems. We also had a Macintosh IIci, a two-page monitor, and the Supercard application for prototyping.

As you will see, our selection of methods was heavily influenced by the following characteristics of the design problem:

1. The design was replacing a pre-existing system, and users would need to transition to the new design. This meant that we would need to understand current operations and system structure in detail as well as uncover needs that were not addressed by the current system.

2. The design would be used by the employees of a single company. This meant that we had the opportunity to tune the design to this specific population and would therefore need to understand in detail the roles and responsibilities of the users.

3. The design would be used by highly trained employees. This meant that we needed to focus on expert use of the system in the context of the highly pressured interactions they had with customers rather than just on initial learnability.

4. The design would cover a large and complex data domain. This meant that we would have to use detailed analytical tools to assure that user needs analysis meshed with data design and migration requirements.

5. The design would need to support two-party negotiations. This meant that we would have to go beyond evaluation of human-computer interaction and investigate the impact of human-human interaction on the system design.

The juxtaposition of the five different design methods made it possible to observe the unique contributions and limitations of each within the confines of the domain of service negotiations. In this paper, we use concrete examples from that domain to illustrate the specific types of information collected with each method, the contributions made by each to the design, the limitations of the methods, and the social impact that the methods had on the design team. You will see that one of these methods alone was sufficient to produce an acceptable design. We discuss the importance of adapting the methods and combining them to meet the practical constraints of a project, based on the type of problem.

The goals for the system design were by no means limited to increasing the effectiveness of the service reps in supporting sales and service. Additional goals included (1) updating the communications network and its links to the databases to reduce installation and maintenance costs and (2) integrating a variety of separate databases to reduce data inconsistency and database maintenance costs. Perhaps the key user interface goal stated at the outset of the project was to allow the service reps to enter data during the dialog with a customer rather than after service negotiation was completed.

On-Site Observation with Current System Review

Our first approach to understanding the user interface design requirements was to visit the service centers. We observed negotiations for establishing, moving, or disconnecting telephone service. We expected that observation of employees using the existing computer systems, forms, and documentation and the expertise of colleagues would very quickly reveal priorities for the new design (Whiteside, Bennett, and Holtzblatt, 1988). Although we did quickly gather many requirements, these observations and interviews were not sufficient to build an acceptable design due to insufficient information about the data domain and goals of the procedures used and the factors that influenced them. We used the series of additional methods to progressively fill in the gaps.

Observation Approach

To determine the scope of the functions that the user interface would have to support, we first interviewed the service reps' supervisors about the reps' responsibilities and asked them to describe their frustrations with the current systems. We found that the reps receive six weeks of intensive training and take many months to become fully competent at the job. We then observed approximately 15 service reps from 4 different sites carrying out their normal activity for a period of 2 to 3 hours. The observations required a total of approximately two weeks for two human factors engineers. We sat down next to each rep at his or her workstation using headphones that allowed us to hear both sides of the conversation. Both videotape and still cameras were used during observation. The still cameras were particularly useful in capturing the detail of the screens and forms, including handwritten annotations. Following the observations, we interviewed the reps about the functions they carried out with each application on the system, the uses of the forms and documentation, and the support they received from other colleagues and departments (for example, getting help on product options from colleagues or information on installation schedules from the engineering department).

Physical Configuration

Even our observation of the physical workplace revealed that a new integrated system could streamline operations and replace manual functions. The service representatives' workstations included a desk with a terminal that displayed blocks of text in response to data queries, a multibutton telephone set, headphones, and a large amount of documentation. In the drawers of the desk were a wide range of forms as well as files for storing notes on orders in progress. Eliminating the need for forms and extensive documentation became a priority.

Operations Overview

We observed the general procedures the reps used in carrying out negotiations. Telephone calls were routed to the reps when they pressed a button indicating they were ready to receive a call. During the calls, the reps collected billing addresses, credit verification information, service addresses, desired services and installation dates, directory listing information, and a small amount of demographic information (such as type of business for small business customers). This could involve getting in and out of as many as five separate databases and referencing as many manuals.

During the conversations, many topics were brought up in different orders. Such topic switches contribute to cognitive overload (Bannon et al., 1983). The new user interface would have to be designed to keep up. In some cases, the topics involved considerable complexity. Business customers, for example, were likely to select a complex combination of services, including multiple telephone lines with multiple features (such as voice messaging), cross-line services (such as hunting between lines), and specialized billing arrangements. We anticipated screen real estate problems handling this level of complexity.

Complex or unusual orders required the rep to use the many volumes of documentation. For certain problems (for example, specifying the appropriate billing structures for 800 service), the reps asked for the assistance of co-workers in the same room or called specialists in other departments. Calls were also made to schedule installer visits for complex orders and to obtain telephone number assignments, among other various activities. Integration of these functions into the computer system would require cooperation of the application architects and the operations managers.

Constraints of the Current Systems

The constraints of the current systems provided clear motivation for user interface improvements. For simple orders, information was entered into the forms-based applications in a strict order. For more complex or unusual orders (such as for Centron service with call forwarding that is shared across multiple lines), the information was entered into an older line-oriented application or onto paper forms that would be typed into that application later by order typists. In these cases, reps needed to recall highly interdependent Universal Services Order Codes (USOC) or look them up in a list thousands of items long. Eliminating the need to memorize codes would dramatically reduce training time.

The observations showed that the reps had significant problems entering data while keeping up with the conversation. Users needed to access multiple block mode applications, yet they were forced to complete data entry in one before switching to another. If they left an application without completing data entry, they had to re-enter the data for that application. Data was often lost because of these transitions. Users were also forced to re-enter the same data in multiple applications. All of these difficulties inhibited the flow of conversation with customers. The navigation on the current systems was so cumbersome that many of the negotiations were done using paper and later entered into the linearly ordered computer screens. This greatly increased the amount of time required per customer order. Interviews confirmed that these were significant problems.

The primary problems we observed were that users (1) kept notes on paper because the order of their screens was incompatible with the dialog with customers, (2) entered products by code and recalled or looked up cross-product constraints (for example, that voice mail was incompatible with the call-waiting feature), (3) logged in and out of multiple databases while answering a single question, (4) used different formats for entering different product types on screens and forms, (5) lost unbuffered data when they left a screen to find other critical context information (for example, pre-existing service), (6) re-entered the same data in multiple applications, (7) referred to paper documentation to determine product constraints such as availability by region, (8) made lengthy telephone calls to obtain key pieces of data, and (9) initiated complex database transactions to view a small subset of retrieved information.

Implications for User Interface Design

We could see that a new graphical interface had the *potential* to alleviate the problems we observed There was a clear need for windowing to reduce the amount of navigation between applications and to preserve context information needed for problem solving. The new user interface needed to store tentative data captured in one application while users worked in another. There was also a clear need for a comprehensive point-and-click catalog of all product lines and consistent product labeling that would eliminate the need to memorize codes. We also wanted to find ways to reduce the number of calls made to other departments. But these observations were not enough to specify the details of the user interface components.

A prioritized list of generic solutions to these problems was included in the first draft of the functional requirements document for the project. Also included was a preliminary detailed design based on these interviews and on detailed study of the current screens, database content, and current system documentation. This textual design listed combinations of the data elements from the multiple applications in a single user interface made up of product menus, directory listing forms, and so forth.

Social Impact

A key social need early in the project was to establish our credibility with the application architects and data modeling teams and to gain sufficient domain knowledge to communicate with the clients who were funding the project. We presented a slide show reviewing current problems found at the sites and potential solutions to the primary clients. The problems we identified had been recognized by the business management, so this contributed to our credibility with both the developers and the clients. The clients were happy that a detailed design was available but did not spend much time critiquing it in its textual form. In general, the user interface chapter in the requirements document was well received.

Limitations of the Method

The observations and interviews did illuminate problems with manual operations and the current systems that could be addressed with a graphical user interface. However, the solutions we generated were at a fairly general level. For details, we went to the current systems' screens and documentation, using their data groupings. Though this design was completed within the deadline for the functional requirements draft, it was not driven by specific task sequences and therefore could not be guaranteed to support those tasks efficiently. We were concerned that these detailed designs would perpetuate problems for the service reps unknowingly, so we attempted to involve the users themselves in the design process, focusing on the typical tasks they had to carry out.

Active Participatory Prototyping of UI Based on Detailed Example Scenarios

We invited three methods analysts (former service reps and experts in the details of current business office operations) and a system administrator to assist in the design of the new system. None of the participants had extensive experience with graphical user interfaces though some had been briefly exposed to windowing systems.

Scenario Development

Karat and Bennett (1991) have noted that scenarios can be very efficient ways to drive out task-oriented requirements (see also Bias, Gillan, and Tullis, 1993). We asked the four contributors to produce a list of the four most frequent scenarios that the reps encountered. The scenarios included (1) adding new lines to an existing account, (2) moving service from one location to another, (3) adjusting bills, and (4) adding a new product to the database (for system administration to be designed in the future). They were then asked to select one of the four scenarios to guide a prototyping session.

Each participant was brought into a room in which the prototyping equipment was set up. They were first asked to list all the detailed steps that would be required to complete the scenario they had selected, and these were recorded on a white board. They were encouraged to add as much complexity as possible. Fictitious names of customers and other details (like financial relationships between roommates) were chosen to make the scenarios concrete. In this case, none of the participants brought reference material with them. The detailed scenarios were documented on videotape prior to the prototyping sessions.

As an example, the steps identified for moving service from one location to another included:

1. Obtain new address.
2. Obtain existing telephone number.
3. Pull up the existing account.
4. Determine status of recent bill and credit information.
5. Determine content of new directory listing.
6. Obtain mailing address if different.
7. Obtain address for delivering directory if different.
8. Determine what services can be provided at the new address.
9. Negotiate installation date.
10. Negotiate disconnect date for old line.
11. Negotiate transfer of calls if new number is required.
12. Review the order with the customer.
13. Call up the rates.
14. Offer installment billing.
15. Close the contact.

The specifics for this example were that "Rob Public" was moving from Denver, Colorado, where he had standard flat rate service, to Bailey, Colorado, where he would be forced to accept a four-party line and additional mileage and construction charges. He would need a new telephone number as well.

Although the three service negotiation scenarios were quite different from one another, they shared components (such as capturing the service address). We encouraged each participant to provide detail on different aspects of the interaction to assure we covered a large number of issues (for example, one focused on obtaining listing information, whereas another focused on scheduling installer visits).

Prototyping Technique

We used a fast prototyping tool (Supercard on an Apple Macintosh) to quickly mock up screens to support the complex tasks. The participants described the type of information needed (service address, billing address, available products, and the like) and then described how it should be displayed for each step in the scenario. As an example, the participants indicated they wanted to view the current data for an account, including addresses and products, and be able to type over any changes. For moves of service, they wanted the current service configuration to be automatically copied to the new address. If particular services weren't available, they wanted automatic warning messages explaining this and providing advice on alternatives.

The prototyping sessions were restricted to two hours per participant. The human factors team prepared a set of nonfunctioning widgets in advance with Supercard. Sets of widgets with different formats were presented to the participant on the fly, and the participants were given the option to choose a widget, request it be changed, or design their own. Many of the interaction methods were new to the participants, and they questioned whether they were realistic with the constraints imposed by current architectures. The human factors team members attempted to be as neutral as possible in interpreting requests. Our questions primarily were in the form of prompts for more information rather than eliciting value judgments on the solutions. We did request that they not restrict their thinking to current architectural constraints and that they be as creative as possible. These two approaches help drive out key system requirements. For example, we were surprised that the participants were skeptical about the use of intuitive menus with English labels because they were concerned that those menus would hide all the intricacies of the complex codes they had memorized. They indicated that they would rather be able to enter those codes than use menus that would be ambiguous. These codes were available for all product lines in the current systems, whereas only a limited number of products were available from menus in the existing forms-oriented applications.

The participants were also requested to specify screen organization. This included positioning fields, error messages, and so on. We attempted to obtain recommendations for the behavior of the widgets and documented this behavior directly on the Supercard windows with typed annotations (for example, one rep requested that charges for installations be automatically calculated and that installers' schedules be viewable when negotiating dates). Occasionally, the participants designed new widgets that were not within the Motif widget set (such as pull-down menu selections with multiple buttons). When all four sessions were complete, the "dead" widgets were brought to life using the Supercard scripting language. Pull-down menus produced forms, for example.

Although the participants were enthusiastic about the design sessions, they were not satisfied with the results. The four participants critiqued each

others' designs with considerable frustration. They had a good deal of difficulty developing consensus on how to organize the screens, often stopping in
frustration and joking that they wanted to see all the data at once. This prototyping effort was completed within two weeks.

Design Implications

These prototyping activities confirmed key design requirements that were
gleaned from the on-site observation. The prototyping, however, produced
much more detailed information about specific screen layout requirements.
Users designed screens with (1) queries to multiple data sources from within
the same window (such as telephone number availability and product availability), (2) access to related applications based on current application state
(such as installer work schedules based on chosen installation date), (3) access
to multiple accounts simultaneously (such as for old and new services),
(4) product incompatibility error messages (such as voice mail and foreign
exchange), (5) automatic recalculation of prices based on tentative product
selections, (6) automatic time stamping of credit information updates, and
(7) a WYSIWYG directory listing editor. Although many of the data elements
they created had counterparts in the existing screens, their presentation was
very different (for example, using pull-down menus instead of forms-based
multipage menus). Their relative screen positioning and the amount of navigation between them was much more supportive of the task scenarios than
the current systems' screen layouts. In some cases, the participants discovered ways of minimizing or even avoiding certain types of data entry
altogether (for example, automatic time stamping of credit updates). These
additional needs were added to a revised version of the functional requirements document.

Social Impact

The participatory prototyping established a partnership with the methods
analysts. This approach had a much stronger impact on building rapport than
on-site observation because it clearly established the mutual design roles of
the methods analysts and the user interface designers. It was a mutual learning situation (Kyng, 1991) where the human factors team was being exposed
to details of the tasks and their current problems, and the methods experts
were being exposed to the range of user interface options that were available
in Motif.

Limitations of the Method

The sessions produced several versions of preliminary prototypes, but it was clear that they were not satisfactory to the participants. It was immediately clear to us that this set of two-hour sessions was insufficient to produce a comprehensive design. This method did not allow the human factors staff to see the structure of the overall domain because it focused on a single thread, through several complex tasks. The design needed to support a wide range of unpredictable combinations of tasks. The participants recognized this but could not use this tacit knowledge to build the design during prototyping sessions based on linear scenarios. Hierarchical decision tree interviews were initiated to obtain a more comprehensive top-down view of the task domain.

Top-Down Decision Tree Analysis

Although we at first hoped only to gain a top-down, integrated view of the tasks that we had already identified by observation or in the participatory design sessions, this method revealed important information that was not obvious from either of the previous methods. As we shall see, it revealed invisible goals that structured the dialogs independent from the users' interaction with the current computers. These goals revealed new opportunities for computer support.

Interview Method

Six service representatives were interviewed individually about the decision process they use when negotiating service. The focus was explicitly on the dialog between the service rep and the customer, not with the system. The structured decision trees (Nilsson, 1971) were written in pencil on 20 × 34-inch easel pad paper as the interviews progressed (Figure 1).

The reps were asked to describe the first thing they said to the customers when they answered the phone and how they decided what to say next. This question led the reps to reveal how they categorize the customers and how these classifications led them to ask different questions. The categories became the prominent nodes in the decision trees. The reps were asked to estimate the relative frequency of encountering each subcategory.

The interviews involved combinations of following depth-first and breadth-first expansion of the decisions paths. Each rep focused on a

FIGURE 1

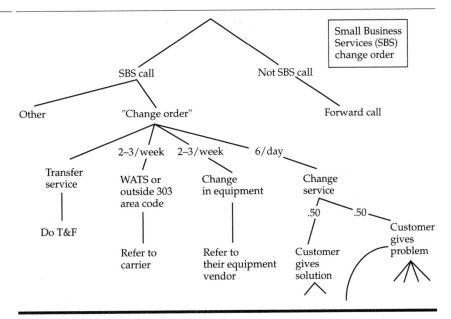

Example component of decision tree.

different branch of the overall decision tree. It was easier for the reps to follow a particular example to completion (following a depth-first description of the steps required to move service), but our prototyping experience showed us that we needed to maintain a comprehensive view of the decision space, so we guided the reps to return to top-level decisions and to expand on options at each level of decision. The interviews required approximately four weeks of effort.

Decision Tree Structure

The structure of the decision trees would be used to map out screen real estate that would support multiple tasks. The reps' first goal was to determine whether the callers had reached the appropriate department. If not, they told them to contact the right resource (for example, long-distance carrier). This node at first seemed outside our project's scope. But this information was needed for planning screen real estate for co-existing applications (for example, call transfer application).

The decision trees revealed that the reps did use the standard order classifications that were the basis of the universal service order codes (such as new connects, moves, change orders, disconnects) to guide their sales strategies but that it was dangerous to break up the user interface according to those classifications. The reps first determined whether the customer was interested in a new account, change of service, move of service, or a change in a record. However, we found that categories could change during negotiations. For example, a "change order" code needed to add a new phone line would have to be changed to the code for new service near the end of a negotiation if the customer requested a separate bill for the line. In the current systems, this often meant starting the data entry over again.

The structure of a tree was sometimes revised radically when it became clear that certain classification schemes dominated others. For example, part way through an interview it became clear that the reps needed to identify credit risks early in their conversations. Such customers were transferred to the collections department, making discussions of services a waste of time.

Often specific sales strategies came out early in the decision trees even though they were not immediately revealed to the customer. For example, the reps could anticipate the type of service needed on the basis of the type of business that was calling in. If a retail store called in, they recognized that there was a high potential need for telephone lines to handle charge card verifications. A manufacturing company, on the other hand, was more likely to have a need for a line to support a security system for a warehouse.

These hidden strategies had implications for both information display and information capture in the new user interface. The classification schemes (business expanding, family with teens, and so on) were obviously very important for identifying solutions that met the customers' needs. Compiling this information was also important for the company for building marketing strategies. This lost information could also be used to streamline follow-up calls with customers who wanted to expand their service. Our observations at the work site showed that most of this information was not captured in the computer systems but rather jotted down on slips of paper.

Quite often the sales representatives would think of configurations of services as the customers were describing their needs. These tentative configurations were also not captured by the existing systems. Only the final list of sold services was captured. The tentative services had many dimensions that interacted with one another. For example, companies that were losing business because of missed calls could either get an additional telephone line or obtain various features like voice mail for the line they already had. The complexity taxed the reps' memories, and they again resorted to notes on paper.

Our evaluations of the current systems showed that they forced the reps to enter the characteristics for each individual telephone line on separate screens. The interviews revealed the nature of the negative impact of this separation. It was very difficult to juggle between multiline solutions and single-line feature solutions. The interviews revealed that the reps made different negotiating decisions depending on the extent to which the customer was concerned about expenses. Often discussions of expenses led the reps to review the last few months' bills (displayed in an independent set of application screens) and to discuss alternative billing plans that could relieve the pressure of expenses but still allow the customers to purchase new services.

Multiple types of customer strategies also became evident. Some customers called in with a concrete solution in mind. In such cases, the reps attempted to get to the problem behind the solution to assure that all sales opportunities were covered. Other customers (secretaries, for example) were only representing the decision makers and therefore had very little information about the nature of the problem or any budget latitude. The reps sometimes requested that the decision maker find the time to call and discuss options. Finally, some customers called in with no understanding of possible solutions and only a fuzzy understanding of their own problems. The reps could be particularly helpful here, asking questions about the nature of the business and educating customers about solutions. These distinctions needed to be captured since they influenced selling strategies (follow-up calls).

Only when the negotiations settled on specific configurations did the reps focus on capturing the necessary data to complete an order (for example, listings and billing addresses, selected telephone numbers). It was clearly a goal of the reps to spend as little time as possible entering data. This was not obvious from the prototyping session, where data entry was the primary focus.

Design Implications

Even as we interviewed the representatives, we were noting user interface implications. The reps needed means for capturing customer characteristics that would guide their sales strategies. They needed to have sales strategies prompted. They needed a location to enter their tentative configurations. They needed to be able to see both line selection options and feature selection options simultaneously. Finally, they needed to be able to move quickly from service selection displays to displays of the customers' recent bills. Seeing the clear impact that the reps' decisions had on the discourse structure highlighted the design requirements much more clearly than the earlier observations or prototyping effort.

Toward the end of these sessions, user interface designs for supporting these dialogs emerged in our minds that we shared with the service reps. A key concept was the "negotiation worksheet" that presented a two-dimensional matrix of product offerings. This worksheet concept would allow the reps to keep track of how the customers planned to use multiple lines (voice, fax, computer modem, credit card verification), as well as possible features that might be needed with each individual line. The need for this user interface component was not revealed by the earlier prototyping sessions. Yet, when a pencil sketch of this idea was presented to the interviewees, they responded with great enthusiasm.

The interviews revealed that new data elements (such as status of business) needed to be included in the design that were not revealed by analysis of the existing screens or by the initial participatory prototyping session. The specific adjacency needs for particular data elements and groups of data elements were also much clearer (see our discussion of screen design).

Social Impact

The decision trees (there were approximately five pages of diagrams per interviewee) demonstrated to the clients our strong commitment to detailed understanding of the user domain. We taped examples of the decision tree diagrams to the walls during all subsequent demonstrations of the prototype to illustrate the relationship of the emerging user interface to the users' goals.

Limitations of the Method

These diagrams captured the end users' representation of the negotiations they carried out. This representation did not reflect future marketing strategies, product offerings, or pricing packages that were under development. Nor did the users have complete knowledge of the complex account structures and product lines of the current business. They depended on documentation or colleagues to handle unusual cases. We, therefore, needed to gain a more comprehensive understanding of the structure of the business and plans for the future in order to assure the new system design covered these options.

Semantic Net Analysis

The decision tree data was supplemented with an analysis of the background semantics of the business. The business had very complex product lines, inventory management, account structures, billing policies, customer demographics, and regional variants. We found that many of the specifics captured in these interviews were only vaguely understood by the end users. Often the structure of the business was driven by historical precedent or system constraints that were beyond the vision of the reps.

Interviewing Method

The semantics of the domain were again captured on large sheets of easel paper as informal semantic nets (Figure 2). These networks are close to the *concept diagrams* used by Novak and Gowin (1984). They are informal variants of the *active structural networks* of Norman and Rummelhart (1975). The key requirements analyst who was part of the project team provided detail on each of the topics and their highly complex interdependencies. The interviews required approximately four weeks of intensive work.

Overall topics were selected by reviewing lists of product lines and USOC lists. The requirements analyst was asked to describe what he or she knew about a particular topic. While describing the topic, the requirements analyst would mention objects, their attributes, and their relations to other objects. The objects, attributes, and values became the nodes in the semantic net, whereas the relations connecting objects, attributes, and values became the arcs of the net. The arcs were annotated to reflect the cardinality of the relations.

FIGURE 2

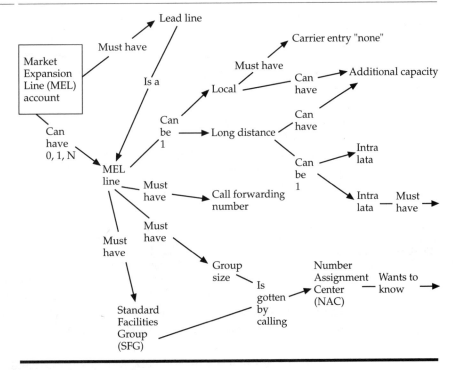

Example component of semantic net.

The requirements analyst was asked to talk about a topic or subtopic while the diagram was being created. Since the diagram contained other objects, relations, and attributes for the topics, it made it easy to prompt and capture relations between objects.

The semantic diagrams were not restricted to internal system elements and tended to incorporate contextual topics outside the domain of the data model (such as roles of office workers). Nevertheless, the information that was relevant to the data model was confirmed and adjusted by the independent team of data modelers who were working with a wide range of experts in each of these areas. For the purposes of the user interface design, we used the pencil drawings of the informal semantic nets to guide the design of cross-functional constraints in the user interface. For example, product incompatibilities were noted and represented as error messages, and product dependencies were represented as simultaneous highlighting of elements in adjacent user interface panels.

Data Collected

This set of interviews provided the fundamental structural information needed for the user interface design. Some of this information had appeared during other interviews and during prototyping sessions, but only in the form of isolated examples. The topic interdependencies were driven by hardware constraints (for example, of telephone switches), multiple public utilities commissions' regulations, and complex business procedures needed to manage the accounts. Many inconsistencies were found that were caused by regional differences and historical accidents.

Design Implications

These interviews assured that the user interface addressed the primary categories and subcategories of data required for negotiation. Completeness of design was assessed iteratively by reference to the existing database model embodied in the universal service order code model. The interviews also contributed to key design decisions in the application architecture as well as the user interface. Plans were put in place to make the previously inconsistent account structure more consistent allowing us to use a hierarchical account navigation scheme in the user interface. The product constraints promoted the integration of an expert system rule base that would automatically display constraints with various forms of highlighting. Thus, these comprehensive nets allowed us to spot generic types of constraints in the business and provide the users with access to them through the user interface design.

Social Impact

These interviews were again very important in establishing our credibility with both the clients and the parallel data modeling team. The data modeling team used the diagrams as verification of their own work and used them and the emerging prototypes to begin to model some of the database processing constraints.

Limitations of the Method

Such interviews are useful to gain "declarative" information about the relationships between elements in the domain but not sufficient input for user interface designs. They do not incorporate key procedural information gained from the on-site observation (for example, we observed their use of pen annotations to update incorrect and outdated information in manuals), and they provide no help in determining data adjacency requirements (for example, what topics are likely to be addressed sequentially). These semantic interviews were again based on the current organization of the business. Future requirements had to be obtained from both the marketing and product management departments.

The Translation of Multiple Requirements to Design

When this round of decision tree and semantic analysis interviews was complete, the human factors team developed a textual compilation of the user interface components that was called the User Interface Component Hierarchy. The outlining capabilities of our word processor made this work more efficient. This hierarchy included all data elements that appeared in any of the semantic nets or decision tree diagrams, as well as all the data elements that appeared in the initial prototype. Thus they included not only product lists but also all the user characteristics that were only in the heads of reps that they used to help identify needed services. Based on our accumulated knowledge of the procedures that would be used to access and update those data elements during live negotiations with customers, each of the 752 elements was assigned to a particular dialog type, as follows:

General menu bar

Window

Tab: used for navigation between panels

Tiled panel

Pop-up panel

Local menu

Field group

Field with menu options

Field without menu options

Button within a form

Multidimensional worksheet

Column heading

Row heading with menu options

Row heading without menu options

Some of these elements were traditionally captured as free-form "remarks" and were converted into explicit choosable data elements (for example, in menus) although it was clear that there was a continuing need for note fields in the user interface. Groups of data elements were clustered into higher-level elements. The interdependencies between the elements helped guide the selection of user interface components.

Once the data elements were assigned to dialog types and clustered, they were reviewed by the key requirements analyst who was part of the project team. A very intensive prototyping effort was then initiated, using Supercard as the prototyping environment. The first version of the prototype (for small business customers) required about six weeks of intensive effort for three people. The authors were joined by the lead user interface software engineer for this second prototyping effort. Decisions were made about the relative positioning of the windows, tiled panels, and pop-up panels, and the navigation techniques for moving between them. We then fleshed out the design of the various panels of the interface one at a time.

The specifics of the prototype were influenced by the preliminary prototype, but the designs ultimately were very different. Several new displays were designed that had not appeared in the existing systems or in the preliminary prototype in any form. These included a mouse-operated panel for capturing customer characteristics and a summary panel for displaying tentative configurations of multiple lines. This panel provided sections for entering lines according to their use. It also provided a condensed view of the features that could be associated with each line. This would allow the reps to view

multiple solutions involving both lines and features. Familiar data groupings were also used, including billing, credit, and listing information, and a
help panel.

The decision trees showed that many of the components would be shared
by multiple scenarios. Whereas some data elements clustered neatly, others
had multiple affinities. For example, the listing, billing, and service addresses
each had to be captured but were often identical. The related items were juxtaposed. Panels were organized so that context information (for example, customer characteristics) was visible for problem solving in other areas (for
example, selection of the number of lines). The navigational techniques were
chosen to support very quick movement between the subareas. The traditional categories (move, disconnect, and the like) were blurred. Users could
enter any subtopic in any order, including the information that uniquely classified the order (for example, disconnect date).

Social Impact

The new prototype became a medium for communication itself. Business
office managers came from several states to review it, as did executives of the
company. A videotape of the prototype was used to reach additional managers. The prototype was used extensively by the other developers for planning application architecture and database structure. During demonstrations
of the prototype, a number of operations and development managers
expressed concern about the complexity of the screens. The decision trees
turned out to be very important in justifying the information display. These
displays could be shown to support the multiple task transitions in the phone
conversations with customers. It was relatively easy to demonstrate that
the total number of screen transitions was drastically reduced compared
to the older systems and that the relative position of the information was
remarkably stable so that reps would quickly learn the topology of the information spaces.

Role-Playing Walkthroughs

Perhaps the ideal method for evolving a prototype that is intended to support
two-party dialog is to use it during actual negotiations. But feedback on the
adequacy of the design is needed much before a prototype can be installed in
a real working environment. Standard thinking-aloud protocols are useful but
do not allow two-party dialogs. To get early feedback, we invited three of the

reps to separately evaluate this version of the prototype against a negotiation that they themselves simulated.

The three reps had limited experience with graphical user interfaces. One had none, one had minimal experience with a mouse for controlling terminal emulation windows, and the third had used a Macintosh computer at home. They were each given a hands-on tutorial on mouse usage and the standard widget set that they would encounter.

Role-Playing Method

The role-playing effort and its analysis required about three weeks of effort, not including time required to update the prototype. Before simulating a negotiation, the reps were given a one-hour orientation to the prototype. They were asked to use the mouse to locate a comprehensive set of data fields and menus within the user interface using a thinking-aloud protocol technique (Mack, Lewis, and Carroll, 1983). Any false starts and difficulties were noted and used to motivate design change recommendations.

They were then asked to participate in the role-playing exercise, which was videotaped. The key requirements analyst (a former service rep) simulated a call for new service. A single scenario was chosen with a moderate level of complexity: A lawyer called in to request a new line for his wife who was joining his practice. He needed help in getting his calls answered when he wasn't at home, and he also needed to change his billing address.

The scenario was played out in a natural dialog. The "customer's" questions were given rapidly to simulate a real call. The participants were asked to field the call as they normally would and to focus on keeping up with the customer. We requested that if they felt comfortable, they enter data into the prototype during the conversation.

Evaluating the Fit Between Dialog and Design

All three reps completed the service negotiation, obtaining the information necessary to complete the order, but only one of the three was able to enter any data into the prototype. This can partially be attributed to lack of experience with graphical and mouse-based interfaces, and partially to lack of any training concerning the differences between the organization of the new interface and the organization of their highly over-learned system.

The reps then reviewed the videotape of the dialog, pausing at each new exchange of information, and evaluated the prototype's design. Finally, they were interviewed about suggestions for improvements.

The bulk of the new design input was elicited during the reviews of the videotapes with the reps. This technique allowed them to evaluate in specific detail the difficulties they encountered during the time-pressured interview. This allowed a much more complete analysis than a standard retrospective report and counterbalanced the problem that they were given no time-consuming training on the new user interface.

The reps asked the mock customer questions or were spontaneously offered information about each of the following areas:

What is your type of business?

What is your desired service?

What type of telephone equipment will you use?

Do you have a receptionist?

What approach will you use to handle calls when you're not in office?

Will your wife want to answer your calls? (Need for roll-over capability)

What format do you desire for the name in your listing?

What telephone number would you prefer?

We noted that all these topics had been revealed in the decision trees and that screen real estate was devoted to each in the user interface prototype. The dialogs revealed frequent jumps between topics that were guided by either the customer (for example, discussion of service jumped to discussion of billing address) or the rep (for example, discussion of features jumped to discussion of type of business).

We noted whether the data requested was viewable on the current screen configuration or required a screen transition (for example, a pop-up panel or change of a tiled panel). The large screen allowed display of current services, service address, business characteristics, and a tiled panel area that alternately displayed individual line usage characteristics, listings, and product recommendations. Screen transitions were required to access billing and credit information and the hidden panels.

At the beginning of the call, the customer gave information (such as type of business) before the rep had a chance to pull up the customer's record that contained the location for entering that data. In these cases, the reps later indicated that they could hold the information in memory long enough to enter it but that they would need to ask for the telephone number as early as possible to minimize writing on paper.

Example screen transitions that were required to keep up with the dialog included pulling up the listings panel to enter the name of the wife, pulling up the billing panel to update the billing address, and pulling up the line usage panel to input type of equipment and type of user (receptionist, for example). Each of these transitions required locating a visible pull-down menu, making a selection of the needed panel, waiting for the panel display, and locating the relevant field within the panel.

Implications for Design

This method confirmed that major screen components were visible when needed and that minimal navigation would be required. It also provided opportunities for enhancing the design. A request was made for an easy way to compare current and future services. Additional requests were made to move data to the initial display (for example, billing address) to avoid any transition. The review of the videotapes also led to requests for different default screen configurations. One rep requested that the listings information be displayed as soon as the customer's record was accessed. But another rep preferred to have prompts for sales strategies appear in that section of the window so that they would not be overlooked.

Some of the panels captured information that was never captured by the computer before but was critical to successful negotiations (customer characteristics, tentative product configurations, and so on). We asked whether the reps would be able to use these panels during the conversation (none of the reps used them during the simulation). The reps indicated that they would be very likely to enter tentative configurations. Customer characteristics input by previous reps would be useful, but they were unable to predict whether they would be motivated to enter the information themselves unless their management made such entries mandatory.

Social Impact

This role-playing method re-established the design partnership that was so helpful in the initial prototyping work. But this time, all parties were working from a highly structured design based on multiple inputs. The reps could then fine-tune this design. At this point, the design had established significant credibility with all parties, but more detailed work would be required to fine-tune it. The focus of the discussion was much less on the existing systems and more on the new methods of meeting fundamental needs. This joint analysis helped motivate the reps to provide this additional assistance.

Limitations of the Method

This review was not sufficient to guarantee that the design supported the total range of possible dialogs or that the reps would in fact be able keep up with the dialogs. We noticed that the rep who was able to enter data during the simulation tended to ask questions before accessing the relevant hidden panels. Additional testing with trained users would determine if they would be able to access panels prior to asking particular questions.

The Interplay Between Methods

It was not clear to us that we selected the optimal order for applying the different design methods. Specifically, it may have been more effective to carry out the participatory design work *after* completing the decision tree and semantic net interviews so that we would be able to understand the implications of the users' suggestions for the data model and for the other paths that users would need to follow through the user interface.

What *was* clear was that information gathered with one method had important influences on others. Our on-site observations helped us determine the type of orientation the users would need before participating in prototyping efforts. The fact that they used forms-based and code-based applications predicted that they would have limited insights into graphical user interface solutions. We therefore needed to orient the users to the graphical interface options first. We also realized it would be more efficient if they focused on the tasks while we took on the burden of providing alternative graphic solutions. We observed that many of the reps' suggestions were solutions to the salient problems observed during the on-site observations.

The observations of the current systems were often necessary for interpreting the decision tree interviews and vice versa. And during interviews, we were aware that the decisions the reps made were affected by the practical constraints of the current systems. This knowledge often allowed us to see beyond the current system and focus on needs for new innovations that could better support their needs. For example, we carefully guided users to talk in terms of customers and products rather than application screens and product codes.

The on-site observation also contributed interviewing topics for the semantic interviews. We could document contextual influences that we observed on-site and use these structured representations to influence the details of the prototype design.

Data from the observations, interviews, and participatory prototyping could be combined through the use of the textual user interface component hierarchy. Finally, the decision tree interviews helped us select an appropriate scenario for the role-playing exercise. Overall, we believe that the convergence of the information gained from the different methods actually contributed to the speed of the overall design process, allowing us to focus our information gathering on relevant details and providing us with the ability to cross-reference data to recognize when we had gathered sufficient requirements to proceed. Gathering all the design requirements from participatory design alone, for example, would have taken much longer since each data element was triggered in the mind of the reps in a walk-through of the screens, and many elements might in fact have been left out. Lack of context information from observations would have let us waver between designs promoted by different participants rather than seeing that there was a set of common problems that was being solved with varying suggestions.

The Social Value of the Design Methods

We have seen that each of the methods played an important social role. Good communication can be key to acceptance or rejection of a user interface design by the clients requesting it, the peers responsible for development, or the development management who may have ultimate responsibility for arbitration. Perhaps good communication starts with establishing a high level of credibility. The more we learned about the details of the application domain, the more credibility we gained with all parties. Concrete evidence of this knowledge, in the form of the decision trees and semantic diagrams, was particularly important in justifying the designs that might otherwise be reviewed on an aesthetic basis alone. The diagrams, the user interface component hierarchy, and the prototypes themselves played key communication roles with developers, management, and clients.

Both the participatory prototyping and the prototype role playing established partnerships with the users and methods analysts. These approaches clearly established the mutual design roles of the methods analysts and the user interface designers. Yet such participation was inadequate to the complexity of this domain, both from our perspectives and from the perspectives of the participants. The updated prototypes based on the decision trees and semantic interviews were viewed as much more effective by these participants, who were able to fine-tune them very effectively. Perhaps these later designs were better accepted specifically because they were based on the users' own expertise even though they did not take part in the time-consuming translation of their expertise into graphical user interface concepts.

Selecting and Tuning Methods for User Interface Design

User interface designers select methods on the basis of many factors. Key factors include time and budget available and level of experience with a particular method. This case study seems to make clear that no one method suffices but that combinations of methods are required. The extent to which one method or the other is used depends on the specific characteristics of the projects. This service negotiation case involved:

1. Replacing a pre-existing system—obligating us to understand current procedures through observation and current system analysis. Designing a completely new system from scratch (for example, a typewriter) could call for substantially different approaches, including evaluating related behavior (for example, handwriting), social conventions constraining that behavior (for example, levels of formality in printed information), and readiness for major behavioral change (for example, communication patterns and paths). These two approaches reflect the distinction between designs based on tradition and those based on transcendence of traditions discussed by Pelle Ehn (1988).

2. Employees of a single company—allowing us to focus on this single-user population in depth. Designing systems for the mass market (for example, voice mail) would require sampling from a wide range of diverse user populations and more substantial analysis of the fit between the needs of subgroups and the specific capabilities of the new product.

3. Highly trained users—leading us to focus on task demands in the context of interaction through observation and time-pressured role playing. Designing systems for casual users would require much more intense attention to learning and documentation early in the design process, perhaps dedicating substantially more time to thinking-aloud protocols.

4. A very complex data domain—leading us to devote substantial time to developing semantic nets that would allow us to view data dependencies. Designing systems for more straightforward data domains (for example, desktop videoconferencing application) would require focusing more on

group communication paths and task analysis to assure proper availability of systems.

5. Two-party negotiations—leading us to drive the decision trees with respect to interaction with clients rather than with the system. Designing systems for other social environments (for example, kiosks in public environments) might require focusing more on the social architectural factors influencing comfort approaching a kiosk.

Approaches to particular circumstances will vary significantly, but we believe case studies like this one help illustrate how the value of specific methods may extend beyond individual cases. For example, on-site observation would be appropriate any time there is a chance that contextual information might have an impact on the design. Whiteside and his colleagues (1988) list many different types of context that may have impact on a design, including work, time, motivation, and social factors. How are the users using documentation? telephone conversations? paper forms? Addressing these issues with a new user interface may create some of the largest improvements in overall operations. Understanding the social roles of the workers and how they work together can assure that the new designs of the interfaces fit smoothly into the social environment. Such observations may also provide a critical orientation for the designers prior to other data-gathering techniques, assuring that key topics get addressed.

Fast prototyping using detailed scenarios can be used to bring the specifics of the application domain and the potential of new graphical devices into close contact in the minds of both users and designers. We also found that this was a very fast way of uncovering key architectural requirements for the applications and databases. This method was also a major boon to establishing rapport with the client group. But prototyping focuses on interaction with the computer, leaving out key needs for supporting negotiation or other types of interaction beyond the computer. Our approach also focused on linear tasks that made it difficult to see the hierarchical structure of the domain. Given that this method required only a few weeks effort, it may well be worth the investment even though it is an inefficient way to capture the complete requirements for complex domains like service negotiation. It may be that modification of the technique using alternative approaches to scenario identification and decomposition (Karat and Bennett, 1991) would increase its effectiveness.

The decision tree interviews perhaps provided the most effective input for a design supporting two-party negotiations. The interviewing method was adopted from problem-solving approaches used in both cognitive modeling and artificial intelligence (for example, Nilsson, 1971). In several weeks of interviews and analysis, we uncovered key requirements for supporting negotiations. And though the audiotapes of the interviews were extensive, the paper diagrams were very easy to work with and share with other developers. The diagrams also were converted into interface designs relatively easily. They provided specific benefits of exposing adjacency requirements for the data.

Traditional linear approaches to task analysis (Jonassen, Hannum, and Tessmer, 1989) could not have been used in this case. In fact, earlier attempts to classify the reps' work in terms of standard linear sequences based on order types had caused unacceptable rigidity in the existing user interfaces.

Obtaining a comprehensive view of the semantics of the application is imperative. For data-oriented applications such as ours, it would be possible to gain this from independent data modeling teams, but we feel it is a mistake to attempt a prototype without a solid foundation in this knowledge. In our case, this meant carrying out parallel interviews to those of the data modeling team. The semantic diagrams, adapted from various approaches to cognitive modeling and artificial intelligence, were flexible enough to cover any topic brought up in the interview so that important context information could be included. The credibility that this knowledge brings to the user interface team may alone be worth the work. But designers should be aware that semantic interviews alone provide no insight into the adjacency requirements that are driven by the reps' negotiating strategies.

Using a systematic approach to representing data and translating it into adjacency requirements provided a major efficiency gain. The textual user interface component hierarchy that was used for this purpose was sharable with both clients and other members of the development team.

Some authors have noted that usability evaluations are often too expensive and too late (Nielson and Molich, 1990; Jeffries et al., 1991). We have found, however, that informal usability testing without formal test plans can be carried out with preliminary prototypes to greatly speed their evolution. Thinking-aloud protocols reveal problems with interfaces quickly, and the technique can be modified to fit different circumstances (for example, using thinking-aloud protocols during prototype orientations). For interfaces that support two-party dialogs, role playing can be an important confirmation that the designs actually meet the negotiation requirements. Even if the users are unable to input data and keep up with the negotiations, they can provide very useful information while comparing their own simulations to such prototypes.

Combinations of these and other techniques can be adjusted to fit within the constraints of particular projects. Decision tree interviews may be more important for complex applications (for example, computer-aided design) than for less complex domains (for example, voice response systems or automatic teller machines). On the other hand, more intensive thinking-aloud protocols and role playing may be required for walk-up-and-use applications. Even complex projects with pre-established data and application structures would still benefit from the decision tree interviews, allowing user interface adjustments to support the decision flows. The value or appropriateness of specific techniques for a particular project will often not be predictable in advance of all requirements gathering since the nature of each case (for example, the complexity of the data requirements of the level of dialog between users) is progressively discovered over time, and changes in user interface technologies require practitioners to constantly update methods to take advantage of new capabilities. What is important is to build experience with a variety of techniques so that they can be called on as the circumstances of each project reveal themselves.

Conclusions

It is not surprising that practitioners have no clear guidelines for selecting methods for designing graphical user interfaces. The types of problems that particular designers face are very different. The multiple approaches that are being promoted by different factions will apply in different degrees to different problem types, especially given the nature of the specific application. Practitioners must expand their repertoire of techniques to meet the challenges of particular projects. They will need to be comfortable designing in the context in which the application is carried out. They will need to be prepared to take on in-depth, top-down analysis of the users' domain and of the semantics of the business. They will also need to be facile collaborators with users. Finally, they will need to familiarize themselves with effective prototyping tools that can support design iterations.

Both researchers and practitioners in the human-computer interaction community can support practitioners by helping create taxonomies of user interface problem types and demonstrating the impact of individual approaches for particular problems.

Acknowledgments

We would like to thank the lead user interface software engineer, Bruce Boelter, the requirements analyst, Linda Gertner, the rest of the project team, and the project's clients for both their input and their support for the methods used here. We would also like to thank Ron Perkins, Lynn Streeter, and Dennis Wixon for valuable comments on the manuscript.

Motif is a trademark of the Open Software Foundation. Macintosh IIci is a trademark of Apple Computer. Supercard is a trademark of Allegiant Technologies Inc.

References

Bannon, L., Cypher, A., Greenspan, S., and Monty, M. L. (1983). Evaluation and analysis of users' activity organization. *Proceedings of the ACM Human Factors in Software Conference, CHI '83*, 54–57.

Bias, R. G., Gillan, D. J., and Tullis, T. S. (1993). Three usability enhancements to the human factors design interface. *Proceedings of the Fifth International Conference on Human-Computer Interaction.* Elsevier, 169–174.

Bjerknes, G., Ehn, P., and Kyng, M. (1981). *Computers and Democracy.* Aldershot-Avebury: Avery.

Ehn, P. (1988) *Work-Oriented Design of Computer Artifacts.* Stockholm: Arbetslivscentrum.

Jeffries, R., Miller, J. R., Wharton, C., and Uyeda, K. (1991). User interface evaluation in the real world: A comparison of four techniques. *Proceedings of the ACM Human Factors in Software Conference, CHI '91*, 119–124.

Jonassen, D. H., Hannum, W. H., and Tessmer, M. (1989). *Handbook of Task Analysis Procedures.* New York: Praeger.

Karat, J. (1991). *Taking Software Design Seriously.* Boston: Academic Press.

Karat, J. and Bennett, J. L. (1991). Using scenarios in design meetings. In J. Karat (ed.) *Taking Software Design Seriously.* Boston: Academic Press.

Kyng, M. (1991) Designing for cooperation: Cooperating in design. *Communications of the Association for Computing Machinery*, 52–63.

Mack, R. L., Lewis, C., and Carroll, J. (1983). Learning to use word processors: Problems and prospects. *ACM Transactions on Office Information Systems*, vol. 1, no. 3, 33–42.

Nielsen, J. and Molich, R. (1990). Heuristic evaluation of user interfaces. *Proceedings of the ACM Human Factors in Software Conference, CHI '90*, 249–256.

Nilsson, N. J. (1971). *Problem-solving Methods in Artificial Intelligence.* New York: McGraw-Hill.

Norman, D. A. and Rummelhart, D. E. (1975). *Explorations in Cognition.* San Francisco: W. H. Freeman.

Novak, J. D. and Gowin, D. B. (1984). *Learning How to Learn.* Cambridge: Cambridge University Press.

Olson, J. R. and Olson, G. M. (1990). The growth of cognitive modeling in human-computer interaction since GOMS. *Human Computer Interaction,* 5(3,4), 221–265.

Whiteside, J., Bennett, J., and Holtzblatt, K. (1988) Usability engineering: Our experience and evolution. In M. Helander (ed.), *Handbook of Human-Computer Interaction.* North Holland: Elsevier Science Publishers.

Wolff, A. S. and Bruner, H. (1990). Cognitive Task Analysis and the Design of Intelligent Service Provisioning Interfaces. Proprietary Bellcore report.

Getting Around the Task-Artifact Cycle: How to Make Claims and Design by Scenario[1]

JOHN M. CARROLL, MARY BETH ROSSON[2]

IBM Watson Research Center

ABSTRACT

We are developing an "action science" approach to human-computer interaction (HCI), seeking to better integrate activities directed at understanding with those directed at design. The approach leverages development practices of current HCI with methods and concepts to support a shift toward using broad and explicit design rationale to reify where we are in a design process, why we are there, and to guide reasoning about where we might go from there. We represent a designed artifact as the set of user scenarios supported by that artifact, and more finely by causal schemas detailing the underlying psychological rationale. These schemas, called claims, unpack wherefores and whys of the scenarios. In this paper, we stand back from several empirical projects in order to clarify our commitments and practices.

Introduction

Here is a perplexing contrast. In the world of science, everything is made as self-consciously explicit as it possibly can be. In the world of practice, many things of critical importance are never made explicit. Indeed, some have raised this to a principle of ineffability, claiming that the most important things *cannot* be made explicit (Heidegger, 1962). Design work on human-computer interaction (HCI) is a case in point: lots of scrupulously detailed normal science, lots of implicitly detailed design work. We wish to develop a proactive understanding of the gap between science and practice in human-computer interaction (HCI). Our approach is to try to build science *in the* extant practice, to reify the practical ontology of design so that it can be used more deliberately, interrogated, improved, and applied.

Developing an Action Science

Our project has two goals: to contribute to the development of HCI as a scientific domain and to contribute to the development of design methodology for HCI artifacts. Our interest is to make progress on these two goals conjointly, that is, through the "same" activity on our part. We propose viewing HCI research as an "action science," a science that produces knowledge-in-implementation (Argyris, 1980; Torbert, 1976), and a view of HCI design practice as inquiry. In part, our commitment rests on critiques of the alternatives: the historically disappointing "normal science" paradigm for HCI research (Carroll, 1989; Carroll and Campbell, 1986) and analytic-decomposition paradigm for HCI design (Carroll and Rosson, 1985). More constructively, we are encouraged by modest success at creating an inquiry-based approach to instructional design grounded in an action science of learning (Carroll, 1990a). But it must be noted that though our orienting commitments are not clearly the standard view of HCI, they are at least implicit in an increasing proportion of current discussion about HCI (for example, Ehn, 1988; Landauer, 1987; Landauer, 1991; Thorndike, 1903) and about computer science more broadly (for example, Floyd et al., 1992; Gilb, 1988).

Historically, basic science and technology development have generally had little mutual impact (for example, Basalla, 1988; Kuhn, 1962; Multhauf, 1959). The complexity of modern science and technology have created the need for better integration, and one can cite impressive recent examples of action science, particularly in large industrial laboratories. A good example is the invention of the transistor (Jewkes, Sawers and Stillerman, 1958, 1969, pp. 317–319; Nelson, 1962; Schön, 1983, pp. 177–182).

The physics of the semiconductor effect was well enough understood to have allowed the development of the transistor as early as 1931. However, early work was hindered by pursuing too closely the analogy to vacuum tubes and by an oversimplified *practical* understanding of the semiconductor effect. In "n" (or negative) semiconductors, there are many more electrons (negative charge carriers) than holes (positive charge carriers), whereas in "p" (positive) semiconductors, the majority carriers are holes and the minority carriers are electrons. However, the practical understanding tended to see n semiconductors as simply negative and p semiconductors as simply positive.

In the late 1940s, Bell Labs significantly stepped up work on semiconductors, including the establishment of a small group directed at building a semiconductor amplifier: a practical goal, but one with significant science dependencies and opportunities. The work of this group consisted of embodying various hypothesized mechanisms in prototype solid-state amplifiers. Discrepancies in predicted performance were grist for further hypotheses and prototypes. The project culminated in the recognition that *minority* carrier current flow is a major effect in semiconductor devices and the discovery of the transistor effect (minority flow induced by one point contact back through another).

It is moot, of course, whether a richer practical understanding of semiconductors, one that kept in view the dual nature of semiconductor current flow, might have allowed the development of the transistor in the early 1930s. But it is clear that technology development can be obstructed by incomplete practical understandings. Our work seeks to promote balanced design analysis so that important factors (the HCI analogs of minority current flow) are not overlooked.

Status

Our task-artifact framework seeks to enrich the concepts-in-action that HCI researchers and designers work with by rendering *explicit* the underlying ontology of HCI. Specifically, we construct explicit descriptions of tasks and artifacts in a very concrete and psychology-laden vocabulary. We use these descriptions as scientific analyses, that is, for explanation and abstraction, but also as design rationale—this is the sense in which we are building an action science.

Our approach to task analysis enumerates critical and typical use-scenarios: the things users characteristically want to do and need to do, as well as the momentous events of user interaction (breakthrough insights and errors). All task analysis schemes do this in some sense; however, ours seeks to identify a "basic" task level (Rosch et al., 1976): We are concerned with tasks at the level people construe their work to themselves; the level at which tasks become meaningful to the people who engage in them. Many task analysis schemes focus on a much lower level than this (for example, the unit task of Card, Moran, and Newell, 1983). We believe a good inventory of basic tasks is the best design representation of an artifact (Carroll and Rosson, 1990). Moreover, building such a representation has uniquely empowering design pragmatics: A set of basic tasks are obligatory prerequisites for constructing task-oriented instruction and other user support (for example, Carroll, 1990a) and usability evaluation instruments (Carroll, Singley, and Rosson, 1991; Roberts and Moran, 1983). Such a representation makes it more feasible to convey the design to users—both within the design process (Ehn,

1988) and subsequently. In our approach, an inventory of basic tasks also serves as the fundamental rubric for our approach to artifact analysis.

Designed artifacts (hardware, software, applications, interfaces) can be interpreted as theories, as embodying myriad specific propositions about their users and the circumstances of their use. For example, a self-instruction manual can be seen as embodying a range of assertions about what the learners know, what they do, what they experience, about the nature of the learning tasks and the contexts within which these tasks are carried out, and so on. This view often surfaces in "design memoirs" (for example, Smith et al., 1982), which can play a proactive role in organizing subsequent design efforts by focusing attention on particular issues.

However, such memoirs casually confound "designer intention" (which may or may not characterize the realized artifact) and "design analysis" (in which assertions are systematically grounded in general laws of psychology, specific user data, or other rationale). In our approach, the psychological design rationale of an artifact-in-use is articulated in causal schemas (which we call claims) relating properties of the artifact with specific psychological consequences, under the scope of a basic task usage situation. Thus, for example, including open-ended exercises in an instruction manual supports learning-by-exploration for situations in which the learner wonders what sorts of projects might be appropriate to work on.

Such a claim might have been enabled by a manual *because* the designer intended to do it. However, the claim is neither more nor less true of the artifact in virtue of this intention, and the relevance and truth of the claim vis-à-vis the artifact and its use can be investigated independent of mere intention. Our objective in constructing descriptions and accounts of artifacts and their use is intended to improve the chance that designers will more deliberately manage the causal schemas they embody in their work.

The ontology of HCI is a task-artifact cycle (Figure 1) in which designers respond to user requirements (in the sense of basic level tasks to be enabled or proscribed) by building artifacts, which in turn present or deny possibilities to their users. On the one hand, we seek to support a more thorough and deliberate enumeration and assessment of the basic tasks (versus designing to an over-narrow or plainly mistaken set of use-scenarios), and on the other hand, to support a more thorough and deliberate enumeration and assessment of claim schemas implicit in the design (versus creating unintended and undesirable psychological consequences for users).

Our approach is similar to contextualist (Whiteside and Wixon, 1987), participatory design (Ehn, 1988), and situated action (Suchman, 1987) approaches in that we conceive of computer systems and applications as rich and dynamic contexts for user activity. However, we are more concerned with developing analytic models for understanding and design. Conversely, our approach is similar to modern, efficiency-oriented approaches (for example, Card, Moran, and Newell, 1983) in its concern with analytic models and methods, but different in taking the broader-scope perspective on user activity and experience. Our approach differs somewhat from all these approaches in its action science commitment, in integrating the development of HCI as a domain of study with its development as a domain of design practice.

We have had reasonable initial success at applying this framework to a variety of problems. A scenario-based claims analysis of the Displaywriter (Carroll, Kellogg, and Rosson, 1991) was shown to reproduce the design arguments underlying the Training Wheels Interface. The methodology guided the development of two View Matcher programming environments for Smalltalk (Carroll and Rosson, 1991). Subsequent work applied the methodology to the design of a task browser (Bellamy and Carroll, 1992), a software design environment (Rosson and Carroll, 1992), and an intelligent tutoring system (Singley, Carroll, and Alpert, 1991). Prescriptive design models as "second-order artifacts" (Carroll and Campbell, 1989) can direct credit–blame attributions to models as well as to exemplars, and thus unify design evaluation and model building (Carroll, Singley, and Rosson, 1991).

Overview

The balance of this paper attempts to operationalize the task-artifact framework. It is both more and less than an instruction manual because we may not yet know how best to do what we seek to do, and as a result, we may raise many methodological and conceptual issues (perhaps both wittingly and unwittingly). The initial discussion in the second and third sections draws on the Displaywriter and Smalltalk case studies mentioned; in the fourth section, we sketch a more complete example of the whole process, couched for the design of an instructional manual (which is a less technically demanding design domain than Smalltalk programming environments and broadens the application bounds of the methodology).

Generating Scenarios

Whether analyzing an existent artifact or envisioning an artifact in design, we begin by generating a set of basic-level task scenarios. Each scenario is a description (in text, in a storyboard, and so on.) of the activities a user might engage in while pursuing a particular concern. A set of these scenarios is a concrete representation of the use to which the artifact will be put. For any reasonably complex system, the scenario representation is necessarily incomplete (there is an infinity of possible use-scenarios). Yet even though it may at best be heuristic, the analyst and the designer need to have a scenario set that provides good coverage of the possible use-scenarios.

The Empirical Approach

One obvious method is to collect scenarios empirically. Of course, observing people or asking them what they do often confounds the predictions made on purely analytic grounds. A learner we studied, who was following an exercise to type and edit a lease, made horrendous errors, but continued somehow on the grounds that, not being a lawyer herself, she could not judge what a proper lease ought to look like (Mack, Lewis, and Carroll, 1983). We might have projected the scenario in which she made the errors, but we could never have anticipated the creativity she brought to bear in seeing an obvious and ugly editing disaster as a "lease."

The problem with purely empirical approaches, however, is twofold. First, they are not merely "rich," they are too rich. They generate unmanageably huge scenario sets with no internal structure, no principle for classifying or grouping scenario tokens. They provide no means of saving effort: Each project of scenario development starts with a blank slate. Second, they are necessarily a posteriori: One must already have a system to collect empirical use-scenarios for the system. Often design work is really redesign, and the scenarios collected after the fact for an earlier system version or level *can* be used as a priori guides for subsequent versions and levels. Nevertheless, both problems point to the importance of a complementary, analytical approach to developing scenario sets.

The Analytic Approach

An analytic approach to generating scenarios would start with a theory of the kinds of scenarios there are. These types could be used to organize empirically collected scenarios, but also to generate scenarios. Of course, a theory of scenarios might not classify all empirically obtained scenarios, it might fail to predict even the majority of obtained scenarios, but *still be useful* both for generating scenarios more efficiently than a purely empirical approach and for providing systematic insight into the relations among scenarios.

We have built a typology of use-scenarios by converging several of our design and analysis projects. The first step was to recognize that basic-level use-scenarios cluster around pervasive user concerns. Indeed, when people construe their activities to themselves as being essentially similar, it is typically because in varying activities they are pursuing the same underlying concern. For example, the new user of a word processing system may want to type and print a simple document. This concern can spawn a staggering number of scenarios, even if we restrict attention to those scenarios in which the user is able to mount a thoughtful, measured, and error-free effort. But many of these differences are akin to the various ways of performing a musical piece; we can appreciate the differences, but we are overwhelmed by the similarities (Fodor, 1966).

Also like musical pieces, we have found that scenarios can be classified at multiple levels of abstraction. Thus, the "type and print" concern for word processor learners can be seen as instantiating an even more general concern learners have with determining how to accomplish goals that they (think they) already understand. These abstractions can be very useful: In designing or analyzing a word processor, one can closely link extant psychological design rationales (for example, Carroll, Kellogg, and Rosson, 1991) to new cases; many aspects of the type and print concern are invariant across word processors. More broadly still, one can link analyses and design argumentation generated for "how-to-do-it" scenarios even across application types (for example, between learning the Displaywriter and learning Smalltalk [Carroll and Rosson, 1991]).

In Figure 1, we have listed and exemplified six of the most general user concerns from two of our design and analysis projects. The Displaywriter is a word processor with a hierarchical menu-based interface; we developed a "training wheels" interface overlay that blocked the advanced functions that tended to attract learner errors (Carroll, Kellogg, and Rosson, 1991). Smalltalk is an object-oriented language and environment—programming in Smalltalk consists of the reuse and specialization of a rich library of classes (object types). We developed a tool (the Reuse View Matcher) that presented multiple, coordinated views of an exemplary application using a target class, allowing a programmer to explore concretely a typical usage situation (Carroll and Rosson, 1991).

The first user concern in Figure 1 is "orienting to appropriate goals," the new user of a word processor may know something about the functional capability of such systems, enough to have wanted to switch it on, but may still wonder how the device can help in pursuing document preparation goals, like writing a letter. Analogously, the Smalltalk programmer understands the black box reuse paradigm (for example, Cox, 1986), but still must determine what specific classes can play a role in the particular project under development.

Users pursue a variety of such concerns. They interact opportunistically with the system environment, wondering what the objects they encounter can

| **FIGURE 1** | **A Typology of User Concerns** |

The example concerns come from our task analyses of learning the Displaywriter and reusing Smalltalk classes; the italicized concerns were generated after developing the typology.

ORIENTING TO APPROPRIATE GOALS

- Displaywriter: how can this help me write a letter to Mom?
- Smalltalk reuse: *what classes can contribute to my color mixing application?*

INTERACTING WITH THE ENVIRONMENT OPPORTUNISTICALLY

- Displaywriter: choosing an option in the Create or Revise menu
- Smalltalk reuse: considering reuse of the Slider class

SEARCHING UNDER A DESCRIPTION

- Displaywriter: *finding the menu for page layout*
- Smalltalk reuse: looking for a class that simulates analog input; finding the Slider mouse conversion method

SEEKING HOW-TO-DO-IT PROCEDURAL INFORMATION

- Displaywriter: typing and printing a letter; formatting a letter
- Smalltalk reuse: hooking up a Slider instance to an application; setting a slider's relative width

SEEKING HOW-IT-WORKS EXPLANATORY INFORMATION

- Displaywriter: finding out why nothing has been printed yet; inferring the role of default settings in menus
- Smalltalk reuse: finding out why the slider shows the wrong scale position

REFLECTING ON AND CRAFTING ONE'S OWN WORK

- Displaywriter: *devising a faster way to do a simple buck slip*
- Smalltalk reuse: deciding to subclass Slider; determining what the specialization should provide

do and exploring the consequences of various possible actions. They search for things, text processing functions they imagine might exist, Smalltalk classes and behaviors they think they might need. They wonder how to accomplish procedural goals, how to format a letter or how to hook up a slider to a color mixer. They seek explanations for events and relationships they notice; for example, after losing track of a print job in the word processor queue, they may wonder how the queue works. And they reflect on the design of their own activity, considering how to streamline a word processing task or whether and how to specialize an existing Smalltalk class.

Even such a simple and coarse-grained typology can find use as a heuristic generator of scenario candidates. The italicized user concerns in Figure 1 are ones that we did not consider (Carroll, Kellogg, and Rosson, 1991; Carroll and Rosson, 1991). We generated them from the typology. To some extent, we can understand *why* they may have been overlooked: The "orienting" concern for code reuse raises a particularly ill-defined version of the classic "aboutness" question; it is a critical concern, but it is not clear how to address it, and it is particularly unclear how to address it within an example-based analysis system like the Reuse View Matcher. Similarly, it is easy to imagine a word processor user with the "search" concern, but the Training Wheels design, which hinges on rendering function nonexecutable, may implicitly discourage a designer from attending to that concern. In these cases, it seems that early design commitments (for example, to example-based analysis or to state blocking) can obscure or preempt consideration of plausible user concerns.

It is not surprising that a designer's extant commitments, to a genre like the View Matcher or to an instructional approach like training wheels, can create a sort of "scenario bias" (a term used by Kevin Singley and Steve Payne). Clearly, any designer will have incomplete and skewed knowledge of the usage situations to which the design work is targeted; this is also a source of bias. None of this is a particular problem for HCI design; it's in the background of all design. However, such biases can operate without being recognized. A common example is the tendency to consider only scenarios of routine and expert errorless performance, overlooking the pervasiveness of user scenarios incorporating slips, mistakes, and confusions (Carroll and Campbell, 1986). Such biases can be mitigated by enumerating paradigmatic types of cases, to help ensure that a rich set of possibilities are generated for any particular situation—increasing the chance that typical, critical, and appropriate ones will be in that set.

Figure 2 illustrates a scenario elaboration of one of the concerns enumerated in the typology of Figure 2; we have built a story describing a user's experience of changing an option in the Displaywriter's Create or Revise menu. The learner responds to the "item" prompt opportunistically, trying out the functionality offered, setting and changing a menu option, and perhaps learning something through the interaction, before moving on.

FIGURE 2

FIGURE 2   **Interacting with the Environment Opportunistically, as Exemplified in Displaywriter Option Choice Scenario**

The learner is on the Create or Revise menu, which offers various "items" (format and storage options) to be specified. There is a highlighted prompt: "Type ID letter to choose item; press Enter."; and an unhighlighted prompt: "When finished with this menu, press Enter."

The learner voices an interest in seeing what "items" are like: typing the ID letter of a menu item and pressing Enter. A further menu is displayed, listing various "choices," with a prompt: "Type your choice; press Enter." The "choices" are parameter values for the items, for example, various formats. The user specifies a choice, and the menu and prompt revert to the initial state (i.e., with the original highlighted and unhighlighted prompts displayed). The learner presses Enter to proceed to the Typing Area (the next system state).

An important use of the typology is to pursue hypothetical "what could go wrong?" lines of reasoning. That is, in addition to detailing how the various user concerns of the typology can be instantiated or satisfied, we detail how they can go awry. Thus, the opportunistic interaction scenario for the Displaywriter can, under certain conditions, become self-sustaining, and result in an option loop error (Carroll, 1990a, p. 29 f.; and Figure 3). This complementary use of the typology emphasizes generating error scenarios though it still undergenerates (for instance, it might not generate error scenarios very far off-path like the mutilated lease scenario).

We are not attempting to make scenario generation *automatic*. Using the typology to develop scenarios always requires detailed information or assumptions about the user's prior knowledge and the contexts and situations in which the scenarios might arise. Indeed, the most most important user concerns for a given design project might very well be the ones that do *not* instantiate any of the concerns in our typology. We see the typology only as a heuristic theory of scenarios and as a tool for systematically reifying one's understanding of the user's activity and experience.

Scenario-Based Design

At some point, one has to stop just generating scenarios, or at least diversify efforts, and *do* something with them. To the extent that one is generating scenarios empirically, one might decide to stop when half of the use-scenarios

FIGURE 3 **Interacting with the Environment Opportunistically, as Exemplified in the Option Loop Error Scenario**

The learner is on the Create or Revise menu, which offers various "items" (format and storage options) to be specified. There is a highlighted prompt: "Type ID letter to choose item; press Enter." The learner types the ID letter of a menu item and presses Enter; a further menu is displayed, listing various "choices," with a prompt: "Type your choice; press Enter." The "choices" are parameter values for the items, for example, various formats. The user specifies a choice and the menu and prompt revert to the initial state (i.e., with the highlighted prompt: "Type ID letter to choose item; press Enter").

The learner specifies items and choices over and over, changing options and then changing them back again. The learner expresses frustration and helplessness, can't seem to see a way out, and feels that she has failed in her original goal of typing and printing a letter.

Comment: The learner does not seem to "see" the exit prompt (on the screen all the time): "When finished with this menu, press Enter." (that is, press Enter *without* having specified an item).

observed are ones that have been seen before (to be more conservative, one might set the threshold at three-quarters). To the extent one is generating scenarios analytically, the stopping rule might be that every category of scenario in whatever typology or theory being used has been concretely instantiated (again, to be more conservative, one might decide to stop after generating three exemplars of each type).

Each scenario should be detailed and developed to capture and explore the finer structure of the operative psychology in the situations of use one has projected or observed. Thus, the scenarios in Figures 3 and 4 have been developed beyond merely enumerating the option choice concern of Figure 1. This detailing captures more about the knowledge, goals, reactions, and qualities of experience that inhere in the scenario. The learner in the error scenario does not seem to appreciate the optionality of the original prompt; it is treated as a directive (that is, you must or should type an ID letter). Most of the actions that comprise the elaboration of the option choice concern are not relevant to the learner's goal, and are seen by the learner as being nonrelevant.

Such detailed scenarios constitute a *narrative theory* of the artifact in use. Displaywriter scenarios like those in Figures 2 and 3 helped us envision alternative scenarios like Figure 4 in designing the Training Wheels interface (Carroll, 1990a). Scenarios have the important property that they can be

FIGURE 4   **Interacting with the Environment Opportunistically, as Exemplified in Training Wheels Option Choice Scenario**

The learner is on the Create or Revise menu which offers various "items" (format and storage options) to be specified. There is a highlighted prompt: "Type ID letter to choose item; press Enter." The learner types the ID letter of a menu item and presses Enter; a message appears at the bottom of the screen: "Change Alternate Format is not available on the Training Displaywriter". After trying several other items, with analogous effects, the learner presses Enter to proceed to the Typing Area (the next system state).

---

generated and developed *even before the situation they describe has been created.* Thus, one might have created a narrative theory of the Displaywriter before it was built, working with storyboards or storyboard software. If one had had the scenario typology of Figure 1, one might have generated scenarios for the "choosing an option in the Create or Revise menu" concern; by asking what could go wrong in such a scenario, one might have generated the option loop error scenario in Figure 3.

We believe that use-scenarios can be the principle design representation of an artifact (Carroll and Rosson, 1990) and have used them in the design of various tools for Smalltalk programming (see also Carroll and Rosson, 1991; Rosson and Carroll, 1992). The example scenario in Figure 5 was generated *before* we ever implemented the Reuse View Matcher (Rosson, Carroll, and Sweeney, 1991); the scenario was a key element in the design specification for that implementation.

Constructing Claims

The set of scenarios that a designed artifact affords (and inflicts on) its users entrains a set of specific empirical claims enabled by the artifact: claims that the user will attempt and can achieve a given scenario and claims about the psychological consequences of pursuing the scenario. We may design an instruction manual to support "how to do it" scenarios like the basic one in which a learner wishes to follow the manual to type and print a letter. We may add to this the associated "what could go wrong?" scenarios, for example, the scenario in which the learner fails to coordinate events in the system with "steps" in the manual.

FIGURE 5

Interacting with the Environment Opportunistically, as Exemplified in the Sliders Scenario

A programmer sees Slider in the class hierarchy, and the name sounds like it might be useful to the current project, a color-mixing application. The programmer opens a View Matcher on it, and selects the first example, a football player analysis program. A short demo of the football program is shown, and the programmer sees that sliders are being used to manipulate player characteristics that predict several player success measures. The programmer recognizes that this situation is very similar to the needs of the color-mixer.

From Carroll and Rosson, 1991.

Enumerating typical and critical use-scenarios characterizes the scope of an artifact's use, the inventory of basic-level tasks it facilitates and obstructs. The details of each scenario show how and why that scenario was supported or not supported by the artifact. The scenarios provide a representation medium for exploring and altering the design.

However, from an action science perspective, one wants to facilitate design analysis which can appeal to relevant abstractions, which can generalize from prior design projects. The transistor design group would not have succeeded to the same extent if they had merely discovered how to produce a particular solid-state amplifier. Their greatest success was discovering the right abstraction for understanding a broad class of solid-state devices. The analog for us has been the objective of making the implicit psychology embodied in situations of using an HCI artifact more systematically explicit than it is in an enumeration of its use-scenarios.

We do this by articulating fine-grained causal relationships that inhere in situations of use. We ask, "in this scenario context, what might this feature of the artifact contribute?" Thus, in the scenarios of Figures 2 and 3, we can ask what the highlighting of the "items" prompt (relative to the unhighlighted "exit" prompt) is contributing to the sequence of events in the scenario, and more broadly to the user's understanding of the events, the user's experience of the events, to the user's subsequent recollection and use of these events. Where scenarios provide a *narrative* account, claims provide a *causal* account.

The five claims enumerated in Figure 6 comprise the answer offered in our earlier analysis of the Displaywriter (Carroll, Kellogg, and Rosson, 1991): Each hypothesizes a specific psychological consequence of a system feature (the two prompts, their relative highlighting, and display interaction) under the scope of the option choice concern. The menu prompts explicitly define an action path for the learner in a manner that is consistent with other menus in

FIGURE 6

Psychological Claims Embodied in the Displaywriter Option Choice Scenario

1. Standard "item" and "exit" prompts cue and simplify menu interaction
   (but user may not yet have seen the other menus that use this technique and may assume it indicates something specific about this situation)

2. The item prompt conveys the procedure for changing options
   (but it may be interpreted as a directive by users who are confused or unsure)

3. Highlighting the item prompt makes the possibility of changing options more salient
   (but makes the exit prompt and the possibility of not changing options less salient)

4. Continued highlighting of the item prompt suggests the continuing appropriateness of changing options
   (but may make it harder to recognize that it is also OK to exit)

5. Returning the user to the Create or Revise menu is adequate feedback that an option change attempt is successful
   (but may not be enough feedback for users who are unsure or confused)

From Carroll, Kellogg, and Rosson, 1991.

the Displaywriter interface. But these causal relations also incorporate potential "tradeoffs," or *downsides*. The third claim in Figure 6 addresses consequences of highlighting the item prompt: The possibility of changing options is rendered more salient to the user, but at the cost of rendering less salient the possibility of not changing options. Recall that for the transistor, a key obstacle was the failure to appreciate all the properties of the n and p semiconductors (each type of semiconductor also includes minority carriers which in the other type are the majority carriers). This claim schema is intended to keep attention focused on all aspects of the psychological consequence.

In the scenario of Figure 5, we can similarly ask what the example application is contributing to the user's planning, action, evaluation, and experience of the "considering reuse of the Slider class" concern. In Carroll and Rosson, 1991, interacting opportunistically with paradigmatic examples can provide a powerful learning situation by offering guided discovery in the context of meaningful activity. In the particular scenario of interacting with an application using a slider, the functionality of the object is conveyed directly and concretely. A downside associated with any example-based learning claim is that concepts induced from examples are often over-narrow. A downside specific to the reuse scenario is that users could have trouble isolating the slider's functionality in the football example.

Generating Claims

Making a claims analysis is an analytical process that involves generating and evaluating a set of candidate claims. The chief empirical source for claims, as in the case of scenarios, is observation and analysis of user reports and behavior. But whereas a scenario set is merely an inventory of the typical and momentous things that users do, a claims analysis seeks to get at just *how* the artifact suggests to users that they do something one way or another, how it supports and fails to support their efforts, how it signals progress and error.

Thus, for the option change scenarios, the deployment of highlighting, the specific wording of the prompts, the immediate effects of given user actions all convey crucial meanings to the user, and together can conspire to cause the scenarios of Figures 2 and 3. The scenarios are integrated descriptions of what can happen to the user, and as such they are important pieces of information for understanding the Displaywriter and, of course, for redesigning it. A claims analysis goes further, it offers an *explanation* of the scenarios, an analysis of why the scenarios can occur.

We use the schematic structure exemplified in Figure 6 to stress that a claims analysis is an analysis of tradeoffs:

(artifact feature or technique) CAUSES (desirable psychological consequence) *BUT MAY ALSO CAUSE (undesirable psychological consequence).*[3]

We want to transcend both the uncritical advocacy of design memoirs and the unsympathetic negativity often associated with human factors evaluations. Like Rittel (1984), we assume that the key issues pertaining to a design will involve *both* arguments for and arguments against. Because a claims analysis juxtaposes the *positive* arguments or desirable psychological consequences for an artifact feature with its associated qualifications or downsides, it provides a medium for combining the traditional strengths of designer justification and usability evaluation.

Error scenarios like Figure 3 seem to be particularly good claim generators. When one sees another person snarled in some misconception or unfortunate sequence of actions, one naturally asks "Why?" In the option choice scenario, one might say that the user was misled by the highlighting. But to stop there would misgauge the role of the highlighting (for example, in conveying to the user the possibility of altering multiple options). Thus, the prominence of downside consequences in error scenarios can be a sort of bias and could lead to thrashing. In complex situations, there frequently are not unique causes; if we make a directly remedial design change each time we identify a downside, we will often undermine desirable consequences that might have been less prominent (at least, perhaps, until we have ill-advisedly disturbed them).

Of course, we should exploit the strikingness of error scenarios in helping to call attention to causal relations, but we also need to avoid focusing too narrowly on only certain causal relations in a complex situation. The claim schema, by balancing the desired and undesired entailments of an artifact feature, supports this. More generally, we can broaden the focus of a claims analysis just by generating *lots* of claims.

Figure 7 lists questions one can ask to generate claims from observed scenarios. We built this list by considering Norman's stage theory of action (Norman, 1986). For each stage, we imagined the general kinds of psychological consequences an artifact might have, translating those possible consequences into questions that one might ask about the artifact. The question list can be used like the user concern typology in Figure 1; that is, for a given artifact, one can try to instantiate one or more claims from each question in the figure. For example, the first question under "Goals" in Figure 7 directs our attention to how the artifact suggests a possible goal, and in that sense generates claim 4 of Figure 6; the first question under "Evaluation" in Figure 7 directs our attention to how the artifact conveys completion of a task, and thereby can generate claim 5 in Figure 6.

Generating claims directly from scenarios is demanding. However, given a literature of claims analyses, there is a supplementary method: analogy. In our work, we frequently refer to earlier analyses for suggestions. Particular scenarios, artifact features, even types of applications tend to be associated with particular claims. One has to be careful about overestimating the utility of this method: We may be unusually narrow designers (it seems that almost everything we design involves example-based learning). But then this might not be so atypical. At the least, the possibility of creating apt analogies from one claims analysis to another indicates that this kind of description and analysis can cumulate and generalize.

A stopping heuristic for claims generation is suggested by Figure 7 and by the relation of claims to scenarios. A claims analysis has attained reasonable completeness when it provides some causal account for each critical and typical scenario. One can use Figure 7 to ask whether a given causal account covers every relevant stage of action in a scenario; in fact, one can do this by just posing each of the questions listed in Figure 7. This heuristic will typically lead to a large set of claims, but the claims might be "prioritized" by first ranking scenarios with respect to criticality and frequency, and then ranking individual claims within each scenario according to the importance of their user consequence to the given scenario (for example, weighting consequences involving high-level goals more heavily than those involving low-level goals).

FIGURE 7   **Questions to Ask in Generating Claims, Organized by Norman's Seven Stages of Action**

GOALS

- How does the artifact evoke goals in the user?
- How does the artifact encourage users to import pre-existing task goals?

INTENTION

- How does the artifact suggest that a particular task goal is appropriate or inappropriate? simple or difficult? basic or advanced? risky or safe?
- What inappropriate goals are most likely? most costly?

SPECIFICATION

- What distinctions must be understood in order to decompose a task goal into methods? how are these distinctions conveyed by the artifact?
- What planning mistakes are most likely? most costly?
- How does the artifact encourage the use of background knowledge (concepts, metaphors, skills) in planning a task?

EXECUTION

- How does the artifact make it easy or difficult to perform a task?
- What slips are most likely? most costly?
- How does the artifact indicate progress in task performance?

PERCEPTION

- What are the most salient features of the artifact? what do these features communicate to the user?
- What features are commonly missed and at what cost?
- What features of the artifact change as users carry out a task? what do these changes communicate to the user?

INTERPRETATION

- How does the artifact guide the user to make correct inferences?
- What incorrect inferences are most likely? most costly?
- How does the artifact encourage the use of background knowledge in making inferences?

EVALUATION

- How does the artifact convey completion of a task?
- How does the artifact help users recognize, diagnose, and recover from errors?
- How does the artifact encourage elaboration and retrieval of task goals and methods?

From Norman, 1986.

Justifying Claims

In problem solving, generation is the hardest stage. However, once one generates a set of claims, the next step is to justify them. Because our concern is to develop an action science approach to HCI, we have focused on justification by deductive linking to scientific principles. For the most part, we have limited our consideration to psychology though clearly other sciences are relevant (economics, sociology, physics). Moreover, we must often settle for less than real deduction; basic science, and psychology perhaps more so than most, often leaves boundary conditions inadequately specified. This is the conundrum of getting from the laboratory to the real world; the only general solution for it is a theory of the world.

Our framework bounds the "theory of the world" problem: We depend on basic science only for justification of claim consequences. In cases for which there is no relevant science, our approach converges with deliberately ascientific, argumentation approaches (for example, Conklin and Burgess Yakemovic, 1991). In other words, we are working toward grounding claims in science, but if the science lets us down in the end, we still have the claims, and our design arguments still proceed (justified in this case only within the design context itself and by the utility of the design result).

We also hope that by linking scientific justification to design argument, we can improve the relevance of the science itself. Simon (1981) suggests that psychology is a science of adaptation to "artificial" circumstances. Thus, HCI is a good venue for basic psychology. The justification we build for claim consequences, even if we fail to import anything of value from official academic sources of psychology, is psychological analysis nonetheless. If it proves eventually to be both useful and abstract at all, it is psychological science. In other words, we can try to give some science back to psychology.

Finally, whether or not we are in the position of linking psychology to claim consequences, we believe it is important not to give up the possibility of linkage. If we do this, we are surely on the slippery slope of design memoir with little to ground our descriptions of a design but our intentions, our common sense and, at length, the empirical bottom-line of a design result. We might not be able to do better than this, but we ought to try.

Much psychological theory can be adduced to back up the claims of Figure 6: For example, the advantages of structural consistency in learning were developed in Esper's (1925) work on artificial languages (see also Carroll, 1985) and in Thorndike's 1903 work on common elements (see also Kieras and Polson, 1985). The tendency of persons in low-power roles to take suggestions as directions, the downside of the second claim in Figure 6, is also a fairly broad and basic finding (Grice, 1967, 1975; Milgram,1968). The tendency for the relative salience of one entity in a perceptual field to undermine the salience of others (claim 4) is developed in Gestalt theories of figure–ground organization (Köhler, 1929) and in more modern theories of attentional limits (Kahneman, 1973). Finally, the parsing problems associated with determining the ending of a sequence (claim 5) are very general (Garner, 1974).

Claims are not justified in isolation, either from one another or from the use situations they describe. Besides linking consequences to abstract phenomena, we seek to interrogate the claims themselves. One rule of thumb we use is to deny the causal consequence, and reason from this toward a "contradiction." This is a logically degenerate form of reductio ad absurdum. The highlighting claim in Figure 6, for example, can be denied as "highlighting the item prompt makes the possibility of changing options less salient." This seems overwhelmingly implausible because it encourages some confidence that the original (undenied) claim was right. Or recall the example-based learning claim of the "what do sliders do?" scenario. Denying the causal consequent would yield the new claim: "Paradigmatic examples of an object's use do not support the analysis of its functionality." It is difficult to find a truly paradigmatic usage example that fails to convey something about an object's functionality.

As with any heuristic, one must be careful about using this method too mechanically. Its strength is that it takes a single claim and generates a set of variant claims, not all of which are likely to be true. Thereby, it poses questions to the analyst, which in our experience have often led to the rejection or tuning of a hypothesized claim.

Another heuristic that can help the analyst confront candidate claims is to collect and group consequences that bear tradeoff relations. For example, claim 3 in Figure 6 addresses both desirable and undesirable salience consequences of the relative highlighting of prompts. Grouping these together into a claim schema helps the analyst confront both sides of the tradeoff and thereby the pertinence of the claim as a causal account of what could be salient to a user in an option change scenario. Indeed, a measure of how well consequences are grouped is the extent to which the resulting claim schemas are effective in provoking inquiry.

Note that nothing deep hinges on the labeling of consequences in a claim schema as "desirable" and "undesirable"; this merely provides a heuristic way of organizing claims that bear a tradeoff relation. An alternative to this schema is to merely enumerate the implicit causal relationships engendered by an artifact and list them alphabetically. But collecting related claims into a more encompassing schema makes it easier to compare the bases of relation. Fronting the desirable consequences helps the designer or analyst keep track of what has been "accomplished" in the design—claims currently regarded as true and desirable. Italicizing the undesirable downside claims helps call attention to aspects of the design that may still require work, more analysis or redesign.

The heuristic of grouping related upsides and downsides also has the benefit of helping generate a more thorough psychological design rationale: If one has a claim without a downside or, perhaps, without an upside, one may be moved to more aggressively ask why, to focus more on what the complete rationale could be.[4] There is no guarantee that there will be an answer to the question, but in our experience there often is an answer, and making that bit of rationale explicit helps get out the relevant issues: It is minority and majority current flow in semiconductors again; we do not want to make the mistake of thinking that only the most obvious claims matter—quite often it is just the reverse.

Claims analysis is neither system modeling nor user modeling. Indeed, we feel that separating these two is responsible for the lack of impact either has had on design and design analysis. Our interest is in keeping all the key components causally linked. A system model that organizes artifact features without causal commitments to specific psychological consequences for users is of little interest for HCI design or design analysis; a user model that systematizes psychological capacities and experiences without causal commitments to specific artifact features is also of little interest.

Using Claims in Scenario-Based Design

Claims analysis can produce situated explanations of predecessor artifacts, and these understandings can be used to envision and to craft new scenarios and new artifacts. The amount and fidelity of information that can enter into a claims analysis will be greatest for artifacts and situations that have been implemented and deployed: In such cases, analytic work can be enriched and complemented by empirical observation. However, the method loses little when applied to artifacts and situations that are only designs and not yet implementations (though we may be less likely to "discover" shocking causal relations strictly by analysis, just as we may be less likely to analytically generate shocking scenarios like the mutilated lease). Thus, claims analysis can be strongly proactive in the sense that it can be used to develop and iteratively refine explanations of artifacts that do not yet exist. This sort of use was illustrated in the development of the Reuse View Matcher (Carroll and Rosson, 1991).

Our use of claims analysis in scenario-based design is similar across evolution from an existing artifact and iteration within an artifact under design: Our basic gambit is to remove, mitigate, or alter downsides (undesirable consequences) while maintaining or strengthening upsides (desirable consequences). This is easy to say but more difficult to do for two reasons. First, one does not alter claims directly. Claims are causal relations between artifacts and users. We want to improve the consequences of the artifact for the user, but we can do this only by altering properties of the artifact. The claim schemas guide our attention to relevant artifact features and make explicit the underlying tradeoffs for the user that inhere in using the artifact. We can reason backward, denying a downside, maintaining or strengthening its upside, and projecting a change in the artifact (for example, a change in Displaywriter highlighting) that could bring this about. But we can only alter what is of real interest to us (the user consequence) *indirectly*.

The second reason that claim-driven design can be difficult is the problem of nonunique causes: Suppose we focus our design attention on a particular claim, wishing to improve the consequence for users in some specific way. We turn to the causally relevant artifact feature, reason about its upsides and downsides, and we make a design change, which may lead to a new claim. How confident can we be now that the new claim is justified? The answer depends, at least in principle, on every other claim embodied in the use of the artifact. This web of causality does not inhere in claims analysis or any class of method, it inheres in the nature of design (Rittel, 1984; see Carroll, 1990b; Carroll and Kellogg, 1989 for related discussion).

Claims analysis provides a vocabulary for reasoning about causal relations between persons and design options. This vocabulary *directly* links the classes of things the designer can actually alter (namely, artifact features) with those things the designer really cares about but must alter indirectly (namely, the consequences for users and their basic tasks). Designers will try to do this anyway; they have no choice. However, when they do not have a detailed representation, like a claims analysis, they will use whatever they do have, namely, the (inarticulate) artifact features over which they have direct control.

Thus we will revisit the Displaywriter and Smalltalk reuse claims and illustrate how claim-based reasoning can play a role in design, and in particular, how it can manage the two difficulties of indirection and nonunique causes.

To mitigate the downside of the highlighting claim in Figure 6, the highlighting might be removed or the scenario redesigned so that the user's attention is not so strongly drawn to the item prompt. More dramatically, we could consider scenarios in which the item prompt is not even presented; after all, for new users of the Displaywriter, resetting options is one of those "unrecommended" activities. However, taking this approach has other consequences for the user. For example, the item prompt and the exit prompt are standard dialog components in the Displaywriter interface; hence, altering their relative highlighting or their appearance at all has global consistency consequences (undesirable consequences in other use-scenarios). Even within the scope of the option choice scenario, there are consequences: Without the item prompt, the procedure for changing options would never be presented; without continued highlighting of the prompt the continued possibility of changing options would not be clear; and so on. In sum, these approaches mitigate a particular downside, but they do this by moving the tradeoff elsewhere, possibly worsening the net consequence for users.

One can develop this line of argumentation to "derive" the redesign move that was actually made in this case, namely, the development of the Training Wheels interface (Carroll, Kellogg, and Rosson, 1991). This solution involves a global mode for the system in which requests to the item prompt are intercepted and trigger a special "blocking message" (for example, "Change Alternate Format is not available on the Training Displaywriter," recall Figure 4). This solution is not without some cost: The learner who wants to change alternate format from within the Training Wheels interface will be frustrated. Nevertheless, the design argument and experimental studies indicate that this design move is effective and pleasant.

In designing the Reuse View Matcher, it was salient to us that when programmers wondered what some class they had come across (say, Slider) could do in the context of an ongoing project (an opportunistic interaction scenario), their decision to reuse the class typically involved instantiating it (for example, in a workspace), perhaps embedding the new object in a context of use, and then exploring its behavior and its possible contribution to their project. We summarized this in a claim schema:

an instantiated object supports discovery of its functionality
(*but finding or creating a representative instance may be difficult*)
(*but trying out individual messages may be tedious or distracting to ongoing work*)

In our design argumentation, we tried to maintain the upside of learning from an instantiated example, but mitigate the downsides of having to do the instantiation and orchestrate an illuminating example. We reasoned by analogy to our View Matcher for learning that we might offer the user prefabricated, paradigmatic examples, examples crafted to illuminate the typical use of the target object and animated to minimize the potential distractions to a user who, by assumption, was interested in using the target object in *some other* ongoing project.

This line of design argument converged on the scenario in Figure 5 and ultimately in the Reuse View Matcher system (Rosson, Carroll, and Sweeney,

1991). New scenarios such as this, and the eventual artifact, entrained changes in the claim:

> paradigmatic scripted demos that use an object help programmers analyze its functionality
> *(but the concept induced might be too narrow)*
> *(but users may have difficulty isolating the target functionality)*

The original downsides have been mitigated though they are superseded by other downsides (see the earlier discussion of example-based learning techniques). That tradeoffs remain is unremarkable; the key point is that the claims representation allowed us to keep track of where we were with respect to these upsides and downsides, to deliberately and selectively work on specific issues in the design, and to assess our work.

It is said that the objective of building a principled methodology is that one does not have to think; the thought required is preempted just to the extent that the principles of the methodology do some work. This orientation can easily get out of hand, as in the notorious search for a "figure of merit" in traditional human factors. One wants to get work out of an action science approach, but one neither expects nor wishes to have a rich and complex decision space conceptually bleached.

The Task-Artifact Framework: An Example

In the foregoing two sections, we have presented the main representations and techniques for scenario-based design and for constructing psychological design rationales. In this section, we exchange the analytical view for a more synthetic development; we sketch the "information flow" (Carroll, 1990b; Wright, 1978) in a gedanken design project. We describe the design of an instructional manual for a word processor: First, we generate scenarios (that is, we make a basic-level task analysis of the domain). Second, we use the task analysis as a rubric for investigating the psychological design rationale for an existent manual (artifact). Third, we use the claims analysis to drive the design argumentation to produce a new manual design (that is, a set of redesigned use-scenarios). Finally, we assess the design project by developing psychological design rationale for the new manual. (This example is a pedagogic reconstruction of our early work on the Minimal Manual [Carroll, 1990a].)

Generating Scenarios

In Figure 8, the scenario typology of Figure 1 is used to generate a list of candidate scenarios for a word processor's instruction manual. As "orienting" concerns, the user may wonder about the kind of instructional situation this is and just how the manual will help in accessing and using the word processor functionality. The user may refer opportunistically to the manual: wondering how to make the screen match a given figure on a given page, seeing a

FIGURE 8   **Scenarios for an Instruction Manual Generated from the Typology**

ORIENTING TO APPROPRIATE GOALS

- How should I use this manual?
- How can this help me find out how to write a letter to mom?

INTERACTING WITH THE ENVIRONMENT OPPORTUNISTICALLY

- Using an appealing figure in the book as a goal
- Skipping ahead to the "reformatting" chapter

SEARCHING UNDER A DESCRIPTION

- Looking for the "print" procedure
- Matching the screen state to some figure in the book
- Finding information on the thing that corresponds to a clipboard

SEEKING HOW-TO-DO-IT PROCEDURAL INFORMATION

- Following steps to type and print a letter
- Following a prompt to check the screen for feedback

SEEKING HOW-IT-WORKS EXPLANATORY INFORMATION

- Inferring what text indentation signifies
- Understanding why it is useful to practice creating a lease
- Conjecturing why the "print" procedure was repeated

REFLECTING ON AND CRAFTING ONE'S OWN WORK

- Annotating and highlighting the index
- Learning to ignore indented text

function referred to in a summary or review and then deciding to practice or explore that function (out of sequence). The user may search for terms in the manual or for concepts without being sure of the correct term. In conventional manuals, the user may wonder how to follow instructions and may be unsure about how to coordinate the manual with events in the system. The user may not always immediately see how the manual works, for example, with respect to typographical conventions, and even so, may reflect on the rationale for the manual (perhaps wondering why certain activities and not others were selected as exercises). Finally, the user may reflect on his or her developing skill, about how tasks can be simplified or enriched: what can really be skipped, what is really important.

Of course, the typology will undergenerate, preserving an incentive to augment the scenario set with empirically attested scenarios—for example, the infamous lease mutilation scenario (see also chapters 2 and 3 of Carroll, 1990a).

Psychological Design Rationale for a Manual

Given a decent scenario set, we try to expose and codify psychological explanations for why the scenarios can occur. Consider the central "orienting to goals" and "how-to-do-it" scenarios in following the manual to type and print a letter. (We are assuming a self-instruction manual exemplifying the "systems approach" of Gagne and Briggs, 1979; again, for more details see Carroll, 1990a, chapters 2 and 3.) The learner seeking to create and print a letter is immediately confronted by supporting material that does not directly bear on the type-and-print concern: a description of the workstation hardware, explanations about magnetic storage devices, pointers, displays, and an orientation to the use of word processing equipment in office settings. The learner defers the type-and-print goal to read through (some of) this material. The learner confirms that all the system components are present. At length (about 25 pages later), the learner reaches the procedural part of the manual and is introduced to the use of menus and command keys through some elementary exercises. The learner scrupulously follows each instruction, occasionally feeling some frustration at not making more rapid and tangible progress and occasionally wondering what other things could be done with the screens and menus involved in the exercises, but basically confident that the manual "knows" what it is doing and is willing to follow. After three chapters of this, the learner successfully prints out a first document.

Figure 9 presents claims that generalize and abstract hypothesized causal relations between features and techniques of the manual artifact and consequences for a learner pursuing the type-and-print concern. Perhaps not all the

FIGURE 9   **Implicit Claims for the "Type and Print a Letter" Scenario**

1. A structural description of major system components conveys a mental model of how the device works (which may help ground or rationalize the learner's understanding of how to use it).
   (but the structural description may distract the learner, may frustrate the learner's concern with typing and printing, and may simply fail to support use of the device)

2. Decomposing "typing and printing" into component steps and training each of these in turn allows a complex target objective to be systematically built up from parts.
   (but learners may not tolerate such rote programs or may make errors that corrupt what is learned)
   (but this organization may not facilitate retrieval and application in real task settings)

3. Keeping directive instructions and learner actions in lock-step contiguity allows the learner to know exactly what to do and when (promoting confidence and curtailing uncertainty).
   (but this does not promote reflection or analysis on the part of the learner)
   (but learners must relinquish control)

downsides in Figure 10 are exemplified in the type-and-print scenario described, but it is easy to imagine that they might have been (see Carroll, 1990a, chapters 2 and 3). Each of these claims could be constructed by asking the questions of Figure 7. The first claim is suggested by the third question under "Specification," asking how the artifact encourages the use of background knowledge in task planning. The second claim is suggested by the first question under "Specification," asking about the distinctions needed to decompose task goals and how these are conveyed. The third claim is suggested by the first question under "Interpretation," asking how the user is guided toward correct inferences.

The claims can also be justified by the laws of basic psychology: For example, with respect to claim 1, many studies describe the role of mental models and advance organizers in learning and exercising procedural skills (for example, Ausubel, 1960; Gentner and Stevens, 1983); some have characterized specific boundary conditions on the utility of mental models (Halasz and Moran, 1983). With respect to claim 2, separately practicing skill components can simplify the learning of a complex skill (Gagne and Briggs, 1979). However, making errors during learning can also corrupt what is learned (Terrace, 1963), and some skill decompositions do not prepare learners to apply what they know in performing a whole skill (Lave, 1988).

With respect to the third claim in Figure 9, the utility of closely coordinating feedback with learner actions to facilitate performance has been described (Lewis and Anderson, 1985). But undermining the learner's control of the situation can obstruct learning (Weiner, 1980). Of course, the analysis merely

FIGURE 10   ## A Redesign for the "Type and Print a Letter" Scenario

The learner quickly scans a labeled diagram of the major system components, noting correspondence with the system being used and associating general functional roles with some of the major parts. Some other general information about using the manual, starting the system, and recovering from errors (on the next three pages) is only noted in passing.

The next nine pages detail the type-and-print procedure; the chapter subheadings are named by the major menus and command environments accessed in the procedure. The procedures are couched at a level that compels the learner to notice, remember, and reason about details (for example, the second time the user needs to use the Typing Tasks menu, the instruction merely says "get to the Typing Tasks menu," leaving generation, recollection, or search for the procedural details to the learner).

The manual presents a continuous typing and printing project within which the learner is presented with the core functions. Events on the screen and passages in the manual are explicitly coordinated by interrogative prompts ("Can you find this prompt on the screen?"). The learner reflects on what is happening in the situation, and at one point notices that the prompts do not match. The learner glances up a few lines in the text and notices a special dingbat indicating situation-specific error recovery information, and follows the recovery procedure. Every few pages an open-ended "on your own" exercise is suggested ("Type a letter to a friend..."). The learner chooses to undertake one of these tasks and spends several minutes planning and creating a personal document.

sketched here would be carried out to greater detail in a real design process, and it would be carried out for several or many different scenarios (as in Figure 8).

As we proceed, we confront hypothesized consequences of our claims to try to generate new perspectives and considerations. We reason counterfactually about the hypothesized claim consequences as a sanity check on the analysis (for example, asking whether having instructions and action in lock-step contiguity *does not* help the learner know just what to do and when).

Scenario-Based Design of a Better Manual

The claim representation can be used to fathom the design space and to orient redesign work concretely and comprehensively (again pursuing the transistor analogy, we move on to the task of designing a solid-state amplifier with an explicit theory of semiconductors—including an explicit inscription about minority carriers). Our first heuristic is to focus on the downsides of the claims (in Figure 9), asking how we might redesign the type and print scenario to mitigate these downsides.

Thus, we ask how the description of system components can be less of a distraction, less of a frustration to a user with a how-to-do-it concern; we ask how it might be made more directly useful to someone pursuing that concern. For example, we might consider a type-and-print scenario in which the system description is minimal, perhaps a single picture or diagram. In this scenario, the user quickly scans for information of possible relevance or interest, and more fluidly moves on to the how-to-do-it procedure.

With respect to the second claim, we ask how the instructional sequence could be made less rigid, how the occurrence of errors can be managed so that mistakes are not made, or at least are not misinterpreted as events of instruction and learned! We ask how the practice can better facilitate retrieval and application in real task situations. For example, we might envision scenarios in which the instructional sequences are more flexible, allowing users to follow procedures more loosely. We consider scenarios in which the procedures to be followed are designed to appear to the user "intrinsically" structured (on analogy with the way old-fashioned specification-selection errors were obviated by graphical interfaces). We imagine scenarios for error blocking to preempt confused interpretations and untoward learning, scenarios for error detection, diagnosis and recovery to streamline the process of getting back on track, and scenarios for providing post mortem commentary to clarify how errors were made and how they can be avoided in the future. And we consider scenarios in which potential contexts of real application for a skill being practiced are suggested or scenarios in which the practice occurs in the context of a real task.

With respect to the third claim in Figure 9, we ask how reflection and analysis might be promoted for the learner and how the learner might be encouraged to feel more control. We imagine scenarios in which concept reflection questions or suggestions are intermittently presented to learners throughout the manual. We consider how the illusion of control might be projected to learners or how more real control might be introduced. (Again, this sort of reasoning process would be carried out for many more claims; indeed, each line of scenario reasoning sets constraints for all the other possible scenarios, which in effect structures and simplifies the design space in which one ends up working.)

The flip-side of our heuristic is to maintain or strengthen the upsides of claims, to capitalize on the desirable consequences for users that might have already been secured through given artifact features and techniques. We want to present some structural description of the device to convey a mental model to support learning procedures. We want to decompose the target skill into components, each of which is more easily learned than the whole skill. We want to keep the learner's reading in the manual coordinated with the learner's interaction with the system.

As we proceed, we try to balance this diversity of requirements in the set of use-scenarios we design, reiteratively assessing the impact of design commitments on the design goals and relations embodied in the claims analysis. The scenario in Figure 10 shows part of one design solution; a set of such scenarios—sufficiently developed—could serve as a design representation for a new manual.

Understanding the New Design

We are not only after artifacts though. We want to understand how and why the new manual may be better.[5] Having only just envisioned the new and perhaps improved artifact, we ask more skeptically what is really at stake in this design. Having tried to strengthen and develop desirable consequences for the user, and eradicate undesirable ones, we now try to make explicit the inevitable tradeoffs that inhere in the new design. One of the key properties of true design problems is that they are never finally solved (for example, Rittel, 1984), and our method is deliberately directed at creating possibilities for conversation and consideration, denying the illusion of closed cases, and keeping the open issues in view. Figure 11 presents a claims analysis for the piece of the manual design we have been discussing.

The first claim is a simple case. The course of the design argument addressed the downsides of the corresponding mental model claim in Figure 9, controlling the potential problems of distraction and frustration brought on by a long introductory section, but introducing potential problems of inadequate information. This is a very typical case in which designers move along a curve, trading off one downside for another. The value added by an explicit claims analysis, even in such a simple case, is that the designer is disabused of seeing what happened as merely moving in the design space from a bad situation to a good one, and at the same time is confronted with open issues: To wit, how bad a problem is it that the user cannot diagnose system errors? how can the user be assured that the minimal structural description is adequate?

The second claim in Figure 11 describes the new design's response to problems people have in tolerating rote learning and getting much out of it (problems transferring skill to real settings, a downside of the second claim in Figure 9) *and* to the downside of the third claim of Figure 9 about promoting reflection and analysis. The redesigned manual decomposes tasks into the key menu and command environments users need to access in the task, and presents these components in a more integrated task setting. The claim schema

FIGURE 11   **Claims Embodied in the "Type and Print a Letter" Scenario**

1. A minimal structural description of the major system components (a labeled graphic) conveys an adequate mental model of how the device works to support learning how to use it.
   (but the structural description may be too incomplete for some purposes, for example, diagnosing system problems, or may leave some learners worried that they do not understand enough to go on)

2. Decomposing "typing and printing" into the key menu and command environment components, but training the entire coherent procedure, allows a complex target skill to be analyzed and synthesized at the same time, and may thereby both speed up initial learning and facilitate subsequent retrieval and application in real task settings.
   (but learners used to systems-style instruction could be made uncomfortable or unconfident by not seeing components cleanly split out from one another for separate instructional presentation)
   (but learners could be overwhelmed by the contextual detail of a realistic task)

3. Supporting error detection, diagnosis, and recovery focuses and motivates learners and helps sharpen a concept of correct performance.
   (but errors can be frustrating, can disrupt task goals, and can corrupt what is learned)

4. More realistic instructional tasks, system-manual coordination prompts, error recovery procedures, and "on your own" suggestions encourage learners to reflect on their actions and experiences in the situation and to feel responsibility for and control over what is happening.
   (but learners may be anxious about bearing such responsibilities)

asserts that these features will encourage more analysis during the synthesis of the skill (since a meaningful task is being worked on, it is possible to think about it as a whole), and will facilitate subsequent retrieval and application in real tasks (since the target real tasks and the instructional task are similar). It also claims this will be an efficient rearrangement. The downsides left open pertain to the learners' likely familiarity with system-style decomposition and the possibility that learning by working on a real task will be too difficult.

For the third claim, our reasoning concerning errors in rote learning programs (a downside of the second claim in Figure 9) impelled scenario work on error detection, diagnosis, and recovery. The other downside of that claim, pertaining to transfer to real tasks, moved us to consider scenarios with more flexible and realistic instructional tasks—perhaps inviting other types of learner error. Finally, the downside of the third claim in Figure 9 concerning reflection and analysis further urged more explicit attention to error. Thus, an assortment of downside issues, across two claim schemas, had the effect of raising what finally became a separate issue: error handling. The rote manual implicitly assumed that error would not occur (the steps were so modest, split out from each other and from any context, and the sequence clearly marked).

It is also interesting that this claim schema includes downsides that are not different in kind from the downside that impelled the consideration of errors: frustration, disruption, and the corruption of what is learned. This example makes the point that claims analysis is not cognitive Taylorism (Taylor, 1911): One does not count claims, one thinks about them. What is important about the error claim in Figure 11 is that new considerations were entered into the design argument, new artifact features and techniques were deployed in the manual design, and new potential consequences for users were created. The value added lies in systematically presenting implicit reasoning and rationale to be critiqued and improved.

The final claim in Figure 11 focuses on promoting reflection and analysis, and learner control. The techniques of realistic tasks, explicit system-manual coordination and error support, and open-ended exercises encourage this by giving the learner something meaningful to manage, decisions to make, consequences to evaluate. But of course, people could be anxious about being put in control; it is another case of sliding along the tradeoff curve from one design hazard to another. The structure of this kind of design process is schematized in Figure 12, a more deliberated reconstituting of the task-artifact cycle as an integration of design and analysis.

Toward an Action Science

We must be heedful of a facile and historically mistaken view about the nature of technology evolution, that basic science regularly holds up a beacon to show the way forward (Basalla, 1988; Kuhn, 1962; Morrison, 1974; Multhauf, 1959). In the modern era, the *need* for science-based technology development has dramatically increased: Technology is more complex and it evolves more quickly than ever before.

The opportunity for science-based technology development is also better than ever before. The notion of action science—science that seeks simultaneously to understand the world and to improve it—can be a key to this. As illustrated in the example of the transistor (among many others, for example, Jewkes, Sawers, and Stillerman, 1958, 1969), this paradigm is already up and running in the contemporary physical sciences. The notion has been articulated for the social sciences (Argyris, 1980; Torbert, 1976), but there is a need for compelling exemplification.

This work hinges on the simple argument that if we make the concepts and actions of HCI design work more explicit, we will be better able to manage and to learn from it. We share many of the goals of software methodologists (for example, Brooks, 1975; Floyd et al., 1992; Freeman, 1987; Gilb, 1988) since

FIGURE 12

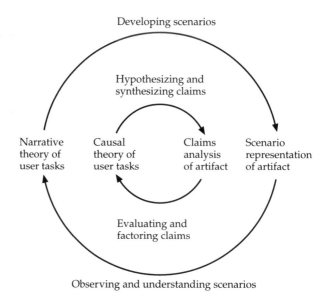

Developing scenarios

Hypothesizing and
synthesizing claims

Narrative | Causal | Claims | Scenario
theory of | theory of | analysis | representation
user tasks | user tasks | of artifact | of artifact

Evaluating and
factoring claims

Observing and understanding scenarios

The task-artifact cycle as an information flow for HCI.

we assume that action science starts and ends with the real experiences and activities of the field: learning, using, and designing computer systems and applications. But we want to pursue these interests in such a way as to construct explanations and generalizations about HCI tasks and artifacts; we want an action science of HCI.

Our work focuses on codifying, sharpening, and applying the concepts-in-action that already typify practice—the arguments developed for design decisions, either within the design process or as design memoir reflections on that process, and the scenarios embodying user concerns and requirements, either attributed as such to users or envisioned as possibilities to be enabled by new artifacts. We seek to refine these concepts-in-action, to make them better practical methods and better abstractions for action science.

The task-artifact cycle reifies the background for practical activity in the field, which sets an appropriate target for scientific abstractions and a context for developing methodology. The notion of user concern allows abstraction of scenarios, better narrative theories of artifacts in use, but also a typology of scenarios that can be a heuristic generator. The yield is a potentially thorough, systematic, and generalizable design representation, and a framework for design analysis that is also richly contextualized.

Psychological design rationale, the implicit psychological claims embodied in the use of artifacts, provides a conceptual framework for distinguishing between designer intention and design actuals, a means of more systematically producing design memoirs (indeed, of producing them in advance of producing the design), but also the conceptual elements of a causal theory of artifacts in use. The yield is an explicit quasi-deductive design argument detailing what was done and why, grounding the design in a framework of prior artifacts and embodied principles.

The minimized and naturalized ontology of tasks and artifacts allows this framework for science-in-design to be bought-into strictly as necessary and as desired. For example, design can focus on scenarios alone, concrete instantiations of basic-level tasks, and problems pertaining to them (see Carroll and Rosson, 1991; Lewis, Rieman, and Bell, 1991; for even stronger positions). The typology of user concerns can be invoked to guide abstraction of a scenario-based design representation. One can go further and detail the claims embodied in scenarios to explain why the scenarios incorporate the phenomena they do. And finally, one can assimilate claims analyses of given artifacts-in-use to other such analyses to draw out and to bound principles and abstractions about HCI, and about psychology more generally.

The key to an HCI action science is to accommodate the background of current practice, adding to it a flexible range of options such that a modest assimilation of the framework is edifying but only modestly disruptive, and such that larger assimilations are no more than proportionately disruptive and perhaps more than proportionately edifying. In this way, designers can pursue projects and make recognizable progress with the confidence of familiarity.

In our own work, we design things that we and others will use, but with a deliberate meta-focus on how we do that work. Thus, we know that the method can be used since through its development it always has been used. Most generally, it helps provide the designer with a framework for developing and interrogating ideas concretely and conceptually at the same time with seemingly little overhead. Using the task-artifact framework has diminished in us the tendency to fix problems tout court by helping us more regularly focus on what is *good* about a current situation and work through the implications a design move under consideration may have for those good aspects as well as for the more attention-getting problematic aspects (cf. Festinger, 1957).

Many challenges lie ahead. For example, in an action science of HCI, knowledge produced, refined, and contextualized in design must be *reused* in subsequent design work. But how is this supposed to happen? It seems questionable whether discursive analyses like those shown in Figures 6, 9, and 11 are suitable, not merely because they are intellectually demanding, but because they do not make explicit the myriad interconnections among user concerns, scenarios, claims, artifact features, types of applications, and so forth. Exploring and investigating these interconnections in the context of a design project is the real vision of an action science: knowledge relevant to action, provided in the context of action (see Fischer et al., 1991).

An important subcase in which analyses of scenarios and claims must be rendered easier to synthesize is in tracking dependencies. Clearly, one cannot expect to improve a design overall by focusing on a single scenario or, by extension, a single claim: Every scenario potentially constrains what other scenarios can be envisioned. We are developing a software tool to help designers manage a set of use-scenarios, by providing explicit connections among the (shared) components of different scenarios, along with techniques for abstracting across a set of scenarios to generate a design model (Rosson and Carroll, 1992).

A third arena of technical challenge is that of developing our understanding of artifacts and situations to better recognize and exploit what generalities there are. For example, as basic tasks can be seen as instantiating general user concerns (Figure 1), artifacts can be seen as instantiating genres (Carroll and Rosson, 1991; Newman, 1988) or prescriptive design models (Carroll, Singley, and Rosson, 1991). Such "second-order artifacts" (Carroll and Campbell, 1989) can be described by the typical and critical scenarios their exemplars "inherit," and by the claims embodied in these scenarios. For example, (Carroll, Singley, and Rosson, 1991), an analysis of the MiTTS minimalist tutorial and tools Smalltalk (Carroll, Singley, and Rosson, 1991; Rosson, Carroll, and Bellamy, 1990) showed how MiTTS inherits claims from both the minimalist model and the systems approach (Gagne and Briggs, 1979).

Several current projects are developing tools and methods for making explicit what would otherwise be implicit justification for design choices (Carroll and Rosson, 1991; Conklin and Burgess Yakemovic, 1991; Fischer et al., 1991; Lee and Lai, 1991; Lewis, Rieman, and Bell, 1991; MacLean et al., 1991). Some of this work shares with ours the specific interest in grounding rationale in scientific principles (MacLean et al., 1991). Other work is directed at developing systematic frameworks for usability evaluation (Lewis et al., 1990; Nielsen and Molich, 1990; Ravden and Johnson, 1989; Wright and Monk, 1989). Some of this work has incorporated a commitment to grounding evaluations in scientific principles (Lewis et al., 1990).

An action science of HCI that embraces and deliberately nurtures what rationality there is and can be in technology evolution could be an important vehicle for constructing rich understandings of human beings and their situations, and for designing appropriate tools and environments to delight and empower them.

Notes

1. A version of this paper appeared in the *ACM Transactions on Information Systems*, 10(2), 1992, 181–212.

2. John Carroll and Mary Beth Rosson are now at the Department of Computer Science, Virginia Tech., Blackburg, VA 24061.

3. Nota bene that this schema is to be interpreted as under the scope of a use-scenario. In some presentations (for example, Carroll and Rosson, 1991), we have incorporated situation description into the identification of artifact features and techniques, which is redundant but perhaps clearer. For a learner exploring the Smalltalk environment opportunistically, we hypothesized:

> exploring demos helps new users learn by doing
> *(but offers little for the user to do)*
> *(but the demos may not be paradigmatic application models)*
> *(but learners may have difficulty finding the corresponding code)*

Striking the word *exploring* fits the claim schema better and is less redundant vis-à-vis the situation of use.

4. There may be several different sorts of trading relationships. For example, psychological consequences derive from variables known to co-vary, a richer display will always be a more complex display. In others, the trading relationship is more poorly understood: Example-based documentation may produce in the learner too narrow a concept, but it is not clear how the degree of example paradigmaticity contributes to or mitigates this tradeoff.

5. Of course, the new manual actually *was* better, and for the reasons enumerated here, among others (see Carroll, 1990a, pp. 143–186), but this is incidental to the present discussion.

Acknowledgments

We are grateful to Steve Draper for observing that Norman's theory of action could provide a framework for our claim questions, and to Bob Allen, Susan Rudman, and the journal's reviewers for comments.

References

Argyris, C. (1980). *The Inner Contradictions of Rigorous Research*. New York: Academic Press.

Ausubel, D. P. (1960). The use of advance organizers in the learning and retention of meaningful verbal material. *Journal of Educational Psychology* 51, 267–272.

Basalla, G. (1988). *The Evolution of Technology.* New York: Cambridge University Press.

Bellamy, R. K. E. and Carroll, J. M. (1992). Structuring the programmer's task. *International Journal of Man-Machine Studies* 35.

Brooks. F. P. (1975). *The Mythical Man-month.* Reading, MA: Addison-Wesley.

Card, S. K., Moran, T. P., and Newell, A. (1983). *The Psychology of Human-Computer Interaction.* Hillsdale, NJ: Lawrence Erlbaum.

Carroll, J. M. (1985). *What's in a Name? An Essay in the Psychology of Reference.* New York: W. H. Freeman.

———. (1989). Evaluation, description and invention: Paradigms for human-computer interaction. In M. C. Yovits (ed.), *Advances in Computers,* vol. 29, 47–77. Orlando, FL: Academic Press.

———. (1990a). *The Nurnberg Funnel: Designing Minimalist Instruction for Practical Computer Skill.* Cambridge, MA: MIT Press.

———. (1990b). Infinite detail and emulation in an ontologically minimized HCI. In J. C. Chew and J. Whiteside (eds.), *Proceedings of CHI'90: Conference on Human Factors in Computing Systems.* New York: ACM, 321–327.

Carroll, J. M. and Campbell, R. L. (1986). Softening up hard science: Reply to Newell and Card. *Human-Computer Interaction* 2, 227–249.

———. (1989). Artifacts as psychological theories: The case of human-computer interaction. *Behaviour and Information Technology* 8, 247–256.

Carroll, J. M. and Kellogg, W. A. (1989). Artifact as theory-nexus: Hermeneutics meets theory-based design. In K. Bice and C. H. Lewis (eds.), *Proceedings of CHI'89: Conference on Human Factors in Computing Systems.* New York: ACM, 7–14.

Carroll, J. M., Kellogg, W. A., and Rosson, M. B. (1991). The task-artifact cycle. In J. M. Carroll (ed.), *Designing Interaction: Psychology at the Human-Computer Interface.* New York: Cambridge University Press.

Carroll, J. M. and Rosson, M. B. (1985). Usability specification as a tool in interactive development. In H. Hartson (ed.), *Advances in Human-Computer Interaction 1.* Norwood, NJ: Ablex, 1–28.

———. (1990). Human computer interaction scenarios as a design representation. *Proceedings of HICSS-23: Hawaii International Conference on System Sciences,* 55–561. Los Alamitos, CA: IEEE Computer Society Press.

———. (1991). Deliberated evolution: Stalking the View Matcher in design space. *Human-Computer Interaction.*

Carroll, J. M., Singley, M. K., and Rosson, M. B. (1991). Toward an architecture for instructional evaluation. *Proceedings of the International Conference on the Learning*

Sciences 1991 (Chicago, August 4–7). New York: Association of Computing in Education.

Conklin, J. and Burgess Yakemovic, K. C. (1991). A process-oriented paradigm for design rationale. *Human-Computer Interaction* 6, 357–391.

Cox, B. J. (1986). *Object-Oriented Programming: An Evolutionary Approach.* Reading, MA: Addison-Wesley.

Ehn, P. (1988). *Work-Oriented Design of Computer Artifacts.* Hillsdale, NJ: Lawrence Erlbaum.

Esper, E. A. (1925). A technique for the experimental investigation of associative interference in artificial linguistic material. *Language Monographs* 1, 1–47.

Festinger, L. (1957). *A Theory of Cognitive Dissonance.* New York: Harper & Row.

Fischer, G., Lemke, A. C., McCall, R., and Morch, A. I. (1991). Making argumentation serve design. *Human-Computer Interaction* 6, 393–419.

Floyd, C., Zullighoven, H., Budde, R., and Keil-Slawik, R., (eds.) (1992). *Software Development and Reality Construction.* New York: Springer-Verlag.

Fodor, J. A. (1966). Could there be a theory of perception? *Journal of Philosophy* 63, 375–395.

Freeman, P. (1987). *Software Perspectives: The System is the Message.* Reading, MA: Addison-Wesley.

Gagne, R. M. and Briggs, L. J. (1979). *Principles of Instructional Design.* New York: Holt, Rinehart and Winston.

Garner, W. R. (1974). *The Processing of Information and Structure.* Potomac, MD: Lawrence Erlbaum.

Gentner, D. and Stevens, A. (1983). *Mental Models.* Hillsdale, NJ: Lawrence Erlbaum.

Gilb, T. (1988). *Principles of Software Engineering Management.* Reading, MA: Addison-Wesley.

Grice, H. P. (1967, 1975). Logic and conversation. In D. Davidson and G. Harman (eds.), *The Logic of Grammar.* Encino, CA: Dickenson.

Halasz, F. G. and Moran, T. P. (1983). Mental models and problem solving in using a calculator. In A. Janda (ed.), *Proceedings of CHI'83: Conference on Human Factors in Computing Systems.* New York: ACM, 212–216.

Heidegger, M. (1962). *Being and Time.* J. Macquarrie and E. Robinson (trans.). New York: Harper & Row.

Jewkes, J., Sawers, D., and Stillerman, R. (1958, 1969). *The Sources of Invention.* New York: Macmillan.

Kahneman, D. (1973). *Attention and Effort*. Englewood Cliffs, NJ: Prentice Hall.

Kieras, D. E. and Polson, P. G. (1985). An approach to the formal analysis of complexity. *International Journal of Man-Machine Studies* 22, 365–394.

Köhler, W. (1929). *Gestalt Psychology*. New York: Liveright.

Kuhn, T. S. (1962). Comment. In *The Rate and Direction of Inventive Activity: Economic and Social Factors*. Universities-National Bureau Conference Series, No. 13. Princeton: Princeton University Press, 450–457.

Landauer, T. K. (1987). Psychology as a mother of invention. In J. M. Carroll and P. P. Tanner (eds.), *Proceedings of CHI+GI'87: Human Factors in Computing Systems and Graphics Interface*. (Toronto, April 5–9). New York: ACM, 333–335.

———. (1991). Let's get real: A position paper on the role of cognitive psychology in the design of human useful and usable systems. In J. M. Carroll (ed.), *Designing Interaction: Psychology at the Human-Computer Interface*. New York: Cambridge University Press.

Lave, J. (1988). *Cognition in Practice: Mind, Mathematics, and Culture*. New York: Cambridge University Press.

Lee, J. and Lai, K.-Y. (1991). What's in design rationale. *Human-Computer Interaction* 6.

Lewis, C. H., Polson, P., Wharton, C., and Rieman, J. (1990). Testing a walkthrough methodology for theory-based design of walk-up-and-use interfaces. In J. C. Chew and J. Whiteside (eds.), *Proceedings of CHI'90: Conference on Human Factors in Computing Systems*. New York: ACM, 235–242.

Lewis, C. H., Rieman, J., and Bell, B. (1991). Problem-centered design for expressiveness and facility in a graphical programming system. *Human-Computer Interaction* 6.

Lewis, M. L. and Anderson, J. R. (1985). Discrimination of operator schemata in problem solving: Learning from examples. *Cognitive Psychology* 17, 26–65.

Mack, R. L., Lewis, C. H., and Carroll, J. M. (1983). Learning to use office systems: Problems and prospects. *ACM Transactions on Office Information Systems* 1, 254–271.

MacLean, A., Young, R., Bellotti, V., and Moran, T. P. (1991). Questions, options and criteria: Elements of a design rationale for user interfaces. *Human-Computer Interaction* 6.

Milgram, S. (1968). Some conditions on obedience and disobedience to authority. *Journal of Abnormal and Social Psychology* 6, 259–276.

Morrison, E. (1974). *From Know-How to Nowhere*. Oxford: Blackwell.

Multhauf, R. P. (1959). The scientist and the improver of technology. *Technology and Culture*, xx, 38–47.

GETTING AROUND THE TASK-ARTIFACT CYCLE **267**

Nelson, R. (1962). The link between science and invention: The case of the transistor. In *The Rate and Direction of Inventive Activity: Economic and Social Factors.* Universities-National Bureau Conference Series, No. 13. Princeton: Princeton University Press.

Newman, W. M. (1988). The representation of user interface style. In D. M. Jones and R. Winder (eds.), *People and Computers IV.* Cambridge, U.K.: Cambridge University Press, 123–143.

Nielsen, J. and Molich, R. (1990). Heuristic evaluation of user interfaces. In J. C. Chew and J. Whiteside (eds.), *Proceedings of CHI'90: Conference on Human Factors in Computing Systems.* New York: ACM, 249–256.

Norman, D. A. (1986). Cognitive engineering. In D. A. Norman and S. W. Draper (eds.), *User Centered System Design.* Hillsdale, NJ: Lawrence Erlbaum, 31–62.

Ravden, S. and Johnson, G. (1989). *Evaluating Usability of Human-Computer Interfaces: A Practical Method.* Chichester: Ellis Horwood.

Rittel, H. W. J. (1984). Second-generation design methods. In N. Cross (ed.), *Developments in Design Methodology.* New York: John Wiley & Sons, 317–327.

Roberts, T. L. and Moran, T. P. (1983). The evaluation of text editors: Methodology and empirical results. *Communications of the ACM* 26, 265–283.

Rosch, E., Mervis, C. B., Gray, W., Johnson, D., and Boyes-Braem, P. (1976). Basic objects in natural categories. *Cognitive Psychology* 7, 573–605.

Rosson, M. B. and Carroll, J. M. (1992). Extending the task-artifact framework. To appear in H. R. Hartson and D. Hix (eds.), *Advances in Human-Computer Interaction* 4. Norwood, NJ: Ablex.

Rosson, M. B., Carroll, J. M., and Bellamy, R. K. E. (1990). Smalltalk scaffolding: A case study in minimalist instruction. In J. C. Chew and J. Whiteside (eds.), *Proceedings of CHI'90: Conference on Human Factors in Computing Systems.* New York: ACM, 423–429.

Rosson, M. B., Carroll, J. M., and Sweeney, C. (1991). A View Matcher for reusing Smalltalk classes. In S. Robertson (ed.), *Proceedings of CHI'91: Conference on Human Factors in Computer Systems.* New York: ACM, 277–284.

Schön, D. A. (1983). *The Reflective Practitioner: How Professionals Think in Action.* New York: Basic Books.

Simon, H. A. (1981). *The Sciences of the Artificial.* 2d ed. Cambridge, MA: MIT Press.

Singley, M. K., Carroll, J. M., and Alpert, S. R. (1991). Psychological design rationale for an intelligent tutoring system for Smalltalk. In S. R. Robertson (ed.), *Empirical Studies of Programmers,* IV. Norwood, NJ: Ablex.

Smith, D. C., Irby, C., Kimball, R., Verplank, B., and Harslem, E. (1982). Designing the Star user interface. *Byte* 7(4), April.

Suchman, L. A. (1987). *Plans and Situated Actions: The Problem of Human-Machine Communication.* New York: Cambridge University Press.

Taylor, F. W. (1911). *The Principles of Scientific Management.* New York: Harper & Row.

Terrace, H. (1963). Errorless transfer of a discrimination across two continua. *Journal of Experimental Analysis of Behavior* 6, 223–232.

Thorndike, E. L. (1903). *Educational Psychology.* New York: Lemke & Buechner.

Torbert, W. (1976). *Creating a Community of Inquiry.* New York: John Wiley & Sons.

Weiner, B. (1980). *Human Motivation.* New York: Holt, Rinehart and Winston.

Whiteside, J. and Wixon, D. (1987). Improving human-computer interaction—A quest for cognitive science. In J. M. Carroll (ed.), *Interfacing Thought: Cognitive Aspects of Human-Computer Interaction.* Cambridge, MA: Bradford/MIT Press, 337–352.

Wixon, D., Holtzblatt, K., and Knox, S. (1990). Contextualist design: An emergent view of system design. In J. C. Chew and J. Whiteside (eds.), *Proceedings of CHI'90: Conference on Human Factors in Computing Systems.* New York: ACM, 329–336.

Wright, P. (1978). Feeding the interface eaters: Suggestions for integrating pure and applied research on language comprehension. *Instructional Science* 7, 249–312.

Wright, P. and Monk, A. F. (1989). Evaluation for design. In A. Sutcliffe and L. Macaulay (eds.), *People and Computers,* V. New York: Cambridge University Press, 345–358.

Mapping the Method Muddle: Guidance in Using Methods for User Interface Design

JUDITH S. OLSON
University of Michigan

THOMAS P. MORAN
Xerox PARC

A great deal of progress has been made in developing methods that designers can incorporate in appropriate places in the design process with the goal of producing interfaces that are easier to use and learn. This book represents another step in this line, reporting on emerging methods for designers. However, we have not yet succeeded in making user interface methods an established part of software design practice. Many designers claim they do not have enough time for usability. Even when designers *want* to design for usability, they find that the literature on design methods is a muddle, making it difficult to figure out if there are methods that are appropriate for their situations. They need to know what they can do, and when. The purpose of this paper is to provide that guidance.

In 1983, there was a similar effort. The National Research Council's (NRC) Committee on Human Factors published the proceedings of a workshop entitled, "Methods for Designing Software to Fit Human Needs and Capabilities" (Anderson and Olson, 1985). Table 1 lists the methods included in that report.[1]

TABLE 1
Methods for User Interface Design Listed in the National Research Council's 1983 Report

Questionnaires and *interviews, diaries, natural observation* of task performance, *activity analysis, logging and metering* for understanding the old situation

Task analysis for understanding the requirements for the new task

Design guidelines, user reactions, and *theory-based judgments* to assess the initial design, with support from *toolkits* to guide designers to select from some well-established design pieces, such as dialog boxes preconfigured and menu bars into which to put command names

Formal analyses of interfaces using *structured walkthroughs, decomposition analysis, object–action analysis, metaphor analysis, mental model* assessment, *GOMS–keystroke analysis,* and *grammar analysis*

Building a prototype through *facading, Wizard of Oz,* or *rapid prototyping*

Using these prototypes in *usability tests*

Running the proposed final design in friendly *field tests* (similar to beta test sites for the system code)

Although the major methods used today are the same as those in the NRC report (Nielsen, 1993), there are some new additions. The collection of papers in this book updates that list to include not only more methods, but also to illustrate their successful use in real design projects. Yet designers still need some help sorting through the methods in order to choose those applicable to the design situation at hand. This help is needed even more so now because the set of methods has grown, some are quite sophisticated, and they differ in applicability to the stage of design and to the kind of task being designed for.

To help orient designers, we begin by a characterization of the design process as consisting of several activities. Methods are then described in abstract form (there are too many to detail here) and associated within the appropriate activity. We then lay out a way for the designer to choose the methods appropriate to key features of the task and users in their design situation: the speed of performance expected of the user, the amount of information content in the task domain, and whether the focus is on rapid learning or expert performance. It is not expected that designers will choose to use only one of these methods, but rather that they will select a set of coordinated methods. We illustrate the use of the methods with scenarios of two contrasting design situations. We end with a discussion about the methods and recommendations for further development of design methods that carry with them the appropriate cost-benefit to the designers.

What Is a Method?

We use the term *method* as meaning "how to go about designing something." A method implies a systematic, repeatable way to design. There are macro- and micromethods. A macromethod is a methodology that organizes the whole design process. Software engineering methodologies, like Jackson System Diagramming and Object-Oriented Methods, tend to be macro. Large companies usually advocate or even require formalized design methodologies to manage large-scale design projects. Micromethods are methods that address only subproblems of design. An extended design process would employ several micromethods, which would be used in combination as needed. In this paper, we discuss only micromethods.

A complete method would include:

- A statement of the *problem* that this method addresses
- A *device* (a tool, technique, model, or representation)
- A *procedure* for using the device
- A *result*

For example, a method called Cognitive Walkthrough (Lewis et al., 1990; Rieman et al., 1991) is complete. It addresses the *problem* of designing a system to be easy to use when the user first walks up to it. It has a set of forms for the designer to fill out (the *device* is a representation) that describe the user's steps in performing a task and a *procedure* for "walking through" the steps, asking questions about how easily the user will discover how to do the next step. The *result* is a list of aspects of the user interface that are likely to give the user trouble, which guides the designer to areas of the interface that should be altered.

There are very few complete methods for user interface design. Usually, there is a technique or model or representation, but no explicit procedure for using it. Sometimes the problem addressed is vague, and sometimes the result is implicit. Often these missing aspects can be supplied by the designer in the context of a particular design situation. Therefore, we simply refer to "methods" in this paper, even if they are incomplete.

What Can Be Done to Improve Design?

The key to good systems is the commitment of time and expertise to the user-oriented aspects of the design. The designers have to know more than computer science and technology; they need training and experience in making systems useful, usable, and acceptable. Methods help guide this effort.

A system has *utility* when it meets users' needs and solves problems that users have. To accomplish this goal, we need to understand the users' practices and work setting, including what their goals are and how they go about accomplishing those goals. The new system must provide appropriate functionality to meet the needs in the context of the work setting (fitting the organizational culture, the established communication patterns, and the incentive structure, among other things).

The functionality must be offered through a *usable* interface. The system must be understandable and learnable, relative to the skills of the users and the resources available for learning. The system must have the right performance characteristics: Users must be able to do the tasks fast enough and accurately enough to meet their needs.

Finally, the system must be subjectively *acceptable* to the users. They must perceive benefit from it and perhaps even enjoy using it. Such acceptance comes from both a well-designed system and a design process that successfully targets the right market and involves users in the design and deployment of the system.

Design methods can help achieve better design. System design is an art that mixes creativity and discipline. Most of the methods listed here help with the discipline, not with the creativity. Of course, regular methods that help with brainstorming ideas and structuring and evaluating them apply to the design process (for example, Adams, 1979). But the design methods reviewed in this chapter are more specific and engineeringlike. They:

- Focus attention on users' needs and capabilities
- Provide tools to represent and build designs
- Encourage thorough thinking and analysis by systematizing design activities and bringing theory and knowledge to bear where it can be useful
- Foster testing and measurement

Focus Attention on Users' Needs and Capabilities

The key feature of good design methods is that they focus on the user. One way to do this is to include users themselves in the design process. When new designs are proposed, users should be involved in testing them. Since users cannot always articulate what they know about a procedure or its goal, it is sometimes important to observe users in their current practice. Even better, users should participate in the creation of the new system, defining requirements, constructing prototypes, and so forth. Almost all methods discussed in this chapter can be enhanced by having users themselves involved.

Probably the most important step in designing good systems is getting the functionality right. It is most important to clearly understand the needs early in the process. Design methods can help investigate the users' task domain and current work practices. One can distill important user scenarios, making clear what the critical criteria are. Most methods rely on having a set of tasks or scenarios. Choosing the right ones is important. It is useful to have a mix of *core tasks* (those that are most central or frequent), *critical tasks* (those that illustrate the new capabilities), and *benchmark tasks* (those that can be used to compare the new system with other systems).

Provide Tools to Represent and Build Designs

Design methods provide useful representations for design. Good representations are important for many reasons. Representations help us see a proposed design in a particular way and come to an understanding of it from that view. Concrete representations help with communication between members of the design team and between designers, users, and other stakeholders. Some representations, called *models*, allow calculations of properties of the design, such as the number of new things to learn or the time the user would be expected to execute a task.

Prototyping is important in that it provides an understanding of many issues at an early stage, when something can still be done to deal with them. Some design methods provide tools that make it easier to build prototypes and even final implementations.

Encourage Thorough Thinking and Analysis

Often the greatest value of a representation comes in the effort to create it, which requires careful thinking through of particular issues. Reflecting is an integral part of design. Design methods can aid reflection both by providing representations that "talk back" (Schön, 1983) and by disciplining the designer to be concrete and complete. Methods such as checklists and walkthroughs promote good reflection and thorough analysis of aspects of the design that might cause users difficulty.

Foster Testing and Measurement

We must never assume that designs will work as planned. They need to be tried and tested. Some design methods provide ways to test and measure prototypes and implementations. Methods codify other designers' experience by prescribing particular tests and measures that have been shown to be informative for discovering difficulties and pointing to areas that need redesign.

The Activities That Designers Engage In

System design is a complex process that varies from situation to situation. For example, designing a generic new product for which there is only a description of a market is quite different from designing a custom system for a specific user in a specific setting. The process must accommodate both these large-scale differences and the specifics of the tasks and settings within them. Nevertheless, there are many recurring activities in design, for which the methods reviewed in this chapter are intended to provide support. We here consider seven common activities:

- *Define the problem.* As we have stressed, the most important thing is to get the problem right. Design theorists (Simon, 1981) have described design as an *open problem* in that the problem is not given from the start but is clarified as the solution is being formulated. Part of defining the problem is understanding the task domain and current work practices of the user community. From this, the designer must figure out what the needs are that can be met with a new system. Defining the problem is not just an analytic endeavor; it opens up possibilities.

- *Generate a design.* Once there is some sense of the problem and at least a general notion of the kind of system needed, a more detailed design can be created. Generating a design is very much a creative and constructive activity, involving the building of concrete representations showing what the system would be like.

- *Reflect on the design.* Once any part of the design is represented, it has to be assessed. This is done by reflecting on it—living with it in the imagination, analyzing it, challenging it, and so forth. This leads to new ideas. Thus, generating and reflecting are tightly coupled activities.

- *Build a prototype.* A prototype is a concrete representation for which some aspects "work." It could be a physical mockup, a set of pictures, or running software that can portray the design in a way comprehensible by someone other than designers.

- *Test the prototype.* The point of a prototype is to "try it out" informally or to test it more systematically with potential users. The goal here is to discover fatal flaws, new issues, and aspects of the design that seem to work especially well.

- *Implement the design.* Building the real system involves a commitment to a lot of decisions since the flexibility to alter the design rapidly becomes less practical. Following software engineering principles can help not only with efficient implementation, but also with modularity that will preserve some flexibility.

- *Deploy the system.* As soon as the system implementation reaches a usable stage (well before it is complete), it can begin to be deployed in different ways. There are several strategies for trying it out in limited ways, both to learn if it will serve the intended needs and to get the user community prepared for its installation. One must also be conscious of the fact that once deployed, the task changes; this leads to the need to evaluate iteratively and inform the next generation of products.

We cannot stress enough that these activities are *not* stages in the design process. The course of design involves continual jumping back and forth between the activities. There is iteration in which feedback from activities later in the list inform those earlier.

Although these activities are common in design, they do not define a complete design and development process. We present them here to provide an organizational framework for the design methods reviewed.

The Methods

The collection of methods for user interface design have clear relevance for different stages in the design cycle. Some methods help the analyst at the beginning of the project to understand the task and the setting in which the new system will reside. Other methods help generate the working design. Still others are intended for analysis of the proposed design, to help in suggesting improvements in learnability and usability. Methods are clustered and ordered according to the seven activities.

Each section that follows begins with a summary table listing the methods, several descriptors that should guide the designer in deciding whether the method is useful, and references that describe the method's use in a design setting or show how to do it. The two descriptors we offer at this stage are estimates of how long it takes to do this method (effort) and how much training is required in order to make the prescribed assessments (training). The training is assumed to consist of a short course or tutorial (for example, from the conference called Computer Human Interaction, CHI) plus some exercises and apprenticeship. The person being trained is either a designer or a human factors person, typically someone with a bachelors degree. The effort is an estimate of how long the analysis or method would take the person so trained. Both of these estimates come from the authors' experience in using these methods as well as teaching these methods and observing their use in a variety of settings.[2] Although many contextual factors, such as background of the analyst and complexity of the application, affect the time estimates, these estimates, at a minimum, show relative values for effort and training.

Define the Problem

Method	Effort	Training	References
Naturalistic observation (diaries, videotape, etc.)	2 days	3 months	Hill et al., 1993
Interviews (including focus groups, decision tree analysis, semantic nets)	1 day	1 month	Rudman and Engelbeck, this volume; Nielsen et al., 1986
Scenarios or use cases (including envisioning)	1 day	1 month	Jacobson, 1992; Carroll, in preparation for 1995
Task analysis (including operator function model)	2 days	3 months	Johanssen, Hannum and Tessmer, 1989

A variety of methods center on detailing the tasks for which the system will be built. In some of the methods, the analyst watches the users do their work through *naturalistic observation* or *analysis of work practice*. Data on these activities can be collected by videotaping workers or by workers keeping *diaries*. In all these methods, the analyst is interested in understanding the practicalities of how the work actually gets done in the current system, the details of the task requirements, the order in which the users do subtasks, what material or information they need, how they communicate with each other, how much time each subtask takes, and the physical, social, and organization setting in which this work takes place.

Another set of ways of gathering requisite information involve asking users directly about their needs. *Focus groups* or one-on-one *interviews* are included in this set of methods. When the task to be supported is entirely new, potential users are encouraged to imagine the new setting and capabilities and are asked what they would do with it and how it would be used, a method called *envisioning*.

Several innovative methods are introduced in this book. Interviews can elicit from the task performer the particular mental steps they go through, which can be represented in a *decision tree*. Rudman and Engelbeck (this volume), for example, attempt to reconstruct the sequential cognitive processing that users perform in solving complex problems, such as configuring telephone service for home users in the face of a myriad of offerings and billing arrangements.

For those tasks that have a nomenclature that is complex and foreign to the analyst, *semantic nets* can represent the organization of objects and the terms used in the task domain. This technique (used by Rudman and Engelbeck [this volume]; see also Gillan and Breedin, 1990) complements the decision tree analysis in that it uncovers complex data structures in the user's vernacular, whereas the decision tree analysis represents the processes that operate on that data. Knowledge engineering methods could potentially be applied to uncover the kinds of strategic activities and knowledge structures people use in domains that are unfamiliar to the designer, as suggested in Olson and Biolsi (1991).

Narrative descriptions of complete tasks are often called *scenarios* or *use cases* (McDaniel, Olson, and Olson, 1994).[3] While gathering these, there is also opportunity to elicit and discuss the problems users have noted with the current system and their wishes for the future.

Information from these observations can be represented in terms of *activity* or *task analyses*, where subtasks are coded and summarized into flow charts, frequency tables, and state-transition diagrams (see, for example, Sasso, Olson, and Merten, 1987). These diagrams can then be used to suggest new ways of accomplishing the same goal. When measures of performance like time or quality are collected as well, these can be used to compare the old system with the new.

The *operator function model*[4] is a specific method for displaying a detailed task analysis. It makes explicit what information the operator or user needs at each moment in the task and the sequence of subtasks that the operator goes through (and the branches, the different things that could be done). This then can be used to suggest what information must be displayed at each moment, what steps the user should be able to go through, and what options should be presented to the user in an easy-to-access command sequence. It is a relatively small step to go from this detailed specification to an actual prototype. Furthermore, it could well serve as the input to a rapid prototyping system such as ITS (Gould, Ukelson, and Boies, this volume).

Generate a Design

Method	Effort	Training	References
Building on previous designs (steal and improve, design guidelines)	1 day[5]	1 month	Perlman, 1988; Tetzlaff and Schwartz, 1991
Represent conceptual model	1 day	2 months	Moran, 1983
Represent interaction (GTN, dataflow, etc.)	2 days	2 months	Kieras and Polson, 1983
Represent visual displays	2 days	3 months	
Design space analysis (QOC, decomposition analysis)	3 days	1 month	MacLean et al., 1991

Design is essentially evolutionary. New designs borrow from and improve on previous designs. Even radically new designs are reactions to existing designs. This is a practical matter of the "reuse" of designs that already work and that users are familiar with. Thus, designers do not have to start from scratch, and users do not have to learn yet again.

There are two distinct "modes" of borrowing: global and local. One can start by adopting the global models of existing systems. Card (this volume) calls this *steal and improve*. For example, there are many common concepts among word processing systems, among database systems, and among spreadsheet systems. You would want to think hard about how and why you would want to be different if you were developing one of these kinds of systems. You can also adopt localized design components, such as user interface "widgets," many of which appear in toolkits. When the designer adopts a *toolkit*, other design decisions are already made as well. For example, in the Macintosh toolkit, the designer has no choice about how menus appear and how selections are made. And embedded in the toolkit instructions are guidelines on how to make some interface features match other systems of similar type, such as the guide to make Macintosh applications all have Apple, File, and Edit as the leftmost three menu items.

Design guidelines exist for some significant portion of the components of a user interface, which are helpful to this initial design. For example, guidelines offer prescriptions about how to organize items on a set of menus, with ordering either by conceptual category (for example, editing commands) or by frequency of use (for example, Smith and Mosier, 1984). Other guidelines suggest the consistent placement of help and warning messages on the screen, and general use of gestalt principles of proximity and dissimilarity to capture and guide the user's eye to appropriate portions of the display.

Although borrowing can often provide a starting place for design, especially in domains where there are existing systems, the goal of design is to create a system that addresses the particularities of the problem at hand. Generating a design involves creating descriptions of the design, and different kinds of design representations are essential for this activity.

A conceptual model is the set of conceptual entities that the system represents, that the user needs to understand to effectively use the system. It is important that the designer be clear about this and explicitly represent the conceptual model (Newman and Sproull, 1979). For example, understanding the hierarchical nature of text objects (characters, words, sentences, paragraphs, sections, chapters, documents) separately from the features of layout (font, line, page, margin) helps construct appropriate actions and associated specifications. Moran (1983) proposed a representation of the relationship between the concepts in the users' work domain (uncovered, say, by interviews or some form of semantic analysis) and the conceptual model embodied by the system. A useful specific version of this is an *object–action* analysis. For example, Moran used this kind of representation to assess the differences between line-oriented and full-screen editors, showing that the conceptual model of the former (strings of things to be replaced) required a translation from the conceptual model of the way we normally think of text.

In Object–Action analysis, the nouns and verbs of the domain and task are arrayed in a table. For example, in text editing, the table would show objects such as letters, words, sentences, paragraphs, pages, and documents on one dimension, and actions such as copy and delete on the other. The table shows the complete matrix of commands that have to be offered. But the analysis shows additional features of the domain model—how characters and sentences are to be treated differently from layout features like lines and pages. These tables encourage completeness of actions on all objects and consistency where appropriate. Such an analysis was one of the key design methods used in the construction of the Xerox Star system, which resulted in the use of various "universal command keys," such as delete and copy (Smith et al., 1982).

Once the domain is known and the objects and actions specified, it is useful to represent dynamics of the interaction. *State transition diagrams* are the most common form of representation of interaction. They are networks of states (screens or modes) where all the possible actions that can be taken at each state are drawn leading to the next states. A simple form of this is the diagram of connected menu items that some training manuals show as a summary of the system's functionality. A more sophisticated representation is the generalized transition network (Kieras and Polson, 1983), which accommodates the hierarchic nesting of contexts.

The commands and flow of the interaction are depicted in the representations described earlier. The *visual display* is best represented by renderings of the display on paper or other media. In PICTIVE, analysts give participants various "pieceparts" of interfaces made out of paper or plastic (for example, menus, dialog boxes, scroll bars, and windows) to arrange in an interface layout. When these pictures (full screenshots) are displayed on a board in the order in which they will appear, they are called a *storyboard*, similar to those used in the construction of films. The closer the representation to the final embodiment of what the user will see, the better the analyses of the arrangement, its attention-getting abilities, and the ease of finding what the user needs to know at each moment.

Design involves discovering and evaluating many different possible designs—a "design space"—and discovering the critical issues or questions that must be addressed. Often it is useful to keep track of the possibilities so that it is clear why particular design decisions are made. Formal analyses of these possibilities come from two methods: *Design Space Analysis* and *Decomposition Analysis*. Both involve systematic processes by which various issues or questions about the design are raised and recorded, and then different alternatives, options, or solutions are offered and analyzed with agreed-on criteria. Design Space Analysis takes many forms; QOC (for Questions-Options-Criteria) serves as a good example (MacLean et al., 1991). In QOC, the designer(s) systematically documents the questions to be addressed. Attached to each question are the various alternative solutions. Appropriate criteria (for example, consistency and ease of programming) are then applied to each alternative, leading to a design decision. Decomposition Analysis is similar, except less formal and at a coarser grain (Olson, 1985). Here, the major components of the interface are the representation of the underlying data structure, the command entry style, the provision of memory aids, the access to help, and so on. Each is examined in turn, alternatives are generated, and they are evaluated by any of a variety of means. In both of these methods, it can be seen that generating a new design and reflecting on it are tightly intertwined.

Reflect on the Design

Method	Effort	Training	References
Checklists	1 day	1 week	Shneiderman, 1992
Walkthroughs	2 days	3 months	Lewis et al., 1990
Mapping analyses (task action, metaphor, consistency)	2 days	2 weeks	Douglas and Moran, 1983; Payne and Green, 1986
Methods analyses (GOMS, KLM, CPM, CCT)	3 days	1 year	Card, Moran, and Newell, 1983; Kieras, 1988
Display analyses	3 days	1 year	Lohse, 1991

Once we have some explicit representations of the design, there are a variety of ways to begin to assess the projected usability of this design as well as the ease of learning it. The methods listed here can also be used to some extent in generating designs. But these methods are detailed and require a fairly specific representation of a design to work on. They can be used either by analysts working alone, with users as part of the design team, or by analysts watching users trying to use a representation of the interface to perform some test task.

The quickest way to evaluate a first-cut or set of alternative components of the design involves answering a set of questions from a *checklist* (Shneiderman, 1992; Nielsen, 1993). Checklists and usability heuristics serve as memory aids to designers, reminding them about prescriptions for the ease of learning and ease of use for each of the major components.

Just as programmers do a code walkthrough to check how the flow of the communication proceeds in the program and to check for things missing or conflicting, user interface designers perform a *walkthrough* of the user interface (Weinberg and Freidman, 1984). Here, however, the flow is from the user's perspective, where the user has goals in mind and tries to perform the actions necessary to accomplish those goals. With a good set of core tasks as test cases, a number of errors can be detected, especially in the flow of actions (whether they fit the order in which the user thinks of the actions) and in the availability of all the subfunctions needed.

Two variants of the walkthrough are the *cognitive walkthrough* (Lewis et al., 1990; Rieman et al., 1991) and the *claims analysis* (Carroll and Rosson, this volume). Like the walkthrough, they begin with the analysts generating a core set of common tasks and the detailed step-by-step listing of what the user has to do to accomplish these. The analyses that follow, however, are much more explicit than in a standard walkthrough. The methods provide sets of questions the analyst is to ask about the interface. These questions are designed to highlight those aspects of the interface that are known to be difficult or error inducing. Claims analysis additionally encourages an explicit discussion of design tradeoffs, similar in style to the decomposition analysis.

Task-mapping analysis begins with a formal representation of the goal–action mapping that the user conceives of and lays alongside it the goal–action mapping that the system requires (Polson and Kieras, 1985). The analysis of the side-by-side diagrams shows mismatches that can turn into difficulty for the user to learn or execute. For example, a system that makes you move a range of text by selecting the range to be moved first, then the target, then the action "move," mismatches the normal English command sequence that begins with the word *move* and continues by specifying the target material and the "move-to" location. Although most word processors today follow the noun–verb format for commands, the novice in word processing must *learn* that particular word order since it is not fitting the order they have learned from spoken language.[6]

Similarly, Douglas and Moran (1983) suggest a careful *analysis of the metaphor* chosen for learning a new piece of software. They showed that by lining up the goal–action pairs of a target system (for example, a text editor) and a metaphor system (for example, a typewriter), there were a number of mismatches, some of which could significantly impede a new learner's understanding of the system. Since new learners will construct a metaphor or mental model even in the absence of instruction (Halasz and Moran, 1983), care should be taken to choose a helpful one and to teach it early.

Object–action analysis and *state transition diagrams*, described earlier, can have benefit in analyzing designs as well as in generating the first design. *Analysis of the grammar* of the command language, such as Moran's Command Language Grammar (CLG) (1981), Reisner's formal grammar (1984), and Payne and Green's Task Action Grammar (TAG) (1986), first represent the rules by which components form to produce a language of commands. Argument is made that the smaller the number of rules in the grammar, the easier the system will be to learn. The importance of these mapping analyses is that they focus the designer on the relationship between the elements of the system being designed and the users' task domain and previous knowledge rather than viewing the design in elegant but unnatural isolation.

Card, Moran, and Newell (1983) generated various ways to assess the moment-by-moment cognitive/perceptual/motor resources being used when interacting with a particular device, pioneering the field of cognitive engineering. The core idea is that for certain kinds of well-learned tasks, one could model the goals the user had, the methods offered by a system to satisfy these goals, the choices people made in varying circumstances, and the operator sequences that followed. From this model, called *GOMS*, and a related, more detailed model called the *Keystroke Level Model*, one can fairly accurately predict how long a task will take (Olson and Olson, 1991). John (1988) introduced *Critical Path Analysis* which, in contrast to the GOMS model that assumes a sequential flow of cognitive processes (the recognize–retrieve–act cycle), recognizes that some tasks involve some cognitive processes that occur in parallel. This is often appropriate when the task to be modeled is performed repeatedly and rapidly in a high-performance situation (see Atwood, Gray, and John, this volume).

Cognitive Complexity Theory, another important extension of the original cognitive engineering modeling of Card, Moran, and Newell, represents the knowledge needed to perform these tasks. Using this theory, Kieras and Bovair (1986) were able to predict how long a task would take to learn. All these detailed analyses highlight the portions of the task that will take longer than necessary (for example, too many things to remember or an overloaded working memory that generates errors), focusing redesign efforts to concentrate on very particular interaction details.

Several methods have arisen to assist in *display analysis*. Tullis (1988) and Mackinlay (1986) developed programs to assess the crowding and thus readability of various aspects of a display. And, more recently, Lohse (1991) has constructed a perceptual simulation that will take a display as input and calculate how long it will take to answer a particular question about the display or to find certain critical features.

Build a Prototype

Method	Effort	Training	References
Prototyping tools	1 month	3 months	Wilson and Rosenberg, 1988
Participatory prototyping	1 week	2 months	Muller, 1991

These methods analyze the plans or requirements of the system. They are conducted by the analyst, without direct involvement with the users of the system. To date, no one has found these analyses to be sufficient to find all the design difficulties (Nielsen, 1992; Karat, Campbell, and Fiegel, 1992). All comparative studies of methods of design of user interfaces have found value to having users actually attempt to perform a realistic task using some form of the interface.

Further, although representations of designs produced in the initial generation are sufficient for the analysis of Reflection, they are not concrete. They can be understood only through the narrow lenses of the particular analyses. A concrete working prototype is needed in order to obtain rich empirical and experiential feedback.

The system used in these evaluations need not be the final system. The prototype can be presented effectively with *paper, storyboards,* and other media. One can produce either sequences of screens similar to a movie production storyboard or a complex book of printed screens whose sequencing is controlled by a human analyst. These allow rapid testing for flow of control, visual clarity, and so on, without having to program a system to be fully operational. A variant of these simple prototypes is embodied in PICTIVE (Muller, 1991). When the end users put the requisite pieces of the interface together, it is called *participatory prototyping* (Poltrock and Grudin, this volume). Although this kind of prototyping might work at this stage, it is more likely to be effective as a first cut that can then be further refined through analysis.

Toolkits provide easy, cost-effective ways to construct a working interface for analysis and testing (Perlman, 1988; Hix and Schulman, 1991). ITS (Gould, Ukelson, and Boies, this volume) discusses ways to display the dialog design with various visual options.

Test the Prototype

Method	Effort	Training	References
Open testing (storefront or hallway, alpha, and damage testing)	1 week	1 month	Gould et al., 1987
Usability testing	2 weeks	1 year[7]	Gould, 1988

Once the system is mocked up using one of these methods, the users are asked to work through a sample realistic task while the analysts collect various forms of data about users' performance. These can be reactions to attractiveness or appeal, ease of learning how to use it, or other characteristics of the user's ease in performing basic tasks. This method is variously called *storefront* or *hallway testing,* best exemplified in the design process used for the Olympic Messaging System (Gould et al., 1987). In *alpha testing,* the prototype is given to associates, who then give feedback to the designers about usability; in *damage testing,* users deliberately try to break the system, giving feedback to the designers about the system's robustness.

More formal analyses involve full-fledged *usability tests,* in which users are taught the system (which itself provides an early test of the training materials) and asked to perform a set of tasks. Early tests of the system often involve "critical tasks" that push the system and the user's capabilities so that they would be sure to see its fragile points. In other situations, when the goal is to find expected times to learn and perform, more conventional, common tasks are used, called benchmark tasks.

A whole variety of measures are possible, including the time to learn, the time to perform particular tasks, individual keystroke times (for assessment of match to predictions from the Keystroke Level Model), error types and frequencies, thinking aloud (for assessment of goals and problem-solving strategies), preference, and satisfaction. The data from usability tests are relatively easy to collect; one can tell fairly quickly whether there are major design errors. More detailed comparison of moment-by-moment keystroke times with those projected from cognitive engineering allow designers to focus on those aspects that seem to present difficulties to the user. What is not easy is fixing these difficulties, especially since every design decision involves trade-offs; each fix changes some other aspect, the overall change needing retesting or analysis.

Implement the Design

Method	Effort	Training	References
Toolkits (Motif, NeXTstep, Apple, etc.)	3 months	6 months	Perlman, 1988

The advantages of building the prototype in a full-scale toolkit center on the fact that the interface is not only easy to build, has style guidelines built in, and is relatively easy to change after usability testing, but also that toolkits generate production code, unlike prototypes built in some system like

HyperCard. With toolkits, it is not necessary to rewrite the interface into the language of implementation.

Deploy the System

Method	Effort	Training	References
Internal testing	1 week	1 month	
Beta testing (logging, metering, surveys)	2 weeks	1 month	Mackay et al., 1989

Once a system is judged satisfactory, it is typically tested further, first in the local environment and then in an outside friendly environment, often a site that would like to be an early adopter of the technology in exchange for feeding back discovered bugs and mismatches in design. These tests are often called *beta testing*. At this point, data are often collected, but data of a less fine-grained sort. Two good sources are cataloged queries that come in on a help line and answers to questionnaires sent to customers or end users. It is also possible, in some situations, to log or meter the new system, just as one would do on an existing system. With keystroke data collected, for example, one can infer both what common tasks are being done efficiently or not and overall use of system features.

What the Designer Needs to Know to Choose a Method for the Right Time and the Right Task

The organization of the methods in the preceding list conveys that they apply to different activities of the development process. They also differ in the amount of time they require, the amount of detail uncovered, and the accuracy of the conclusions that result. For example, using a checklist on the current or proposed design takes several hours and produces general recommendations about usability and learnability. The checklist can help determine which of two competing software packages might be easier for the end user, but will not provide enough detail to determine how long the task will take or what skill or domain knowledge the end user will have to behave accurately and with reasonable speed. In contrast, GOMS analysis and its partners, CCT and Keystroke Level Model, require a great deal of time, but provide the detail necessary to say what users will have to know to perform the tasks well, roughly how long it will take to learn, and how long representative tasks will take to perform.

We also noted that the methods differ in how much the designer needs to know about human cognition, perception, and motor movement. Task analyses require very little such knowledge, as do some forms of checklists or guidelines and the cognitive walkthrough, whereas claims analysis, Cognitive Complexity Theory, and Keystroke Level Model require a great deal.

That is, the methods differ in:

The amount of time they take and the concomitant level of detail and risk associated with the findings

The knowledge the analyst is required to have about basic cognitive processes of users

Some methods are particularly suited for some kinds of users and tasks and less so for others. This is probably the most difficult thing for the designer to assess. For example, tasks such as information retrieval, financial planning, piloting an airplane, and rapid transcription of text are very different in how sequentially and deliberately the user goes through the steps in the task. There have been numerous attempts to develop a task taxonomy (see, for example, Lenorovitz et al., 1984 for a short review), but in general the taxonomies are far too detailed for the use we wish to put them to here. However, the analyst does need some guidance on which of the methods suits the particular user's tasks under consideration.

For our purposes, the following seem to be the major dimensions on which a wide set of users' tasks differ:

1. The task is performed either as a set of sequential steps or as a rapidly overlapping series of subtasks.
2. The task involves either high information content, with consequent complex visual displays to be interpreted, or low information content, where simple signals are sufficient to alert the user that the next step is to proceed.
3. The task is intended to be performed either by a layman without much training or by a skilled practitioner in the task domain.

The first dimension has to do with whether the user's actions are deliberate and single-minded, much like using a spreadsheet. This contrasts with tasks such as air traffic control, where attention rapidly shifts between input streams and where goals are intertwined. Air traffic control similarly is high in information content, the second dimension, whereas the task of assigning a student a workstation in a computer lab is low in information content, much more like reacting to a simple signal (the request of the student). The third dimension reflects the assumed knowledge or skill level of the users. A bank teller machine has to be recognizable by any customer, whereas a computer-aided design (CAD) system is specific to a professional domain with its own shared vocabulary and can be designed with the assumption that the designer will be trained in its use.

Most of the methods are applicable to both sequential and overlapping tasks. The one major exception is the GOMS-CCT family of models and accompanying analyses. They fit those tasks that comprise subsets of sequentially performed operators (either mental or motor). The Critical Path Analysis grew from this set of models to explicitly accommodate rapid-fire tasks that most likely involve cognitive and motor components that overlap in time (see Atwood, Gray, and John, this volume).

When tasks are rich in information content, it is important both to determine the structure of the information as the user understands it and to display it in a representation that visually maps well to that understanding. Therefore, those methods that assess the organization of information objects and actions, the mental model of the system, and the analysis of particulars of the perceptibility of visual displays are particularly relevant.

Interfaces for tasks that are designed for casual use by the layperson, that do not assume knowledge in a particular domain, should be assessed in particular for their learnability and the provision of information on the screen that suggests to the user what to do next. Several methods, such as the cognitive walkthrough, storefront analysis, and claims analysis, are particularly relevant for assessing this aspect of the interface.

If the task will be performed by a large work force of dedicated users, then the more detailed methods, like GOMS, grammar analysis, and Critical Path Analysis, will likely provide significant payoff. For example, there is a significant work force that reconciles mismatches in customer-claimed deposits and the accounting ledger in a bank "back room." These people work full days at a rapid pace. It is particularly important in this task that the information that the user needs to access to solve a problem be placed on the screen in tandem and that the key information is readily readable. Careful analysis of eye movements, clarity of font, and keystroke or command sequence is very important to a good design in this task so that information is not lost out of the user's working memory and so that extra scans are not required to "line up" the aspects of the accounting that mismatch. Good screen design can shorten each reconciliation task by seconds. Although mere seconds are saved, when multiplied by the number of tasks accomplished per day and the number of operators doing such a task, the savings could accrue to millions of dollars.

Some of the methods, like GOMS, CCT, Keystroke, and grammar analysis, require weeks to do for any medium-size task and system. They are very detailed, cataloging not only the action steps of the potential user, but the cognitive/perceptual/motor steps as well. They provide, however, a great amount of detail. They are therefore appropriate only when that kind of investment in time will reveal important details of the speed of interaction or complexity that might produce significant errors. They have shown value in situations where new operator workstations are being designed for high-speed work (Atwood, Gray, and John, this volume) and for situations where errors are very costly, such as wrong business decisions caused by the wrong data being retrieved from a large database because of its complex user interface (for example, Smelcer, 1989).

These time-consuming methods often also require detailed knowledge about cognition. GOMS family of models and methods require the analyst to know facts about when in a task information might reside in short-term memory and how far an eye movement will jump on a visual display of certain size. Even the claims analysis requires intuition about these processes to help discover what the appropriate and inappropriate claims are that the artifact embodies. In contrast, methods like checklists and walkthroughs often can be conducted by people without an intimate knowledge of cognition and perception, and are therefore at the same time faster to accomplish and less accurate. User testing often takes several weeks to accomplish (including building the prototype, watching the users, and analyzing the results), but can be done by careful, though not necessarily trained, observers.

Summary of Costs and Benefits

To provide guidance to the designer, we have prepared Table 2, which highlights four characteristics:

The *type* of the method—some collect data (empirical), some are analyses of the structure of the task and interface (analytic), and some construct various representations of the interface (constructive)

The *benefits* of the method in terms of what aspect of the interface the method is particularly suited to reveal—the task steps, the performance or learnability, or the user's acceptance of the system (called tasks, perform, learn, or accept in the table)

Two aspects of the *costs* of using the method—the *effort* to use it (which often correlates with amount of detail) and the *training* needed

Table 2 provides a rough assessment of these characteristics. It was constructed and synthesized by the authors, guided by input from the members

TABLE 2   **Summary of Costs and Benefits of the Methods**

Method	Type	Benefits	Costs—Effort	Costs—Training
DEFINE THE PROBLEM				
Naturalistic observation (diaries, videotape, etc.)	Empirical	Tasks	2 days	3 months
Interviews (including focus groups, decision tree analysis, semantic nets)	Empirical	Tasks	1 day	1 month
Scenarios or use cases (including envisioning)	Analytic	Tasks	1 day	1 month
Task analysis (including operator function model)	Analytic	Tasks	2 days	3 months
GENERATE A DESIGN				
Building on previous designs (steal and improve, design guidelines)	Constructive	Tasks, perform, learn, accept	1 day	1 month
Represent conceptual model	Constructive	Learn	1 day	2 months
Represent interaction (GTN, dataflow diagram)	Constructive	Perform, learn	2 days	2 months
Represent visual display	Constructive	Perform, learn	2 days	3 months
Design space analysis (QOC, decomposition analysis)	Analytic	Tasks, perform, learn	3 days	1 month
REFLECT ON THE DESIGN				
Checklists	Analytic	Perform, learn	1 day	1 week
Walkthroughs	Analytic	Perform, learn	2 days	3 months
Mapping analysis (task action, metaphor, consistency)	Analytic	Perform, learn	2 days	2 weeks
Methods analysis (GOMS, KLM, CPM, CCT)	Analytic	Perform, learn	3 days	1 year
Display analyses	Analytic	Perform, learn	3 days	1 year
BUILD A PROTOTYPE				
Prototyping tools	Constructive	Testable system	1 month	3 months
Participatory prototyping	Empirical	Tasks, accept	1 week	2 months

Method	Type	Benefits	Costs—Effort	Costs—Training
TEST THE PROTOYPE				
Open testing (storefront or hallway, alpha, damage testing)	Empirical	Perform, learn, accept	1 week	1 month
Usability testing	Empirical	Perform, learn, accept	2 weeks	1 year
IMPLEMENT THE DESIGN				
Toolkits (Motif, NeXTstep, Apple, etc.)	Constructive	Fully testable system	3 months	6 months
DEPLOY THE SYSTEM				
Internal testing	Empirical	Perform, learn, accept	1 week	1 month
Beta testing (logging, metering, surveys)	Empirical	Tasks, perform, learn, accept	2 weeks	1 month

of the workshop at Boulder. The table is intended to advise when a method will or will not be useful.

Examples of Coordinated Use of the Methods

Table 2 provides some guidance to the selection of methods for the particular design task at hand. But just as good cookbooks give not only selection criteria for individual dishes but also suggest combinations of dishes to create a pleasing meal, we provide here two such "meals." The first illustrates the use of quick methods for a simple walk-up-and-use system, such as an ATM. The second illustrates the set of design methods at the other end of the continuum, where the interface is information rich, and speedy, accurate real-time performance is critical to the operator's success.

The literature contains several other descriptions of a coordinated set of methods. Gould's description of the development of the Olympic Messaging System (Gould et al., 1987) demonstrates the coordinated use of several methods for walk-up-and-use interfaces, and the description by Rudman and Engelbeck (this volume), about the development of an interface for the operator's support for configuring new telephone service, demonstrates coordinated methods for an information-rich, interactive system involving customer conversation. McDaniel, Olson, and Olson (1994) describe the use of a combination of HCI methods, those from Business Process Redesign (Hammer and Champy, 1993) and from Object-Oriented methodology (Jacobson, 1992) in the design of a system to help space physicists access remote sensors and converse about them across several continents (McDaniel, Olson, and Olson, 1994).

Coordinated Methods for Quick Evaluation of a Walk-Up-and-Use System

An ATM is an example of a system that:

Has simple sequential task flow (that presents information on choices the user has, each of which leads to new choices)

Is relatively low in information content (mainly verbal selections, for example, about withdrawal or deposit and how much)

Is targeted for the layman

Because the task is performed by untrained users at their own pace, the emphasis is on the ease with which the user can learn to operate the device. Obviousness of what action to take next and error recovery are prime. Moreover, since the business objective of this system is not rapid performance of tasks, but rather widespread use leading to offloading clerical tasks to the customer, the budget for construction and evaluation is likely small. Fast methods will do, and the designer should not be expected to have a Ph.D. in cognitive psychology.

To discover the components of the task, simple *questionnaires* might suffice, asking the potential customers what kinds of choices they might be interested in. Often marketing has the basics of this information collected already, and use of this for the interface objects, actions, and flow will serve well. Since lots of ATMs exist already, it would also be appropriate to do some *naturalistic observation*, where designers observe current users at existing machines.

The initial design, guided by prescriptions from *guidelines* and assessed quickly with *checklists*, might be printed on paper and displayed as a *storyboard*, for analysis of flow, screen display, and so on without users. Designers can view the storyboard for aspects of ease of learning, using in particular a *cognitive walkthrough*. The flow of the system could be assessed with a simple *generalized transition network*, to assure consistency in the use of error recovery and navigation commands.

For *hallway testing*, a mockup of the entire display might be constructed, with a *rapid prototyping system* (such as HyperCard) embodying the design. Designers can observe the test users' difficulties or get them to think out loud while they attempt to use the system.

After several such short analyses and redesigns, the system, in its penultimate form, can be installed at a friendly test site, and some basic *system monitoring* data can be collected for analysis of gross usability and preference characteristics.

Coordinated Methods for Detailed Evaluation of a High-Performance System

At the other end of the spectrum is a system that supports back-room workers at a bank who are reconciling the machine-read check register with what the customer wrote on the back of a deposit slip. The task:

Requires the overlapping activation of the user's mental and physical capabilities (scanning the next set of materials while the previous tasks' corrections are keyed in)

Is relatively high in information content (side-by-side displays of the deposit slip's handwritten entry and a list of the checks accompanying the deposit, both machine read and scanned in true copy)

Is targeted for the dedicated, skilled user

Because the task is performed all day every day by skilled users, there is considerable payoff from having detailed, somewhat time-consuming analyses. The outcome has to be detailed enough to recommend changes to the interface that may bring about seconds of savings in each task completion. But because of the high volume of performance of each task, savings accrue rapidly. Budget for construction and evaluation of this kind of system can be quite large, given the anticipated payoff.

To understand the task, which in this case is not particularly obvious to the system designer, several discovery techniques should be employed. If there is a previous system in place (check balances are reconciled in *some* way before this new system is built), the designers can engage in some *natural observation*, plus interview the workers about aspects that are difficult or annoying. More detailed discovery of the objects and actions of the task domain and the kind of thinking that goes on during the execution of the task can come from *semantic net interviews, decision tree interviews,* and other techniques from the area of knowledge engineering. A detailed *task analysis* is performed next, showing the order of subtasks and the kinds of information that are needed at each moment so that the user can perform requisite cognitive tasks to accomplish the goal. The task analysis may take the form of an *operator function model,* with details of the knowledge necessary in the form of a *GOMS model* or some parts of the *Task Action Grammar.*

Once the task is fully understood, a series of design and evaluative iterations follow. The system can be generated and displayed as a *Generalized Transition Network* or a working prototype, using one of the more sophisticated toolkits like *ITS.* This design is then analyzed in detail for the cognitive and motor movements required to accomplish the task using the *Critical Path Analysis* (CPA) variant of the GOMS family of models. Since the system has high information content, detailed analysis of the *visual display* is also warranted. *Usability tests* follow, with particular emphasis on the fit of the CPA to the actual timing of the task, to hone both the model's accuracy and to show where the system does not fit the predictions of optimal performance afforded by the model. The design iterates until the users' performance meets preset target criteria for skilled performance.

Discussion

The preceding synthesis and Table 2 are intended to be helpful, not to provide a detailed critique of each method for its usefulness. There are methods, for example, that have the goal of being useful and usable by designers but, at present, are in a form that makes them difficult to learn or awkward to use. For example, one of the motivations for providing the Cognitive Walkthrough was to make knowledge that is gleaned from GOMS and other empirical investigations accessible in a method usable by designers.

Further, the table format masks the potential synergy between methods, those useful links that can occur between methods. For example, the Operator Function Model is a detailed analysis of the object, actions, and flow of control necessary for task performance. On inspection, we discovered that its outputs are exactly what are needed for input to ITS. Thus, whereas one method might be effective only on its own, others may have useful links between them.

It is also the case that the table makes only crude assessments of the kinds of tasks that it can be applied to and coarse-grained estimates of how much effort it takes and how much training the designer has to have in order to use the method successfully. Of particular concern is the implication that those methods that take a short time but give you broad coverage of evaluation are higher on the cost–benefit curve and therefore more valuable. Some of the methods, such as GOMS, although they take a long time to specify, have a large payoff for several different aspects of the design process. For example, once the task is specified in a GOMS terminology, not only is it possible to estimate how long a task will take (by using parameters in the Keystroke Level Model), but you also have the basic information necessary to write effective documentation (Gong and Elkerton, 1990). The GOMS model forces the analyst to understand the major tasks and the recommended procedure to accomplish those tasks, the basic elements of writing good training material.

A listing of methods misses some of the more global design process principles that successful designers offer. For example, it has been widely recognized that an effective management procedure for assuring adequate attention to the user interface is to incorporate metrics of user acceptability into the same set of metrics that software designers are used to having to determine if the performance of the software itself is acceptable (Good et al., 1984). There are other principles for effectively using the methods in the design process. Having the software developers themselves on the team that runs a usability evaluation is recommended because they can see for themselves in real time that aspects of a current design provoke repeated difficulties across users. Summary reports do not convey the same weight for such conclusions as do real-time experiences. And it has long been recommended that users themselves sit on the design team to assure adequate input of task vocabulary, completeness of features, and flow that fits the way the user thinks about the task progression. Many of the methods listed could benefit from users being on the design or analysis team.

This overview shows that there is considerable progress in providing ways to design useful, usable, and learnable user interfaces. Many new methods have been developed since the 1983 NRC report, and recent studies have compared the cost-benefit of various methods (Nielsen, 1992, 1993). We have provided a framework for seeing the roles of different methods, but more work is needed on a detailed cost-benefit of the methods. Not only do the methods need to be assessed for their usefulness, but new methods need to be developed that are more complete and usable.

Notes

1. Of the participants in this book, many were also participants in the NRC Committee on Human Factors workshop in 1983. Stu Card, Jack Carroll, Judy Olson, and John Whiteside were at both. Others in the 1983 workshop included Nancy Anderson, Elizabeth Bailey, Alphonse Chapanis, Rex Hartson, David Lenorovitz, Marilyn Mantei, Dick Pew, Phyllis Reisner, Janet Walker, and Bob Williges.

2. Published reports (for example, Nielsen, 1992; Karat, Campbell, and Fiegel, 1992) include other numbers as estimates of the time to perform some of these analyses, but they are reporting actual times for specific, small design situations. The numbers here are intended to be more wide ranging, applying to more real-world design situations.

3. Use cases are essential components of the new Object Oriented Methods, now increasing in favor in the software design community (Jacobson, 1992).

4. Christine Mitchell presented the operator function model at the workshop but that paper is not included in this volume. See Mitchell (1987); Mitchell and Saisi (1987); Dunkler et al. (1988); Jones, Rubin, and Mitchell (1989); Smith, Govindaraj, and Mitchell (1990); and Chu, Mitchell, and Govindaraj (1989).

5. This may take longer. It requires the analyst to know the previous designs, for example, from competitive analysis, which normally take at least a week.

6. This analysis, of course, depends on what you take as "natural." English imperatives may be verb-noun, but manually, one first grabs a thing and then does something with it, that is, noun-verb.

7. This estimate is for "delux" usability testing. "Discount" testing (Nielsen, 1992) is much faster to learn.

References

Adams, J. L. (1979). *Conceptual Blockbusting: A Guide to Better Ideas.* New York: W. W. Norton.

Anderson, N. and Olson, J. Reitman (eds.) (1985). *Methods for Designing Software to Fit Human Needs and Capabilities: Proceedings of the Workshop on Software Human Factors.* Washington, DC: National Academy Press.

Atwood, M., Gray, W., and John, B. Project Ernestine: Analytic and empirical methods applied to a real-world CHI problem. (This volume.)

Card, S. Pioneers and settlers: Methods used in successful user interface design. (This volume.)

Card, S. K., Moran, T. P., and Newell, A. (1983). *The Psychology of Human-Computer Interaction.* Hillsdale, NJ: Lawrence Erlbaum.

Carroll, J. and Rosson, M. B. Getting around the task-artifact cycle: How to make claims and design by scenario. (This volume.)

Chu, R. W., Mitchell, C. M., and Govindaraj, T. (1989). Characteristics of an ITS that evolves from tutor to operator's assistant. *Proceedings of 1989 IEEE International Conference on Cybernetics and Society.* Boston, 778–783.

Douglas, S. and Moran, T. (1983). Learning text editor semantics by analogy. *CHI'83 Proceedings of the Conference on Human Factors in Computing Systems.* New York: ACM, 207–211.

Dunkler, O., Mitchell, C. M., Govindaraj, T., and Ammons, J. C. (1988). The effectiveness of supervisory control strategies in flexible manufacturing systems. *IEEE Transactions on Systems, Man and Cybernetics,* vol. SMC-18 (March/April), 223–237.

Gillan, D. J. and Breedin, S. D. (1990). Designers' models of the human-computer interface. *CHI'90 Proceedings of the Conference on Human Factors in Computing Systems.* New York: ACM, 391–398.

Gong, R. and Elkerton, J. (1990). Designing minimal documentation using a GOMS model: A usability evaluation of an engineering approach. *Proceedings of the Conference on Human Factors in Computing Systems.* New York: ACM, 99–106.

Good, M., Whiteside, J., Wixon, D., and Jones, S. (1984). Building a user-derived interface. *Communications of the ACM 27,* 1032–1043.

Gould, J. D. (1988). How to design usable systems. In M. Helander (ed.), *Handbook of Human-Computer Interaction.* Amsterdam: North-Holland, 757–785.

Gould, J. D., Boies, S. J., Levy, S., Richards, J. T., and Schoonard, J. (1987). The Olympic Messaging System: A test of behavioral principles in system design. *Communications of the CACM 30,* 758–769.

Gould, J., Ukelson, J. P., and Boies, S. Improving user interfaces and application productivity by using the ITS application development environment. (This volume.)

Halasz, F. G. and Moran, T. P. (1983). Mental models and problem solving in using a calculator. *Proceedings of the Conference on Human Factors in Computing Systems.* New York: ACM, 212–216.

Hammer, M. and Champy, J. (1993). *Reengineering the Corporation: A Manifesto for Business Revolution.* New York: HarperCollins Publishers.

Hill, B., Long, J., Smith, W., and Whitefield, A. (1993). Planning for multiple task work—An analysis of a medical reception worksystem. *Proceedings of the Conference on Human Factors in Computing Systems.* New York: ACM, 314–320.

Hix, D. and Schulman, R. S. (1991). Human-computer interface development tools: A methodology of their evaluation. *Communications of the CACM 34(3),* March, 74–87.

Jacobson, I. (1992). *Object-Oriented Software Engineering.* Reading, MA: Addison-Wesley.

John, B. E. (1988). *Contributions to engineering models of human-computer interaction.* Dissertation, Carnegie Mellon University, Department of Psychology.

Jonassen, D. J., Hannum, W. H., and Tessmer, M. (1989). *Handbook of Task Analysis Procedures.* New York: Praeger.

Jones, P. M., Rubin, K. S., and Mitchell, C. M. (1989). Validation of intent inferencing by a model-based operator's associate. *International Journal of Man-Machine Studies,* 177–202.

Karat, C. M., Campbell, R., and Fiegel, T. (1992). Comparison of empirical testing and walkthrough methods in user interface evaluation. *Proceedings of the Conference on Human Factors in Computing Systems.* New York: ACM, 397–404.

Kieras, D. E. (1988). Towards a practical GOMS model methodology for user interface design. In M. Helander (ed.), *Handbook of Human-Computer Interaction.* Amsterdam: North-Holland, 135–157.

Kieras, D. E. and Bovair, S. (1986). The acquisition of procedures from text: A production-system analysis of transfer of training. *Journal of Memory and Learning* 25, 507–524.

Kieras, D. and Polson, P. G. (1983). A generalized transition network representation for interactive systems. *Proceedings of the Conference on Human Factors in Computing Systems.* New York: ACM, 103–106.

Lenorovitz, D. R., Phillips, M. D., Ardrey, R. S., and Kloster, G. V. (1984). A taxonomic approach to characterizing human computer interfaces. In G. Salvendy (ed.), *Human Computer Interaction.* Amsterdam: North-Holland, 111–116.

Lewis, C., Polson, P., Wharton, C., and Rieman, J. (1990). Testing a walkthrough methodology for theory-based design of walk-up-and-use interfaces. *Proceedings of the Conference on Human Factors in Computing Systems.* New York: ACM, 235–241.

Lohse, J. (1991). A cognitive model for the perception and understanding of graphs. *Proceedings of the Conference on Human Factors in Computing Systems.* New York: ACM, 137–144.

Mackay, W. E., Malone, T. W., Crowston, K., Rao, R., Rosenblitt, D., and Card, S. K. (1989). How do experienced users use rules? *Proceedings of the Conference on Human Factors in Computing Systems.* New York: ACM, 211–216.

Mackinlay, J. (1986). Automating the design of graphical presentations of relational information. *ACM Transactions on Graphics* 5 (April 2), 110–141.

MacLean, A., Young, R., Bellotti, V. M., and Moran, T. P. (1991). Questions, options, and criteria: Elements of a design space analysis. *Human Computer Interaction* 6, 201–250.

McDaniel, S. E., Olson, G. M., and Olson, J. S. (1994). Methods in search of methodology—Combining HCI and object orientation. *Human Factors in Computing Systems: CHI'94 Conference Proceedings.* New York: ACM.

Mitchell, C. M. (1987). GT-MSOCC: A domain for modeling human–computer interaction and aiding decision making in supervisory control systems. *IEEE Transactions on Systems, Man, and Cybernetics,* vol. SMC-16, no. 4 (July/August), 553–572.

Mitchell, C. M. and Saisi, D. S. (1987). Use of model-based qualitative icons and adaptive windows in workstations for supervisory control. *IEEE Transactions on Systems, Man, and Cybernetics,* vol. SMC-16, no. 4 (July/August), 573–593.

Moran, T. (1983). Getting into a system: External-internal task mapping analysis. *Proceedings of the Conference on Human Factors in Computing Systems.* New York: ACM, 45–49.

———. (1981). The Command Language Grammar: A representation for the user interface of interactive computer systems. *International Journal of Man-Machine Systems* 15, 3–50.

Muller, M. J. (1991). PICTIVE—An exploration in participatory design. *Proceedings of the Conference on Human Factors in Computing Systems.* New York: ACM, 225–231.

Newman, W. M. and Sproull, R. F. (1979). *Principles of Interactive Computer Graphics.* New York: McGraw-Hill.

Nielsen, J., Mack, R. L., Bergendorff, K. H., and Grischkowsky, N. (1989). Integrated software usage in the professional work environment: Evidence from questionnaires and interviews. *Proceedings of the Conference on Human Factors in Computing Systems.* New York: ACM, 162–167.

Nielsen, J. (1992). Finding usability problems through heuristic evaluation. *Proceedings of the Conference on Human Factors in Computing Systems.* New York: ACM, 373–380.

Nielsen, J. (1993). *Usability Engineering.* Boston: AP Professional.

Olson, J. S. (1985). Expanded design procedures for learnable, usable interfaces. *Proceedings of the Conference on Human Factors in Computing Systems.* New York: ACM, 142–143.

Olson, J. S. and Biolsi, K. J. (1991). Techniques for representing knowledge. In A. Ericsson and J. Smith (eds.), *Toward a General Theory of Expertise.* Cambridge, England: Cambridge University Press.

Olson, J. S. and Olson, G. M. (1991). The growth of cognitive modeling since GOMS. *Human Computer Interaction* 5, 221–266.

Payne, S. J. and Green, T. R. G. (1986). Task-action grammars: A model of the mental representation of task languages. *Human Computer Interaction* 2, 93–133.

Perlman, G. (1988). Software tools for user interface development. In M. Helander (ed.), *Handbook of Human Computer Interaction.* Amsterdam: North-Holland, 819–833.

Polson, P. G. and Kieras, D. E. (1985). A quantitative model of the learning and performance of text editing knowledge. *Human Factors in Computing Systems, Proceedings of the CHI'85.* New York: ACM.

Poltrock, S. and Grudin, J. Organizational obstacles to interface design and development: Two participant observer studies. (This volume.)

Reisner, P. (1984). Formal grammar as a tool for analyzing ease of use: Some fundamental concepts. In J. Thomas and M. Schneider (eds.), *Human Factors in Computer Systems*. Norwood, NJ: Ablex.

Rieman, J., Davies, S., Hair, D. C., Esemplare, M., Polson, P., and Lewis, C. (1991). An automated cognitive walkthrough. *Proceedings of the Conference on Human Factors in Computing Systems*. New York: ACM, 427–428.

Rudman, C. and Engelbeck, G. Lessons in choosing methods for designing complex graphical user interfaces. (This volume.)

Sasso, W., Olson, J. S., and Merten, A. (1987). The practice of office analysis: Objectives, obstacles, and opportunities. *Office Knowledge Engineering* 2, 11–24.

Schön , D. A. (1983). *The Reflective Practitioner: How Professionals Think in Action.* New York: Basic Books.

Shneiderman, B. (1992). *Designing the User Interface: Strategies for Effective Human-Computer Interaction.* 2nd ed. Reading, MA: Addison-Wesley.

Simon, H. A. (1981). *Sciences of the Artificial.* Cambridge, MA: MIT Press.

Smelcer, J. B. (1989). *Understanding user errors in database query.* Unpublished doctoral dissertation, University of Michigan, Ann Arbor.

Smith, D. C., Irby, C., Kimball, R., Verplank, B., and Harslem, E. (1982). Designing the Star user interface. *Byte* 7(4), 242–282.

Smith, S. C., Govindaraj, T., and Mitchell, C. M. (1990). Operator modeling in civil aviation. *Proceedings of 1990 IEEE International Conference on Cybernetics and Society.* Los Angeles, 512–514.

Smith, S. L. and Mosier, J. N. (1984). Design guidelines for user-system interface software. Mitre Corporation Report ESD-TR-84-190. Bedford, MA: Mitre Corporation.

Tetzlaff, L. and Schwartz, D. (1991). The use of guidelines in interface design. *Proceedings of the Conference on Human Factors in Computing Systems.* New York: ACM, 329–334.

Tullis, T. S. (1988). Screen design. In M. Helander (ed.), *Handbook of Human Computer Interaction.* Amsterdam: North-Holland, 377–411.

Weinberg, G. M. and Freidman, D. P. (1984). Reviews, walkthroughs, and inspections. *IEEE Transactions on Software Engineering* SE-10(1).

Wilson, J. and Rosenberg, D. (1988). Rapid prototyping for user interface design. In M. Helander (ed.), *Handbook of Human-Computer Interaction.* Amsterdam: North-Holland, 859–876.

Real-World Context

Organizational Obstacles to Interface Design and Development: Two Participant Observer Studies[1]

STEVEN E. POLTROCK

Boeing Computer Services

JONATHAN GRUDIN

University of California, Irvine

The development of human-computer interfaces was studied in two large software product development organizations. Researchers joined development projects for approximately one month and participated in interface design while interviewing other project participants and employees, recording activity in meetings and on electronic networks, and otherwise observing the process. The two organizations differed in their approaches to development, but in each case, development practices interfered with the successful application of accepted principles of interface design. The obstacles to effective design included the inability of interface designers to obtain access to users, prototyping tools that allow minor changes to be tested but that constrain innovation, resistance to iterative design that results from people noticing and being affected by interface changes, and a lack of communication among those sharing responsibility for different aspects of the interface. All these are serious concerns that seem rooted in widespread organizational structures and practices.

Interface Design Practices Are Not Well Documented

> It is difficult to develop good user interfaces. We know this because there is no shortage of bad user interfaces, even in products where developers tried to incorporate "user friendliness." (Perlman, 1988).

The poorly designed features that handicap most interfaces are common targets of criticism, but their origins are largely unexamined. Descriptions of particularly successful or innovative development are few, and the contributions in this volume are a welcome addition, but careful analyses of more typical design and development are virtually nonexistent. Accounts of the successful use of new interface design methods and tools are valuable, but we also need detailed accounts of the existing design practices that the new methods and tools are to displace. This paper includes two such accounts.

It is not surprising that developing good interfaces is difficult. Interactive systems are something new: Millennia of artifact design did little to prepare us for the challenges that they present. Even within the computer field, many organizations that develop interfaces today originally developed systems that did not have a significant human-computer interface. Possibilities for interface expression are mushrooming. Computational power permits more media to be combined in more ways, and on the other side of the interface, the nature of user populations is changing just as rapidly. Finding an appropriate fit is a challenge.

Do bad interfaces arise because we do not know *how* to develop good interfaces? Or do we know how, but fail to practice it? In our view, principles and methods for developing good interactive systems are known and are rapidly being refined, so it is a matter of execution. This raises a second question: Could the principles and methods be applied in a straightforward manner, or are there fundamental organizational barriers? In this paper, we identify widely accepted principles of design and then describe detailed studies of development practice in two software development projects. The projects succeeded, in that the products were built and marketed, but the product interfaces were far from perfect. Obstacles to applying accepted design principles and methods were evident. These obstacles are a direct consequence of interface development practices, which are, in turn, a consequence of organizational structures and processes. In the end, we are left to ponder what combinations of new methods, new organizational structures and processes, and new tools will best move us forward.

One goal in identifying problems or bottlenecks in current interface development practices is to inspire tools that will contribute to greater productivity and quality. Prototyping tools that allow designers to explore design alternatives, demonstrate the advantages of a design to management, and test designs with users can increase usability and decrease the cost of development. Other tools could enhance communication and coordination. But the effectiveness of such tools might be highly dependent on organizational context; in fact, some problems or bottlenecks might be more easily repaired just by changing organizational practices. Interface design and development have only recently become a respected area of software specialization. Many software development organizations do not yet recognize the unique requirements of interface design. In some cases, significant improvements will be achieved by changing an organization's design practices. The discrepancies between interface design principles and practices described here suggest opportunities for such changes.

Interface Design Principles

Gould and Lewis (1983, 1985) proposed principles of interactive system design that have had the benefit of repeated application and refinement (Gould, 1988; Gould et al., 1987; Gould, Boies, and Lewis, 1991). Their four principles currently are:

- *Early focus on users.* Designers should have *direct* contact with intended or actual users—via interviews, observations, surveys, and participatory design. The aim is to understand users' cognitive, behavioral, attitudinal, anthropometric characteristics—and the characteristics of the jobs they will be doing.

- *Early—and continual—user testing.* The only presently feasible approach to successful design is an empirical one, requiring observation and measurement of user behavior, careful evaluation of feedback, insightful solutions to existing problems, and strong motivation to make design changes.

- *Iterative design.* A system under development must be modified based on the results of behavioral tests of functions, user interface, help system, documentation, training approach. This process of implementation, testing, feedback, evaluation, and change must be repeated to iteratively improve the system.

- *Integrated design.* All aspects of usability (for example, user interface, help system, training plan, documentation) should evolve in parallel, rather than be defined sequentially, and should be under one management (Gould, Boies, and Lewis, 1991, p. 75).

Gould (1988) notes some similarities of these principles to those proposed by others and lists methods for implementing them. Researchers have successfully used the principles to develop working systems (Gould et al., 1987; Hewett and Meadow, 1986). Presented with these principles, systems developers consider them to be obvious (Gould and Lewis, 1985). However, many people, including Gould and his colleagues, find that developers rarely follow them. Most designers report giving some consideration to users, but few involve users directly in the design process or plan for design iterations.

Investigations of the interface development process and of developers' disregard for these principles have relied primarily on interviews, surveys, and direct reports of experience (for example, Goransson et al., 1987; Gould and Lewis, 1985; Grudin and Poltrock, 1989; Hammond et al., 1983; Rosson, Maass, and Kellogg, 1988). Gould and Lewis (1985) suggested that the rules are not applied because designers underestimate diversity in the user population, believe that users do not know what they need, have faith in the power of reason to resolve design issues, and believe that the right design can be achieved the first time. They also allude to "obstacles and traditions" that stand in the way. Gould (1988, p. 776) later noted the principles "are hard to carry out, mainly for organizational and motivational reasons." Others have noted that design decisions are based on faulty "common sense theories" of users rather than on observations of actual users (Hammond et al., 1983), late contact with users (Rosson, Maass, and Kellogg, 1988), and lack of communication among different interface specialists (Grudin and Poltrock, 1989).

These reports strongly suggest that there is a mismatch between the needs of interactive systems development and existing systems development practices. To address this problem effectively, we needed to know whether it arises from insufficient awareness of what is required to develop interactive systems or is an inherent consequence of existing organizational structures and practices. Such a determination required detailed examinations of development practices in specific organizational contexts.

Two Case Histories Based on Participant Observation

Participant–observer studies were carried out at two major computer companies. In each case, an investigator joined a software development organization within the company that consisted of 70 or more people responsible for the development of a major product or product line that is sold internationally. The group being studied was designing a new version of an existing product.[2]

The investigators joined interface teams. Over the course of a month, they participated in interface design and interviewed people throughout the organizations, primarily people who contributed directly or indirectly to interface design or development. Each investigator interviewed about 25 people, starting with the interface team and later expanding to include other developers, members of technical support groups, and managers. As members of an interface team, the investigators acquired firsthand an appreciation of the methods and tools used in that period. Through interviews, the investigators learned about preceding activities and planned activities, and explored the perspectives of other members of the development organization. Issues investigated included the organizational context for interface development, the tools used in the organization, how those tools affect the work, which different disciplines are involved in interface development, how people from different disciplines coordinate their contributions, and how the organizational structure affects interdisciplinary coordination.[3]

Case 1[4]

Case 1 centered on a CAD product that started as a university project and then survived more than five years in a dynamic marketplace. Some new functionality and small changes to the interface had appeared in periodic releases, but as the product aged, maintenance and modernization became increasingly difficult, and it was rapidly losing ground to competitors' newer products. The organization had anticipated this problem years earlier and set up a small research project to design a new product, but after a year they were disappointed with its progress and canceled the project in favor of major modifications to the existing product. For two more years, they vacillated between the strategies of building a new product and modifying the old one. As time passed, a sense of urgency grew, and these projects were allocated greater resources. The projects provided some product enhancements but failed to produce an acceptable long-term development plan.

As recounted by those who had been involved, these projects were overwhelmed by the difficulty of deciding what to do. The same issues arose repeatedly, with little sense of moving toward a consensus. Every option could be the topic of seemingly endless discussion, and any decision could later be overruled by someone outside the group deciding that it did not fit the organization's marketing strategy. Frequent reorganizations and some staff reductions contributed to both the indecision and the sense of urgency.

This unproductive state of affairs was overcome by a "super designer" brought in from a group that supported the product at a distant site (see Curtis, Krasner, and Iscoe, 1988, for a description of the roles of super designers in software development). He had a strong technical background that included experience customizing the product for a major customer and a thorough understanding of this customer's needs based on contacts with managers and users. He joined the vice-president's staff after persuading the vice president that the product could be made competitive within a year.

This leader knew exactly what he wanted to do. He had a vision of an innovative release and how it would be built, and his vision drove the interface design. To realize his vision in a year would take extraordinary effort and commitment from everyone and could not wait for the usual cycle of reviews, consensus building, and approval. Working without formal authority, he hand-picked developers without consulting their managers, assigned them tasks, and then reviewed their progress and problems daily. This hands-on approach was a significant change from standard practice, and it irritated many managers and developers. But when anyone complained, the vice-president backed the super designer.

Early reports indicate that the new product was a success in the market-place. But the procedures that made this success possible were subsequently abandoned. At the time of our study, the vice-president had left, the super designer expected to leave, and the management structure had been reorganized. When the new managers were interviewed, they talked about the importance of following standard software development management prac-tices to control the product design and to ensure coordination across the proj-ect. These practices would enable them to meet reliability criteria and schedules, goals that seemed more important than further innovation.

During our study, an interface development team was designing the inter-face for the next release. This team did not use the product and did not have the experience working with customers that was apparently the basis for the super designer's vision for the product. They could not involve users in the interface design, and no usability testing was planned.

Case 2

The Case 1 and Case 2 products were about equally old, but the Case 2 prod-uct, an office system, had a very different history. It had evolved from a field service group's successful solution to a specific customer's problem. A devel-opment group within the company had built a similar product, but they had not started with a particular customer in mind, their progress had been slow, and the result, although technically sound and reliable, was unsuccessful on the whole. Wishing to develop and market new, improved versions of the sys-tem that Field Service had produced for one customer, the company reas-signed the development group to extend it. At the time of the Case 2 study, this group was supporting two releases of the system, implementing a third version, designing a fourth version, and planning a fifth.

Why had Field Service been able to develop a more successful product? One manager suggested that the software development group was hindered by requirements and procedures that slowed product development and disconnected it from user inputs. He believed that the field service group knew the needs of their customer and could quickly respond to the customer's requests. This lesson was apparently not lost on the development organization, whose procedures changed considerably after their failure. User input became a central part of the design and development process. At the time of our study, human factors engineers designed and evaluated the interfaces and tested their designs using prototypes as early in development as possible. They learned about users' needs by using the product themselves, visiting customer sites, talking to customer representatives, and demonstrating and evaluating the product and prototypes.

The Case 2 organization aggressively sought ways to introduce innovations in their product, planning how to integrate them over the series of product revisions. A group was established to serve as technological gatekeepers (Allen, 1977; Allen and Cohen, 1969; Allen, Tushman, and Lee, 1979), looking for innovations both inside and outside the company and working with the interface designers to plan the integration of these new features. Taking this long view allowed them to develop or commission development of prototypes that would demonstrate the value and feasibility of new features.

Not long after this study was completed, the Case 2 organization responded to budget constraints by reducing the interface design staff, discontinuing user testing, and disbanding the group of gatekeepers. The interface design staff had grown rapidly and made an attractive target for budget cuts.

The Organizational Context

Figure 1 shows a partial organizational structure similar to those of our two cases. It includes only the organizational elements that are most relevant to interface development. We are defining interface broadly to include documentation and training, as well as the software and hardware interface. The groups in italics had especially direct involvement in some aspect of interface design in the organizations studied, the other groups were more tangential. For example, Performance Analysis and Quality Control groups were not heavily concerned with interface design issues. Performance analysts focused on issues affecting total system performance, not user performance,[5] and Quality Control groups did not critique or evaluate the interface unless, as one engineer put it, "the interface is truly awful." The structure shown does

FIGURE 1

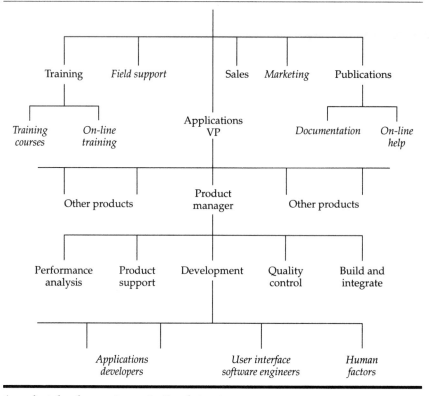

A product development organizational structure.

not exactly reflect either case; for example, Case 1 did not have a team of human factors engineers.

The purpose of Figure 1 is not to endorse this organizational structure but to guide our exploration of the ways in which organizational structures can influence interface development. Pressman (1987) notes that "there are almost as many human organizational structures for software development as there are organizations that develop software." Some issues of generality are discussed in the conclusion.

Little is known about the relationship between organizational structure and productivity, but organizations do impose a structure on formal communication that influences its frequency and quality (Curtis, Krasner, and Iscoe, 1988). More communication generally occurs among people at a given hierarchical level than across levels. Communication tends to decrease in frequency and increase in formality as organizational and physical distances increase (Allen, 1977). Communication across organizational boundaries can be limited or impaired by being channeled through managers or other intermediaries, by a reduced incidence of informal contact, and by the difficulty of overcoming physical distances.

Figure 1 suggests reasons for interface developers to be concerned about the effects of organizational distance on communication. People responsible for different aspects of the interface—documentation, training, and software—are far apart organizationally. Field Support and Marketing, which can also contribute to interface design, are organizationally distant from the interface developers. Note that this structure violates the fourth design principle, which calls for placing all aspects of usability under one management. Indeed, we observed problems arising from communication breakdowns between organizationally distant groups.

Within this broad framework, details of an organization's structure, as well as the managers responsible for the organizational entities, may change frequently. Such changes are often accompanied by changes in direction, which can adversely affect the interface design among other things. One manager described the effects of organizational changes as follows:

> I don't think anybody's figured it out yet! I don't think anybody has taken the time. Everybody's working so hard at defining their perch. I've got this image that you've got this big bird cage, and everybody has their perch. And then along comes a new vice-president, and bang they hit the cage with their base-ball bat, and all the birds fly up in the air. And they take out a couple of perches, and then everybody comes down to land. And they work real hard at getting their perch stabilized, and now I got a job definition, and I'm building my empire again. And just about the time everybody gets settled and starts singing again, here comes the next king, right? The king's dead, long live the king. BANG! They hit the bird cage again, and everybody flies up, and it's just crazy! You never have consistency.... Any time you change the organization all the commitments are gone! And what the hell's the customer do with that!

Design decisions have a political component; they are often compromises between competing forces. Management changes often shift the political balance, reopening design issues and forcing revisions in partially completed designs. Changes in management and even in organizational structure can mask an underlying perpetuation of high-level structures, dynamics, and practices in an organization. Readers may benefit from comparing their own organizational structures, organizational dynamics, and design practices to those we observed.

Interface Design Practices

Now we turn to the interface design practices of our two case studies. Keeping in mind the principles for building effective interfaces noted in the introduction, we first look at each organization's "theory" of the interface design process and how it maps onto the organizational structure. Then we compare these principles and each organization's theory with its actual practices.

Case 1: Theory

> Well, the theory of this organization structure is that Marketing is the primary one working with Sales and customers to understand market requirements. The Design group works with customers to understand the technical details of the requirements. And Development should be able to get that information from the Design group without having to go out and work with the customers as well. You know, certainly Development will always have the argument, "Well, gee, if we could do that, we'd understand it better." Well, yes, that's true! But you can't have everybody going out to the customers all the time. You should focus on doing development and respond to those design requirements.... When once they write the User Interface Specification, then the Design group may come in and say, "No, we should have done something else. You did not meet the intent."

A theory describing how the organization coordinates interface design and development was extracted from interviews with several people. Figure 2 depicts the flow of information, according to this theory, between customers and elements of the organization. Marketing defines product requirements, including new product features, based on information about customers' needs acquired directly from customers and indirectly through field support. Marketing communicates these requirements in the form of specifications to a Design group, which in turn specifies how the features will function in more detail. Such a Design group does not appear in Figure 1 but is similar to the product manager in that figure. The Design group interacts with customers as needed to produce a specification of a high-level product design. This specification may call for new interface features but does not define such details as methods for accessing the features.

A group of software engineers within Development designs the software interface based on specifications from the Design group and produces an

FIGURE 2

A theory of information flow for interface design that is widely held in the Case 1 organization.

interface design specification. As noted by the design group manager quoted earlier, this User Interface group is intended to have no contacts with customers or users.[6] The Design group reviews the interface specification to determine whether it meets the intent of their high-level design specification. Then the software engineers implement the interface in accordance with the approved interface specification. Later, an Evaluation group ensures that the interface matches the interface specification. Thus, formal specifications are the primary means of communication among Marketing, the Design group, Development, and Evaluation.

Case 1: Practice

> The general consensus is that our Marketing group is next to worthless.

In theory, Marketing is the primary source of information about customers and drives the entire design process. Designers and developers, however, had low regard for Marketing, and most had relatively little contact with them. Developers were unable to reach users directly. One developer met an experienced user at a trade show who complained about communications with Development. The user was quoted as saying:

> It's really a shame the way that [you] decide what to do in the product. I have to talk to Marketing, who really sometimes don't have the foggiest idea what I'm talking about. They pass the information on as best they can to the Design group, who might not have any idea what Marketing is talking about either, so now we've got it even that much more garbled. And then it gets to you guys, and you have no idea what it is about; you don't know where it came from, and you don't know how to contact me.

By examining Figure 2, you might guess another approach taken by designers and developers anxious for more information about users:

We tried to get Field Support involved in design reviews, because Field Support has a lot of involvement with customers through the support they're providing and potential customers through the demos and benchmarks, etc. We always had difficulty getting the time from the Field Support people to be involved in those design reviews and the planning of the features.... Then Field Support moved under Marketing, and the Marketing approach was that they didn't want Field Support working directly with Development or the Design group. They wanted it to come through the Marketing people....

Thus, the theoretical flow of information did not work, yet there were efforts to enforce it. We will now discuss the effects in detail in terms of the Gould and Lewis principles.

Product Definition and User Involvement

As we noted, Marketing was viewed by Development as ineffective at getting the information needed to define product requirements:

The biggest problem area is the fact that the Marketing organization is not very strong.... They really don't have very many people at all that understand marketing or how to determine market requirements, and so that's the biggest danger, that we may respond very effectively to the market requirements as defined by Marketing, but those may not be what we should have been doing to capture the market and be successful in that industry.

One can easily understand how Marketing, the principle communication channel to customers, could acquire this reputation. Marketing's primary role is to determine what is needed to sell systems, not what is needed to make systems usable. Were Development to seek guidance from Marketing about users' needs, Marketing would lack the information required for a constructive reply. Their contacts are with the customers' management; Marketing rarely communicates with users or with field support about users' needs. Information from customers' management may be adequate to define high-level objectives, but it cannot support the understanding of users' tasks that is required to design and develop effective interactive systems. Neither customers' management nor Marketing have sufficient experience or intuition with the newly important and rapidly changing area of interface design. This communication paradigm may have been sufficient when the interface was an unimportant part of their products, but it is inadequate to support interface design.

Given that Marketing is not highly regarded, who actually defines product features? A great many of the features were proposed by members of the development organization, including the Design group. In fact, many features were proposed and added to the design during development. Often these features were motivated by customers' requests. The development managers maintained their own informal, unofficial contacts with customers' management and used these contacts to bypass Marketing and acquire ideas for new features. A member of the Marketing group complained that Development "is very intimately involved with a lot of our customers, they make commitments personally for features." These contacts with customers provide Development with limited information about users' needs, but it should be noted that Development's source of information, customers' management, does not use the products. Formal analyses of users and their tasks played no role in the definition of product features.

Although development management maintained some contacts with customers, rarely did individual interface developers or users bypass the consciously interposed intermediaries such as Marketing and Field Service. A few customers were acquainted with specific developers and in that way bypassed or supplemented communication with Marketing, and opinions could be expressed at trade shows or user group meetings. Several justifications for these barriers were offered. Some managers worried that developers would be excessively influenced by requests for features from customers who are not representative of the marketplace. Others worried that developers, who often have a reputation for lacking social skills, would damage customer relations. Still others believed that it is important to protect developers from distractions so that they can be productive.

These barriers may be well motivated, but they clearly stand in the way of the first two design principles and equally clearly had negative consequences for interface design. The software engineers responsible for designing the interface were not informed about the intent of the features they were designing. The specifications provided by the Design group did not indicate what problem the features were intended to solve or the context in which the features would be used. As one software engineer said, "They give us a solution, and they don't tell us what the problem is." Consequently, the software engineers were uncertain how to design the interface. When adding new features, the software engineers had to decide which menus would provide access to the features without information about why or when the features would be used.

As we noted, to acquire information about the purpose and use of features, the User Interface group interacted informally, though somewhat infrequently, with field support staff who had experience using the products. Discussions with Field Support were not a recognized part of the interface design process and consequently often occurred after part of the design was completed. One software engineer reported, "I mean, I was just today talking with a fellow [from Field Support] about a feature and how he thought it ought to work, and I've had to start from scratch just based on talking to him."

Some people did realize that the absence of user involvement had consequences for the interface. A member of the Marketing group said, "Development doesn't even know how to build a friendly user interface because they don't know what a user is. And that really is, I think, a real key right there in how you make something user friendly." This Marketing representative went on to describe in more detail the limitations of contacts between customers and Development:

> They should have very close knowledge and connection with a user, a user, not the companies but the user. What happens is not this, it's that management of Development goes out and gives presentations to management of customers. This is what actually happens. They want a new feature called "undo." They call development management and say, "Goddamn it, your product ought to have undo." Management says, "Yeah, we're going to put in undo." The poor little developer sitting there never gets to talk to the goddamn user down here of what really undo is.... We don't even have our own internal users talking to our developers.

The problem is of course even more strongly recognized by some of the software engineers who design and implement the interface. One software engineer said:

> What I'd really like to do as a user interface designer, if the Marketing people could at least provide some major direction, some areas that we want to address, and I think they have done some of that, and then, I wish they would identify some customers that we could go to and work with.

Indeed, this software engineer suggested that all of Development could benefit from observing users at work. He recognized that users provide a resource that can be tapped only with some ingenuity and with a global view of their work:

> I think it would be worthwhile if all developers would spend maybe a couple of hours a year seeing how the product is used by those customers. Just watching them. And while they're watching them the customer would say, "I don't like the way this works," and noting those things.... You need to see how they use it. You need to understand, first of all, what they're doing. So you need them to give you a little background, and then watch how they accomplish it, and see the totality of it, especially. How they fire up, the whole structure

of their day. And then use that information to give you a global sense of how to help them out. You can't help them without understanding how they work. And not to ask them so much, "What do you want to see?" Because they don't know.

A couple of hours a year! Some software engineers and the Marketing representative clearly recognized the importance of involving users, one of the principles of interface design. Nonetheless, the development organization persisted in applying a theory of design that prevented this involvement.

Prototyping and Iterative Design

In the absence of user feedback, iteration has less utility, but the software engineers did prototype their designs. These prototypes were constructed by changing the product code, not through use of prototyping tools. The prototypes were not evaluated through tests conducted with users; in fact, they were not implemented to evaluate the interface design, but to estimate more accurately the time that would be required to implement the interface. The developers did informally evaluate prototypes by showing them to their colleagues and to management. However, in the absence of evidence favoring a design, such demonstrations could have unwelcome effects. An interface developer commented that at design review meetings, "unqualified people make lots of comments off the top of their heads." The interface developers hoped to find a way to limit the involvement of other project members by requiring written review comments.

Even the finished product was not evaluated by users before it was shipped to customers. Some people realized that the tests conducted by Quality Control to ensure that the product matches the specification were not sufficient. One manager noted:

> I would say that testing should be done by a group outside Development. 'Cause Development knows how the code works, and even though you don't want it, your subconscious makes you test the way you know it works.... See, those people in the Quality Control group have nothing to do with customers. They're not users.

In fact, two members of Field Support were reported to have found more bugs than the Quality Control group in the latest release, and they had accomplished this by working with the product as they imagined that users would. Testing by Field Support was an innovative experiment, however, and not part of the accepted development process:

The Quality Control group has a lot of systematic testing, and you need some of that, but at the same time, you need somebody who is essentially a customer. It is as if you had a customer in house who uses it the way a customer would every day, and is particularly tough on it and shakes all these things out. That's what these two guys did, and it was just invaluable.

Integrating All Aspects of Usability

The fourth principle encourages the concurrent development of all aspects of usability under one management. Until shortly before our visit, all software engineers shared responsibility for designing and implementing the interface. Maintaining a consistent software interface style had thus been a serious challenge on previous releases; the software engineers had been more concerned with the data their programs needed from users than with the usability of the programs. All software interface design and development was now centralized in a single group, which included some engineers with training and interest in interfaces. However, the organization had no involvement of interface specialists such as human factors engineers or industrial design engineers, and Documentation and Training were handled in organizationally distinct groups. In a separate survey of interface development practices that included the two companies observed here, we found that documentation and training are typically developed late and in isolation from software development (Grudin and Poltrock, 1989). In this organization, one developer enjoyed writing and worked closely with the Documentation group. Interface specifications were the primary sources for the technical writers, but these were supplemented with frequent face-to-face meetings.

Communication with Performance Analysis and Quality Control groups was less frequent. To construct automatic performance or quality tests required information about typical user interactions, but users were not consulted directly. Manuals and specifications were used by Quality Control to construct an interaction scenario. Quality Control reported bugs formally using databases accessed by the developers.

A more serious integration problem resulted from sharing design responsibility across Marketing, Design, and Development organizations. Specifications were management's coordination mechanism. As Curtis, Krasner, and Iscoe (1988) observed, specifications are an important but unsatisfactory communication medium. As noted earlier, the User Interface group complained that the specification provided by the Design group failed to explain the reasons for the features it described. Clarification of the specifications was made difficult by the separation of the groups:

The design requirements are written specifically as, "This is what will be done." And it doesn't try to justify why that should be done. And they don't come back and say, "Well, let's have a meeting with the Design group and discuss and understand why these things are requirements." ... There still is somewhat of a barrier there to effective communications in that we are physically in different parts of the building here.

These groups were in the same building—in another instance, a small group located in another state developing part of the product was eventually disbanded because of communication problems:

That whole communication there was real difficult, trying to keep in synch.... It was very difficult to keep the standards the same because it was a small group so far away. It was very difficult. The code that came back was hard to work with and hard to integrate, and then if we had to iterate real quickly on something when we were trying to release, the long-distance communications just slowed everything down. We had a lot of teleconferences, but I think you do miss a lot [that is] in the face-to-face.

Physical distances as well as organizational distances that foster competition for limited resources and power can erode the trust required for effective communication. A manager attributed some communication problems to both distance and lack of trust:

There are two primary things. One is just the historical lack of respect and trust or whatever between different organizations, Development, the Design group, and Marketing. The other is being in separate physical locations. For most of the time that the division has been in existence within the company, Marketing was at one site, Field Support was at another site, Development was at a third site.... And there was always the desire to have all three of those groups together, but there was never economic justification for making those moves up until fairly recently.

The management role of serving as a communication channel among groups, selecting and distributing information or establishing direct contacts at lower levels, is impaired when trust erodes. Some managers restrict any communication with their subordinates, perhaps to protect them from outside distractions or perhaps simply to control the flow of communication.

The Design group was composed of experienced software engineers charged with translating Marketing's requirements into a high-level design. Their role as designers gave them a stake in the outcome and perhaps impaired their effectiveness as pure communication channels. Developers seemed reluctant to approach the Design group for more information about users. The tension that existed between the Design group and developers was revealed in a statement that a Marketing manager attributed to a member of the Design group:

> Camels complain whether you put one straw on their backs or a whole bale of straw on their backs, they complain about the same. They make as much noise and braying and all that. It's just a lot of goddamn weight. No matter what you put on their back, it's an enormous undertaking to do that, and that's the camel's nature. And it's real hard for you to tell whether the camel's really carrying a lot of weight or if the camel is just passing gas, right? And so you load the camel up until it just about collapses and then you say, "Oh, that's about the load the camel can take." And then you drive the camel that way.... The same thing happens in Development. Everything you ask them is too hard, it takes too long, and it's just an enormous undertaking, it won't work. And some of that's real and some of it isn't, and it's really hard to determine what is and what isn't. And it's the nature of the beast to do that. It's got nothing to do with personality or anything else. It's just the way all of the management and the culture has been built in the development group.

Managers face the problem of maintaining effective communication despite obstacles such as incomplete specifications, distance, and distrust. The super designer of the previous release accomplished this by usurping the organizational design process. He constructed the high-level design himself and bypassed the usual management chains of communication, personally talking to each developer daily, even several times per day, during the design and development of the product. Describing this coordination task, he said, "I ran around like a living information system between all the subprojects and checked them against the master project." His close supervision ensured smooth communication, though many of the developers resented it. At the end of the project, management was eager to return to "a standard development process."

What are the consequences for interface quality of the standard design practices? A middle manager in the development organization said, "Relative to user interface, we don't have the best in the world, I know that."

Case 2: Theory

The Case 2 theory of interface design, summarized in Figure 3, is less Marketing-driven than in Case 1. Marketing writes a specification suggesting

FIGURE 3

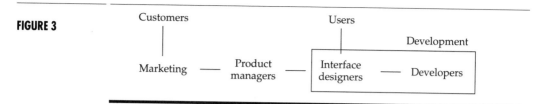

A theory of information flow for interface design that is widely held in the Case 2 organization.

features that meet existing and potential customers' needs. Marketing's primary source of information is again management in major customer organizations. A Product Manager then negotiates an agreement between Marketing and the development organization and writes a performance requirements specification that includes their agreement about the features to be implemented.

In theory, features can be proposed by Marketing, Development, or Product Management. But unlike the Design group of Case 1, Product Managers are selected for both their communication and technical skills. They conduct regular meetings of the management team as facilitators, not as advocates, and thus may be more effective in communicating user needs to developers.

The development organization includes the interface designers and the developers who implement the design. The former, a group of human factors engineers, has given considerable thought to the interface design process and the role of users. They solicit comments from users on the initial designs, build prototypes that are evaluated by user testing, and then iterate the design. The final design is specified in a document delivered to the software engineers who implement it. As new features are implemented, they are evaluated in benchmark tests against usability criteria.

Case 2: Practice

Product Definition and User Involvement

Marketing in Case 2 was not highly regarded, though perhaps more highly than in Case 1. Two differences between Cases 1 and 2 may explain why the relationship with Marketing seemed more strained in Case 1. First, Development in Case 2 was less dependent on Marketing for information about users that would influence product requirements. Through the Interface

Design group, Development had its own source of information about users, and this group contributed significantly to product requirements. Second, the role of Marketing in defining the product requirements was given less prominence in the theory of Case 2, a historically engineering-driven company that recognized Development's contributions to product definition.

The role of the Product Managers was analogous to the Design group in Case 1, in the sense that both mediated between Marketing and Developers. The Product Managers, however, did not specify a design; their role was to negotiate the product requirements. The developers retained responsibility for the product design. Indeed, they claimed to have primary responsibility for determining which features would be implemented. Developers even claimed responsibility for their unsuccessful products:

> If the product doesn't sell, it's Engineering's fault. They very much have total responsibility for the product, including sales, in a sense.... The fact that Marketing told me to build a product is no defense. If I were stupid enough to do what they told me, then I failed.... There's a tension always there, because they always want more than you can do, and they may want, in some ways, the wrong thing.

The human factors engineers in the Interface Design group met with users from a small subset of customer organizations throughout all phases of product development. They rarely visited customer sites to observe how the product was used but frequently invited users to their laboratories. This communication channel was managed by the account manager for that customer, who often accompanied the users during visits to Development. The visits were planned to serve the needs of both Development and the customers, who apparently were interested in monitoring and influencing future product directions. Development requested users with skills that would test particular components of the product, but customers also sent managers or software engineers interested in technical aspects of the product.

Design ideas were tested by presenting them to users. For example, the terms to be used in a menu system were tested by asking users to explain what each term seemed to mean, then to supply an alternative term for the intended meaning. In other instances, a series of screens were constructed to simulate the appearance and behavior of a new feature, and users were invited to critique the design. Product usability was measured by users' performance in benchmark tests and by their responses to questionnaires. Prototype or product testing was always followed by general discussions of the product, in which users were invited to describe features they would like to see in future versions and problems they encountered in the current version.

The result was that both Development and the customers benefited, and a stronger relationship was forged:

> We get three or four customers to come in and take part in our software evaluations. They will come in, and they'll be doing half-hour benchmark tasks for part of the day, but for the other part of the day we'll just sit down and really discuss their general concerns about the product, what they like about it and what they don't like about it. Each session generally has a theme of some kind. There will probably be some area that we will really want to go into detail with them. And we get other people in, their software engineers and architects come in to talk to us as well, and we'll also answer their technical questions.... We generally ask for particular skills.... The problem is that maybe a manager is interested in finding out what the company is doing with the product, so he is going to come along anyway and he's not, maybe, the representative user we want. So you have some difficulty in terms of guaranteeing that the customer sends exactly the right people. They see it as an opportunity for a day out to ask a lot of deep questions. They maybe don't want to just send a half dozen users because they don't feel that's going to be so useful even though it's what we're really after. So, it works out. I think we get three out of four of the right people for the study, and there are always this other 25 percent that have just come along. And we have no quarrel with that. Much of this has to be a kind of relationship-building exercise, showing that we are doing this kind of work, and we're interested in what these customers are saying.

Although greater collaboration is imaginable, with developers spending more time at user sites, a broad survey of product development organizations found that they rarely achieved this level of contact (Grudin and Poltrock, 1989).

Prototyping and Iterative Design

Prototyping and user testing were integral parts of interface design and development practices. Interfaces and their prototypes were constructed using tools built into the product that permitted changes to the appearance and to some behaviors of the interface. As in Case 1, small interface changes could be quickly prototyped and evaluated, possibly even before the design was reviewed and approved. But innovative changes beyond the capability of the existing tools required implementing new functionality. Prototypes of innovative features were either programmed without the benefit of tools or were delayed until new tools could be implemented. In either case, their construction and evaluation were postponed until later in development when design iteration faced greater resistance.

In addition to facilitating user testing and design iteration, prototypes helped the designers sell their ideas, again as in Case 1. Innovative designs are not only harder to prototype, they are harder to sell (Poltrock, 1989). The designers were able to introduce one innovative feature because they had previously implemented it in a product that had been canceled early in development. One designer said, "Having that prototype was a tremendous weapon to get that into the product because we wouldn't have done it if we hadn't had that already working so people could look at it." This feature required substantial changes in the interface construction tools. The prototype of the canceled product was essential to persuade management of the value of the new design:

> ...it gave us a working model of the feature that we could show to people and having got somebody really enthusiastic about it, it was then sort of sold to various other people in marketing and various other levels of management.... You know, people just looked at it and said, "That's great, we've got to do that." I think without that, it was such a phenomenal amount of work to do, I really don't think we'd have done it. So having that prototype was wonderful.

The Interface Design group knew that the remainder of their design would need to be prototyped, tested, and iterated, and this could not be completed until late in the development process. Having sold so many people on the initial design, one interface designer expressed concern that there would be resistance to the necessary design revisions that would follow tests of the prototypes:

> There were still a lot of things that had to be designed with no prototyping or anything at all.... We'd made a commitment to a very, very large specification of the interface with a lot of areas that had never seen the light of day and where there had never been any user input whatsoever, there had been no testing or anything, so we were sort of making commitments to initial design, and the problem was that a lot of people had to buy into that.... And it was signed off at all sorts of levels, and I saw that as a problem because we'd made this sort of phenomenal commitment to this design, and the fact is that we'd never tested it. And it wasn't until November that it was actually tested, sort of six months after the design had been written, and people had started to implement it.

This interface designer was also concerned about the visibility of interface iterations. A series of design changes proposed late in development would seem odd to developers and managers who felt that the Interface Design group should have worked through design problems much earlier. As Gould and Lewis (1983, 1985) noted, many system designers believe that the design can and should be done right the first time. This perception is compounded by the fact that small changes in software design generally require no approval and are considered a normal part of debugging. But any change in the interface design, no matter how small, must be reviewed and approved because it affects other parts of the development project. There is no equivalent concept of debugging the interface design. The interface designer described this problem saying:

> I think one of the biggest problems with user interface design is, if you do start iterating, it's obvious to people that you're iterating, you know. Then people say, "How is this going to end up?" They start to get worried as to whether you're actually going to deliver anything, and they get worried about the amount of work it's creating for them, and people, like [those in] Documentation, are screwed up by iterations. Whereas software, you can iterate like mad underneath, and nobody will know the difference.

Another problem with interface visibility is that more people in the development organization have and express opinions about the interface than about other aspects of development outside their area of expertise. One developer commented:

> If you put up an architectural model, not many people will come back and comment on architecture. But if you actually put up screens and ask people to comment, everyone from the managing director downwards use the product and has their own personal idea, and you get as many ideas as people in the room....

Everyone in the organization needs a chance to comment, but as emphasized by Gould et al. (1987), the interface designer must be prepared to defend the design and communicate why it is right. The same developer went on to say:

> The person who has designed the user interface sits there in a meeting and gets bludgeoned by a person 17 levels higher than them who just says, "I want my feature to behave like this."

Of course, some developers recognize that effective interface designs emerge from iterations. A development manager, asked what communication problems are encountered between interface designers and implementers, responded that iteration in the interface design is the main problem, yet he recognized that the problem is currently unavoidable:

> [It] is not a communication problem at all. It's a technology problem, or at least a methodology problem, the way the user interface gets designed. At the moment, we don't seem to be able to design, test, and freeze off the user interface sufficiently far ahead in the development cycle. So we are continually trying to refine the user interface at the end of the development cycle.

Resistance to iterations late in product development was partly due to scheduling. Usability testing was scheduled a few weeks before field test, when the interface would be frozen—too late to make any major interface changes. Fortunately, the Development schedule slipped significantly, providing the time needed to revise the interface:

> The user interface testing went fairly well, and, as it happened, we did identify some key areas that we needed to fix, and those areas have largely been addressed, fortunately. I mean, looking back now we actually evaluated the product at quite an early stage, but we didn't know that. I mean, our assumption was that when we began testing, the user interface would be frozen in three or four weeks. In fact, the functionality hasn't quite been frozen yet [many months later].

Hoping to avoid this problem, the designers of the next version began prototyping and testing the design much earlier.

One episode demonstrated both the organization's reluctance to iterate the interface design and a problem with benchmark usability tests. A new feature had performed well in the usability tests, but problems in its design appeared when developers began to use the product. The design had been optimized for situations that were infrequent in typical work, and the usability tests had assessed performance in these atypical situations. When developers, including interface designers, began using the product, they soon realized the design should be changed. Management first opposed this late change because of its impact on the development schedule—in fact, a documentation set had already gone to press—but eventually approved it. But in general, coordination requirements can block iterations in the interface that occur late in development.

Integrating All Aspects of Usability

At a high level, the same integration issues affected Case 2 as Case 1: Management reliance on specifications to coordinate activity, the separation of teams working on different aspects of usability, and the distributed responsibility for design. But a more detailed picture reveals some noteworthy differences.

Software engineers implemented the interface in accordance with a specification prepared by the Interface Design group. This specification was intended to describe every possible user action and its consequence for every product component. Some software engineers contributed to the product design, reviewed the interface specification, then used it as a reference. Other software engineers, who joined the project later, had difficulty using the specification, with one suggesting that interface designs can never be adequately described in a specification:

> You just can't specify in words what your intentions are when you design a user interface. You can produce a spec which defines what you want and there's no saying it's right until you use it. So there isn't a technology that we have currently that allows people to write down definitions of user interfaces that are complete. I've seen people wanting to specify user interfaces by defining objects and hierarchies of widgets and so on in which you can build up a user interface. That still doesn't mean it's going to be a good user interface at the end of the day, and it still doesn't mean that it's going to turn out to be the interface that you thought you were writing down when you wrote the spec.

An interface designer was more specific about the problems and also felt that they are unavoidable:

> The specs are far from complete. There's absolutely no doubt about that. There are always holes in the specifications. I think the user interface specification is, as a whole, quite a good specification in that it goes into quite a lot of detail, although there are mismatches between different chapters. There are obviously ambiguities and so forth, and sometimes we've found that people have implemented things in a way that we didn't expect because they've misinterpreted the spec.

Curtis, Krasner, and Iscoe (1988) found "little evidence that documentation had reduced the amount of communication required among project personnel." The interface designers recognized the inevitable need for supplemental communication about requirements and designs. For their next interface design, they planned a series of presentations that would include (1) videotapes of users reacting to the existing and redesigned interface, (2) prototype demonstrations, and (3) explanation of the design rationale. Of course, the design would still be described in a specification, and they still expected to spend a lot of time answering questions:

> It's an environment where people just come and ask you. I mean, a lot of my

time is just spent handling queries, "Oh, what did you mean by this?" "What did you mean by that?"

As in Case 1, although interface specifications were the primary sources for the technical writers, they enjoyed a good working relationship with other developers. The technical writers were located adjacent to the Interface Design group, and some members of the Interface Design group had experience as technical writers. One technical writer contributed to the interface design, wrote part of the design specification, then wrote the user manual. When writing the user manual, the design specification was an indispensable resource. Furthermore, interface designers reported that the technical writers helped find problems in the specifications: "Once they started writing the books, it became obvious where the holes were even before the developers had gotten to a lot of things."

This relationship, perhaps unusually good (Grudin and Poltrock, 1989), did not extend to training development. There was little coordination between the Interface Design group and even the on-line training developers located on the opposite side of the building. The Training group had access to interface specifications and communicated with software engineers about implementation details, but there was no direct communication with the Interface Design group about users' training needs or interface design strategies, nor did the Interface Design group evaluate the on-line training. The common response when asked about coordination with the Training group was that on-line training was funded separately from development and was not even subject to the same design review process. In fact, the Interface Design group was beginning to recognize the importance of communicating more effectively with the Training group and had just assigned a person to establish closer relations with them.

The on-line training provided an example of how this communication bottleneck can adversely affect the interface. A new interface for one component of the product provided several ways of easily accessing functionality while retaining the old, more awkward interface to provide backward compatibility. In some future release, the old interface was to be retired. The only interface option described in the on-line training, however, was the awkward one most consistent with the old interface. It seemed that the Training group was not aware of the overall interface design strategy.

As in Case 1, communication with Performance Analysis and Quality Control groups was not frequent, but Quality Control did draw indirectly on Development's experience with users. Quality Control obtained a scenario from the Interface Design group that was based on observations of users working with previous versions and expectations regarding the use of new features. Because the automatic tests detected all changes affecting screen displays, Quality Control consulted with the Interface Design group regarding interface changes. All examples in the user manual were tested for correctness, requiring communication with Documentation. Also as in Case 1, Quality Control reported bugs formally to Development.

The development organization was located thousands of miles and several time zones from Marketing, the Product Managers, its parent organization, organizations that translated the products for foreign markets, and organizations developing related products. To retain group and project cohesion and a shared context, members of different teams communicated frequently, including by electronic mail, a computer-conferencing system, telephones, and voice messages. Meetings between teams were generally more formal and structured than within-team meetings. They were scheduled in advance and focused on specific issues. For example, two or three interface designers and software designers met frequently to discuss the functionality and interface for specific product components. Even within a team, physical separation led to greater formality: Some members of the Interface Design group, in a different building from their Development peers, used electronic mail to discuss issues, either addressing or copying messages to all members of the group. In one instance, two group members used electronic mail to discuss a planned audit of their product even though they could have talked directly to one another by just turning their chairs. They purposefully used electronic mail because it allowed them to keep all group members informed, as though the audit was discussed in a meeting.

To enhance their ability to serve as communication channels, managers cultivated personal relationships with managers at other sites and maintained these relationships by means of phone calls, visits, and electronic messages. Apparently, personal relationships contribute to cooperation among managers in much the same way they contribute to collaboration among researchers (Kraut, Egido, and Galegher, 1988; Kraut, Galegher, and Egido, 1986). Establishing and maintaining personal relationships with colleagues at other sites was viewed as part of the work in Case 2. One manager said, "Most afternoons I would guess I'm on the phone probably two hours. I put a fair bit of effort into that. . . . I sort of tend to have a certain list of people that I get in touch with every now and again, one way or another."

To understand the value of these personal relationships, consider what would happen if this manager only called his colleagues when they had a conflict of interest. Soon, his calls would not be welcome and their relationship would be built on a history of past disagreements. Through routine phone calls and visits to other sites, he established a positive foundation for coordinating work and resolving conflicts.

Integrating all aspects of usability can be challenging because usability issues have fuzzy organizational boundaries and potentially unlimited scope when related products are considered. In Case 2, similar products were implemented on several machines with different operating systems and interface capabilities. The names and target markets for all these products were the same, and Marketing wanted the products to be interchangeable so that customers could gradually replace their older equipment without retraining. Development concluded that this degree of compatibility was not possible. Even ensuring that the interfaces were *similar* was a significant challenge. The interface designers of these products frequently discussed the differences in their designs, seeking to convince one another of the superiority of their own design or seeking a compromise that would meet the needs of both projects. Occasionally, management became involved in these design decisions, particularly when political issues were involved. Describing how he became involved, one manager said, "To manage the thing politically, so that it becomes acceptable to go that way. If they [the interface designers] think this is the right engineering solution, but they think politically it's unacceptable, they'll look to me to sort out the politics involved."

Communication across projects occurred at all organizational levels; interface designers, developers, and managers interacted with their respective counterparts in other projects. Electronic mail, a computer-conferencing system, telephones, and teleconferences were the primary methods of communication. International communication in both cases relied on electronic mail because time differences made telephone conversations inconvenient. Despite its inconvenience, the telephone was still used for some long-distance and international communications, especially by managers. The risk of communication failures (either no communication or miscommunication) was greatest between projects that were organizationally and physically distant, with personnel differing in culture and background, and in the context of competition for limited resources.

Design Principles Revisited

What emerges from these studies is further validation of the desirability of following the recommended principles of designing interactive systems, together with a description of organizational factors that can block their application. Even developers who fully support the principles can encounter great difficulty following all or even most of them.

Access to real users is at the heart of three of the four principles: early focus on users, early—and continual—user testing, and iterative design. Large product development organizations have consciously insulated developers from customers, delegating customer contact to marketing, customer support, field service, training, and other specialists. This policy may be beneficial when developing products with little or no human-computer interface, but those benefits become obstacles to carrying out structural or procedural changes to promote user involvement in interactive system development. Further, some people fear that by exposing features and functionality that are under development, user involvement can discourage customers from buying the current product version, create false expectations if features are not implemented, risk legal rights to software patents, and give competitors information about product plans. Obtaining access to users can require overcoming these concerns.

In current practice, most contacts are with buyers or customers and not the actual end users. Marketing may be tasked with conveying information about customer needs to developers, but they are not equipped to do so at the level of detail required for interface design. Even in Case 2, where for a period these obstacles were overcome, communication with customers was carefully managed and developers rarely observed users performing real work to appreciate how users' tasks differ from the benchmarks.

In the organizations observed, achieving an early and continual focus on users was complicated by the fact that Marketing was the first to be involved in product definition. Marketing's focus is on competitive products and on the buyers or customers (who are often distinct from the users). Its primary goal is marketability rather than usability, so, for example, features from competitors' products might be desirable whether provably useful or not. Its expertise in usability issues is limited: Usability has long been in the shadow of functionality from a marketing perspective and is only now becoming important in its own right.

Ongoing participation of users in designing or evaluating interface elements is also problematic. Organizations have delegated external contacts to groups other than development and have concerns about changing that arrangement. In addition, Marketing (or other design groups) has a stake in a product they have defined: From their perspective, developer–user contact may result in claims that Marketing erred in product definition or in failing to provide sufficiently detailed design information. Particularly in an engineering-driven company, committed developers can overcome these obstacles, as in Case 2, but the abandonment there of user involvement as part of a reorganization shortly after the study further suggests that inherent forces work against such arrangements. Changing the situation will require both a determination that greater usability is of enough importance to warrant change and knowledge of what is required to achieve usability. (Further obstacles to direct user contact in product development are described in Grudin 1991b, and comparisons with contract and in-house development contexts are described in Grudin 1991a).

Iterative design faces unique problems due to the visibility of the interface—changes are very evident to many people—and due to the dependence of the integrity of the interface design on a range of people involved in hardware, software, documentation, training development, marketing, and other professions. Software interfaces are the foci of training, user documentation, and marketing campaigns, so changes in them affect other people. And though user feedback should ensure that iterations will lead to improvements, the very concept is not easily accepted in engineering environments conditioned to stress the importance of thorough up-front design.

Iterative design also faces a fundamental, historical engineering challenge: the success of noniterative design for many *noninteractive* systems. Most software does not involve human-computer interfaces. Management and software designers have learned to approach design as a rational, highly analytic process that can be done right the first time. But the introduction of users has consequences that Gould and Lewis (1985) describe as follows:

> Adding a human interface to the system disrupts this picture fundamentally. A coprocessor of largely unpredictable behavior (i.e., a human user) has been added, and the system's algorithms have to mesh with it. There is no data sheet on this coprocessor, so one is forced to abandon the idea that one can design one's algorithms from first principles. An empirical approach is essential. (p. 305)

Even in Case 2, where iteration occurred, there was some distaste for it. One software engineer stated his belief that every design issue could be resolved by logic. And the development schedule did not explicitly include interface iteration, which subsequently made abandoning it easier.

The ability to exploit the contributions of interface specialists and users can be limited by the available tools. In both organizations, prototype construction was difficult and largely limited to exploring minor changes by changing the product, either by revising the code or through use of limited tools built into the product. Sometimes prototyping was postponed until late in development when resistance to design iteration was greatest. Both organizations would benefit from powerful rapid prototyping tools that allow them to explore new interface designs early; the Case 1 organization planned to incorporate an interface management system in their product that would provide this capability.

Perhaps the most difficult principle to apply is to carry out all aspects of usability concurrently under one management. The organizations we observed have a long tradition of independently developing hardware, software, documentation, and training. Coordination with developers of on-line training and documentation is particularly critical because these interface components stand between the users and the product. However, the requisite specialists are often geographically distributed and assigned to projects at different times. They may also be viewed as having different funding sources. In Case 2, product development was funded by sales of the product, whereas on-line training was funded by the training organization, which sells training as a support function.

Contributors to the interface (in addition to software engineers) included human factors engineers, technical writers, training specialists, marketing representatives, field support, performance analysts, and quality control. Their involvement in interface development varied greatly in time and extent, making it more difficult to envision bringing them under one management. Matrix management models, in which specialists effectively have more than one manager, is one approach. In practice, we observed specifications used as the principal medium of project-level communication about interface issues. Face-to-face communication outside management meetings was relatively rare, despite the inadequacies of specifications as a communication medium and the resulting breakdowns. Certainly communication tools could help, but organizational change is required to bring usability concerns under one management.

In support of the potential usefulness of the concept of integration, we observed relatively few within-team communication and coordination problems. Constant communication in face-to-face meetings, including regularly scheduled team meetings and impromptu meetings of two or more team members, established a shared context and personal relationships that facilitated communication. Although team members had different educational backgrounds, they had similar professional experience, goals, and knowledge of interface issues, particularly issues relevant to their products. In addition to interface design and development issues, procedural and organizational issues were often discussed. Part of the work was to produce formal documents that were distributed outside the team, and each team supported this work by reviewing paper or electronically distributed drafts.

Integrating under one management would facilitate direct communication; instead, both cases relied on written specification documents as a communication medium. Marketing specified the marketing requirements, the Design group in Case 1 and Product Management in Case 2 produced the performance requirements, and both these specifications influenced the interface design. Design and Product Management served as communication channels between Marketing, Development, and other organizational units during development. As we described earlier, the roles of the Design group and Product Managers were distinctly different, however, with consequences for their effectiveness as communication channels. The interface specifications were reviewed and approved by managers and technical leaders throughout the projects. During a project, requirement and design changes were continuously proposed and reviewed. But many researchers and developers feel that written specifications cannot adequately convey interface information (Curtis, Krasner, and Iscoe, 1988). Gillan, Breedin, and Cooke (1992) found that software engineers understand key interface concepts very differently from human factors engineers. Such differences, which plausibly apply to other professionals as well, could undermine the efficacy of written specifications and be exacerbated by the physical separation of those involved.

These studies examined the development of new releases of existing products. Different challenges face the developers of a new product. Identifying and accessing prospective users can be even more difficult, and prototyping by modifying existing code (with its virtues and vices) is impossible. Similarly, developers of interactive systems for in-house use or under contract face different constraints. The eventual users are often more easily identified, but obstacles to their involvement can be as great (Grudin, 1991a). Many of our findings will extend to other settings, but not all will generalize, so they should be taken as possibilities to consider in a given setting. In fact, a product development company that grew up in the past decade, in the era of interactive systems, may be organized differently and more effectively than the older organizations we studied.

In summary, adopting widely recognized and accepted principles of interface design in a large project requires an organizational commitment. Interface designers and developers may recognize the value of these principles but lack the authority to recruit users or to plan for design iteration. Change will not be quick or easy. Training is required to maximize the benefit from access to populations of users. The development schedule must accommodate iterative cycles of design, prototyping, and testing with users, and the development organization must learn to tolerate the instability that results from iterative interface design. One way to minimize uncertainty is careful prioritization and the use of concrete usability objectives and measures (Butler, 1985; Carroll and Rosson, 1985; Whiteside, Bennett, and Holtzblatt, 1988; Wixon and Whiteside, 1985) that prevent never-ending design iterations, just as system performance and reliability are measured and controlled. Of course, without a thorough knowledge of users' tasks, it may not be possible to set meaningful usability objectives.

Can we go beyond general encouragement to work around obstacles to applying the guidelines? Can we recommend specific organizational change? Often we hear calls for placing human factors and software engineers together, or for fostering much tighter collaboration among developers and marketers. These are consistent with the principles but may not work well everywhere. We see positive signs that in some companies younger than those described here, virtually all employees take usability seriously. Such changes in attitude are an important first step.

Acknowledgments

Thanks are due to William P. Jones, who contributed to the planning and studied one of the organizations. Thanks also to Randolph Bias, Rob Kling, Bill Kuhlman, Jean McKendree, and dedicated anonymous reviewers for comments on early versions. Special thanks are due to Jim Hollan, who encouraged this research, to MCC, which supported it, to the two companies studied, and to the members of the two software development organizations for their hospitality and cooperation.

Notes

1. This paper is based on a series of Technical Reports from the MCC Human Interface Laboratory, Austin, TX. The report numbers are ACA-HI-346-87-P, ACA-HI-288-88-P, ACA-HI-013-89, ACA-HI-024-89, ACT-HI-088-89-P, ACT-HI-125-89, and ACT-HI-162-89. Another version has appeared in *ACM Transactions on Computer-Human Interaction*, 1, 1, 1994, 52–80.

2. This is typical of product development projects, but care must be taken in generalizing our findings to other kinds of projects. This is discussed in the conclusion.

3. Participant observation is a widely used field study approach. Anthropologists cannot avoid participating in the life of the communities they study. A fear is that by participating, the investigator may be less objective; on the other hand, the investigator can obtain a much richer sense of the experience. In our studies, the investigators' involvement was limited in time, they did not work on critical aspects of the project, and they had less stake in the project outcome than other team members.

4. The names of organizational units in both cases have been changed to protect their anonymity.

5. Of course, system performance influences user performance, and interface designs can affect system performance. In Case 2, interface designers made a simple modification without the assistance of the developers. Unfortunately, the performance analysts found that this simple change imposed a 1 percent cost in total system performance. Although this design change provided an attractive interface feature, it was removed.

6. There is an important distinction between customers and users. Customers purchase software systems. A customer is generally a company or other organization that purchases the systems, but the customer is personified in the managers responsible for the purchasing decisions, such as the managers of an MIS organization. Users are the people who actually interact with the product and may include people within the software development company, even members of the development team. Customers may be users, but often are not.

References

Allen, T. J. (1977). *Managing the Flow of Technology*. Cambridge, MA: MIT Press.

Allen, T. J. and Cohen, S. (1969). Information flow in R&D laboratories. *Administrative Science Quarterly* 14, 12–19.

Allen, T. J., Tushman, M. L., and Lee, D. M. S. (1979). Technology transfer as a function of position in the spectrum from research through development to technical services. *Academy of Management Journal* 22, 694–708.

Butler, K. A. (1985). Connecting theory and practice: A case study of achieving usability goals. In *Proceedings CHI'85: Conference on Human Factors in Computing Systems*. New York: ACM, 85–88.

Carroll, J. M. and Rosson, M. B. (1985). Usability specifications as a tool in iterative development. In H. R. Hartson (ed.), *Advances in Human-Computer Interaction (Vol. 1)*. Norwood, NJ: Ablex, 1–28.

Curtis, B., Krasner, H., and Iscoe, N. (1988). A field study of the software design process for large systems. *Communications of the ACM* 31(11), 1268–1287.

Gillan, D. J., Breedin, S. D., and Cooke, N. J. (1992). Network and multi-dimensional representations of the declarative knowledge of human-computer interface design experts. *International Journal of Man-Machine Studies* 36(4), 587–615.

Goransson, B., Lind, M., Pettersson, E., Sandblad, B., and Schwalbe, P. (1987). The interface is often not the problem. *Proceedings of CHI+GI'87*. New York: ACM, 133–136.

Gould, J. D. (1988). How to design usable systems. In M. Helander (ed.), *Handbook of Human-Computer Interaction*. Amsterdam: North-Holland, 757–789.

Gould, J. D., Boies, S. J., Levy, S., Richards, J. T., and Schoonard, J. (1987). The 1984 Olympic Message System: A test of behavioral principles of system design. *Communications of the ACM* 30(9), 758–769.

Gould, J. D., Boies, S. J., and Lewis, C. (1991). Making usable, useful, productivity-enhancing computer applications. *Communications of the ACM* 34(1), 74–85.

Gould, J. D. and Lewis, C. H. (1983). Designing for usability—Key principles and what designers think. *Proceedings CHI'83 Conference on Human Factors in Computing Systems*. New York: ACM, 50–83.

———. (1985). Designing for usability—Key principles and what designers think. *Communications of the ACM* 28(3), 300–311.

Grudin, J. (1991a). Interactive systems: Bridging the gaps between developers and users. *IEEE Computer* 24(4), 59–69.

————. (1991b). Systematic sources of suboptimal interface design in large product development organizations. *Human-Computer Interaction* 6(2), 147–196.

Grudin, J. and Poltrock, S. E. (1989). User interface design in large corporations: Coordination and communication across disciplines. *Proceedings CHI'89 Human Factors in Computing Systems.* New York: ACM, 197–203.

Hammond, N., Jorgensen, A., MacLean, A., Barnard, P., and Long, J. (1983). Design practice and interface usability: Evidence from interviews with designers. *Proceedings CHI'83 Conference on Human Factors in Computing Systems.* New York: ACM, 40–44.

Hewett, T. T. and Meadow, C. T. (1986). On designing for usability: An application of four key principles. *Proceedings CHI'86 Human Factors in Computing Systems.* New York: ACM, 247–252.

Kraut, R., Egido, C., and Galegher, J. (1988). Patterns of contact and communication in scientific research collaboration. In *Proceedings of the Conference on Computer-Supported Cooperative Work* (Portland, September 26–29). New York: ACM, 1–12.

Kraut, R., Galegher, J., and Egido, C. (1986). Relationships and tasks in scientific research collaborations. In *Proceedings of the Conference on Computer-Supported Cooperative Work* (Austin, December 3–5), 229–245.

Perlman, G. (1988). Software tools for user interface development. In M. Helander (ed.), *Handbook of Human-Computer Interaction.* Amsterdam: North-Holland, 819–833.

Poltrock, S. E. (1989). Innovation in user interface development: Obstacles and opportunities. *Proceedings CHI '89 Human Factors in Computing Systems.* New York: ACM, 191–195.

Pressman, R. S. (1987). *Software Engineering: A Practitioner's Approach.* New York: McGraw-Hill.

Rosson, M. B., Maass, S., and Kellogg, W. A. (1988). The designer as user: Building requirements for design tools from design practice. *Communications of the ACM* 31(11), 1288–1298.

Whiteside, J., Bennett, J., and Holtzblatt, K. (1988). Usability engineering: Our experience and evolution. In M. Helander (ed.), *Handbook of Human-Computer Interaction.* Amsterdam: North-Holland, 791–818.

Wixon, D. and Whiteside, J. (1985). Engineering for usability: Lessons from the user derived interface. *Proceedings CHI'85 Human Factors in Computing Systems.* New York: ACM, 144–147.

System Design Practice, Emerging Development Acceleration Strategies, and the Role of User-Centered Design

R. JAY RITCHIE, JUDITH A. LIST

Bell Communications Research

Introduction

Competitive pressures, productivity erosion, and rapid technological changes are forcing computer-based system designers toward shorter product development life cycles (Evanczuk, 1990; Brown,1990). At the same time, there has been an increased awareness that system success depends on product quality improvement, ease-of-use, and end user acceptance. This awareness has been catalyzed in part by the community of researchers and practitioners devoted to the development of human-computer interfaces (HCI) and product usability through user-centered design (UCD) system design approaches. The community of HCI experts, based in disciplines such as human factors engineering and computer science, has tended to pursue HCI design improvements through development of new tools and design methodology (Eason, 1991).

Although collaborative and iterative design techniques and rapid prototyping tools extend the power of the user interface designer, continued improvements in HCI design tools and methodology do not necessarily result in successful, usable products. Engineering management decisions, influenced by a number of system development constraints and approaches, can greatly influence the success or failure of user interface design. Product development constraints such as design practice, cost, schedule, requirements, priorities, and competition will continue to influence the final product design. HCI experts, like other engineering disciplines involved in the system development process, are subject to the same constraints and pressures from management decisions. In addition, HCI experts may face special organizational barriers that can affect the ability to integrate and practice HCI methods and techniques in the overall design and development process (Meister, 1987; Grudin and Poltrock, 1989; Grudin, 1991).

Actual design practice within our own organization for specific engineering projects was observed to have many of the constraints and barriers mentioned (List, 1990). In order to determine how a user-centered design approach could be integrated as part of the engineering process and to determine if such inclusion would result in effective change, we began (1) to examine current and emerging states of design practice, (2) to understand how HCI experts interact within the product development life cycle, and (3) to identify new methods we could use to effect change.

During this analysis, described in the second section, we concluded that ensuring significant successes of HCI design in the pragmatic context of engineering will depend primarily on the full commitment to the practice of a systems design approach by the engineering organization. This approach requires that the engineering organization understands the relationships of actions and effects of all underlying design elements and structures as well as the organizational linkage between business and engineering processes. Achieving this change will require full integration of HCI methods and techniques into the product development life cycle. HCI experts will need to actively and continuously promote and demonstrate benefits of HCI design techniques to engineering management. Engineering management will need to recognize the benefits of HCI methodology and successfully manage it within the development process.

We wanted to determine if the application of these recommendations would result in a change of the engineering process. During the development of a high-speed data communications service, an approach supporting both user-centered design and accelerated development was successfully applied and is described in the third section. To validate and refine the design of this new service, a series of case studies with potential users was completed. The purpose of these case studies was to develop profiles of representative users likely to purchase the service. The customer profiles were completed using a modified data acquisition method combining market research opinion surveys and job–task analyses. The profiles provided an understanding of how customers may use and manage the new service within their corporate data networks. Acceleration of the design process was confirmed through improved economies of research and analysis time, and early recognition of product improvements and identification of operational bottlenecks supported by different views from the various product development disciplines. Support of user-centered design methods was demonstrated by increased strength of user requirements data, increased customer understanding of the product, and identification of service stakeholder relationships.

System Design Practice and Product Improvement

The current crusade for product improvement and accelerated time-to-market comes from various competitive pressures and has initiated a transformation in general design practice focusing on the objective of the rapid development of usable, marketable products. This transformation has been initiated by different product development disciplines with recurring themes as solutions for poor product design such as multidisciplinary product development teams, focus on the entire product life cycle, and iterative design. However, the assimilation of the basic themes into mainstream engineering has been slow (Meister, 1987).

Changing from Sequential Design Process to Concurrent, Accelerated Development Strategies

In conventional system engineering environments, information typically flows in one direction: from concept to requirements definition to design to implementation to test and evaluation to deployment and operation. Although design iteration may occur in this process to improve original designs, product development is typically fragmented into a series of isolated steps performed by engineering specialities. Further, because of the functional and organizational separation of disciplines, multidisciplinary teams cannot effectively work. This process greatly affects engineering activities downstream since revisions become difficult to accomplish.

Historically, human factors engineering has played a role during each phase of the sequential design process. Human factors engineering professionals perform tasks such as functional analyses, function allocation, identification of human operations activities, and engineering tradeoffs to facilitate total systems operations, assistance with the preparation of training materials and documents, design analyses (for example, workload, task, prototyping), usability evaluations, and operational tests. But the nature of the sequential design process and project cost and schedule constraints often resulted in reduction or elimination of tasks during development unless a specific task was requested by the customer (Meister, 1987). As Eason (1991) has noted, the sequential design process does not easily permit the results from usability evaluations to affect changes in product design. As seen in Figure 1, Moraal and Kragt (1990) identified the design phases where intervention by ergonomic practitioners is most likely to impact the design. The highest impact is during concept development, the earliest stages of which occur in marketing research.

Driven by accelerating the time-to-market and the availability of computer-based design tools, engineering organizations have begun to actively move away from conventional, sequential design practice toward concurrent performance of engineering activities. Through popular support by the electronics design community in concurrent engineering, accelerated development strategies are beginning to re-emerge (Evanczuk, 1990). Although methodology promoting accelerated development has existed for years (for example, "skunk works") (Ziemke and Spann, 1990), the more common sequential development approaches have prevailed (Evanczuk, 1990). The

FIGURE 1

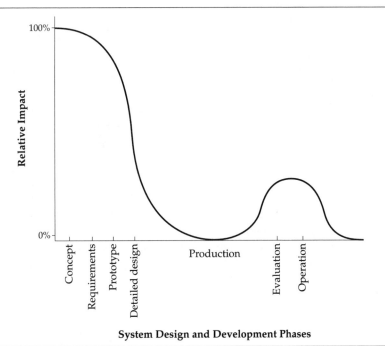

Impact of ergonomics on product design. *From Moraal and Kragt, 1990.*

objective of accelerated development strategies is the rapid, economical design and development of products that meet customer and user needs (McEachiron, 1990).

This objective can be accomplished through an overlap in the traditional design phases. This overlap can be accomplished only through an "information-networked" and multidisciplinary development team. Engineering management facilitates the operation of this team through building a team culture and organization, and providing advanced tools (for example, CAD/CAM, CASE), methods, and training. Although the accelerated development strategy promotes the familiar "user-centered design" principles, its main goal is to reduce the time it takes to put a product to market. Networked teams and advanced tools may certainly accelerate the design process, but will they produce usable and useful products? Where does the role of product quality and usability fit in these new design strategies, and what role will HCI experts play?

The Influence of Usability and Quality-Oriented Approaches on Design Practice

The usability of complex, computer-based systems have become increasingly important. The community of HCI researchers and practitioners have devoted significant resources in developing and practicing empirical approaches to user interface design, such as the development of usability specifications, the concepts of participatory, iterative design, and early prototype development (Carroll and Rosson, 1985; Whiteside, Bennett, and Holtzblatt, 1988; Gould and Lewis, 1985). New approaches, such as contextual design (Wixon, Holtzblatt, and Knox, 1990), continue to support the movement toward integration of user-centered design methods within the product life cycle. In addition to the HCI community, other disciplines have advocated design principles oriented toward user satisfaction and product quality. Disciplines such as quality planning and total quality management (Fine, 1987; Juran, 1988), and engineering management (Eppinger, Fine, and Ulrich, 1990), have defined design principles based on multidisciplinary teams, iterative design, and customer involvement. Although each of these disciplines proposes a slightly different model for improving system design, the following common principles are often mentioned:

- Create multidisciplinary teams and involve them in all stages in the process.
- Understand the product life cycle.
- Incorporate lessons learned from predecessor systems into new designs.
- Include all team members in the planning phase.

- Understand stakeholder needs and operations early.
- Involve users in the design process.
- Improve product design continuously throughout its life cycle.
- Use advanced tools and tool cooperation frameworks.
- Obtain management commitment and support.

These recurring principles support the evolution toward concurrent engineering and product improvement. Although inclusion of these principles in the design process may improve how the user interface is designed, the final product may still fail to have the requisite usability and utility features because of other constraints imposed during the design process. As Eason (1991) has noted, if system specifications are deficient, good user interface design will not ameliorate basic design inadequacies. Energies expended in the application of HCI methods may be wasted or may fail if the organizational setting for product development does not support human–system interaction throughout the entire process. In fact, many of these themes (for example, team formation, team planning, understanding product life cycle, understanding stakeholder needs, management commitment) must be implemented by project management and will likely require changes in the organizational structure. These changes can occur but will obligate both managers and HCI experts to remove the organization barriers that are currently impeding such changes.

Removing Organizational Barriers Affecting HCI Design Practice

Ironically, the community of HCI researchers and practitioners have encountered a number of organizational obstacles when attempting to integrate user-centered design principles and HCI techniques into the system engineering life cycle. Grudin (1991) has reiterated a number of these organizational obstacles that affect interactive system development for CSCW (Computer Supported Cooperative Work) experts. Many of these obstacles are similar to those encountered in the past by human factors engineering professionals, such as engineering management misconceptions about user interface design, inability of product management to consistently and systematically apply design analyses, and lack of emphasis on detailed user interface design in system requirements (Meister, 1987).

Other recent observations also indicate that many of the same barriers continue to exist. Many of the issues still center on the ability of product developers, with the responsibility and skills to perform usability engineering, to convince engineering management that such principles do work and are worth modifying the organization to place them into effect. Some of these observations include:

- Organizations often lack the expertise or management structure to include human factors research (Moraal and Kragt, 1990).

- Current design behavior is nonsystematic, regardless of the design practice policy in place, and based on a number of organizational factors, including dynamics of design team, resistance to change, lack of skills, and perception of low cost-benefit for human factors design (Eason, 1991; Meister, 1987; Mossink, 1990; Urlings, Nijboer, and Dul, 1990).

- The integration of human factors practitioners and marketing professionals into the design process is still inadequate, and these professionals are likely to be excluded from the design process even though they are perceived as being most likely to understand user needs (Grudin and Poltrock, 1989).

- Lack of commitment by the organization to make user involvement work, inability to identify the actual product market prior to development, lack of planning for user involvement during the early product planning stages (Grudin, 1991).

Grudin claims that CSCW researchers and developers are "uniquely endowed with the interests and skills to understand and guide such organizational change." If the HCI community holds the solution to effect changes in the engineering organization ultimately affecting improvements of the development process, why hasn't a solution been defined and implemented?

Integrating HCI Design Practice into Engineering Practice

From the engineering management perspective, other observations imply that engineering management is slow to integrate HCI methods because they perceive that the costs of inclusion of HCI methods outweigh the benefits, if there are any benefits at all. Some of these observations include:

- HCI research does not generate empirical evidence directed at relevant system engineering questions (Moraal and Kragt, 1990; McClelland and Brigham, 1990).

- HCI experts maintain a narrow focus on research and data, and fixate on user interface design rather than focus on development of the entire product solution (Marshall, 1991).

- HCI researchers and practitioners assume their approach is indispensable for system design, but results using the approach are not guaranteed (Mossink, 1990).

The recency of these observations indicate that the views between HCI experts and engineering management on the inclusion of HCI methods are divergent, and resolution of these issues will require responsibility from both groups. Although these observations contradict statements that any improvement is being made in the development process, understanding of the need for new design methods that improve system usability has been recognized by engineering management (Cheney, Hale, and Kasper, 1990; Eppinger, 1990). Successful application of user interface methods and techniques requires acceptance by engineering management, but acceptance will not take place until user interface designers demonstrate that their methods add value to the product and to the system engineering process. Some specific remedies for integration of user-centered design methods into the development process have been identified. These recommendations underscore the dual responsibility of managers and technical staff to promote integration:

- HCI experts need to broaden their range of focus from explicit ergonomic research and practice to include the system engineering process (Algera et al., 1990; Moraal and Kragt, 1990).

- HCI research requires generation of empirical evidence directed at relevant system engineering questions (Algera et al., 1990; Moraal and Kragt, 1990; McClelland and Brigham, 1990). This may be accomplished through usability objectives (Whiteside, Bennett, and Holtzblatt, 1988; Carroll and Rosson, 1985; Gould and Lewis, 1985).

- Human factors engineering should be incorporated in the education of all engineers and managers (Moraal and Kragt, 1990; Cheney, Hale, and Kasper, 1990; Eppinger, Fine, and Ulrich, 1990).

- HCI practitioners need to market their value to the organization by (1) intervening in the design and development process to effect change and (2) translating technical results into usability objectives for designers and into project benefits for management and the organization (Brown, 1990; Lenior and Verhoven, 1990; Lenior and Rijnsdorp, 1990; Marshall, 1990).

- HCI practitioners can act as intermediaries among divergent disciplines, but they must be involved in all development stages and be part of the core team (Regensberg and Van Der Veen, 1990; Hendrick, 1990).

- Attitude and behavior need to be shaped toward a general concept that product developers are 'service providers' within and outside the organization in order to support the systems approach (Kunak, 1990; Urlings, Nijboer, and Dul, 1990).

These observations and solutions imply organizational change, both from the top levels of an organization and from the HCI engineering ranks, and gave us a working model to effect change in our own organization. If the proposed solutions were to be implemented, it seemed reasonable to start at the earliest phase of product development to establish a product team that would prevent some of the problems that typically occur throughout the design and development process. It was our belief that if benefits are demonstrated early in the product life cycle and engineering management understands the impact of those benefits on product development, then integration of user-centered design principles and acceleration of the development process becomes more likely.

Supporting User-Centered Design and Accelerated Development: A Test Case

Initially, to investigate ways to increase the integration of HCI in the product development process, a set of activities aimed at long-term corporate commitment had been underway at Bellcore. A group of middle managers, representing each vice-presidential-level organization in the company, had been convened by corporate officers to develop and oversee the implementation of companywide policies and procedures needed to achieve the corporate goal of ensuring that all products and services had verified usability. This group decided on a strategy of targeting model projects in each VP area for concerted UCD effort. The intent was to concentrate limited resources to develop showcase examples of the effective integration of UCD into the product development process. These examples could then be used as models from which other projects could learn, thereby propagating the UCD philosophy and methodologies. The target projects were chosen in consultation with senior management to ensure their commitment to the approach and the specific examples. It also was considered critical that the target projects be highly visible and strategically important ones from the corporate perspective. A high-speed data communications service was chosen as a target project.

Segments of the telecommunications industry are moving to increase market share of data communication products and services. As part of this movement, a connectionless, high-speed, public packet switched data service to connect local, metropolitan, and wide area networks was developed as a potential service offering by Bellcore client companies. The high-speed data service was designed to support transparent, wide area connectivity for local area networks (LANs) and to provide data throughput at rates of 1.5 to 45 megabits per second. Service features were originally designed to provide customers with LAN-like characteristics:

- Ability to define a "logical private network"
- Access to a range of intermediate bandwidth levels that match user LAN throughput
- Usage measurement capabilities

The approach for developing the service had at the outset followed a common pattern in design practice: use of the engineering model without incorporation of user or task models (Gentner and Grudin, 1990). The product concept was developed (1) without assessing detailed user requirements from specific market subsegments, (2) without assessing potential impact on current customer operations, (3) without mapping potential customer business applications to product features, and (4) without identifying explicit design features desired by the customer.

Identifying the Role of User-Centered Design Within the Target Project

Project management anticipated information on user requirements and preferred design features to come from market research activities. Initial market research identified some new service requirements from the users' perspective, such as LAN-like capabilities, performance parameters, and low impact of integrating new services into existing data networks. However, the early market surveys needed to be complemented with information about performance, feature requirements, how introduction of the service might affect network operations, and how customers make decisions when they migrate to new network services or products. This type of information, as well as explicit feedback on new service features, was crucial to development engineers for service design requirement refinement.

The approach used in the initial market surveys supported Nielsen's (1990) observation that traditional market research does not typically use methods needed to develop usable designs or transfer market research results to system developers. The Yankee Group (1990), a market research organization, has noted that user surveys are inappropriate within the data communications domain because the general data communications population does not fully understand new products' capabilities and has not conducted sufficient analysis to determine how products fit into the corporate communications strategy. Because of the shortfalls in engineering and operations information from initial market research and in order to validate and refine the service offering prior to extensive field trials of the service, it was initially determined that single-customer, in-depth case studies should be performed to capture opinions about the new service.

The intent to assess user needs through the case studies appeared at the same time Bellcore management was identifying target projects. Although immediate convergence might have been expected, this was not the case. In getting started, the HCI specialists confronted many of the aforementioned barriers to successful integration. Initially, the project management and technical staff team did not believe that UCD would provide value-added input to service development; they believed that the users' perspectives had clearly been accommodated in the service design, they were concerned about negative effects on schedule and resources if UCD were incorporated into the project, and they were concerned about the overhead associated with bringing a new project member up to speed on the technology and service. A series of negotiations ensued over a period of five to six months between the HCI manager and the project team to increase understanding of the methods and benefits of UCD and of the service and technology. The project team members were, in some instances, openly hostile during these discussions. These discussions would likely have broken down at several points were it not that senior management was firmly committed to and insistent on integration of UCD into the project.

Identifying Methods to Accelerate the Development Process

There is evidence that pairing usability evaluation methods with traditional market research surveys may strengthen and validate preference findings for new products or services (Mitchell, 1987; Caplan, 1990). However, using these techniques requires access to a tangible product or prototype. In addition, lack of an early and complete task analysis can affect user interface design (Shute and Smith, 1990; Richards et al., 1990). Within the usability engineering life cycle, job or task analysis and customer site visits are considered high priority during the early phases although job or task analysis may not always be performed because of funding or schedule constraints (Nielsen, 1990). In cases where the product is being conceptualized but no tangible prototype exists, it was postulated that if system analytical methods were introduced as part of the early market research process, then similar benefits may be produced.

Market research and early system analyses have a common goal with the systems definition of marketing: finding out what the customer wants, and planning and developing the product that will satisfy those wants (Stanton, 1984). Each process can use similar techniques (for example, on-site interviews, focus groups, telephone interviews) to assess user requirements early in the development process, but differ in the type of information that is gathered. Although traditional market research activities may achieve the goal of providing preliminary information about a proposed product or service, it usually provides a very broad view (for example, market demand, willingness to pay, desired product features, product introduction factors) of the expected market. The type of technical information needed to influence development (for example, quality of service requirements, network configuration parameters, provisioning and maintenance requirements) may not always be gathered in traditional market research though both broad market views and technical information are necessary and complementary components of the product development life cycle. Finally, if any technical information is collected, many organizations are typically not structured to facilitate systematic transfer of marketing information to system developers.

The purpose of the new service application case studies was to collect engineering and customer operations data, in addition to opinions on service features, by focusing on a small sample of prospective customers from representative market segments. Compared with the broad market view, this approach assumed that a detailed perspective from selected, sophisticated users and providers of data communication services could provide the technical and operational information needed to determine if the service is feasible, cost-effective, and suitable for corporate data networks. In order to collect this body of knowledge in a timely and cost-effective manner, it was discerned that two previously separate processes, market research and job–task analysis, could be combined into a single process. Figure 2 depicts how the different perspectives of market research and system-oriented job and task analysis could be combined to support a single development activity. It was anticipated that combining both activities would afford early awareness of customer needs and would provide enough technical information to influence service development and deployment.

Some of the expected benefits from this activity included improving the economies of research and analysis time; improving the strength of the opinion data through analysis of customer operations; understanding the relationships between customer, vendor, and end user classes; ameliorating organizational issues by early inclusion of user-centered design personnel on the multidisciplinary team; and providing a learning instrument for product users (Van Dijk, 1990a) in preparation for future participatory design activities.

Test Case Methodology

The methodology for the test case consisted of a series of preparation, implementation, and analysis steps. The method steps, used for three separate customer case studies, are described next and depicted in Figure 3.

FIGURE 2

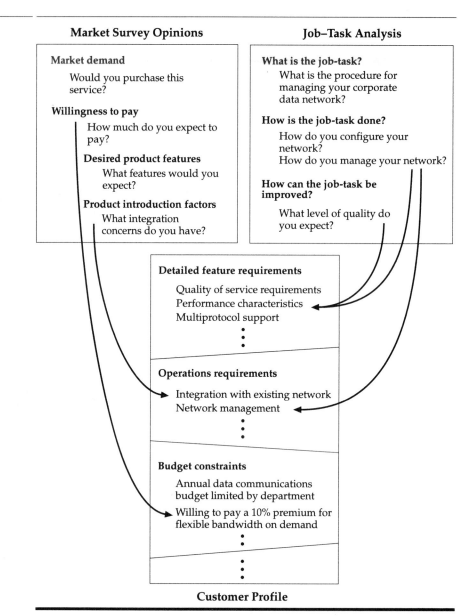

Development of customer profile through opinion surveys and job–task analysis.

Step 1: Promote UCD to engineering management. Management was approached with a description of the basic user-centered design principles and how inclusion of these principles, as well as the modified data collection and analysis method, could lead to results yielding the information they had been seeking. Expected benefits were outlined.

FIGURE 3   Method for developing customer profiles.

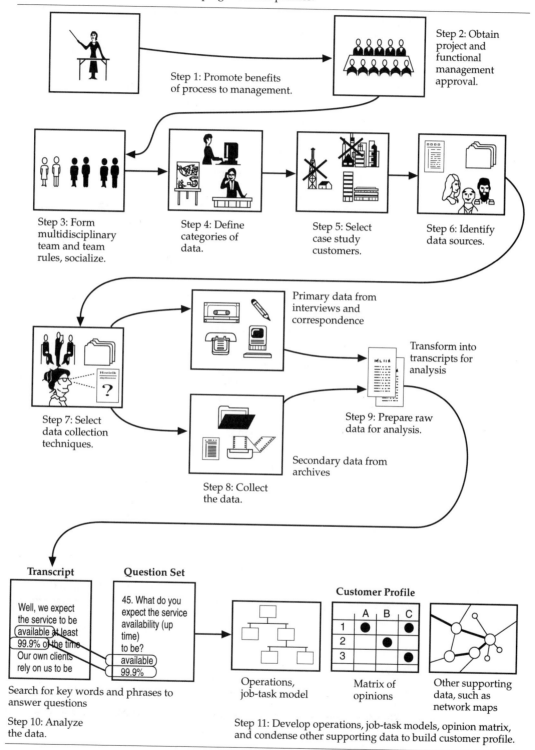

Step 1: Promote benefits of process to management.

Step 2: Obtain project and functional management approval.

Step 3: Form multidisciplinary team and team rules, socialize.

Step 4: Define categories of data.

Step 5: Select case study customers.

Step 6: Identify data sources.

Primary data from interviews and correspondence

Transform into transcripts for analysis

Step 7: Select data collection techniques.

Step 9: Prepare raw data for analysis.

Secondary data from archives

Step 8: Collect the data.

Transcript

Well, we expect the service to be available at least 99.9% of the time. Our own clients rely on us to be

Question Set

45. What do you expect the service availability (up time) to be? available 99.9%

Customer Profile

	A	B	C
1	●		
2		●	
3			●

Operations, job-task model

Matrix of opinions

Other supporting data, such as network maps

Search for key words and phrases to answer questions

Step 10: Analyze the data.

Step 11: Develop operations, job-task models, opinion matrix, and condense other supporting data to build customer profile.

Step 2: Obtain management commitment. Project management was briefed at all levels involved with the project, and they agreed to use the project as a test case to explore the effects of integrating the approach on the development process. This step, management commitment, is essential to the effective integration of user-centered design into projects. However, though strong top-level management commitment is valuable, it is not necessary. Strong commitment can come at any level in the direct project line of management, starting with project management and moving upward. In this case, project management and its immediate management were not supportive initially; however, senior management was insistent. Engineering staff committed to timely delivery of study results.

Step 3: Assemble a multidisciplinary team. In order to cover the wide range of information to be gathered, a multidisciplinary team was established. This pivotal step determines the success of the remainder of the procedure, along with management commitment, since it is the team that determines what type of information should be gathered.

The case study teams comprised individuals with experience and expertise in various disciplines: network design engineering, product management, human factors, market research, and network operations. Although all team members did not necessarily participate in the data collection steps, all members contributed to the other parts of the process, such as the question set design and data analysis. Multiple discipline involvement was crucial in fully interpreting the respondents' opinions about the service and cross-checking facts.

As with most development teams, there was an initial adjustment period for team members to understand each member's special skills and expected contribution to the project. It was critical for the HCI specialist to quickly become an integral member of the project team. This adjustment period was accelerated through early, frequent project meetings, courses in the technology and service, and discussions with key management players.

Step 4: Identify all categories of data to be collected. The fourth step was to determine what categories of data needed to be collected to meet the study objectives. The categories selected for the case studies represented events normally associated with data communication network activities: network engineering, network management, and related operations and administrative tasks. The major data categories for the new service case studies included:

- Business and decision-making strategies for data communications
- Data services used or offered
- Business or end-user applications used in corporate data networks
- General data network operations procedures: provisioning, maintenance, administration

- Network configuration, equipment, and engineering strategies
- Network management capabilities
- Quality and performance criteria
- Relationships among stakeholders (for example, service providers, corporate data network managers, end users, and equipment vendors)

Examples of types of data included network availability (that is, uptime), acceptable delay characteristics, changes in network topology, and product provisioning requirements. Specific information was collected on critical networking tasks and functions, task timelines, and interaction points or information transfer points.

Step 5: Select sample of customers and users. In order to fully examine potential service utility and usability concerns, it was necessary to first identify an environment where information on all stakeholders in the data communications networking hierarchy could be gathered. The potential service stakeholders included end users of high-speed data networks, data communications managers, system integrators, and network component vendors (for example, switches, routers), and interexchange carriers. It was assumed that corporate data communications managers would make the final decision to incorporate the new service into their networks and, therefore, became the studies' focal point.

Using the aforementioned data categories as screening criteria, potential case study sites were examined and selected. The three customer sites were selected from education and computer technology market segments, but other segments (for example, aerospace, insurance) were considered. Prospective customers were selected based on experience with engineering and managing corporate data networks. To understand the context in which the selected customer site operated, supporting data from other stakeholders, such as end users, vendors, and system integrators, were collected as well.

Step 6: Identify data sources. Data sources typically include subject matter experts (SMEs) and various forms of previously documented data. SMEs were considered as the primary data source since they could provide critical information in an accurate and timely manner. Secondary data supporting and validating SMEs' verbal reports were also identified and obtained. These data consisted of traffic statistics (for example, packet counts, bit error rate, number of dropped packets), procedural and policy documents, organizational data and charts, press releases, and campus and regional network maps.

For example, in one case study, policy and procedures documents describing the organization's operations plus initial discussions with personnel from the local exchange carrier were used (1) to establish points of contact and (2) to provide a baseline for the description of operations activities. Thirteen

SMEs were identified for the operational areas of customer interface and account management, network engineering, and network management. The list of SMEs was updated and augmented periodically as the interviews progressed with new points of contact in other areas or facilities provided by SMEs. Local exchange carrier SMEs also were interviewed, with concentration on personnel that engineer and maintain the high-capacity circuits.

Step 7: Select data collection techniques. Various data collection techniques were reviewed for primary data collection, including individual and group interviews, questionnaires, and observation. Interviewing subject matter experts was selected as the primary technique for data collection.

It was assumed that a planned sequence of face-to-face individual and group interviews with subject matter experts would (1) foster an atmosphere for detailed probing of information, (2) allow the respondents to learn about the service, (3) validate information by cross-checking respondents' changes in information, if any, from an individual to a group setting, and (4) permit flexibility in the information-gathering process (Van Dijk, 1990b; Hoffman, 1987; Shute and Smith, 1990). Other techniques such as telephone or mail surveys were not expected to accomplish those objectives (Van Dijk, 1990b). Materials prepared for the interviews included new service descriptions and the structured interview question sets.

Service descriptions varied in content and were presented in various forms throughout the interviewing process, depending on the individual SME or group experience levels. The interview question sets were structured to sequentially elicit (1) information on corporate data network configuration, (2) information on performance of specific SME (data communication managers and engineers) tasks, (3) end-user applications over the data network, (4) opinions on proposed use of the new service and its features, and (5) information that could result in improvements to the existing corporate data network.

Question sets were tailored for each SME interview and were organized by network activities (for example, network management). Questions related to engineering and management activities of the existing network system were fielded prior to questions asking for opinions on the proposed service. Basic question structure for engineering and management activities was derived from job and task analysis methods (Carlisle, 1986) and were generally open-ended (for example, "What tools do you use to manage your data network?" or "Describe your current network topology"), permitting the respondent to freely describe an activity. Prompts were provided in some cases when the respondent was unable to formulate complete answers. Opinion questions on the new service features focused on specific engineering information (for example, "What traffic statistics should be collected: packet counts, number of invalid addresses, address screening errors,...?"). Although the initial set of questions had attempted to adequately cover most of the areas, questions

TABLE 1	**Samples of Interview Questions**

SAMPLES OF JOB–TASK ANALYSIS QUESTIONS

- Please indicate what type of network(s) your organization has.
- What type of data networks are installed?
- How important to your company is interconnecting different proprietary networks (for example, TCP/IP to DECNet to SNA)?
- When performing network design activities or selecting data communications services or products, what are the relevant decision-making criteria? (Examples: cost; flexibility and growth; standardization, interoperability, and connectivity; control and management; performance; reliability; security; new or additional applications; confidence in technology or product)
- What are the primary business applications of the end users in your multiple-location interconnected LANs?
- What traffic statistics do you collect? (Examples: packet counts; number of dropped packets; error rate; source and destination; number and types of alarms)
- How do you track network troubles?

SAMPLES OF OPINIONS ON NEW SERVICE QUESTIONS

- What limitations of the new service do you believe will be drawbacks in the service and would cause you not to consider it in your network? (Examples: data traffic only, no voice; purchase of interface hardware; T1 as lowest bandwidth; involvement of IEC across LATAs)
- What would you expect the availability (% time available) to be for the new service? What is your own availability number for your corporate network?
- How do you feel about using the public network solution for your wide area data interconnections compared to a private network solution that you build and maintain yourself?

were added or deleted to the original question set as interviews progressed. Samples of questions are provided in Table 1.

Step 8: Collect the data. Verbal reports obtained from the SMEs during structured individual and group interviews were the primary data source. Archival data collected from the respondents augmented the verbal reports.

In summary, the interviews were conducted for the new service case studies according to the following procedure:

1. Briefly discuss the nature of the study and set interview ground rules.

2. Present the service description.

3. Ask respondents about general data communications tasks and network configuration, working toward more detailed questions on data network planning procedures.

4. Introduce questions on opinions about the new service, repeating service descriptions as necessary to clarify questions and answers.

5. Ask respondents for relevant supporting documents that would help complete the question set.

6. Follow-up with respondents to complete partially answered questions.

For all case studies, this procedure was performed in both individual and group settings. This was done to determine if opinions about the service would change significantly by individuals from one setting to another.

Team members were generally assigned various roles in the interviewing process for each interviewing session based on the technical or operational area (for example, network engineering, network management). One team member was designated as session facilitator with the remaining members acting as listeners or interpreters and scribes. However, any team member could ask questions during the interviewing period. If respondents required further details on service features during questioning, they were provided, and the question was restated.

The interviews were generally limited to two hours per session. The process usually required at least two interviews per SME to gather and validate all the information. At the end of each interview, the respondents were asked for any relevant documentation, such as network maps and work flow diagrams, that might clarify or validate the verbal reports. The number of interviews among the three case studies varied depending on the type of customer and the number of available SMEs. The range varied from 4 interviews over a 7-month period to 20 interviews over a 5-month period.

Where possible, interviews were tape recorded to facilitate analysis. However, in some cases tape recording was prohibited. Interview notes from interviewers substituted for tape recordings in these instances. Since at least two interviewers were always present, notes were cross-checked and corroborated. Questions that were not answered during formal interviews were addressed in follow-up sessions via face-to-face interview, telephone, or electronic mail.

Step 9: Prepare raw data for analysis. Data from verbal reports, either tape recordings or notes, were transformed into transcripts for analysis. Supplementary material from secondary sources (for example, documents, reports) was reviewed and highlighted for key phrases that answered specific questions.

Step 10: Analyze the data. The data were analyzed by extracting key words and phrases that answered specific questions on the interview question set The number and type of responses were tabulated for those questions. Information extracted during analysis was used to define operations, job and task models, and a matrix of opinions on service features.

Step 11: Develop customer profiles. Responses were compiled into written descriptions and graphic representations that supported respondent statements or inferences. Figure 4 illustrates the work flow model for data network development from one customer. These models provided a comprehensive view of customer data network operations processes and interactions among the various stakeholders in the data network engineering and management process. The models were also used to identify procedural bottlenecks, recurring problems with the current data network configuration, needs for improved service delivery, and policies that might influence data network engineering and management decisions.

For example, during one case study, it was established that flat rate billing was the preferred method of billing (flat rate only {N=18}, usage-based only {N=0}, or some combination of flat rate and usage-based {N=2}). The rationale for the selection of flat rate was that researchers on the Internet would feel restricted in the ability to communicate and perform work at remote sites if they had to pay by the packet. The task model revealed that both flat rate and usage-based billing schemes were administered by the organization, with flat rate being the predominant method. Based on these results, it was concluded that the new service usage measurement capabilities for billing will probably not initially be used by this type of customer.

The customer profiles were the tangible results of the case studies. These profiles were used by engineering management to validate or modify service requirements. Although the preceding steps represent the data collection and analysis method used in the case studies, the series of activities leading to the customer profiles occasionally resulted in the beginning of development activities. In one case study, the customer SMEs, the LEC, and the interviewing team participated in a joint network design exercise to determine the impact of using the new service in their regional data network. The differences in network design, which were expected to give the customer improvements in network interconnectivity while maintaining expected data throughputs (DS1 at 1.5 megabits per second, DS3 at 45 megabits per second) and potentially reducing costs, are illustrated in Figure 5.

Case Study Results

Following the study, it was concluded by project engineering management that new and useful information had been gathered and that it would affect service definition. Comparison of individual and group interviews revealed convergence for all opinion data, except for service cost recovery procedures. Based on the customer profile, which included a composite of their business operations and their opinions about the service, mismatches between the

FIGURE 4

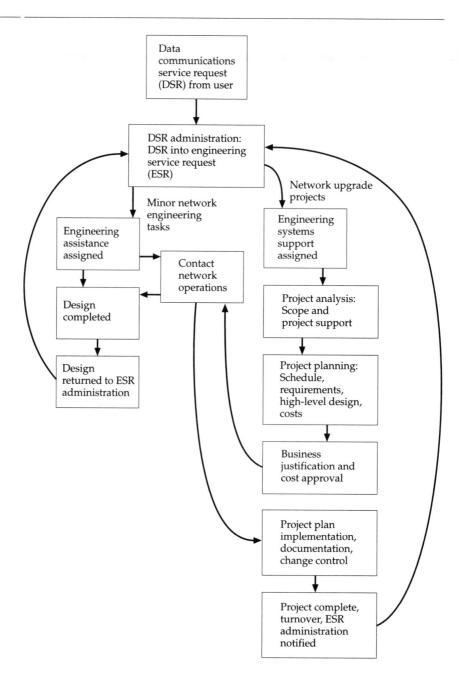

Sample of a customer network engineering job–task flow.

FIGURE 5

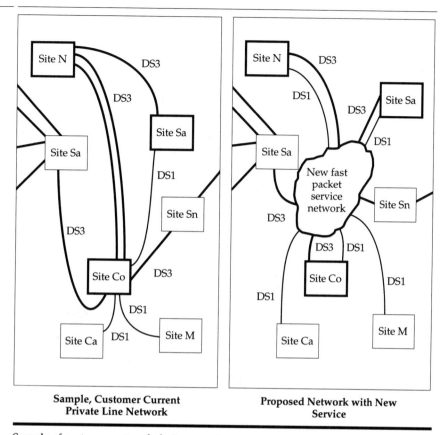

**Sample, Customer Current
Private Line Network**

**Proposed Network with New
Service**

Sample of customer network design exercise.

engineers' concept of the service and the customers' and end users' requirements were discovered. These mismatches included:

- Service availability requirements
- Network configuration requirements
- Expectations about service provisioning, maintenance, administration

Operations issues were uncovered in provisioning and maintenance activities, such as placement of data communication experts on customer account teams and the need for improved mean times to restore service. Proposed changes in the service and its provisioning were discussed with the customer to understand how to minimize the impact of service introduction on current operations. The job–task analysis had provided information about customer and user operations and their methods for designing and managing networks. This information provided the background and rationale for statements of opinions about proposed service features.

A final development of the interviewing process in one case study was the design of a sample network with the new service in place. This design was achieved with joint participation between Bellcore, the LEC, and the study respondents. Participatory designs during the final portions of the interviewing process imply that early discussions with customers using a peer level team may act as a catalyst for service introduction.

Engineering management concluded that insertion of a systematic process of extracting detailed customer knowledge from a potential customer affected service design and anticipated service operations, and that concurrent performance of marketing research and front-end analyses can provide tangible savings in resources. Engineering management commitment and use of a flexible, interdisciplinary team were crucial components of successful application of this method.

The results indicated that linking the analysis of customer business activities with opinion surveys validated the service and identified areas for change in the service requirements. Other benefits also were realized using this method:

- Improving the economies of research and analysis time
- Providing a learning environment for potential customers
- Establishing a working relationship between stakeholders
- Enhancing interdisciplinary engineering activities among team members

Economic Benefits

Both broad and focused views of the market are necessary and complementary, but the approach used in the case studies could conceivably be used to predict the broad view, resulting in potential cost and resource savings. Market research efforts prior to these case studies took place over a 2-year period with approximately 60 staff months of effort. The data collection and analysis periods for the case studies ranged from five to eight months in duration. The total expenditure in staff resources for the 3 studies was approximately 40 staff months. However, the magnitude of the improvements identified here is based on an assumption that specific engineering and market research information from a small sample of prospective customers from specific market segments supplements market research approaches that seek to supply a broader view of the market by sampling a large number of prospective customers.

Additional formal study is required to determine (1) if these types of case studies can be used to predict general market trends and (2) if the average contribution of savings in engineering staff hours can be consistently decreased by using this service validation technique. A modified version of this method, further reducing interviewing time, is now being tested at a broader level across multiple customers by interdisciplinary market research teams.

Educating the Customer

Study respondents stated that they had learned more about the new service than they would have without the interviews. Using the studies as a learning instrument for customers was a benefit that may have had a more significant impact than initially realized. In a post-interview survey, respondents indicated that the interviewing procedures had helped them better understand the new service and had increased their level of understanding and knowledge of the high-speed data networking in general. In addition, they were able to discuss the placement of the new service within their corporate data networks. Although not rigorously tested in these studies, one implication of this learning effect is that gathering opinion data without sufficient understanding of a product by the customer may not result in valid or useful information.

As indicated by the respondents, there will be a limit to full understanding without actual and extensive experience with the proposed product. Two customers of the case studies actually used the service on a trial basis, but all features of the service were not activated, and therefore, a complete comparison between service opinions pre-trial and post-trial was not made.

Understanding Stakeholder Relationships

Although focusing on a single customer cannot support predictions of broad trends in the marketplace for this service, it was evident that concentrating efforts on a representative customer permitted deeper understanding of the relationships between customer, vendor and end-user classes. For example, respondents typically requested that service providers maintain a provisioning and maintenance staff well versed in data communications technology. This is not currently provided, and this information was deemed to be a crucial factor in successful service implementation.

Building More Effective Project Teams

The studies provided an opportunity to explore the effects of using a multidisciplinary team. Some early conflicts in study direction, due to the different disciplinary orientation of team members, were resolved as the team worked together. The socialization process was a necessary part in helping team members understand one another's skills and experience. The respondents viewed the multidisciplinary team approach as a desirable attribute: They would like to see such teams as part of the new customer service support staff. Although the test case demonstrated a single step toward resolving the organizational barriers and supported development process acceleration, it was evident that the process of learning how to incorporate UCD into design practice will be long term and may not be easily transferable across projects that often replace team members.

Summary: Aspects of Design Practice Influencing HCI Design Success

In summary, the results of the test case imply that user-centered design can be mainstreamed early into a conventional, sequential design process. Constraints in the application of HCI design techniques are manifested in engineering management decisions and may be perpetuated either by management or by technical staff. Successful application of user interface methods and techniques requires acceptance by engineering management. Acceptance may not take place until user interface designers demonstrate that their methods add value to the product and to the system engineering process. HCI practitioners must understand the product development life cycle and maintain a working knowledge of project-related disciplines.

In addition, the test case demonstrated that market research activities and early usability analyses can be performed in tandem. These joint efforts can smooth the path to acceptance by engineering management by demonstrating conservation of resources, identifying user requirements early in the development process, and reinforcing the importance of completing relevant analyses. A prerequisite for success of this method is early management commitment and formation and maintenance of the multidisciplinary team.

There may be additional challenges for integrating HCI methods into accelerated design strategies. Although it appears that engineering management obstacles are generated in organizations that practice only sequential development strategies, it is still possible that simultaneous engineering techniques also may not generate totally usable systems. Automated tool frameworks will still operate under management directive. As accelerated system development models evolve, the likelihood of being able to complete requisite user interface analyses, design and prototyping activities, and evaluation cycles may be diminished. This may already be occurring. For example, Hutchinson and Hoffman (1990) and Boyle (1990) indicate that for concurrent engineering to function efficiently, multidisciplinary teams require consistent and compatible resources and capabilities, but an imbalance of tools and resources for capture of user requirements and knowledge exists.

The full integration of engineering support structures (management procedures, the product development process, and the tools and techniques used during the process) will ensure consistent design success. Although this integration has already been advocated as part of the concurrent engineering process, realization of the integration objective will require an active transition from recognition and understanding to actual change by all those that practice engineering.

Acknowledgments

The authors would like to thank Bellcore Network Services management, the market analysis and research staff, and the technical staff that contributed to the design and execution of the case studies.

References

Algera, J. A., Reitsma, W. D., Scholtens, S., Vrins, A. A. C., and Wijnen, C. J. D. (1990). Ingredients of ergonomic intervention: How to get ergonomics applied. *Ergonomics* 33(5), 557–578.

Boyle, E., Easterly, J., and Ianni, J. (1990). Human-centered design for concurrent engineering. *High Performance Systems* 11(4) (April), 58–60.

Brown, O. B. (1990). Marketing participatory ergonomics: Current trends and methods to enhance organizational effectiveness. *Ergonomics* 33(5), 601–604.

Caplan, S. (1990). Using focus group methodology for ergonomic design. *Ergonomics* 33(5), 527–533.

Carlisle, K. E. (1986). *Analyzing Jobs and Tasks.* Englewood Cliffs, NJ: Educational Technology Publications.

Carroll, J. M. and Rosson, M. B. (1985). Usability specifications as a tool in iterative development. In R. Hartson (ed.), *Advances in Human-Computer Interaction.* Norwood, NJ: Ablex.

Cheney, P. H., Hale, D. P., and Kasper, G. M. (1990). Knowledge, skills and abilities of information systems professionals: Past, present, and future. *Information & Management*, Vol. 19. Amsterdam: Elsevier Science Publishers, 237–247.

Eason, K. D. (1991). Ergonomic perspectives on advances in human-computer interaction. *Ergonomics* 34(6), 721–741.

Eppinger, S. D., Fine, C. H., and Ulrich, K. T. (1990). Interdisciplinary product design education. *IEEE Transactions on Engineering Management* 37(4) (November), 301–305.

Evanczuk, S. (1990). Concurrent engineering, The new look of design. *High Performance Systems* 11(4) (April) 16–27.

Fine, C. H. (1987). Managing quality improvement. In M. Sepehri (ed.), *Quest for Quality: Managing the Total System.* Atlanta, GA: IE&M Press.

Gentner, D. R. and Grudin, J. (1990). Why good engineers (sometimes) create bad interfaces. *Proceedings of the Conference on Human Factors in Computing.* New York: ACM, 277–282.

Gould, J. D. and Lewis, C. H. (1985). Designing for usability—Key principles and what designers think. *Communications of the ACM* 28, 300–312.

Grudin, J. (1991). Obstacles to user involvement in software product development, with implications for CSCW. *International Journal of Man-Machine Studies* 34, 435–452.

Grudin, J. and Poltrock, S. E. (1989). User interface design in large corporations: Coordination and communication across disciplines. *Proceedings of the Conference on Human Factors in Computing.* New York: ACM, 197–203.

Hendrick, H. W. (1990). Factors affecting the adequacy of ergonomic efforts on large-scale-system development programs. *Ergonomics* 33(5), 639–642.

Hoffman, R. (1987). The problem of extracting the knowledge of experts from the perspective of experimental psychology. *AI Magazine,* no. 8.

Hutchinson, K. and Hoffman, D. R. (1990). Implementing concurrent engineering. *High Performance Systems* 11(4), 40–43.

Juran, J. M. (1988). *Juran on Planning for Quality.* New York: The Free Press–Macmillan.

Kunak, D. V. (1990). Backing into the system: From the marketing concept to human factors in product design. *Ergonomics* 33(5), 535–540.

Lenior, T. M. J. and Rijnsdorp, J. E. (1990). Systems design and organizational design and management: Introduction and prospects. *Ergonomics* 33(5), 579–582.

Lenior, T. M. J. and Verhoven, J. H. M. (1990). Implementation of human factors in the management of large-scale industrial investment projects: A management point of view and ergonomics practice. *Ergonomics* 33(5), 613–619.

List, J. A. (1990). User-centered design discussion and demonstration at the 1990 Bellcore Technology Seminar. Del Lago, Texas, March.

Marshall, C. (1991). Ergonomics is dead: Long live ergonomics. *Bulletin of the Human Factors Society* 34(4) (April), 3–4.

McClelland I. L. and Brigham, F. R. (1990). Marketing ergonomics—How should ergonomics be packaged? *Ergonomics* 33(5), 519–526.

McEachiron, N. B. (1990). Speeding new products to market: Strategies and tactics. SRI International Briefing on Quality and Productivity Management, June 5.

Meister, D. (1987). Systems design, development, and testing. In G. Salvendy (ed.), *Handbook of Human Factors*. New York: John Wiley & Sons, 17–42.

Mitchell, P. P. (1987). Ease-of-use testing and marketing research: 1+1=3. *Journal of Data Collection* 27(2) (Fall), 23–26.

Moraal, J. and Kragt, H. (1990). Macro-ergonomic design: The need for empirical research evidence. *Ergonomics* 33(5), 605–612.

Mossink, J. C. M. (1990). Evaluation of design practice and the implementation of ergonomics. *Ergonomics* 33(5), 613–619.

Nielsen, J. (1990). The usability engineering life cycle. *Bellcore Technical Memorandum,* No. TM-ARH-018126, Bell Communications Research, December.

Regensburg, R. E. and Van Der Veen, F. (1990). Marketing ergonomics within multi-disciplinary project teams. *Ergonomics* 33(5), 553–556.

Richards, R. E., Byers, J. C., Kuipers, D. G., Gilbert, B. G., and Haney, L. N. (1990). Substituting rapid prototyping for task analysis for a major system upgrade project: Lessons learned. *Proceedings of the Human Factors Society.* Santa Monica, CA: Human Factors Society, 1098–1102.

Shute S. J. and Smith, P. J. (1990). Knowledge acquisition techniques: A case study in the development of a knowledge-based system for document retrieval. *Proceedings of the Human Factors Society.* Santa Monica, CA: Human Factors Society, 320–324.

Stanton, W. J. (1984). *Fundamentals of Marketing.* New York: McGraw-Hill, 7.

Urlings, I. J. M., Nijboer, I. D., and Dul, J. A. (1990). Method for changing the attitudes and behaviour of management and employees to stimulate the implementation of ergonomic improvements. *Ergonomics* 33(5), 629–637.

Van Dijk, J. A. G. M. (1990a). Delphi method as a learning instrument: Bank employees discussing an automation project. *Technological Forecasting and Social Change,* Vol. 37. Amsterdam: Elsevier Science Publishers, 399–407.

———. (1990b). Delphi questionnaires versus individual and group interviews: A comparison case. *Technological Forecasting and Social Change,* Vol. 37. Amsterdam: Elsevier Science Publishers, 293–304.

Whiteside, J., Bennett, J., and Holtzblatt, K. (1988). Usability engineering: Our experience and evolution. In M. Helander (ed.), *Handbook of Human-Computer Interaction.* Amsterdam: Elsevier Science Publishers, 791–817.

Wixon, D., Holtzblatt, K., and Knox, S. (1990). Contextual design: An emergent view of system design. *Proceedings of the Conference on Human Factors in Computing.* New York: ACM, 329–336.

The Yankee Group (1990). The Market for High-Speed Network Equipment.

Ziemke, M. C. and Spann, M. S. (1991). Warning: Don't be half-hearted in your efforts to employ concurrent engineering. *Industrial Engineering* (February), 45–49.

Bringing Usability Effectively into Product Development

PETER F. CONKLIN[1]

Digital Equipment Corporation

In today's competitive environment, most project managers believe in the value of good human factors in the systems they build. They understand that the customers for their products will insist on products that are immediately useful. This implies that the products should be readily learned and provide appropriate function needed for effective use. But in practice, few projects take full advantage of the kinds of insights and suggestions for practical action potentially available from a usability expert.

In this paper, I offer a product manager's perspective on this issue. I illustrate the problems that now occur in handling usability. I then relate these problems to the classic model of the development process that today guides product managers' thinking. Finally, I suggest a new model of development that promises to improve the treatment of usability in development by reframing the resource allocations decision managers must face.

What Happens to Usability Today: Two Examples

Terminal Setup

Each generation of video terminal has introduced many more options to allow it to be set up and adjusted to meet computer interface and human preferences. The number of features controlled by the setup screen has grown by a factor of three or four per generation to the point that today's terminal has several hundred options presented on multiple screens. Many of these options have more than two values, resulting in even more complexity. Furthermore, a terminal must be set up suitably before the user can start accessing and using the computer system and become productive.

A typical terminal development project runs two years and has an engineering development budget of several million dollars. A significant part of the terminal design is about various ergonomic features, including scan rate, character size and resolution, tilt-swivel, and so on. These features are part of the marketing requirements and hence receive much attention. Frequently, strong commitments are made just to secure project funding. And in the highly competitive terminal market, schedule becomes a dominant factor.

Despite the user frustrations dealing with terminal setup, the setup screen usually receives little attention. In a recent project, the first usability expert was brought in for setup review only during product qualification. The investment was less than one half percent of the overall project budget. Although the resulting report and demos were well received, the product was not modified.

System Enclosure

This project to develop a new system enclosure (hardware package) was initiated in response to its predecessor having insufficient space and expandability. We determined that we needed more cable interfaces and capacity. Since the system would be used in offices and small businesses, we knew the importance of good human factors.

During the 18-month development cycle, we spent 5 months in planning, 9 months in design and implementation, and 4 months in qualification. The product shipped on schedule although later than upper management would have liked.

Usability consulting was not originally budgeted. However, we subsequently spent approximately 2 percent of the project engineering budget on usability consulting. The engineers had already spent significant design effort on the layout of the enclosure to ensure easy service access for maintenance and expansion. Special considerations had been given to cabling for the disks and the communication adapters.

The usability inputs were followed for the shipping package and documentation. However, recommendations were rejected for control panel design, device location and orientation. Subsequent customer feedback indicated that device orientation, especially for the tape and diskette devices was confusing. Although the proper orientation of the removable media was clearly documented, users were consistently confused about the correct orientation for insertion.

The Pattern in the Examples

These examples illustrate an often repeated pattern in development.

The project manager says that he or she wants good human factors in the product. Frequently, this is even referred to in the original product specification. This might take the form of "good ergonomics" or "meet the customers' needs." In the initial project proposal, everyone agrees that this will be important to the success of the product. However, we do not usually find included in the specification a metric for these qualities.

After the project is underway, a usability expert is brought in and introduced to the project. The project team welcomes the usability expert anticipating that the expert will help them address the project's goals.

After intensive testing on project prototypes, the expert issues a formal report. Everyone agrees that the report is thorough and that the recommendations make sense. However, the recommendations are not followed for the most part, and the product ships without most of the recommended changes.

Post Mortem

In retrospect, the usability expert observes that the project's budget for usability design was insufficient or nonexistent; besides, the resources were scheduled too late in the project. We also notice that the original functional specifications were insufficiently precise to allow for earlier usability analysis.

So the project had problems from the start. But why weren't these problems recovered from? Why did the project invest in expensive testing and a thorough study of usability, and then not act on the results? The project manager's response is that the report was excellent but that the changes recommended were too large to implement so late in the project. Then we are particularly frustrated when, after the product ships, the problem reports from the customers reflect exactly what the report identified.

Analysis

Because the specifications for good human factors in our hypothetical project did not include metrics that were recognized by those making the specifications, a serious investment in human factors study was not in the original project proposal. In many projects, the original proposal just covered the direct engineering resources. The funding for the usability consulting was taken subsequently out of the project manager's discretionary fund.

Typically, the usability expert was not involved in the project planning. After all, so the logic goes, why would you need a usability expert when you don't even know the design of your product? The project members view the expert as someone to review the specifications to correct usability errors.

The developers frequently leave the detailed design of the human interface to the end. Sometimes the interface design ends up reflecting the designer's view when the code is developed. In other cases, it just turns out to be the way the code works. That is, the human-computer interaction frequently follows accidents of the code structure or the arbitrary sequence in which code was written.

In other cases, the product is a successor of another. So the presumption (untested) is that its interface would be the same as the predecessors. But of course many new features have been added, so the interface now has many more parameters for the end user to set, change, or even just review.

For all these reasons, when the human-computer interaction (HCI) design is done late in the implementation stage, the usability expert's review and report arrives when the product has entered its qualification phase.

Now the key problem appears: Late in development, investing in usability is quite likely to delay product delivery. And late delivery is the cardinal sin in product development.

Example: Trying to Do Better

Here's an example of a project in which we tried to forestall this problem by better planning of usability work up front. In a large project specifically working on a set of products implementing a new user interface, one of the primary goals was to have an excellent human interface. This multiyear project specifically budgeted approximately 1 percent of the total project budget for formal usability design. The consulting started at the beginning of the project and continued throughout.

During the planning phase of the product set, the usability experts helped project members prototype major parts of the screen and keyboard interactions. These prototypes were all done as throwaway code. All the component products of the set were prototyped and user interactions measured. The prototypes' screens were also key parts of the design reviews of each component. The cross-component reviews ensured that all products had a consistent look and feel.

Later in the project, formal performance goals were established and measured. These goals were based on usability principles, and many measurements were taken to confirm the specific targets. The results of measuring individual products during the qualification stage were reported to the developers. The final user-system performance of the resulting product set was substantially improved as a result.

The resulting product set has been well accepted in the market. The product set is consistent, and many other products have been added since. Key elements have been adopted as industry standards, and many third-party products have been developed to the same interface standards. The usability is substantially above that of its predecessor.

So there is good news in this example: Usability objectives were met. But there is bad news, too. Meeting usability objectives caused several delays in the project, partly because the objectives were not set until well into the project. These delays were frustrating to developers who were working hard to keep to an aggressive schedule. Although everyone agreed that the resulting product was much improved, the delays left a legacy of pain.

Easing the Pain: Changing the Model of Development

Why are these developers unhappy with what could be seen as a great success? Why are they so concerned about the delays that they question the value of what they agree are considerable usability improvements?

Within the classic well-managed product development model, we concentrate on "time to market." This is usually measured from the time that resources are first applied to the project until the product is shipped to the marketplace. The conventional wisdom is that this concentrates the developers' attention on the aspect of the business that they can best influence.

FIGURE 1

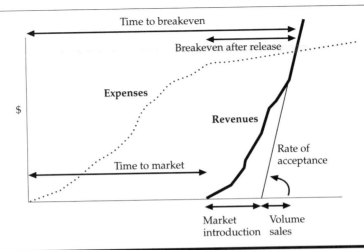

Time to breakeven includes time to market and the subsequent period needed to recover expenses.

To ensure that schedule commitments are met, the experienced project manager controls the progress of the project by ensuring that it is done in sequential steps of goal setting, design, implementation, and qualification. In this model, usability design is frequently viewed as a part of the product qualification; hence, it occurs well after the design is complete. Since time to market is the operative metric, substantive usability critique is too late to be used.

A New Development Model

Business is in the process of adopting a new development model. It is exemplified by "The Return Map: Tracking Product Teams" by Charles H. House and Raymond L. Price (1991). The cost of a schedule overrun has been understood for years. What is now emerging is a better understanding of the criticality of the elapsed time from the start of a project until profit (that is, just after the recovery of all investment costs). This is known as "time to breakeven" instead of "time to market" (Figure 1).

Time to breakeven is the sum of time to market and breakeven after release. The former continues to be the interval from project inception to product release. The latter is the time from release until profit margins have offset the development costs. This is heavily dependent on the rate of sales and, hence, of market acceptance of the product.

Using the examples from that article, three projects had investigation time of 8–16 months, development times of 19–36 months, and breakeven-after-release times of 17–27 months. Thus, the breakeven times are at least a third of the total time to recover the investment. And when the time value of the investment is measured (interest plus opportunity cost over time), the breakeven time represents approximately one half of the impact on the return.

How the New Model Can Affect Developers' Outlook

How would the developers in our example project feel about the usability work on that product if they were using the new model? Quantitatively, the parts of the product for which usability objectives were set late slipped an average of three months. But what is the impact of that slippage on time to breakeven? If the usability improvements were large enough, it could be that taking the time to make them could actually shorten time to breakeven.

How Usability Affects Time to Breakeven

It is useful to divide the interval breakeven after release into two subintervals. Market introduction is the time from product release until significant volume sales begin. We'll call the remaining interval to breakeven the volume sales interval. The time required for market introduction is strongly influenced by early adopters and people who influence the market. If these important early users rave about a product, and if they develop a positive opinion rapidly, the market introduction period will be dramatically shortened. Usability can directly affect early users' judgments and the speed with which they come to appreciate the value of the new product.

During the volume sales interval, progress is determined by rate of sales and by price. Superior usability can affect both factors by attracting more customers and by supporting a higher price. Even a 10 percent increase on dollar volume for a product can have as large an impact as the three-month potential schedule savings that concerned the developers in our example project. Such a volume increase is not at all implausible. In fact, even in the system enclosure example, presented earlier as a failure to capitalize on usability work, the impact of the usability improvements that were made is estimated as high as 50 percent on volume. Once the project team saw those results, it made sure usability design was budgeted in subsequent projects!

Lessons for Managers

It is impossible to provide hard, dollars-and-cents figures to guide specific management choices about usability. Products and markets vary too much. There will always be arguments about whether a given usability improvement, with a given cost in resources and schedule, is or is not a wise investment. But the shift from time to market to time to breakeven can establish a better framework for addressing such questions. When attention is focused on time to market, usability improvements look like pure costs: Their benefits are left out of the equation. Usability advocates in a project then appear to the rest of the product team as people seeking to hold up everyone's progress because of their specialized concerns.

Focus on time to breakeven changes the picture profoundly. Now the potential benefits of usability work, in shortening market introduction and increasing sales volume, are part of the discussion. Usability people have the opportunity to argue their case in such a way that everybody on the project can see what may be gained from usability improvements that can balance or outweigh the costs.

Lessons for Usability Experts

Usability people need to frame their arguments not just in the technical language of human-computer interaction, usability engineering, or contextual inquiry, but also in the language of development: time to market, time to breakeven, and profit. The time to breakeven development model can provide a useful framework in which to view and present their work. If they do this, all members of the development team can work together toward the mutual goal of acceptance and profitability of their product.

Note

1. Sadly, Peter Conklin passed away while this book was being readied for publication. Conklin's willingness to take time from an extraordinarily busy schedule as a senior manager at Digital Equipment Corporation to share his experiences and perspectives at the workshop was very much appreciated by the participants. His voice will be greatly missed in the usability community.

Reference

House, C. H. and Price, R. L. (1991). The return map: Tracing product teams. *Harvard Business Review*, January–February, 92–100.

Accepting the Challenge

JOHN L. BENNETT

IBM Almaden Research Center

Introduction

In the final session of the workshop, the focus shifted to examples of current practice in the real-world environment. The question of generalization had been an undercurrent of discussion throughout the three days. We had recognized that the success cases described and the methods that emerge from those experiences are situational. Generalizing from the cases and establishing broader value of the tools depend highly on the context in which work is done. At the close of the workshop, it was time to hear descriptions of the kinds of environments and constraints that would support—or hinder—future successes. The goal was, in part, to identify the climate for carrying forward in a general way the specific work reported on the previous days.

As authors prepared their papers for the workshop, they had been challenged by questions asked by the organizers:

- What is the current state of interface design practice in particular domains (for example, the aerospace industry)?

- What aspects of this practice need to change?

- What are the relative costs (in time, expertise, and so on) and benefits of the approaches discussed?

- How do these costs and benefits fit in with organizational concerns about budgets, schedules, and so on?

- How can successful design models and methods be incorporated into the design process and integrated into complex design organizations?

- What levels of management influence interface design, and what is each level's role in delivering an interface?

- How do groups of designers communicate?

- What role do users play in interface design?

- How does work in user interface design and development accommodate real-world organizational, commercial, or practical requirements?

- How could this accommodation be improved?

No one expected any one paper to address all, or even a majority, of these questions. Rather, the questions represent important background issues to be considered when moving from abstract theory and isolated methods into integrated, practical application in a world that is much influenced by factors represented in the questions. In fact, reading the three closing papers with these questions in mind leads to a further question:

- What would have to happen for the isolated instances of successes reported to become a generally observed reality?

The Papers in the Session

In "Organizational Obstacles to Interface Design and Development: Two Participant Observer Studies," Poltrock and Grudin report on their experience while working within two large software development organizations. To meet their goal of identifying tools that could contribute most to future successes if such tools were made available, they gathered data on current interface design practices. Each author worked with a different team (the projects studied included a total of 70 or more people) during a period of a month. Though they sought to be "members of the team," the authors were simultaneously conducting interviews, and it was known to project members that their visit was temporary. As a result, the authors probably were not totally successful in seeing design "from the inside." However, as experienced observers, they give us many valuable comments to ponder.

In documenting their study, Poltrock and Grudin identify development practices and aspects of interface design that act as barriers to successful application of accepted principles. In particular, they cite the principles presented by Gould and Lewis in 1983 and refined in 1985. Observations made by Poltrock and Grudin include:

- Designers are isolated from eventual users by the structure of organizations.

- Current expensive-to-program prototyping tools constrain innovation.

- Wide visibility of potential changes to an interface leads to resistance to such changes, especially if changes are proposed late in the development process.

- Lack of intergroup communication among developers about *overall* system implications of local design decisions leads to less-than-adequate design results.

They emphasize that principles of good design are available, and sometimes the principles are well-known to members of the development team. The issue is how to create a climate for effective application of the principles in the development environment.

By using quotations from interviews, Poltrock and Grudin provide a wealth of insights on cultural and conventional values in development organizations. These reinforce perceptions of technology managers who are all too experienced with visible, obvious present costs. The studies highlight the tendency of these costs to overshadow the invisible, subtle future benefits.

The Ritchie and List paper titled "System Design Practice, Emerging Development Acceleration Strategies and the Role of User-Centered Design" describes a project that served as a demonstration pilot. The work was intended to show how the combination of market research, opinion surveys, and job–task analyses performed by a multidisciplinary team could lead to reduced development time and to a better understanding of customer requirements for a high-speed data communications service. Though the work reported does respond to the principle of bringing human factors skills to the requirements stage prior to design, and though it did help make designers aware of user needs, it is not clear that HCI-specific issues were addressed in the work reported.

Ritchie and List emphasize throughout the importance of management support for the kinds of changes needed to integrate "user-centered design" practices into current engineering processes. In this, they echo Poltrock and Grudin as they describe cultural factors in the development environment. In their view, these factors are significant barriers to successful integration into effective teams of people with human factors skills and teams of people trained in the domain technology. They also mention the importance of skills needed to work successfully in multidisciplinary teams.

They offer a revealing account of the process they followed in obtaining support for the work that they saw as needed. Even gaining recognition for the potential value of the proposed work required several months of negotiation facilitated by intervention and support of senior management. This reinforces a concern expressed by many people at the workshop: Participation by people seen (from the perspective of existing team members) as "nontechnical" will be considered an obvious cost to team productivity (time and resources) with little or no visible benefit in return.

As reported in this study (and in others described at the workshop), much effort was needed to overcome a widespread perception (also found in many other organizations) of ineffective cost–benefit ratios for investment in HCI-oriented activities. Engineering takes place in a world of tradeoffs relating to:

- Pressure to provide functions and features required for marketing success
- Need to manage costs to keep product prices low
- Demand for early delivery (schedule) to gain market share

Conklin is especially effective in pointing out these constraints. A new mindset is needed that includes usability as an integral quality of the function.

Current perceptions may well be related to the historical role of human factors people who provided evaluation critiques as contrasted with providing a recognized contribution of valuable design ideas. This perception creates a double challenge in the campaign to gain engineering management acceptance for investment of resources in HCI activities. Practitioners must demonstrate to the satisfaction of management that use of HCI methods adds value to the product. Practitioners must also show that the value can be realized within the function, cost, and schedule constraints on resources.

Ritchie and List suggest that, under a concurrent engineering emphasis, activities once carried out sequentially now need to be done in parallel. But the obstacles in the real world of engineering hinder integration of HCI techniques that should co-occur. Under conventional wisdom and present-value economics, it is cost-effective to postpone "nonessential" activities until late in development.

As a result of their work, the authors report that the multidisciplinary team was effective and that the following benefits were demonstrated:

- Reduced research and analysis time
- Produced user requirements data in a form useful to engineering
- Showed how to make product improvements early in the cycle

- Identified potential operational bottlenecks
- Increased customer understanding of the (eventual) product
- Increased mutual respect and understanding among those in the team coming from different development disciplines

However, Ritchie and List caution that lasting change is slow, requiring a fundamental shift in beliefs and understandings. In the three years since the workshop, a poll they made of some of the individuals who were involved in their project is revealing. These people consider the pilot project to have been successful, but these same people have a difficult time convincing others in new projects to adopt similar innovations. We see a continuing mismatch between what our experience indicates is required for the development of interactive systems that meet user needs and what we observe as continuing development practices (implicitly or explicitly) in many organizations (as cited, for example, by Poltrock and Grudin).

In the final paper in the session, Peter Conklin speaks as a high-level engineering manager in his essay on "Bringing Usability Effectively into Product Development." This was a rare opportunity for workshop participants to interact directly with a person who has major responsibility for allocating product development resources.

Conklin made a special trip to Colorado to participate in the last day of the workshop. Though workshop participants were not aware of it at the time, he was in the middle of managing the Program Office for the Alpha AXP project, "the largest in Digital's history and one of the largest in the computer industry" (Conklin, 1992). As Software Director, Advanced Systems Group, he and his team of 7 managers began coordination of 22 software engineering groups and 10 hardware engineering groups in 1989 to achieve successful release of Alpha late in 1992.

Conklin states that managers often "believe in" good usability for systems. As Poltrock and Grudin point out, it is easy for management to assume that developers will naturally "get it right the first time." After all, no one ever sets out to build a product that is *not* useful and usable! But Conklin outlines the circumstances leading to failure to take full advantage of human factors skills that were available in several projects that he had managed.

As he points out, engineering is based on managing scarce resources to achieve results. Any quality without a metric often will lose out to one with an established performance criterion. In current practice, usability metrics are not established early. If objectives related to high-quality user interfaces appear in an original project proposal, then people can see the need for including staff trained in usability skills as part of the product development team. In the cases cited, a usability expert was "brought in" only after a project was well underway, when a project budget was insufficient for significant usability design, and usability resources were scheduled too late to influence (economically) the final design.

Note that Conklin, probably without meaning to do so, reinforces the perception that usability work is not "essential" by citing the examples of the terminal setup project and system enclosure project that were "tremendous sales successes" even though the usability advice was not fully followed. When recommendations became available, the (immediate) cost of implementing was seen as much larger than the (potential) benefit. He does go on to say, as an unusually perceptive and far-seeing product manager, that additional value could have been obtained if it had been feasible to act on the results generated by the usability activities. He agrees that this was frustrating to all concerned because subsequent reports from customers validated recommendations that were made but not followed.

To succeed in making a difference, Conklin suggests that human factors practitioners must:

- Enroll product management in the economic value of implementing recommendations
- Help establish accepted metrics during planning
- Provide competent information, advice, and results as respected members of the development team
- Show how that work contributes to the overall product success

Usability experts need to enroll the project team's manager in both the value of good human factors and the ability of the people with usability skills to manifest human factors qualities in the particular product. The first part is most easily done by putting the values into the project's framework. The second part can be done by relating the contributions of people trained in human factors to the metrics that improve time to breakeven. In summary, they must convince managers that they as practitioners have the capability to deliver the needed result.

The model that Conklin presents for justifying development expense in relation to early revenue return on product investment is a valuable action point for usability practitioners. He suggests a way to take an overall systems view so that the horizon expands to include the value to the organization of applying resources early in the cycle to gain overall increased return on investment for a product. A campaign to bring this kind of insight into the organizations where usability practice occurs will be a challenge—it will not automatically be successful, but it is an important idea to consider. It offers an opportunity to see how we might position usability tradeoffs in a way attractive to product managers.

Outlining the Challenge

What do all these papers have in common? If we stand back from these specific reports and look at prospects for future effective action, what observations can we make in the large? First, almost all those people in the workshop reporting development experience mentioned the importance of management support for making changes (sometimes revolutionary) in development processes. Second, it is clear that human factors practitioners in industry are affected by the structural changes going on in large development organizations. For example, many large software product development organizations once had large "human factors" or "usability" departments. Now these are often being disbanded, and people with human factors and usability skills are becoming members of development teams.

This need for management support and the integration into software development teams presents a double challenge to individual human factors and usability practitioners. To be fully effective, they must become change agents for the kind of systems thinking advocated by Conklin, they must overcome past barriers to being accepted as full participants in development teams, and they must become "quick on their feet" as effective practitioners. Fortunately, we can recommend sources of ideas on how they might proceed to meet these challenges.

Assisting Management to Take a Systems Perspective

One book that may be particularly valuable for gaining an understanding of managerial concerns and ways of thinking is *The Fifth Discipline* (Senge, 1990). Though a visit to any bookstore reveals a "five-foot shelf" of management books, and though all of them may have ideas that could be helpful, I'll outline here representative opportunities suggested by my interpretation of points in Senge's book.

The five disciplines described by Senge are:

- Systems thinking—learning to think from a systems perspective (for example, performance of equipment and users in a customer environment)
- Personal mastery—building and demonstrating competence in one's technical domain and a willingness to contribute effectively to projects
- Mental models—understanding views of the world represented in current ways of acting, assumptions that may be outmoded. Exploration is successful when conducted in a balance between inquiry and advocacy

- Shared vision—building a commitment to successful results from within through personal commitment and enrollment of others (as contrasted with imposed from outside)
- Team learning—moving beyond current assumptions, recognizing defensiveness, and thinking together to make the vision a reality

Understanding the appeal to managers of such books may help the visionary practitioner "stand in the shoes of the persons you are talking with" (know the users) when inviting changes within organizations.

Clearly, this abstract list does not do justice to Senge's book. But these disciplines can be usefully combined with ideas from another writer on management, John Henderson, to achieve further success of the kind described in the workshop.

Developing Effective Teamwork

Effective teams and partnerships among team members are closely related. John Henderson (1990) provides a descriptive model of partnership and its attributes. This may be useful in responding to the observation of Conklin that "usability experts can become part of the original product proposal... only if the usability expert builds a relationship as a team member within the development group." Following Henderson, we characterize partnership as "a strategy to achieve higher performance and/or lower costs through joint, mutually-dependent action of independent individuals."

Suggestions listed by Henderson, augmented by my thoughts on how they relate to participation of usability experts in teams, include:

- Establish a common goal, a vision of what could be. Partnership requires developing a design vision strong enough to support collaboration despite cultural differences. The vision may evolve as the team members work together to achieve a particular design result, but the goal needs to remain shared. Developing the vision, goals, and objectives requires open negotiation, sensitive speaking, and attentive listening.
- Be predisposed and willing to trust. Willingness to trust is influenced by past performance and personal relationships, a sense of healthy interrelationships, and recognition of consequences that can hurt if trust is broken. Trust must be continually reinforced and maintained through personal relationships in the context of the current project.
- Recognize and respect distinctive competency. Teams are typically formed to include people known to have skills and experience with potential value

in achieving project results. It is important for team members to develop a mutual recognition of the special talents available within the team and to see how complementary skills are needed for project success.

- Share knowledge as appropriate. Each individual on the team must be willing to share knowledge to the degree necessary to achieve the team goals. It is quite realistic to take into account the purpose and bounds of the project when deciding what it is appropriate to share.

- Attend to mutual benefits. To have an effective team, each member needs to develop an understanding of how individual work contributes to achieving the objectives. Then attention is required to see to it that each member of the partnership is served in the collaboration. This requires explicit attention to the benefits that each person may seek. These may differ markedly for each person on the team.

Building on Senge's five disciplines and considering Henderson's analysis of partnership, the effective usability practitioner may discover a synthesis of the two and find ways to:

- Contribute to systems thinking. Human factors and usability people have training that has potential for understanding a system as a whole: relationships of development activities to user satisfaction and the effects of underlying product structures on usability. They are also capable of recognizing recurring structures—parts that are fundamental from a user perspective and that function in relation to each other. They are capable of seeing circles of interrelations rather than linear cause–effect chains. They can develop skills in noticing causes and effects not closely coupled in time or space, allowing for delays between user actions and computer system consequences. As a result of seeing patterns more clearly than others, they can advocate significant and enduring changes effectively.

- Build shared vision. See future possibilities, and learn how to create a vision as a force in people's hearts. Contribute to a climate that encourages personal vision. Interpret and communicate a personal vision to build genuine commitment and enrollment (rather than compliance), respecting freedom to choose. By aiming for the long term, connecting to a larger purpose and to one another, people can come to know that they make a difference.

- Reinforce personal mastery. Continually focus on what one person (or the group) truly wants and is willing to accomplish (material, personal, service results). Keep attention on creating a specific result with intrinsic value; do not confuse results with means and mechanisms, direction, and process. Clarify and deepen personal vision (things that matter most). Develop patience; see current reality "objectively" so as to generate energy for change. Learn how to carry on conversations that balance inquiry and advocacy rather than be dominating. Move beyond reactive–responsive mindsets to see how actions have a creative effect in the world of the project.

- Explore mental models. Be aware of how assumptions, generalizations, and internal world images (some of which may not be conscious) influence how people act. Distinguish genuine data as distinct from questionable interpretations loosely based on data. Change requires us to:

    Become aware of our present way of seeing our world
    Be willing to test assumptions
    Notice judgments and evaluations that shape our actions
    Develop learning skills to see differences between the way we think we act and the way we actually act

- Develop team learning. Assist the team in developing a capacity to achieve extraordinary results not available individually. Support team members growing more rapidly in skills than they would otherwise. Help a team to suspend assumptions and enter into genuine dialogue needed for learning together as a team. Develop acceptable ways to bring to the surface patterns of interaction and defensiveness that undermine learning. Be an agent for seeing a larger picture that lies beyond individual perspectives. Find ways to develop user-oriented representations that provide a shared language for dealing with HCI complexity.

Our focus here is on practice. Can one usability person working alone *begin* to make progress on even a few of these challenges? Probably not—if working alone.

A recommendation that I have made for some time to people in this situation is to find a partner. It can be valuable (perhaps essential) to have someone who shares your vision and who can be a partner with you to provide mutual acknowledgment and support through the worked-for successes and the inevitable failures.

Many people will find the book *The Phoenix Agenda* (Whiteside, 1993) a valuable source of practical ideas for mutual support. Though describing the organizational and personal turmoil currently found in industrial downsizing and rightsizing, the book is really about individuals finding ways to be effective despite the changes. Indeed, people can make use of these changes to bring forth concrete results (described abstractly by Senge) through using the concepts of partnership outlined by Henderson. Whiteside illustrates the 12 items in *The Phoenix Agenda* with many stories drawn from his usability experience at Digital. In particular, I recommend his Chapter 10, "Transformational Coaching," to anyone who creates a partnership as a way to undertake effectively some of the challenges outlined here.

When I talked about this progression from Senge to Henderson as a challenge to practitioners with one acquaintance, he responded, "Who, me? I couldn't do that in my situation!" Perhaps the best response I can give is taken from the close of Whiteside's *The Phoenix Agenda:* "If not you, then who? If not now, then when?"

References

Conklin, P. F. (1992). Enrollment management, managing the Alpha AXP Program. *Digital Technical Journal* 4(4), Special Issue, 193–205.

Henderson, J. C. (1990). Plugging into strategic partnerships: The critical I/S connection. *Sloan Management Review,* Spring, 7–18.

Senge, P. M. (1990). *The Fifth Discipline, The Art and Practice of the Learning Organization.* New York: Doubleday.

Whiteside, J. (1993). *The Phoenix Agenda: Power to Transform Your Workplace.* Essex Junction, VT: Oliver Wight.

Synthesis and Closing Discussion

Respect and Beyond

CLAYTON LEWIS, PETER POLSON

The workshop was held in 1991, roughly ten years after the emergence of ACM's Special Interest Group in Computer Human Interaction, SIGCHI, and after as many years of progress in research and in widening acceptance of usability as a prime issue in systems development. But one theme in the discussions at the workshop sounded a clear echo of discussions of years ago, and we wondered why this was so. Why was this particular theme still vital after all these years of apparent progress in HCI? The theme was *usability people don't get no respect in the computer business.*

This theme was audible in much of the discussion of the various projects that were described at the workshop. Both the presenters in recounting their work and members of the audience in relating the presentations to their own experience often made this point.

Peter Conklin's remarks provided fascinating, and rare, testimony on the theme from the perspective of a product manager. He made clear his intellectual commitment to usability, and gave many illustrations of the trouble he has gotten into over many years by not paying enough attention to usability. But he also observed that he keeps making this mistake, despite his recognition of it, and confessed his unwillingness, despite his intellectual commitment, to change the basic organization of the development process to give usability and usability people a bigger or different role. He presented the concept of time to breakeven as a way to get a more favorable hearing for usability people in the dialog on project goals, but this suggestion itself presupposes the problem: As things are, usability people don't get a hearing.

So what's behind this problem? Why, after a decade of progress in which usability is almost universally recognized as a crucial facet of systems technology, do usability people still make this lament?

Surely one part of the answer is the complexity of the determinants of success and failure in any technical venture, as forcibly argued by Stuart Card. Nobody's contributions to success can be isolated with complete clarity, and it's too much to expect that people working on different aspects of system development will come to agree on the relative importance of each others' work to the success of the whole.

Another factor, related to Card's general point, is that there are no obvious benchmarks for usability that serve to mark progress in usability work in the way that chip densities, processor speeds, or (less visibly) algorithm performance mark progress in neighboring areas of technology. This is a point that John Gould and Stephen Boies have made in their efforts to assist management in appreciating the importance of usability (Gould, Boies, and Lewis, 1991). The simple benchmarks that are used in other fields have their liabilities, but they nevertheless serve as strong drivers for innovation and investment.

Benchmarks work in part by promoting rivalry, which in turn establishes a high value on skills and people that can help an organization win. But in usability work, rivalry is dampened by the need for stability in design. There is a disincentive for sweeping changes in user interfaces, and so the scope for vigorous competition is reduced.

Another complex of factors that contribute to "no respect" is organizational. Usability people are still commonly isolated in special functional groups in an organization ("usability people" are commonly identified and segregated, whereas, say, "algorithms people" are not). This segregation contributes to the problems that Conklin discusses because differences in goals and responsibilities for different people are built into the workaday structure of project groups. Usability people in such a structure are perceived as somewhat helpful at best, compared to the obviously essential system builders, and as obstructionist at worst.

We usability people need to shoulder some of the blame for this situation. Our response to "no respect" is sometimes to seek segregation, with our own managers and our own like-minded colleagues, and with our own "professional" goals, which may visibly depart from the project goal of creating a superior system in the direction of doing publishable studies or otherwise seeking approval from those we see as professional peers rather than from project co-workers. Thus "no respect" can be self-intensifying, with lack of respect producing greater divergence from co-workers, which produces even less respect.

One last factor, which was prominent in the discussion at the workshop, is the lack of managers who understand usability. This is a clear chicken-and-egg situation. As long as usability people aren't respected, they will not be well represented in management. More specifically, connecting back to the previous point, there won't be many usability-conscious managers as long as usability people are organizationally isolated and accept narrow technical roles.

But having picked over the respect issue this much, we want to leave it alone. In fact we'll argue we all ought to leave it alone. It's the wrong thing to worry about, for more than one reason:

1. Outside our personal frames of reference respect is not of value in itself. We ought to be worrying about how people can produce better tools for people to use, not how usability people can get more respect.

2. The concern for usability people is limiting. It accepts the segregation of usability people from other systems people, a segregation that (as argued) actually is part of the problem.

3. The focus on computers, in "Usability people don't get no respect in the computer business," is limiting in that it can lead to investment in inappropriate technology and neglect of better solutions that don't involve computers. Don Norman (for example, in Norman, 1988) has argued forcefully that concern for usability should not be limited to computer-centered things.

4. The focus on the computer business is limiting. As computers become commodities, the computer business is being dramatically restructured. The focus has shifted away from large equipment vendors to software and services vendors, and we may see a further shift toward user organizations rather than supplier organizations. It is in user organizations that computers produce value, and so we can expect that there's where usability work will happen in the long run.

If we accept the broadened and reframed issue, "How can people produce better tools for people to use," what can we do to push on it? One answer flows easily from the foregoing appraisal: We should work more on applications. Ruven Brooks has long called for this (Brooks, 1993), and has pressed the SIGCHI organization to better accommodate application developers.

Part of this effort should be to develop a strengthened intellectual framework for applications work. The efforts of Brooks and others to increase our communal focus on applications are handicapped by this lack. Conference submissions on application development are downgraded by reviewers because they often have limited appeal outside a particular application domain. Ideas developed in one application domain that would be useful in others travel only slowly if at all across domain boundaries, for want of ways to characterize advances in terms that are not application bound. Wehrend (1993) presents an approach to this problem in the visualization area; the idea is to identify classes of data and judgments that can be used to relate analogous visualization problems in different application areas. We could do this more broadly for interactive technology.

Another imperative is to reduce the cost of user interface construction. High costs inhibit investment in applications that are important but whose limited scope of use provides small ammortization of development costs. The fact that it's hard to build user interfaces also creates the separation between people who know about usability and people who can actually build a user interface. This separation, already a bad thing today, will be intolerable in small, application-centered organizations.

Extending this point, our progress in transplanting usability from the computer business to the application business will be faster if we can package usability as a technology people can buy as a block. If somebody wants to exploit embedded microprocessors in something they build, they can read something about them, buy them, and hire somebody who can apply them. We are not there yet with usability, and some might argue that we will never be, or perhaps should never be. But there is a real prospect that soon we could have tutorial material on usability technology that is accessible to managers and technologists that want to know about it; that we could have interface building tools, perhaps not fundamentally different from those now available, but simpler and more robust, so that one would not have to become a specialist to use them; and that we could train people to be technically competent not in just some aspects of usability work, such as testing or design, but in the whole spectrum. One way to frame the goal is with two questions: "How likely is it today that a company could hire one person who would bring in the skills necessary for practical user interface development?" and "What can we do to raise this likelihood?"

Looking ahead to another workshop after another ten years, will we still be complaining about respect? We think not, not because we'll have respect but because the broad terms of our work will have changed in ways suggested here. Usability work will be integrated not only with other areas of computing technology but with work in multifarious application domains. Organizational structures will reflect this and so will individual training and careers. There won't be an "us" to be respected or not, and that will be a good thing.

References

Brooks, R. (1993). The case for the specialized interface. *IEEE Software* 10 (March), 86–88.

Gould, J. D., Boies, S. J., and Lewis, C. H. (1991). Making usable, useful, productivity-enhancing computer applications. *Communications of the ACM* 34, 74-85.

Norman, D. A. (1988). *The Psychology of Everyday Things*. New York: Basic Books.

Wehrend, S. (1993). Taxonomy of visualization goals. In P. R. Keller and M. M. Keller (eds.), *Visual Cues: Practical Data Visualization*. Los Alamitos, CA: IEEE Computer Society Press.

Index

A

AAMRL Virtual Reality System, 124, 125
academic research, CHI theory, 104, 117
accelerated development strategies, 340–42, 377–78
identifying, 348–49
acceptance, of innovation, 66
Actions, 180
action science
defined, 259
HCI, 229–31, 259–62
technology development through, 259
active participatory prototyping, 204–08, 222, 224, *See also* prototyping
active structural networks, 213
activity analyses, 277
ADL, 20
Alpha AXP Project, 379
alpha testing, 285
Alsop, Stewart, 2d, 63
Alto Workstation, 74, 75, 92
analogy, generating claims through, 244
analytic design methods, 151, 154–59
analytic model development, 104
analytic scenarios, 234–38
Apple Lisa. *See* Lisa
Apple Macintosh. *See* Macintosh
application content
defined, 176
experts, 181
user interface style and, 176–78
application development
generators, DEC Rally Version 2, 4
problems in, 176

productivity, 175, 182–96
using ITS, 173–96
arithmetic expressions, 88–89
ARPA, 162
artifacts, *See also* task-artifact framework
action-science approach, 232
altering properties of, 249
scenarios as narrative theory of, 29–40
second-order, 233, 262
ATM, coordinated evaluation methods, 292–93
attitudes, in real-world experiments, 114–15

B

backend functions, 181
Beaudelaire, Patrick, 77
Bell Labs, 230–31
benchmarks
DEC Rally Version 2, 6
Freestyle, 40
GOMS analysis, 107
organizational structure and, 322–23
purpose of, 7
for usability, 390
Bennett, J. L., 204
beta testing, 286
bitmap graphics editors, 77
blocking messages, in claims analysis, 250
Boies, Stephen, 33, 390
borrowing, 278–79
global, 278
local, 278
Bovair, S., 283

Bowman, Bill, 77
Boyle, E., 362–63
Bravo, 76, 129
BravoX, 76
Brooks, Ruven, 391
Brotz, Doug, 77
Brown, J. S., 117
Bush, Vannovar, 72

C

Campbell, P., 93
Card, Stuart K., 63, 96, 278, 283, 390
causal schemas, 232, *See also* claims
checklists
  in coordinated design, 292
  for reflecting on design, 281
  selecting, 286–87, 289
claims, 229
  blocking messages in, 250
  consequences of, 247–48
  constructing, 240–51, 253–59
  defined, 232
  justifying, 246–48
  making explicit, 257–59
  psychology and, 246–47, 254–55
  reasoning toward contractions, 247
  in scenario-based design, 248–51
  tracking dependencies, 262
  tradeoffs (downsides), 242, 247–51,
    256, 257–59, 378
claims analysis, 248–51, 282
  defined, 243
  nonunique causes problem, 249
claims generation, 243–45
  stopping heuristic for, 244
  through analogy, 244
code reuse, in ITS, 182
Cognition MCAE CAD/CAM system,
  89
Cognitive Complexity Theory, 283,
  287–89
Cognitive Walkthrough, 271, 282, 292,
  294
Command Language Grammar (CLG),
  282
commercial success, 133–41, *See also*
  revenues
  of GUI, 127, 129
  of innovation, 129
communication
  computer-conferencing, 329, 330

documentation, 327
electronic mail, 77, 328, 329, 330
fax machines, 63, 65
GUI design methods and, 222–23
integrated design and, 327–30
meetings, 328
network diagrams, 58–60
on-line training, 328
organizational structure and,
  310–11, 318–20, 321, 333–34
personal relationships, 329
telephone, 329, 330
videoconferencing, 65
workgroup networks, 57–60
competency, of team members,
  382–83
computer-aided design (CAD) tablets
  and pens, 43–45
computer-human interface (CHI)
  theory, *See also* human-computer
  interaction (HCI); user-centered
  design (UCD)
  academic research, 104, 117
  as an applied science, 103–04
  corporate research, 103–04, 117
  evaluation, 115–18
  GOMS analysis and, 102–03
  research application, 101–20
concept development, 341
concept diagrams, 213
conceptual models, 279
concurrent design strategies, 340–43
conferencing, 239, 330
Conklin, Peter F., 66, 378–81, 382,
  389–90
content experts, 181
content programmers, 181
content specification files, 181
context sensitivity
  help, 23–24
  menus, 12–13
contextual design, 232, 342
contextual inquiry, 8–9
  DEC Rally Version 2, 7, 8–9, 31
  defined, 8
contextual interview, 36–37
Continental Insurance, 183–84
contradictions, reasoning toward, 247
control groups, 111–12
Cooper-Harper Scale, 133, 134
corporate research, CHI theory,
  103–04, 117

Cosmic Osmo,   132
Cox, Norm,   79
CPM-GOMS,   108–11, 126, 127, 133, *See also* GOMS analysis
    CHI evaluation,   115–18
    performance time predictions vs. trial data,   110–11
    schedule charts,   108
Critical Path Analysis,   283, 294
    critical path,   108–09
    critical tasks,   273, 285
    GOMS extension. *See* CPM-GOMS
    selecting,   288
CSCW (Computer Supported Cooperative Work),   344
CUA style,   186–87
CUA-2 style,   178
cursor keys, mouse vs.,   86–87
Curtis, B.,   327
customer profiles
    development of,   350–51, 356–57
    job-task analysis based on,   357–60
customers, *See also* participant selection; users
    educating through user-centered design,   361
    interviews,   6
    needs of, attention to,   92
    selecting sample of,   353
customization, Freestyle,   41–42, 52–53

D

damage testing,   285
data collection
    categories of,   352–53
    sources of,   353–54
    techniques for,   354–55
Dataland,   124, 125, 132
decision tree analysis,   277
    interviews,   293
    top-down,   208–12, 221–23, 224–25
decomposition analysis,   280
DEC Rally Version 2,   3–34
    expert learning problem,   25–27
    list of values problem,   17–20
    long lists of values problem,   25
    menu navigation problem,   10–17
    planning,   5–6
    preference rating,   27
    product origins,   4–5

programming environment problem,   21–23
    revenues,   30–31
    specific design issues,   27–29
    usability bugs,   29–30
    usability methods,   6–10, 31–33
    useless information problem,   23–24
DeluxePaint,   77
demand pull inventions,   143
dependencies, tracking,   262
design, *See also* graphic design; hardware design; integrated design; interface design; iterative design; software design
    analysis,   232, 280
    borrowing,   278–79
    building prototypes of,   274–75
    deploying,   275, 286, 291
    as evolutionary,   278
    features, evaluating,   27–29
    generating,   274, 278–81, 290
    implementing,   275, 285–86, 291
    memories,   232
    problem definition,   274, 276–78, 290
    process evaluation, Star,   89–93
    reflecting on,   274, 281–83, 290
    testing prototypes for,   275, 284–85
designer intention,   232
design methods, *See also* graphical user interface (GUI) design methods; interface design methods
    analytic,   151, 154–59
    coordinated,   291–94
    development mileposts,   159–62, 165–66
    dimensions of variation,   154–62, 165
    Freestyle,   146–48
    idealization of context,   154, 157, 158
    idealization of representation,   155–59
    invention process and,   141–44
    Meetingware,   145–46, 151
    New TAO Workstation,   144, 151
    patterns of, use,   150–54
    Pioneer Systems and Settler Systems,   162–64
    popularity of,   153–54
    Rally,   144–45, 151
    Star,   148–50, 151
    synthetic,   151, 154–59

design methods *(continued)*
  theft as, 153–54
design process
  acceleration of, 340
  concurrent, 340–43
  influence of usability on, 342–43
  integrating HCI into, 344–46
  sequential, 340–41
design space, 280
desktop customization, Freestyle,
  52–53
desktop metaphor, 70, 71, 94, 124
development mileposts, design
  methods, 159–62, 165–66
discount usability engineering,
  37, 62
display analysis, 283
Displaywriter, 233
  claims embodied in, 241–42
  constructing claims, 241–42
  generating claims, 243
  user concerns typology, 236–38
documentation
  as communication, 327
  iterative usability testing, 49–50
  poor, 304–05
  usability problems and, 11
document-centric design, Star, 91
Doodle, 77
Douglas, S., 282
downsides, *See also* tradeoffs
  claims, 242
  mitigating, 248–51, 256, 257–59
Draw, 77, 129
DynaBook, 75

E

Eason, K. D., 341, 343
edit-object menu structure, 14–15
Ehn, Pelle, 22
electronic mail, 77, 328, 329, 330
Ellis, Clarence "Skip," 77
Emacs, 125, 126, 132
embodiment merit, 136–39
Engelbeck, G., 277, 291
engineering success, 129, 133, 141,
  165
Englebart, Douglas, 72
envisioning, 277
error scenarios, 237–38, 243–44
Esper, E. A., 246

expectations, in real-world
  experiments, 114–15
experimental groups, 111–12
expert learning problem, DEC Rally
  Version 2, 25–27
Expo'92 multimedia visitor services
  application, 187–91

F

familiar skills
  Freestyle, 52
  innovation and, 41, 67n
  support of, 39–40
fax machines, 63, 65
field observation, *See also* observation
  Freestyle, 45–46, 50, 52–53, 61
  hardware design, 45–46
field trials, Project Ernestine, 104–07
Fifth Discipline, The (Senge), 381
Flegel, Bob, 77
flexibility, Freestyle, 41–42
Flyer, 77
focus group interviews, 277
Forbes, 65
forms, DEC Rally Version 2, 4
Free-Hand Drawing, 77
Freestyle, 38–66, 124, 125, 126, 127
  benchmark tests, 40
  design concepts, 38–42
  design methods, 146–48, 151
  evaluation, 62–66
  familiar skills supported by,
    39–40
  features of, 38–39
  field observation, 45–46, 50, 61
  hardware design, 42–47
  innovation, 40–41, 138–39
  invention phases, 142
  iterative usability testing, 48–50
  laboratory testing, 43–45, 54
  rapid prototyping, 50–53
  software design, 47–54
  tutorial, 48–50
  user needs, 55–57
  workgroup support, 54–62
funding, 162, 163

G

Generalized Transition Network, 292,
  294

general-purpose spreadsheet package, 184–85
goal-action mapping, 282
GOMS analysis, 283, 294–95, *See also* CPM-GOMS
  application of, 101–02
  benchmarks, 107
  CHI theory and, 102–03, 115–18
  Project Ernestine, 107–10
  selecting, 287–89
  validating, 118–19
Gould, John D., 33, 291, 305–06, 325, 332, 390
government funding, 162, 163
Graham, M. B. W., 133, 135, 136
grammar analysis, 282, 288–89
graphical object editors, 77
graphical programming, 76
graphical user interface (GUI)
  commercial success of, 127, 129
  development of, 96, 127–30
graphical user interface (GUI) design
    methods, 198–226, *See also* design methods; interface design methods
  active participatory prototyping, 204–08, 222, 224
  combining results of, 215–17
  interplay among, 221–22
  on-site observation, 200–204, 221–22, 224
  selecting and tuning, 223–26
  semantic net analysis, 212–15, 225
  social value of, 222–23
  top-down decision tree analysis, 208–12, 221–23, 224–25
graphic design, in Star design process, 79, 85, 90–91
Grudin, J., 344, 376–77
Gypsy, 76, 129

H

hallway testing, 285, 292
hardware design
  field observation, 45–46
  Freestyle, 42–47
  methods and results, 64
  rapid prototyping, 50–51
Hardy, 77
help
  context-sensitive, 23–24
  iterative usability testing, 50

Henderson, John, 382, 384–85
heuristic evaluations, 37
Hoffman, D. R., 362–63
House, Charles H., 372
Hughes, T. P., 141–43
human-computer interaction (HCI), 36–37, *See also* computer-human interface (CHI) theory; user-centered design (UCD)
  action-science approach to, 229–31, 259–62
  design, 237, 369–71
  hardware methods and results, 64
  methods evaluation, 62–66
  normal science paradigm for, 230
  perceived effectiveness of, 378
  psychology and, 246
  software methods and results, 64–65
  task-artifact framework, 231–33
  timing, 369–71
  workgroup support methods and results, 65
human-computer interface (HCI), *See also* computer-human interface (CHI) theory; user-centered design (UCD)
  broadening of, 345
  effectiveness of, 338–39
  integrating into design process, 344–46
  organizational barriers to, 343–44
  organizational structure and, 343
human factors engineering
  activities, 380
  integrating into design process, 345
  principles, menu design and, 11, 16
  sequential design process and, 340–41
Hutchinson, K., 362–63
HyperCard, 125, 126, 132
hypertext, 73

I

icons
  confusion over, 83–85
  design of, 67n, 79
  development of, 76
  testing, Star, 83–85
icon targeting, Freestyle, 49, 52
idealization of context, 154, 157, 158

idealization of representation, 155–59
idea processors, 73
IEEE Spectrum, 127
Illinois Department of Employment Security (IDES) case study, 195
imitation
  invention success and, 140, 164–65
  theft, 153–54
incentive merit, 133, 136–39
industry trends, 92
innovation, 130, *See also* invention
  acceptance of, 63, 65–66
  criteria, 135
  familiar skills and, 67n
  investment in, 162, 164
  prototyping and, 324
  success of, 133–41, 165
  value of, 40–41
instructional manual. *See* manual (example)
integrated design, 305
  communication and, 327–30
  organizational structure and, 318–20, 326–30
  resistance to, 332–33
interactive responsiveness, 92–93
interface design, *See also* design; iterative design
  commercial success, 127, 129, 133–41
  cost of, 392
  DEC Rally Version 2, 3–34
  deploying, 275, 286
  development of, 173–74
  discovery, 129
  documentation of, 304–05
  engineering success, 129, 133, 165
  evaluation methods, 80–81
  guidelines, 279
  improving, 271–74
  innovation, 130, 133–41, 165
  integrated, 305, 318–20, 326–30, 332–33
  invention success, 129, 130–32, 164–65
  iterative, 305
  methods, 122–66
  organizational obstacles to, 303–35, 339, 376–77
  organizational structure and, 309–11, 312–30

participant-observer studies, 305–09
pioneer systems, 123
poor, 304–05
principles of, 305–06, 330–35
settler systems, 123
successful, 123–27
usable, 272
user contact and, 305, 308, 309
interface design methods, 269–95, *See also* design methods; graphical user interface (GUI) design methods
  activities, 274–75
  building prototypes, 274–75, 283–84, 290
  coordinated use of, 291–94
  costs and benefits, 289–91
  defined, 271
  design improvement and, 271–74
  encouraging reflection with, 273
  generating designs, 274, 278–81, 290
  implementing designs, 275, 285–86
  interviews, 276
  macromethods, 271
  micromethods, 271
  naturalistic observation, 276
  problem definition, 274, 276–78, 290
  prototypes, 275, 284–85, 291
  reflection, 274, 281–83, 290
  as representations for design, 273
  scenarios, 276
  selecting, 286–91
  task analysis, 276
  testing, 274, 275, 284–85, 291
  user needs and capabilities and, 272–73
interface style, 174
  application content and, 176–78
  defined, 176
  rule-based, computer-executable, 179
interface visibility, 324–25
interviews, 276, 277
  for top-down decision tree analysis, 208–09, 222–23, 224–25
  for user-centered design, 355, 356
invention, *See also* innovation
  demand pull, 143
  embodiment merit, 136–39
  imitation and, 140

impacts of, scales for describing,
130–32
incentive merit, 133, 136–39
market merit, 136–39
NOV (novelty) scale, 130
operational merit, 136–39
process of, 141–44
success of, 129, 130–32, 140, 164–65
technology push, 143
Iscoe, N., 327
iterative design, 173–74, 305
for noninteractive systems, 332
organizational structure and,
317–18, 323–26, 332
resistance to, 326, 332
usability testing, Freestyle, 48–50
visibility of, 324–25
ITS, 173, 177–96, 294
background, 175–82
code reuse, 182
Continental Insurance underwriting
application case study, 183–84
CUA user interface style case study,
186–87
Expo'92 multimedia visitor services
application case study, 187–91
general-purpose spreadsheet
package case study, 184–85
Illinois Department of Employment
Security case study, 195
present status, 196
productivity case studies, 182–96
prototyping, 182
time and attendance recording
application case study, 191–94
work products, 179–82
work roles, 179–82

J

Jackson System Diagramming and
Object-Oriented Methods, 271
job-task analysis, 357–60
John, Bonnie, 103, 283
Johnson, J., 91
Jones, Sandy, 126

K

Karat, J., 204
Kawasaki, Guy, 122, 162
Kay, Alan, 72, 74

keystroke data, 285, 286
Keystroke Level Model, 283, 285,
287–89, 295
Kieras, D. E., 283
Kragt, H., 341
Krasner, H., 327

L

labeling studies, Star, 81–82
laboratory testing, Freestyle, 43–45, 54
Lampson, Butler, 76
Laurel, 77
Learning Research Group (LRG), 74
Levine, Stephen, 39
Lewis, C. H., 33, 305–06, 325, 332
Lisa, 89, 92, 94, 124, 129
interface, 124, 129
List, Judith A., 377–79
list of values (LOV)
DEC Rally Version 2, 17–20, 25
in programming environment, 20–21
local area networks (LANs)
Freestyle support, 61
user-centered design, 346–47
Lohse, J., 283

M

McCreight, Ed, 159n
Macintosh, 92, 94, 124, 125, 129
innovation criteria, 137–38
interface, 124, 125, 129
toolkit, 278–79
MacKinlay, J., 283
macromethods, 271
Malloy, Tom, 76
management, *See also* organizational
structure
commitment of, 352, 379–80, 381–82,
389–91
developing effective teamwork,
382–85
promoting user-centered design to,
350
time to breakeven and, 374
manual (example)
claims analysis, 257–59
psychological design rationale for,
253–55
scenario-based design for
improvements, 255–57

manual (example) *(continued)*
  as task-artifact framework example, 251–59
market creation, for innovation, 66
marketing departments
  communications issues, 320, 321
  integrated design and, 318–20
  product definition and, 312–15, 321–22, 331
  role of, 312, 320–21, 331
market merit, 136–39
market research, for user-centered design, 347, 348–49, 360–61, 362
Markup, 77
media richness, 67n
Meetingware, 126, 127, 132
  design methods, 145–46, 151
  invention phases, 142
mental models, 381, 384
menu items, semantic structure of, 15
menus
  context-sensitive, 12–13
  DEC Rally Version 2, 4
menu structure
  DEC Rally Version 2, 10–17
  edit-object approach, 14–15
  jumping across, 13–14
  number of items, 11
  object-operation, 11–13
  redesign, 11–17
  semantic, 15
  stack-based, 13–14
MERMAID, 45
metaphor analysis, 282
Metaphor workstation, 89
micromethods, 271
Microsoft Word, 130
mileposts, design methods, 159–62, 165–66
Minimal Manual, 251–59
models
  analytic, 104
  conceptual, 279
  GOMS, 107–10
  mental, 381, 384
  operator function, 277–78, 293–94
  for user interface design methods, 273
Modified Mercali scale, 130
Molich, R., 80
Moraal, J., 341
Moran, T., 279, 282, 283

mouse
  buttons, 87
  vs. cursor keys, 86–87
  development of, 86–87
  low- vs. high-level handling, 87, 96n–97n
  vs. other pointing devices, 87
  Star, 85, 86–87
multidisciplinary teams, 342–43, 361–62, 377, 378–79
  assembling, 352
multimedia applications
  communication systems, 36–37
  Expo'92 visitor services, 187–91

N

narrative descriptions, 277
narrative theory, scenarios as, 239–40
NASA Virtual Reality System, 124, 125
National Research Council (NRC), Committee on Human Factors, 269–70
naturalistic observation, 276, 292, 293
needs-finding interviews, Freestyle, 56
network diagrams, 58–60
Newell, A., 130, 283
New Horizons Project, 118–19
Newman, William, 77
New TAO Workstation, 126, 132, 133, *See also* toll-and-assistance operator (TAO) workstations
  design methods, 144, 151
  invention phases, 142
Nielsen, J., 80, 347
NLS, 72–73, 74, 124, 125, 132
noninteractive systems, iterative design for, 332
Norman, Don A., 244, 391
Norman's stage theory of action, 244, 245
NOV (novelty) scale, 130
Nutt, Gary, 77

O

object-action analysis, 279–80, 282
object-operation menus, 11–13

objects-and-actions design
    methodology, 78, 90
observation
    field, 45–46, 50, 52–53, 61
    naturalistic, 276, 292, 293
    on-site, for GUI design, 200–204,
        221–22, 224
OfficeTalk, 77–78
Olympic Messaging System, 37, 62,
    124, 125, 126, 132, 285, 291
on-line training, 328
on-site observation, for GUI design,
    200–204, 221–22, 224
Open Software Foundation, Open
    Look, 89
operational merit, 136–39
operator function model, 277–78,
    293–94
organizational structure, *See also*
    management
    changes in, 311
    communication and, 310–11,
        318–20, 333–34
    HCI and, 343–44
    integration issues, 318–20, 326–30
    interface design practices and,
        312–30
    interface design principles and,
        330–35
    interface development and, 309–11
    iterative design and, 317–18,
        323–26
    obstacles created by, 303–35, 339,
        376–77
    physical distances, 319
    product definition and, 314–17,
        321–23
    prototyping and, 317–18, 323–26
    removing barriers created by,
        343–44
    theory and practice, 312–14
    user involvement and, 314–17,
        321–23
overlapping windows, 95

P

paint programs, 77
Palo Alto Research Center (PARC),
    74–78, 89–90, 92, 129
Pareto chart, 7
participant observer studies, 305–09

participant selection
    customers, 353
    factors affecting, 111–12
    random assignment, 112–13
    in real-world experiments, 112–13
    users, 93, 353
participatory prototyping, 204–08,
    222, 224, 284, *See also* prototyping
partnership, *See also* project teams;
    teamwork
    goals for, 382
Payne, Steve, 237
PC/Computing, 63
PenPoint, 124, 125, 132
pens, design, 43–47
performance time, predictions vs. trial
    data, 110–11
Perin, Constance, 60
personal computer, use of term, 74
personal mastery, 381, 383–84
personal relationships, 329
Phoenix Agenda, The (Whiteside),
    384–85
physical metaphors, overreliance on,
    93
PICTIVE, 280, 284
Pioneer Systems
    defined, 132
    design methods, 162–64
    impacts of, 167
    interface design, 123
    invention phases, 142
    investment in, 162–64
    timing of, 166–67
pointing devices, 87, *See also* mouse
Poltrock, Steven E., 376–77
PowerPoint, 131
Pressman, R. S., 310
Price, Raymond L., 372
problem definition, 274, 276–78, 290
problem tracking, 10
product definition
    organizational structure and,
        314–17, 321–23, 331
    user involvement in, 314–17
product development, *See also* project
    development
    accelerated development strategies,
        340–42, 348–49, 377–78
    bringing usability into, 367–74
    system enclosure, 368–69
    terminal setup, 368

product improvement
  demand for, 340
  system design practice and,
    340–46
productivity
  application development and, 175
  case studies, 182–96
    Continental Insurance
      underwriting application,
      183–84
    CUA user interface style, 186–87
    Expo'92 multimedia visitor
      services application, 187–91
    general-purpose spreadsheet
      package, 184–85
    Illinois Department of
      Employment Security, 195
    time and attendance recording
      application, 191–94
  measuring, 182
programming
  environment problem, DEC Rally
    Version 2, 21–23
  with graphical elements, 76
  languages, 20
project development, *See also* product
    development
  concept development, 341
  development mileposts, 159–62,
    165–66
  time to market, 340–42, 371–72
  usability studies and, 369–71
Project Ernestine, 101–20
  analytical model development,
    104
  background, 101–03
  as a CHI success story, 115–18
  field trial, 104–07
  GOMS analysis, 107–10
  performance time predictions vs. trial
    data, 110–11
project teams
  competencies, 382–83
  effective, 383–85
  mental models, 384
  multidisciplinary, 342–43, 352,
    361–62, 377, 378–79
  personal mastery, 383–84
  systems thinking, 383
  teamwork, 382–85
  trust, 382
property sheets studies, Star, 82–83

prototyping
  active participatory, 204–08, 222, 224
  building prototypes, 215–17, 274–75,
    283–84, 290
  DEC Rally Version 2, 9
  defined, 9
  innovative products, 324
  in ITS, 182
  organizational structure and,
    317–18, 323–26, 332
  rapid, for Freestyle, 50–53
  role-playing walkthroughs, 217–21,
    222
  Star, 80–89
  testing, 275, 291
  tools, effectiveness of, 305
  user interface design methods, 273
psychology, claims and, 246–47,
    254–55
Pygmalion, 76

Q
QOC (Questions-Options-Criteria),
    280
quality planning, 342

R
Rally, 126, 127, 132, 133
  design methods, 144–45, 151, 159
  invention phases, 142
random assignment, of participants,
    112–13
rapid prototyping systems, 292
Raskin, Jeff, 67n
real-world experiments, 111–14
  evaluation, 116–17
  experimental and control groups,
    112–13
  organizational attitudes and
    expectations, 114–15
  participant selection, 112–13
recognize-retrieve-act cycle, 283
Red Book (Star Functional
    Specification), 78–79
reflection, 273, 274
reports, DEC Rally Version 2, 4
Reuse View Matcher, 235, 237, 248, 250
revenues, *See also* commercial success
  interface design and, 289–91, 392
  usability improvements and, 30–31

Ritchie, R. Jay, 377–79
Rittel, H. W. J., 243
Rogers, E. M., 67n
role-playing walkthroughs, 217–21, 222, *See also* walkthroughs
Rooms, 124, 125
Rudman, C., 277, 291

S

scenario bias, 237, 243
scenarios, 276, 277
  analytic approach, 234–38
  constructing claims for, 240–51
  defined, 233, 243
  empirical approach, 234
  with errors, 237–38, 243–44
  generating, 233–40
  generating claims from, 243–44
  as narrative theory of artifacts, 29–40
  stopping generation of, 238–39
  tracking dependencies, 262
  typology of, 234–38, 252–53
schedule charts, CPM-GOMS, 108
science
  action, 229–31, 259–62
  normal, 230
  technology development and, 230
scrolling problems, Freestyle, 49
second-order artifacts, 233, 262
Seismic Scale of Innovation (SSI), 130–32
semantic net analysis, 277
  for GUI design, 212–15, 223, 225
  interviews, 293
semantic structure, of menu items, 15
semiconductor development, 230–31
Senge, P. M., 381
sequential design process, 340–41
Settler Systems, 133
  defined, 132
  design methods, 162–64
  interface design, 123
  invention phases, 142
setup screens, 368
shared knowledge, 383
shared vision, 382, 383
SIL, 77
Silva, Dan, 77
Simon, H. A., 246
Simonyi, Charles, 76

Simula, 124
Singley, Kevin, 237
situated action approach, 232
Sketchpad, 72, 77, 123, 125
skills, familiar, 41, 52, 67n
  product support of, 39–40
Smalltalk, 74–76, 77, 124, 125, 129, 233
  programming in, 235
  user concerns typology, 235–37
Smith, David C., 76
social factors
  in active participatory prototyping, 207, 222
  in GUI design, 217, 222–23
  in on-site observation, 203
  in role-playing walkthroughs, 220, 222
  in semantic net analysis, 215
  in top-down decision tree analysis, 212, 222–23
software design
  Freestyle, 47–54
  methods and results, 64–65
software developers, usability studies involving, 295
spreadsheets
  expressions, in Star, 88–89
  general-purpose, 184–85
Sproull, Bob, 77
SRI International, 72
stack-based menu structure, 13–14
stage theory of action, 244, 245
Stanford Research Institute, 72
Stanley, J., 93
Star, 70–96, 124, 125, 126, 127, 129, 132
  design methods, 148–50, 151, 159
  design process, 71, 78–80
  design process evaluation, 89–93
  desktop metaphor, 70, 71, 94
  document-centric design, 91
  forerunners, 72–78
  graphic design, 79
  graphics selection methods, 85
  icon tests, 83–85
  influence of, 70, 73, 89
  influences on, 73
  innovation criteria, 136–37
  invention phases, 142
  labeling studies, 81–82
  mouse use, 85, 86–87
  object-action analysis, 279–80
  property sheets studies, 82–83

Star *(continued)*
prototyping, 80–89
purpose of, 71
text selection methods, 85
tiled vs. overlapping windows, 95
user testing, 80–89
writing arithmetic expressions, 88–89
Star Functional Specification (Red Book), 78–79
state transition diagrams, 280, 282
Steele, Lowell, 50, 67n
storefront testing, 285
storyboards, 280, 284, 292
style, interface, 174, 176–89
style designers, 181
style implementation routines (SIRs), 182
style programmers, 181–82
style specifications files, 181
subject matter experts (SMEs), 353–54
subject selection methods, 93
SuperCard, 205–06, 216
SuperPaint, 129
surveys, user, 347
Sutherland, Ivan, 72
synthetic design methods, 151, 154–59
system enclosure, 368–69
Systems Development Department (SDD), Xerox, 78
systems thinking, 381, 383

T

tablets
design, 42–47
rapid prototyping, 50–51
tag language, 181
Task Action Grammar (TAG), 282, 294
task analysis, 276, 277, 293
action-science approach, 231
task-artifact framework, *See also* artifacts
constructing claims, 240–51, 253–59
defined, 232
example, 251–59
generating scenarios, 233–40, 252–53
manual design, 253–59
purpose of, 231

status of, 231–33
value of, 260–61
task-mapping analysis, 282
tasks, time needed to perform, 283
team learning, 382, 384
teamwork, *See also* project teams
developing, 382–85
technical writers, 328
technological development
process of, 63, 65–66
science and, 230, 259
technology push invention, 143
terminal setup, 368
Tesler, Larry, 76
text selection methods, Star, 85
theft, as design method, 153–54
"theory of the world" problem, 246
think-aloud protocols, 225–26
Thorndike, E. L., 246
tiled windows, 95
time and attendance recording application, 191–94
time to breakeven, 372–73
defined, 372
management and, 374
usability and, 373, 374
time to market, 371–72
acceleration of, 340–42
timing
of HCI, 369–71
of Pioneer Systems, 166–67
of usability studies, 369–71
toll-and-assistance operator (TAO) workstations, 102–04, 105–07, *See also* New TAO workstation
evaluating with CPM-GOMS, 126, 127
GOMS models, 107–10
toolkits, 278–79, 284, 285–86
top-down decision tree analysis, 208–12, 221–23, 224–25
total quality management, 342
Totals, workstation development, 191–94
Touch Illinois, 195
tracking problems, DEC Rally Version 2, 10
tradeoffs, 378
claims, 242, 243, 247–48
Training Wheels, 233, 237, 250
transistors, 230–31, 241, 242, 255–56

transition networks, generalized, 292
try-to-destroy-it tests, 42–43
Tullis, T. S., 283
tutorial, iterative usability testing of, 48–50
type-ahead, DEC Rally Version 2, 4
typewriters, 63

U

Unix, 124
Unix Shell Scripts, 125, 126
upsides, strengthening, 249, 256–57
usability
  benchmarks for, 390
  bringing into product development, 367–74
  bugs, DEC Rally Version 2, 29–30
  influence on design practice, 342–43
  integrating all aspects of, 318–20, 326–30
  management commitment to, 379–80, 381–82, 389–91
  rating problems, 10
  respect for, 389–91
  time to breakeven and, 373, 374
  tracking problems, 10
usability engineering, 5, 7–8, 31
usability experts, separation of, 390–91
usability studies, 174
  DEC Rally Version 2 case study, 3–33
  involving software developers, 295
  labs, 174
  with limited participants, 37
  tests, 285, 294
  timing of, 369–71
  using market research with, 348–49
  value of, 225–26
use cases, 277
useless information problem, DEC Rally Version 2, 23–24
user-centered design (UCD), 338–39, 377–78, See also computer-human interface (CHI) theory; human-computer interaction (HCI)
  accelerated design strategies and, 342
  assembling multidisciplinary teams for, 352

customer profiles, 356–57
customer/user sample selection, 353
data analysis for, 356
data collection for, 353–56
economic benefits of, 360–61
educating customers through, 361
effectiveness of, 362–63
identifying role of, 347–48
interviewing for, 355, 356
management commitment to, 350, 352
market research for, 347, 348–49, 360–61, 362
perceived value of, 348
supporting, 346–57
User Interface Component Hierarchy, 215
user interface design. See graphical user interface (GUI); interface design
user interface design methods. See graphical user interface (GUI) design methods; interface design methods
User Interface Management Systems (UIMS), 177–78
users, See also customers; participant selection
  contact with, 305, 308, 309
  designer understanding of, 305, 306
  identifying needs of, for Freestyle, 55–57
  involving in design process, 272–73
  involving in product definition, 314–17, 321–23, 331
  needs and capabilities of, 272–73
user surveys, 347
user testing
  early, 305
  selecting users for, 93, 353
  Star, 80–89, 91
use-scenarios, 233–38
utility, defined, 272

V

variable names, long, list of values (LOV) problem, 17–20
Verplank, W., 85, 91
videoconferencing, 65
videophones, 65

video terminal setup, 368
View Matcher, 233
ViewPoint, 77, 79, 92, 95, 96
VisiCalc, 125, 126, 132
vision, shared, 382, 383
visual display, 280, 294
voice controls, Freestyle, 52

W

walkthroughs, 292, 294
 for reflecting on design, 281–82
 role-playing, 217–21, 222
 selecting, 289
walk-up-and-use ATM system,
 292–93
Wang Laboratories, 38, 63, 65,
 138–39
Wehrend, S., 392
Wells, Doris, 79
White, G. R., 133, 135, 136
Whiteside, John, 126, 224, 384–85
windows, tiled vs. overlapping, 95
Wixon, Dennis, 126

work-arounds, 22
workgroup processes, 57–61
workgroup support, 54–62, 65
work practices, analysis of, 276–77
workstations
 performance time predictions vs. trial
  data, 110–11
 for toll-and-assistance operators
  (TAOs), 102–04, 105–07
 Totals, 191–94
WYSIWYG text editors, 76

X

Xerox
 PARC, 74–78, 89–90, 92, 129
 Systems Development Department
  (SDD), 78
Xerox Star. *See* Star
X protocol, 124, 125, 132

Y

Yankee Group, 347